Praise for *A Wild and Sacred Call: Nature—Psyche—Spirit*

"Who but the huge-hearted Will Adams could have written this work? There are many fine volumes on the confluence of eco-psychology, spiritual practice, and ecology. Here, however, is a genuinely talismanic text that enacts the healing it so carefully elucidates. This is a quiet masterwork of both scholarship and sensitivity, one that carries the reader into the depths that it gently discloses shimmering around us. A book of simple power that, like a struck prayer bell, keeps reverberating in the hollows of the body, dissolving the shackled habits that block our eyes and ears and heart from really noticing, really attuning to, really *feeling* what meets us in the relational thick of the present moment."

— David Abram, author of *Becoming Animal: An Earthly Cosmology*

"This book combines a lyrical invitation with an insistent demand. Both involve taking seriously our kinship with the earth and with all our fellow-species, whether we understand this call to become part of a mystical/transpersonal whole, or—in a pluralistic spirit—to respond to the other and the others. In either case, Adams insists, we are called to exit from our own self-centered and possessive egoism, to take up our responsibility for the widow, the orphan and the stranger, as well as for other species and for our shared home."

— Donna M. Orange, author of *Climate Crisis, Psychoanalysis, and Radical Ethics*

"This work is perhaps the most comprehensive and ambitious text in the fledgling field of ecopsychology, extending its tableau to include transpersonal, literary, and spiritual wisdom sources. Most importantly, it enacts the healing for which it calls."

— Jason M. Wirth, Seattle University, author of *Mountains, Rivers, and the Great Earth: Reading Gary Snyder and Dōgen in an Age of Ecological Crisis*

"Our twenty-first-century Earth community is in deep trouble, heading toward destruction due to the violence perpetrated by humans against one another, and due to the violence wrought against the natural world brought about by human hubris and greed. *A Wild and Sacred Call* addresses our critical situation, offering a worldview grounded on the fundamental interconnectedness of nature, the human psyche, and spirit. To convey its powerful message, this work deftly combines scholarly erudition with poetic imagery and insight, using stories from the author's own personal life as well as from the store of rich narratives from various cultures."

— Ruben L. F. Habito, Guiding Teacher, Maria Kannon Zen Center, Perkins School of Theology, Southern Methodist University, and author of *Be Still and Know: Zen and the Bible*

"This is an insightful, in-depth inquiry into the psychological and spiritual dimensions of healing in troubled ecological times. As one of its many precious gifts, the book provides a vivid demonstration of how classical and contemporary sources of spiritual wisdom are directly relevant in our day-to-day lives."

— James Finley, Center for Action and Contemplation and author of *Christian Meditation: Experiencing the Presence of God*

# A Wild and
# Sacred Call

SUNY series in Transpersonal and Humanistic Psychology

Richard D. Mann, editor

# A Wild and Sacred Call

## Nature–Psyche–Spirit

Will W. Adams

FOREWORD BY DAVID R. LOY

SUNY
**PRESS**

Published by State University of New York Press, Albany

For information, contact State University of New York Press, Albany, NY
www.sunypress.edu

### Library of Congress Cataloging-in-Publication Data

Name: Adams, Will W., author
Title: A wild and sacred call : nature–psyche–spirit | Foreword by
    David R. Loy
Description: Albany : State University of New York Press [2023] | Series:
    SUNY series in transpersonal and humanistic psychology | Includes
    bibliographical references and index.
Identifiers: ISBN 9781438492056 (hardcover : alk. paper) | ISBN 9781438492070
    (ebook) | ISBN 9781438492063 (pbk. : alk. paper)
Further information is available at the Library of Congress.

10 9 8 7 6 5 4 3 2 1

*With boundless gratitude and love, this book is dedicated to*
*Holly, my beloved sweetheart;*
*Lily Claire, my sweet full moon;*
*Eli, my shining son;*
*and all our glorious, vulnerable other-than-human companions*
*who grace this one wild and sacred earth.*

# Contents

# Foreword

Are we now living in the most dangerous moment in human history? That's according to Noam Chomsky in a 2020 article, and it's difficult to argue with him: what we do (or don't do) in the next few years will have serious repercussions for many generations, maybe for many centuries. Although he was interviewed during the coronavirus pandemic, Chomsky didn't even mention COVID, which (horrible though it has been for so many) doesn't compare with the Black Plague in the fourteenth century that killed maybe one third of the people in Europe alone. He did cite rising authoritarianism and the growing threat of nuclear war, but first on his list is the climate crisis. That by itself is arguably the greatest challenge humanity has ever faced, but nonetheless it is only part of a much larger ecological catastrophe that includes (among many other things) biodiversity collapse, worldwide soil degradation, as well as increasing toxins in the sea and the air, in the earth and our bodies. As Will Adams writes in this book: *Our world is wounded, and it wounds us in return.*

The tragic irony is that, just when humanity has achieved a truly global civilization, that civilization seems to be self-destructing. "The day of reckoning has come," said the ecotheologian Thomas Berry. "In this disintegrating phase of our industrial society, we now see ourselves not as the splendor of creation, but as the most pernicious mode of earthly being."

Surely this changes everything, right? . . . Well, not yet, anyway. The most extraordinary aspect of this unprecedented predicament is our collective inability to address it with the attention and determination required. Despite all that we now know about what is happening, and all the resources available to us, our collective response continues to be self-stultifying. Daily life for most of us continues much the same as before. And even if carbon emissions can be radically reduced, that by itself will not be sufficient, because it becomes ever clearer that the deeper problem is humanity's dysfunctional relationship with the rest of the natural world. As Will says: *In trying to master nature we are trying to master the great mystery, to control what is intrinsically beyond our control.*

That deeper problem is the topic of this timely book, which persuasively makes the case that the fundamental issue is alienation: from our own bodies, from each other, and from the earth. One of its key insights is that the ecological emergency is not only a social (political, economic, technological) crisis but also a spiritual emergency that challenges us in various ways. This book shows how the three alienations are not separate problems but different aspects of the same problem, and all three dissociations need to be addressed. They require a healing that can happen when we reconnect with what we have been denying or overlooking—when we realize that our true nature is both earthy and spiritual, because the two are not really incongruous. Will again: *Potentially, today's ecological breakdown is summoning forth a radical psycho-spiritual-cultural breakthrough.*

A book about a new way of thinking, feeling, and living also needs to be written in a new way, which in this case not only describes but illustrates what it is talking about. In what follows, diverse academic fields and specializations converse with each other, as the different chapters weave together overlapping insights from Christian mysticism, Zen Buddhism, existential philosophy, hermeneutic phenomenology, and psychotherapy. Just as important is the way that the text transcends the usual division between serious-minded scholarship and personal experience, with poetry and storytelling that bring the issues home to our own lives in a more direct and intuitive fashion. The juicy result is a transpersonal version of ecopsychology—more joyful as well as more nondual—that escapes all the usual disciplinary boundaries in the process of revisioning what life could be. *Knowledge acts upon us to sponsor new ways of being and understanding and loving.*

At the heart of that vision is the letting-go of ego-self, a psychological and social construct that is inherently insecure because it feels separate from the rest of the world. *Our conventional sense of self is an intrinsically delusional, paranoid, and greedy structure, yet ultimately an illusory one.*

The alternative is experiencing and understanding our innate relatedness, not only to each other but to the natural world. *In each encounter the being of others ceaselessly becomes part of our very being; and our being becomes part of theirs.*

But how does embodied attunement to the natural world help us address our dangerous situation today? This is the most crucial part of the book, in my opinion. Realizing our relationality is not only personally healing; it sensitizes us to the ethical appeal of the natural world. As we open up to our interconnectedness, we become aware that we are called upon to respond appropriately. Engagement then is more than a task of moral responsibility: it is what we *want* to do. *Our well-being and that of others turns on how we take up such appeals.*

Another word for this back-and-forth ethical appeal-and-response is love, flowing from the recognition that this world is sacred, and that its sacredness includes us and our actions, since we are an inescapable and irreplaceable part of it. *This shared world is inherently holy and complete just as it is, for the time being. Now go work with all your heart to transform the world. You are inherently holy and complete just as you are, for the time being. Now go work with all your heart to transform your self, your consciousness, and your way of being with others.*

The issues discussed in this book become more urgent each day, and they deserve our full attention. I have quoted liberally from this book, because I can't improve on Will's words. But see for yourself.

# Preface

## Deep Calls to Deep:
## Hallowing Our Relationship with Nature

There is another world, and it is inside this one.

—Attributed to Paul Éluard

We are here to awaken from the illusion of our separateness.

—Thich Nhat Hanh (in Loy, 2008, p. 103)

We are human only in contact, and conviviality, with what is not human.

—David Abram (1996, p. ix)

Early one morning I walked into my study and came upon the marvelous encounter depicted in the photograph. I was able to catch the moment with my phone camera, quickly and in dim light. The image is blurry, but its meaning is clear: two toddlers from the neighborhood, drawn to each other in mutual fascination. The four-legged animal is a white-tailed deer fawn. The two-legged animal is my son, Eli. This experience, and similar ones with squirrels, rabbits, birds, and butterflies, primed him for another encounter that occurred many years later. By that time we had moved to a new (yet rather old) home in the woods. Eli had just turned ten. He and I were driving away from our house when the event took place. Catching sight of a white-tailed doe leaping high over a fallen tree, Eli exclaimed with a big beaming smile, "Dad, that deer was falling from heaven! Like, like, floating!" I too had seen her gliding in a graceful arc, as if "in slow motion" (as Eli put it). Such occurrences are common where we live, and thoroughly awesome at the same time. Even before Eli's remark I had already been taken up into the wonder of the doe's flight. Yet his poetic comment called forth something I had not explicitly named. Spirituality is important in my family, but "heaven" is a word we rarely use. The only time I can recall is when I told my kids that I am with Saint Catherine of Genoa when she proclaims, "All the way to heaven is heaven" (Day, 1948, p. 17).

I was surprised that Eli spoke of heaven, but it did convey a sacred or holy ambiance that was present in our contact with the deer. By this I mean that Eli and I were touched by the depth dimension of existence shining through that ordinary event; that we were granted access to something profoundly precious, meaningful, powerful, alive, and enlivening; that we were pulled out of our usual preoccupations and into caring involvement in a beautiful, inter-responsive, and (at best) responsible life, a seamless, indivisible, conversational life that goes infinitely deeper than our supposedly separate self and species. Gary Snyder (1990)—poet, naturalist, Zen practitioner, scholar—provides an exquisite articulation of what I am alluding to: "The point is to make intimate contact with the real world, real self. *Sacred* refers to that which helps take us . . . out of our little selves into the whole mountains-and-rivers mandala universe" (p. 94). For Zen Buddhism, "mountains-and-rivers" means the whole wide earth and beyond, precisely as it is being embodied in the tangible intimacy of the present encounter. Whether our relational partners are human or otherwise, when we realize their sacred nature we are *freed from* our merely self-interested individualistic self and *freed for* conscious loving engagement. I saw this clearly in Eli's response. After the season's first snowfall a few days later, he asked me with heartfelt concern: "How do deer survive in the winter? They don't hibernate, and their fur isn't long like Lela's [our beloved dog]."[1]

"The point" that Snyder invoked above is the point of our very existence; or more aptly, the *coexistence* we share with all the diverse beings and elemental natural presences who grace this glorious and troubled world. In letting another move us deeply—receiving their overture beyond the habits, conventions, and defenses of our small, contracted, ego-centered self—understanding, love, compassion, and justice flow freely in response. Strangely, such open care goes against the grain of today's dominant cultural values. I feel sad suggesting that *authentic love is a countercultural quality*, but we are living in disorienting days. In our relationship with each other and with the rest of nature, it is clear that we have lost our way. Still, the capacity for kind, sensitive attunement is always available. William Blake (1988) famously encouraged us to see "Heaven in a Wild Flower" (p. 490), and my 10-year-old son did essentially that! The deer around our home are quite familiar to Eli. Yet by allowing the doe's astonishing glide to really touch him, he saw into the depths of what he ordinarily takes for granted. We know how easy it is to be swept along by our conventionally self-absorbed approach. But here the momentum of Eli's usual mode was instantaneously interrupted, and a more wondrous existence was revealed. Sensing heaven in the wild deer's flight, Eli discovered another world, another self, another way of being together.

"*There is another world, and it is inside this one.*"[2] Infinitely deep, sacred, beckoning our gratitude and love: This "other world" exists in and *as* the heart of our everyday world. It is always living latently there, there in the gesture of a stranger who needs a hand at the grocery store, or in the radiance of our beloved's smile; there in a rare natural marvel witnessed once on a trip far from home, or in the sparrow singing right outside our window; latent, in fact, as an infinitely charged potential in every single encounter of our life. Yet, all too often it is unwittingly obscured by our supposedly separate, ego-centered stance. Fortunately, there are far more gracious ways of welcoming contact with others. Stated differently, "another self" emerges intimately with this "other world," an alternative mode of consciousness or way of being that encompasses and permeates our usual egoic one. We each have the ability to listen and see from such a deeper consciousness, to appreciate the corresponding depths of our relational partner, and thus to reply with understanding and compassion. Awakening to the other world within this one is an opportunity—in fact, responsibility—that is built into the nondual, conversational, call-and-response structure of our very (co)existence. The sacred depths of our companions are ever appealing for discovery, like a geode found on a riverbank: a lumpy old rock that when cracked open reveals beautiful crystals inside. Or, because this latency is not fully formed in itself, objectively there to be uncovered, it is more like those "magic eye" images that appear only when we shift our conventional awareness and see more subtly.

The point I am making is this: the "other world" is a metaphor for the reality of our fellow humans, the rest of nature, and the larger existence we are co-creating together. All are imbued with a depth dimension that yearns to come to life in relationship with an appreciative partner: namely, us. This other world is precisely no other than the world of our daily lives, but met freshly, intimately. As Snyder (1990) attests, "There's a world behind the world we see that is the same world, but more open, more transparent, without blocks" (p. 164). Then he stresses the crucial fact: "We are always in both worlds, because there really aren't two" (p. 165). Whether this deeper world will actually be disclosed, honored, and served is contingent upon our consciousness and responsive follow through. This is life's core ethical calling, sent forth in our inherent involvement with other people and with the wild, sacred, imperiled earth.

My work in ecopsychology arises in response to this great summons. The aspiration of this book is to articulate some key aspects of the psychology and spirituality of our relationship with the rest of nature, so as to return readers freshly to their own personal and professional lives. This study endeavors to craft an approach that works in consonance with the nature of nonhuman beings and elemental presences; with the nature within each person and culture; with the nature that transpires between us by way of interpersonal, sociocultural, and spiritual relationships; and with the nature of the great mystery of life. In this spirit, we would do well to heed the wisdom of three teachers who appeared in my opening story. One of them is my son, who in this case exemplifies the sensitive intelligence and kindness with which we are all gifted. Such attunement is common in children until it gets cultured out of us by the excessively busy, stressed, acquisitive lifestyles that now dominate our world. The white-tailed doe is another mentor who deserves to be honored. Her ancestors roamed Eurasia as far back as twenty million years ago. Deer are blessed with a participatory intelligence developed across all those years, one that lets them thrive in this marvelous and dangerous world. In contrast, we humans are the youngsters here on earth! The call-and-response sensitivity of that neighborhood doe; her ability to craft a cooperative coexistence with her human and nonhuman fellows; her wariness over the intrusion of techno-corporate culture (appearing in the guise of my car): these are a few lessons I gleaned in that encounter. Yet, when I pay attention, I realize that such teachings are always being given freely. I often come upon mother deer and fawns contending with a human-dominated world, especially with cars being driven too fast by people encapsulated not only in their armored machines but in their constricted self and anxious preoccupations. In watching these moms I am learning something about tending my children's well-being while letting go of my wish to fully protect them from dangers that inevitably come in an engaged life. We are an immensely talented species, as evidenced by our savvy for social collaboration, art, literature, music, science, technology, philosophy, spirituality, and intersubjective intimacy. At the same time we have so much growing up to do, as evidenced by personal irresponsibility, the ecological crisis, perpetual war, racism, and other pernicious structures of oppression.

We can also hearken yet another great mentor from my story, one that is unimaginably ancient—timeless, in fact—and always freshly coming into being. This one is difficult to speak of because it is truly ineffable. No name can really suffice. We could call it the holy depths of life. Alternately, we could call it the conversational community of this wise and loving earth. That is, all the animals, plants, fungi, and earthy-airy-fiery-watery elements—including humans—in their inter-dependent, inter-responsive relationship with each other and with the embracing ecosphere. Inclusivity is a key for ecopsychology, and to be all-inclusive could even speak of the whole dynamic cosmos, manifest and unmanifest. But, staying grounded, what I am really talking about is this: the earth supporting our every step, the smiling face of a cherished friend, a glowing iris—all expressions of a mysterious reality that goes infinitely deep. The great depths also summon us in painful ways, say, in the haggard face of a homeless woman; in a living mountain under assault by the coal company; in yet another Black person murdered by police or White supremacists; in wilderness handed to corporations by politicians and judges; in children poisoned by toxic emissions from fracking wells near their schools and sports fields.

Confusion, fear, and greed are rampant today, afflicting our well-being together with that of the rest of nature. The primary source of these maladies is a fundamental relational rupture: we human folk conventionally presume that we are separate from nature's other folk, and from other people as well. From this dissociated and fear-filled stance, we act as if we are divorced from and an exception to the natural order. We imagine ourselves superior to all other life forms. Not understanding the real source of our fear—the illusory but haunting sense of separation— we often feel entitled to ravage the rest of nature for convenience and profit. In a grievous twin betrayal, we wreak havoc on our nonhuman companions while debasing ourselves and generations to come. However, we know ruptures in connection can be healed, relationships renewed and carried further. In this great endeavor we need an interdisciplinary psycho-spiritual-cultural "therapy." I will offer proposals for this transformative work as we go along, but here I want to articulate one of its key constituents: that is, an appreciation that something infinitely deeper than our self-contained ego and species is the ever-present source of our existence, is in fact the real therapist after all. Herein, we discover ourselves to be significant yet humble participants in the great mystery of life and the life of the one great mystery. Nature's primary gift to us, its primary teaching, its primary healing power, its primary ethical summons, is its seamless, indivisible, inter-responsive, conversational functioning—painful and dangerous at times, yet thoroughly awesome, beautiful, wise, and loving. Realizing it directly, not merely cognitively but deep in our embodied heart, we awaken from the fundamental delusion of humankind, the felt-sense of separation from others and the rest of nature; and we awaken into responsibility toward the sacred depths of life. This intimate relationship is at the heart of what it is to be human. And let us not fool ourselves: when it is lost or destroyed our humanity is diminished. So too is the rest of the world. As David Abram (1996) emphasizes, "We are human only in contact, and conviviality, with what is not human" (p. ix).

In ancient times people experienced the sacred depths in their daily contact with the meaningfully expressive powers of the natural world. Over time, with an intuition that the whole world is an expression of infinitely vast cosmic or spiritual processes, these natural depths came to be called the Dao or buddha-nature or God (among other classic appellations). They also came to be known as our deepest heart, our true or real self (as the mystics say). Soon I will comment on my use of spiritual language. To put it briefly for now, I will be crafting a largely existential and transpersonal approach to ecopsychology. Across the ages, the spiritual mystics were the ones with the greatest knowledge of what we now call transpersonal psychology. Indeed, the mystics were the world's indigenous psychologists. By way of meditation and contemplative prayer, they were the ones devoting careful attention to the workings of our mind and heart.[3] Long before psychology came into being as a research and clinical discipline, the mystics were exploring perennial psychological concerns. Who am I? What is this challenging, perplexing, dangerous, and beautiful life? Who are these others with whom I am involved, both human and more-than-human? How can I best serve all my fellow beings, this animate earth, and the one great mystery? How can I handle the suffering sent our way? How can I live well, love well?

Speaking personally and as a scholar, I take my guidance from inter-responsive involvement in everyday life, both with other people and the natural world; from longtime Zen practice; and from the traditions of phenomenology, psychoanalysis, and contemplative/mystical spirituality (especially Buddhism and Christianity). Given this orientation, it follows that *intimate attunement to actual lived experience will serve as our primary method of inquiry in this book*. As Mary Oliver (1992) avows: "I don't know exactly what a prayer is. / I do know how to pay attention" (p. 94). That is really the heart of the matter: careful awareness in the present moment, and the love that follows spontaneously. Similarly, the Zen poet Matsuo Bashō (1966) offers this advice to his students (and now to us): "Go to the pine if you want to learn about the pine. . . . And in doing so, you must leave your subjective preoccupation with yourself. Otherwise you impose yourself on the object and do not learn. Your poetry issues of its own accord when you and the object have become one—when you have plunged deep enough into the object to see something like a hidden glimmering there" (p. 33).[4] Be assured, Bashō is talking not only about poetry. He is inviting us all into the kind of encounter that transpired spontaneously for my son. Touched intimately by the gliding deer, Eli surely did not meet her from the position of a detached, self-preoccupied observer. And it is fair to say that he saw a kind of "hidden glimmering" there. Such experiences are aesthetic, but not only that. They also carry profound ethical implications. We can hear this from a participant in a phenomenological research study I conducted on the confluence of contemplative prayer and socially engaged activity for ecological well-being. In Nora's poignant words:

I know that the earth is in a desolation. So the world that the mystery has brought forth is in a desolation. . . . So my contemplative practice now, it is not just the bucolic world—let me get into my garden and be in my paradise mind. . . . I feel like I'm coming as a nurse, tending a patient, something that is injured. . . . I always felt held because I felt like this was the great embrace of the mother. And now, I feel, oh my God, my mother is dying. . . . I never thought I would live to see this happen to the life systems of the planet, to the body that is the great body, that is the mother body. That is for me the sacrament of God. I do not know what is going on in the rest of the universe. I don't know how many of these little blue gems there are. But for me, it is an attack on God. I almost cannot even say more than that because I could burst into tears.[5]

Nora's eyes did well up with tears. So did mine. She herself is desolated, earth is desolated, two inseparable "sides" of one (co)existential emergency. As her eloquent comments intimate, coming from the perspective of mystical Christianity, the animate earth—this "little blue gem" glowing in space—is a precious form of the deep reality we call God. How could she not cry when she knows that an attack on the body of the earth is an attack on the body of God? On her body too. And make no mistake, it is your body, my body, the body of all our brothers and sisters, human and otherwise. There is really only one great body, after all, of which we are all indivisible expressions and co-creative participants.

I am mourning with Nora and with this wild and sacred earth. Grief-work is a crucial constituent of ecopsychology. *Our world is wounded, and it wounds us in turn.* Yet our world is also unsurpassably glorious: the caress of a lover, the saturated hues of a sunset, the cooing of a baby, the nighttime howling of an unseen wolf. The whole of life, in all its splendor and suffering and everything in between, calls to be met with attentive and reverent care. Life asks that we celebrate its beauty, bear the pain that inevitably comes our way, prevent the suffering that is not necessary, and minister to the anguish that is present. When it comes down to it, this is what makes it crucial that we discover a holy world inside the one we take for granted. Holiness, wholeness, healing, and health, all intertwined not just linguistically but existentially.

Following the dominant ethos of modern Euro-American culture, the earth is usually seen as an objective resource to exploit; an impediment to our self-centered, species-centered, or corporation-centered wishes; or simply absent or irrelevant. This reductionistic view precludes real empathy and care, leaving the natural world to be assaulted from the depths of oceans to the upper atmosphere. In vast contrast, it is heartening that people like Nora see deeply and love the earth as holy, even as the tangible body of God. The ecotheologian Thomas Berry emphasizes that every historical era calls upon people to collaborate in a "Great Work," a life-changing, consciousness-changing, culture-changing venture that is distinctive to the beckoning circumstances of each particular age. "The Great Work now . . . is to carry out the transition from a period of human devastation of the Earth to a period when humans would be present to the planet in a mutually beneficial way" (Berry, 1999, p. 3). The rampant desecration of the earth comes from pathological, fear-inducing confusion in human consciousness and culture. Maladies of ecology and climate (affecting all) and economic/political aggrandizement (benefiting the few) are disastrous symptoms of an even more radical disaster, an *ethical crisis* driven by insidious psychological and sociocultural forces. For the great work to succeed, we need a profound transformation of consciousness and culture. A key "therapeutic" ingredient must be the psychospiritual dimension of existence. "The difficulty is that the natural world is seen primarily for human use, not as a mode of sacred presence primarily to be communed with in wonder and beauty and intimacy" (Berry, in Deignan, 2003, pp. 18–19).

I realize that conventional religion simply does not speak to many of us today. Even more disturbing are versions of religion that devalue this earthly life for an imagined otherworldly one, or versions that sanction violence against those not in one's tribe. (The terrorism of so-called "holy" wars might be the first thing that comes to mind. But let us also think of the violence the human tribe is wreaking upon the nonhuman world.) Across history, spirituality has brought forth the best and worst in people. Atrocities committed in the name of "God" are too numerous to list. Thus many contemporary citizens understandably eschew terms like sacred, holy, and (especially) God. Nonetheless, anyone can tap into an *experience* of what these classic words disclose (at their best). The great humanistic psychologist Abraham Maslow (1971) was an avowed atheist, yet he argued that "desacralizing" was one of the most pernicious defense mechanisms of modern life. Alternately, "resacralizing" our everyday experience is a critical element in living a healthy, self-and-other-actualizing existence (pp. 49–50).

The natural world has forever been a primary locus for psychospiritual realization. When Abram (1996) was visiting a family in Bali, his hostess placed tiny mounds of rice outside her home, commenting that these were "offerings for the household spirits" (p. 11). Later, upon witnessing black ants carrying the rice away, a revelation came to him. *These common ants were the very "spirits"* for whom his hostess was providing devoted care! If not for these daily gifts to the spirits, the woman's home would have been invaded by ants. In Euro-American culture, we have come to think of spirits as disembodied, supernatural beings. Images of humanlike ghosts often come to mind. But Abram realized that "the 'spirits' of an indigenous culture are primarily those modes of intelligence or awareness that do *not* possess a human form" (p. 13). No wonder these people were so carefully attuned to the meaningful expressions, forceful powers, beauty, love, and ethical solicitations of the "more-than-human world" (in Abram's felicitous phrase). Similar stories are found in ancient myths from Africa and native "America" (or "Turtle Island," as the Haudenosaunee tradition names it). And today's well-known religious traditions were initiated by their founders' transformative encounters in the natural world. Recall Moses with the burning bush; Krishna in the forest; the Buddha under the bodhi tree, awakening with the morning star; Christ in the desert wilderness; and Muhammad in a mountain cave. Whether we deem our sensibility to be spiritual or secular, we can appreciate that nature is infinitely deep and irreplaceably precious; that it is dynamically alive and enlivening for us and all our relations; that it *draws us out* of our contracted captivation by a narrowly human world and ego-centered identity; and that it *draws us into* intimate loving contact with our kindred companions in the shared earth community. But since we are often dashing around with nary a pause, this is a far cry from how we usually perceive the world of nature.

I began this preface by celebrating the awesome wonder of nature. Yet a shadow lurked there from the start. From the small instance of my car disturbing the white-tailed deer to the monstrous corporate-political pillaging of ecosystems, when we open our heart to the natural world we are surely touched by immense suffering along with immense beauty. Today's human-generated eco(psycho)logical crisis is unprecedented, multifaceted, and pervasive. Our fellow species are being massively extinguished, habitat destroyed for human convenience (in the name of progress and profit), the world overheated and climate disrupted dangerously, floods and droughts amplified, sea levels rising, air and water poisoned with industrial toxins, drinkable water becoming scarce, fish and insect populations gravely threatened. Every day we are confronted with more agonizing news. But we are far less aware of the *psychospiritual affliction* wrought by the desecration of the natural world. Due to lifestyle changes, we humans are abdicating our consistent conscious contact with our companions in the rest of the natural world. Such involvement has nourished our health since the dawn of humankind, and given us an *experiential source of care* for our nonhuman fellows. And it is now being severely impoverished. We are only beginning to awaken to the magnitude of this trauma.

Today we are suffering two profound losses: our ancient relational partners are vanishing; and with the ones still left, we have forgotten how to listen to their intelligent, revelatory, gift-bestowing voices. It is not a matter of going "back" to nature, because *we humans are nature*. We, each of us, are an incarnation of the animate and wise earth (while existing as cultural beings as well). The words *human* and *humus* come from the same ancient Latin root, pointing to the fact that we humans are earthlings. Humble and humility also share those earthy roots. While we do well to learn from older ways, we are not being called to go back in time but to settle more deeply, consciously, and compassionately into our present time, so as to serve all our relations now and for generations to come. This is what Eli did when he let that soaring deer speak to him. After all, it is (*still*) in our human nature to be sensitively attuned to nature.

Our estrangement from and destruction of the natural world, and our enduring awe in the face of its wildness and beauty: both of these circumstances are what called ecopsychology into being. Everyone living today has been thrown into an eco(psycho)logical catastrophe we did not choose. But crises have a way of requiring the best of individuals and societies (while sometimes bringing out the worst). *Potentially, today's ecological breakdown is summoning forth a radical psycho-spiritual-cultural breakthrough.* There are incipient signs that we are discovering/creating a mutually enhancing coexistence. People are (re)learning how to listen to the depths of life, to welcome messages from their most authentic self and from the larger natural world. This "great work" may well be sponsoring a momentous "great turning" of consciousness and culture (Korten, 2006; Macy & Johnstone, 2012).

"Deep calls to deep in the voice of your waterfalls" (Psalm 42:7).
I take this poetic line as a revealing formulation of our (co)existential
condition, and of the responsibility inherently given with it. It provides
an intimation of what is needed for the metamorphic turning that
ecopsychology is endeavoring to foster. In just a few words, the psalm
conveys the guiding ethos of this book. Although usually obscured by
our conventional ways of being, the depths of the natural world are
always already present. These sacred depths are ever calling upon us,
asking something of us, and awaiting our rejoinder. To reply skillfully,
we must listen, see, and feel with our own depths, beyond our egocentric, anthropocentric stance. Surrendering our exclusively self-interested
individualism, our heart can welcome the deep appeals of nature. The
intertwining of these twin depths thereby becomes the dynamic source
from which our responses flow.

This can take place when we are solicited by the rumbling voice
of a waterfall or the subtle whisper of a breeze moving through leaves,
by a beloved forest being clear-cut or a fledgling robin near death after
crashing into our window. If we avail ourselves of the opportunity, we
can be touched deeply by any experience at all. As Martin Buber (1948)
avowed, "There is no not-holy, there is only that which has not yet
been hallowed, which has not yet been redeemed to its holiness, that
which we shall hallow" (pp. 135–136). We could say that everything is
always already holy or sacred, intrinsically so. But since nature is being
plundered with unprecedented ferocity and with little other than personal,
political, or economic self-interest deemed as holy, I appreciate Buber's
ethical call for us to consciously "hallow" or consecrate all our relationships. "Everything desires to be hallowed, to be incorporated into the
holy . . . everything desires to become a sacrament. The creature seeks
us, the things seek us on our ways; what comes in our way needs us for
its way" (p. 144). What if we actually realized that every single one needs
our sensitive response for the fulfillment of their own authentic way?
We can opt to treat others as an "It," as a mere object or commodity
that we use instrumentally for our own self-centered gratification. But
there is always a radical alternative: meeting them as a "Thou," listening
deeply, and caring for them in their inconceivable, irreplaceable, and
holy depths. Life continually presents us with opportunities to move from
a utilitarian I-It mode to an I-Thou mode, to be *with and for others* in
a genuinely open, loving way. Buber celebrates three forms in which a
potential I-Thou partner may appeal for our caring contact: other people,

God, and (perhaps surprisingly?!) the natural world. "It by no means needs to be a man of whom I become aware. It can be an animal, a plant, a stone. . . . The limits of the possibility of dialogue are the limits of awareness" (Buber, 1965, p. 10).

Our relationship with the rest of nature is a real relationship, a true call-and-response dialogue. This fact was always completely obvious until we began ignoring it a few hundred years ago. Now humankind is mostly lost in a repetitive monologue, one based upon the dream/nightmare of dominating, mastering, controlling, and exploiting the earth. This is a core pathology of a culture gone terribly awry. Thus, the "limits of awareness" are a major concern for ecopsychology. Yet we humans are gifted with the ability, indeed the urgent responsibility, to deepen our awareness. We act destructively not because we are evil, but because we are confused, frightened, and misguided. Our most basic, suffering-inducing confusion is that we (mis)take ourselves to be merely separate sovereign egos. This inevitably gives rise to fear and greed. Our mistaken identity operates in a mutually reinforcing manner with collective, sociocultural condition-ing, especially with *stories and practices of separation* that elevate humans to a position of superiority above the rest of nature and that authorize exclusively self-serving structures of oppression (economic, political, legal, technological). We and all our relations are betrayed in this process. But there is another way: we can realize that we are inter-responsive beings. Awakening to our inherent inseparability is crucial but does not take us far enough. The point is not only that we coexist inextricably *with* each other, but that we can do so *in the caring service of* each other. Ancient animate mountains glowing red-orange-yellow in autumn, the same moun-tains seen as a mere commodity and thus annihilated by mountaintop removal coal mining; osprey hunting in a once thriving, later toxified, and now revitalized lake; bees pollinating our vegetable plants, bee colonies collapsing due to the abuse of pesticides; beautiful rivers winding through our hometowns, those rivers flooding due to climate disruption; the animate earth—including people—with all its resplendence and bountiful gifts; the animate earth—including people—afflicted by humankind's ecocidal beliefs and actions. Life is imploring us to deconstruct and reconstruct our self-sense and society so that we may fulfill the most essential responsi-bility of all: allowing humans and the rest of nature *to live and love well together, with* each other, and *for* each other.

Today's eco(psycho)logical crisis is a symptom of a culture gone mad. But history has taught us that radical change is an ever-present possibility. Lest we lose hope in this perilous era, we can imagine the unimaginable "great flaring forth" of our universe (Swimme & Berry, 1992, p. 17). Spirit or energy formed into stardust, into our precious living planet, into single-celled organisms, into waterfalls and trees and whales and all of earth's wildly diverse beings and presences, including the Buddha and Christ and you and me. What radical changes we have already been through! But it was not just once, 14 billion years ago, that things flared forth transformatively. They are always flaring forth: a maple seed twirls to the ground, a baby is born, racial justice movements are born and reborn, a psychotherapy patient becomes free from shame. In your very own life, perhaps, recall the blessed shift from a place of alienation and despair to one of receiving love and becoming able to love once again. It is not only that transformation can happen, but it is happening all the time.

Impermanence—which, described differently, is the mutually responsive co-arising of all phenomena—is the very structure and functioning of life itself. This means that everything is always already changing and ever open for further metamorphosis. *Our task is to join consciously and compassionately in life's conversational unfolding,* harmoniously offering our distinctive gifts (as individuals and societies). I am wary of grand notions of "Progress" with a capital "P." Much violence has been wrought in the guise of goodness and growth. There is no way to know what will happen in the years and centuries to come. Things are precarious. Confusion, fear, and greed could win the day. Nonetheless, it does seem that a great turning is underway, a deepening of consciousness and culture that honors the well-being of all. I am not claiming this as a fact, because I am far from certain. Rather, I am telling a story that—with devoted collaboration and courage—we may be able to make into a reality.

Dr. Martin Luther King Jr. (1968) famously avowed, "We shall overcome because the arc of the moral universe is long but it bends towards justice." It grieves me to know that things surely do bend in the opposite direction at times. Today the ravaging of earth is operating hand in hand with the exploitation of those deemed "other," that is, other than oneself and the tribe one identifies with. People are being assaulted based upon fear-filled fantasies about their race or class, their gender identity or sexual orientation, their religion or lifestyle, their values or country of origin, and on and on. Faced with such intersecting forms of violence and oppression, the anthropologist Ruth Behar (1996) set forth an urgent challenge that goes right to the heart of ecopsychology:

research "that doesn't break your heart just isn't worth doing anymore" (p. 177). That spirit imbues all that I am sharing in this book. I feel heartbroken over the rapacious destruction being executed in the name of progress and profit. In the midst of anguishing grief that knows no bounds, I am always sent back to the relationships that comprise my very (co)existence. Right now I am remembering a young fellow who is immensely dear to me, my shining son Eli. Here is a boy who, like so many in his generation, enjoys staying indoors to play video games. Yet he is also one who was deeply touched by earth's wild and sacred call. Thrown like we all are into a wounded and wounding world, another world opened in Eli's heart of hearts. This is a small example of the revolutionary, evolutionary transformation of consciousness and culture that the animate earth is summoning forth. A countercultural, counter-consciousness movement is underway. It is heartening that the world's youth are stepping up with real energy and action. In one notable case, 16-year-old climate activist Greta Thunberg urged leaders to meet the challenge: "I want you to act as if the house is on fire, because it is" (Hertsgaard, 2019). Life is asking each of us to join in this great work in our own unique, irreplaceable ways.

Yes, my heart is breaking. Since you are reading this book, I imagine your heart is breaking as well. With the earth under assault, sadness, grief, anger, and despair are welling up in ways that can feel unbearable. *And yet, and yet: I can sense that our hearts are not really breaking, but breaking open.* Bearing anguish as best I can, and bearing love even more so, this very book is springing forth from my broken-open heart. Correspondingly, my hope is that you let my offering find its way to your own heart, through which you will bring into being some as-yet-unknown but transformative response. Our deepest heart is infinitely resilient. For the sake of the forsaken earth, for of all our relations both human and otherwise, let us draw upon this resilience and nurture our heart's authentic responses—awe, gratitude, joy, grief, anger, love, compassion, justice, and more—as they emerge from and *for* life's wild and sacred depths.

# Introduction

## Transpersonal Ecopsychology by Way of Phenomenology and Contemplative Spirituality

All important ideas must include the trees, the mountains, and the rivers.

—Mary Oliver (2016, p. 18)

I like to play indoors better, 'cause that's where all the electrical outlets are.

—A young boy (Louv, 2008, p. 10)

The Tao that can be told is not the eternal Tao.

—Laozi (Mitchell, 1988, p. 3)

## Overture

The shared earth community is sending us a wild and sacred call, beckoning us to cultivate a mutually enhancing relationship between humankind and the rest of nature. In response to this summons, the present book will articulate a largely transpersonal, contemplative, nondual approach to ecopsychology. Our explorations will weave together insights from peoples' lived experience, mystical/contemplative spirituality (especially Zen Buddhism and Christian mysticism), phenomenological philosophy, psychoanalysis, and transpersonal psychology, with plenty of illustrative poetry along the way.

1

## Conscious Contact with the Natural World:
## It All Begins Here

Perched on a low branch of a maple tree next to our driveway, a hawk caught my daughter's attention. We were playing soccer, and the raptor made her pause from her favorite game. "That's cool!" she said. We watched for a brief time until the big bird grew restless with our gaze and flew into the woods. "Do you know what that was?" I asked. "A hawk," Lily Claire replied. "What kind?" I said, casually intimating that different species share this wooded land with us. "I don't know, let's play!" I slipped in "broad-winged" while passing her the ball. Just a bit later we heard a rousing interplay of bird cries. Resounding squawks were coming from various places across the creek, and single high-pitched screeches were sounding in evident response. "What's happening over there?" I wondered aloud, stretching my luck with a teenager in hopes of nurturing her budding ecological awareness. I was glad to hear her quick reply: "That hawk is hassling some crows, and they're trying to scare it away. Now come on Dad, kick me the ball!" Soccer was more important that day, which was fine. It's a great game and we were having fun. I trusted that she had been touched by the hawk, and that his presence would live on in her in some mysterious way. I also knew she would meet him again. He is our neighbor after all!

The fabric of human life has always been woven with experiences like this. Always, until recently. Encounters with wildly diverse beings and elemental presences have helped comprise our very existence, just as our involvement has helped comprise theirs. Of course, the other-than-human natural world is immensely powerful and at times deadly dangerous. To idealize nature as all beautiful and nurturing is as deceptively alienating as seeing it merely as a threat or material resource for human exploitation. Yet the natural world is vital in bringing us into being and sustaining our lives in healthy ways. It cannot be otherwise. But many of us now go about our daily existence without appreciating the significance of this core (co)existential fact. Sometimes we actively repress it so as to avoid painful realities, or for temporary convenience or self-aggrandizement. Prime examples are the widespread denial of global warming and people's lack of awareness that the earth is now suffering a mass extinction of species. Both of these are human-generated perils, symptoms of humankind's confused, fear-filled estrangement from the rest of nature. Culturally sponsored beliefs, values, and lifestyles have created a world dominated merely by interactions with other people and human artifacts. Most of us are losing the daily, conscious contact with the natural world that has nourished us since the very incipience of our species. We are now infecting ourselves with a malady unprecedented in human history: "nature-deficit disorder," in Richard Louv's (2008) foreboding phrase. The designation, a darkly ironic twist on attention-deficit disorder, is not a formally designated psychological disorder. Not yet. But we are definitely plagued by an insidious deficiency in the quality, amount, and consistency of attention we give to the natural world. As one fourth grade boy put it, "I like to play indoors better, 'cause that's where all the electrical outlets are" (Louv, p. 10). Ominously, we know this young fellow is not alone in his sentiments. In most so-called developed countries, people's lifestyles are (mostly) based on the (mostly) unconscious fantasy that we can detach ourselves from the rest of nature and still live well. Albeit normal today, this is delusional and unsustainable. By delusional I mean a false belief that is held rigidly in the face of clear evidence to the contrary. Our ecopsychological affliction is far more grievous than any officially designated psychopathology. In response to this crisis, the present book will offer a diagnosis of current maladies and opportunities—indeed, responsibilities—for healing and transformation.

If conscious contact with nature continues to decline, if the narrowly human world is all that young people experience, this depleted condition will become the unquestioned norm, simply the way things are and have to be. Nature will be further impoverished and so will we, but without even realizing what we are missing. What remains will be a haunting feeling that something is wrong, something important is absent. And it will be difficult to name. Anxiety, sadness, disorientation, irritation, and unhappiness will be exacerbated, but such symptoms will be attributed to sources unrelated to our alienation from the natural world. Such a deprived state ensures that ever more animals, plants, and natural places will be banished from our lives, driven away by climate disruption and habitat destruction (such as massive deforestation), poisoned by chemicals we spread, or totally vanquished at the hands of a nature-estranged culture dominated by unconstrained capitalist expansion and excessive (but ultimately unfulfilling) consumption. In a vicious circle, contact with nature will further decrease and distress will increase.

It is clear that we are in the midst of a severe ecological crisis. The fact that we are correspondingly undergoing a psychological, spiritual, and cultural crisis is less clear but even more dangerous. We humans are intrinsically relational beings. Our well-being is enhanced and our suffering is healed largely by way of our interactions with others. So let us remember that the beings and presences of nature are relational partners who have forever graced our lives. *When we lose these natural companions and our relationships with them, we are losing something essential in human existence.* We are just beginning to reawaken to a fact that has been obvious to indigenous peoples across eras and cultures: conscious involvement with the natural world fosters our well-being and that of our nonhuman fellows, inseparably so and reciprocally so.

## Introducing Ecopsychology

Ecopsychology is a relatively new field that explores the psychological dimension of our relations with the rest of nature and the ecological dimension of human psychology. Via theory and applied practice, eco-psychology is devoted to fostering a new turn in consciousness and culture, a psycho-spiritual-cultural transformation that enhances the *mutual well-being* of humankind and the rest of nature. The health of humans and the natural world co-arise in concert. So too the lack of well-being. We all flourish, or not, together. By well-being I mean truly holistic health: physical, psychological, sociocultural, spiritual, and ecological, with all these dimensions working synergistically with each other. While the biological world is being ravaged unconscionably, it is increasingly apparent that our current ecological maladies are not only biological ones. Looking just under the surface, we see that they involve a fundamental psychocultural and psychospiritual pathology. Our lives are being afflicted by a misguided (and misguiding) dissociation, particularly the *supposed separation of one's self from others and of humankind from the more-than-human natural world.* Such feelings of disconnection sponsor fear toward all those who appear separate from us. Overcompensating in the face of this exaggerated threat, we presume ourselves superior to the rest of nature, elevated above the so-called "lower" animals (not to mention plants, mountains, oceans, deserts, atmosphere, and on and on). This creates a felt-belief that we are entitled to exploit the natural world, with little empathy, conscience, or care. But when we abuse the natural world, we abuse ourselves, our children, and generations to come, because all of these are inextricably involved with the rest of nature. This is the urgent crisis of consciousness and culture calling to us today.

The most commonly proposed solutions to our ecological maladies are technological: renewable energy, green buildings, desalination, seeding the atmosphere with small particles to block incoming radiation and reduce global warming, even colonizing Mars. Some, like the first three, are quite valuable. Some, like the last two, are based upon notions that created the ecological crisis in the first place: the wish that humans could master and control the natural world, or the wish that we could escape and avoid our real challenges. But no technology addresses the root causes of our suffering. That is where ecopsychology and allied approaches come in. The most crucial step is growing beyond our fantasy of separation. We find a similar ethos in indigenous cultures; in the nondual, contemplative branches of the world's spiritual traditions; and in phenomenological philosophy. Throughout this book I will weave together insights from Zen Buddhism, Christian mysticism, existential and hermeneutic phenomenology, and psychoanalysis, including key ideas from the practice of psychotherapy. In doing so, I will craft a largely transpersonal—nondual, nonseparatist—version of ecopsychology that is complemented by existential and psychoanalytic insights. The present work aspires to help us heal our *supposed, apparent, or presumed* dissociation from the nonhuman natural world. The qualifiers in italic are important because our felt-sense of separation is a socially constructed belief, a collective fantasy that operates much like an individual delusion. It temporarily attenuates our anxieties—dread of death, lack of control over our lives, the sense that something is lacking—while creating far more suffering over time.

Because we will often return to the core endeavor of surpassing this afflictive sense of separation, let me share what I mean by "separate" and associated words. Separate can serve as a synonym for "particular" or "individual," as in a separate self or tree. But that is not how I use it in this book. Of the dictionary meanings that I do hope to evoke, as a verb, separate means to sever a connection, divide, detach completely, force apart, disunite. (These readily transpose into adjectives.) As an adjective, separate signifies something apart, by itself alone, disconnected, divided from the rest. Two connotations from Middle English are especially pertinent for us: to be "cut off from the main body," and, for marriage partners, to be "estranged."[1] All of these meanings apply, depending on context, not to reality but to our (often unconsciously held) felt-beliefs about our relationship with the natural world. To be clear, every person and the whole human species are different in many ways from nature's other beings and presences. We can honor such differentiation while knowing that we can never really be separate, severed, or cut off from the great body of the animate earth. In Wilber's (1977) words, each of us is "'different,' but *not* separate" from every other (p. 107). To draw another metaphor from the etymologies I just shared, it is not uncommon for married couples to undergo a trial phase of "separation." But in humankind's intrinsic (yet often disavowed) marriage with the rest of nature, it is painfully obvious that our experiment with separation (or even presumed divorce) has been an utter disaster. We could say that ecopsychology is now stepping in as a kind of marriage therapist.

However, until recently, psychological research and clinical practice have mostly ignored our relations with the natural world. This very fact is an expression of humankind's experiential dissociation from the rest of nature. Psychologists have long worked to alleviate suffering that comes from biological, existential, interpersonal, intrapsychic, and sociocultural adversity. Biologically, we are conditioned by our genetics and the intrinsic vulnerability of our tender animal bodies. Existentially, the ordinary circumstances of life are difficult and painful (and marvelous too). Each of us will struggle with injuries, accidents, illnesses, and aging. We will inevitably lose everyone we love most dearly, as they will die before us or we before them. Interpersonally, people will hurt us and we will hurt them, often unintentionally and sometimes maliciously. Intrapsychically, in our relations with our own self, we can fall into patterns of tyrannizing ourselves with confusion, fear, self-doubt, shame, self-loathing, mistrust, and self-constriction. Here we bind ourselves with our own rope, as an old Zen saying has it. Social, cultural, economic, political, and legal forces support us in countless ways. Yet they can also be terribly oppressive, often reinforcing inequities of power, privilege, wealth, and justice. Think about matters such as racism, classism, sexism, homophobia, religious intolerance, militarism, consumerism, homelessness, unconscionable forms of corporate capitalism, and so on.

The field of psychology has studied and responded to all these painful challenges. However, only in the last couple of decades has it begun to work with the suffering associated with our alienation from and destruction of the animate earth. Ecopsychology now is helping us embrace the health-enhancing possibilities and ethical responsibilities that come with our interdependent involvement with the natural world. Immersed in life's beauty and its pain, it is evident that we coexist with all other beings and presences. Taking the next crucial step, ecopsychology supports us to be in this life not just with each other but *for* each other, in the service of each other. Psychology and other fields are increasingly focusing on how nature can bolster human well-being: encouraging exercise, designing work environments that include natural phenomena, bathing in the fresh air of a forest to enhance our mood, procuring ingredients for new medicines from natural habitats, and so forth. Such initiatives are tremendously valuable. However, they can be one-sided, unintentionally reinforcing the exclusively human-focused bias that generated our eco(psycho)logical crisis. Therefore, ecopsychology endeavors to foster psychological, cultural, and spiritual capacities that ally with the rest of nature in a *mutually* enhancing way. I keep saying "the *rest* of nature" because we humans are natural beings. (Nature includes culture, as I will discuss.) When nature is ill, we too are ill. When children breathe polluted air, their bodies become polluted and respiratory illnesses tend to follow. When people are deprived of conscious contact with nature, anxiety, depression, and other psychological maladies arise. Conversely, when humans are ill—psychologically, culturally, spiritually—the nonhuman natural world will be ill. Alienated by the fantasies of human exceptionalism and self-interested individualism, governments, corporations, and individuals continue with business as usual even when confronted with disasters such as global warming. In a countercultural move, ecopsychology understands that taking care of the natural world is simultaneously taking care of human well-being.

## Brief Overview of Chapters

Each chapter begins with pertinent epigraphs and an introductory "Overture." The book is organized thematically such that a single chapter might offer views from Buddhist psychology, Christian mysticism, phenomenology, and psychoanalysis on a distinctive concern. Our partners in dialogue will be David Abram, Matsuo Bashō, Thomas Berry, William Blake, Martin Buber, Shākyamuni Buddha, Eihei Dōgen, Meister Eckhart, James Finley, Jane Goodall, Jesus Christ, Emmanuel Levinas, David Loy, Joanna Macy, John Muir,[2] Maurice Merleau-Ponty, Thomas Merton, Thich Nhat Hanh, Gary Snyder, Mary Oliver, Ken Wilber, and others.

Chapter 1 celebrates joyous, pleasurable, revelatory, transformative experiences with the natural world. This will help us appreciate earth's healing, life-enhancing qualities, thereby sponsoring the kind of gratitude and care that are so often lacking in today's nature-estranged world. Chapter 2 explores the rampant death and destruction of the natural world currently taking place. By creating experiential access to the reality that the earth is suffering a mass extinction of species, the chapter guides us into working with grief as a key constituent of ecopsychology. Chapter 3 considers the fact that humans are inherently relational beings. By plundering nature, we are vanquishing relational partners who have forever graced our lives. In abdicating conscious contact with nature, we are disavowing crucial relationships. Both of these moves destroy something essential at the heart of being human. Chapter 4 considers how the historical and cultural conditions of the modern era amplified the socially constructed view that humans are separate from, elevated above, superior to, and thereby entitled to dominate and exploit the rest of nature. Chapter 5 looks at the development of the ego or separate self-sense (in childhood and beyond) in order to deepen our understanding of the way we humans are afflicted by stories, feelings, and actions of separation. Chapter 6 offers a transpersonal, contemplative approach to ecopsychology by way of the Christian mystical tradition. A crucial transformative element involves seeing ourselves and the rest of nature as an expression of the infinite depths of life. Relatedly, the mystics advocate a psychospiritual metamorphosis wherein we surrender or transcend our exclusive identification with our supposedly separate, autonomous ego, and thereby realize an infinitely deeper, transpersonal sense of self and way of being. Chapter 7 works with the writings of the Zen poet Bashō in order to craft a contemplative therapy for our eco(psycho)logical maladies, one that fosters a movement from ego-centered alienation to eco-centered intimacy. The chapter includes ecopsychological insights from Buddhist psychology. Chapter 8 shows how humans and the rest of nature are always participating in and creatively contributing to a nondual, transpersonal, conversational, ecological form of consciousness, one that transcends yet includes our conventional individual consciousness. Awakening in this participatory conversation, we may realize that nature's dynamic inter-responsive field is simultaneously who we are and that for which we are summoned to loving care. Chapter 9 explores the common malady of bodily desensitization and disidentification, a key variant of our overall dissociation from the rest of nature. We will show how the natural world can foster embodied relational attunement; and, correspondingly, how such conscious attunement can be mutually healing for the rest of nature and for ourselves. Chapter 10 explores how the natural world is ever calling upon us, and that each of us is irreplaceably responsible for answering that call. Our well-being and that of others turns on how we take up such appeals. Countering our conventional, separatist stance, chapter 11 explores how love is our nature, our calling, our path, and our fruition. The culminating coda freshly gathers the book's major ideas and envisions ways to take further steps.

## Placing Powerfully Charged Words in Context(s): Nature and the Natural World

I want to affirm the mysterious, complex, indeterminate, evocative quality of key words, and especially of the *lived phenomena* to which they point. The preceding heading alludes to "charged" words: nature, mystery, reality, spirit, buddha-nature, true nature, true self, the Dao, the way, God, sacred, holy, nonduality, contemplative, mystical, ethical, love, life, and so on. Each holds a powerful energetic and disclosive charge. Given these words, truly offerings for mutual contemplation, an author and a reader have a reciprocal task, one that is far more important than quibbling over strictly preestablished and fixed meanings. Our responsibility is to release the latent charge of these words (and associated stories) so as to foster fresh understanding and loving interactions. In this way, an overly familiar term can come alive as a transformative "turning word." This is a Zen expression for a word (or phrase) that is welcomed so openly and deeply that it sponsors a real turning of our consciousness and way of being.

"Love" and "compassion" will often be used interchangeably because I understand the second to be a variant of the (more inclusive) first. With *compassion*'s Latin roots evoking a sense of deep care and "suffering with" another, sometimes I opt for this term when the context involves our response to pain. I will often speak of the "beings and elemental presences" of the natural world. I use "beings" for biological organisms and "presences" for all other differently animate forms of nature. For the latter, I mean variations of the classic elements of air, earth, water, and fire: presences that are airy (sky, wind, breath), earthy (soil, stone, bone), watery (rain, oceans, tears), and fiery (sun, lightning, the firing of synapses). Most presences are conventionally deemed inanimate and insentient, but it only takes a little shift in awareness to sense their dynamic liveliness. For example, I once heard a woman tell of a powerful encounter on a mountain path. Walking along she was suddenly struck by the way an immense rock wall rose sharply up from the trail. This stopped her in tracks instantly. Gazing in awe at the sheer stone face of the cliff, she said she felt "the living presence of God." Experiences like this are why I say that these phenomena are differently animate. Similarly, each presence is really a "presencing." This unusual locution conveys the vivid dynamic (inter)activity we feel when meeting, say, a flowing stream, cold wind rushing through our hair, or a dancing campfire. This is much like the connotations already built into the word "being," invoking not merely a reified objective entity but its lively shining forth, its being. All presencing includes hidden, implicit, unmanifested, or not fully manifested (yet nonetheless intimated) dimensions.

The word "nature" is far more mysterious, intrinsically resisting any prescribed, delimited, firmly fixed, readily graspable definition. "Nature is perhaps the most complex word in the language" (Williams, 2015, p. 164), as one scholarly survey of the most significant English words concluded. I have done plenty of foolish things in my time but I am not so foolish as to try to precisely define the word nature. The depths of what it refers to, how it functions, and what it can summon forth in us are truly ineffable and infinite. One cannot de-fine something that is in-finite, de-limit something limitless. Nonetheless, to suggest the interrelated network of meanings that this word carries, I will offer a few remarks. The *Oxford English Dictionary* (OED) tells us that it derives from the Latin *nātūrā*, which means "birth, constitution, character, course of things"; and from *nascī*, "to be born," thus highlighting its dynamic, nonreifiable quality. The dictionary goes on to articulate 15 different definitions, beginning with "the essential qualities or properties of a thing" (1971, p. 1900). Other variants include: "the general inherent character or disposition of mankind [sic]"; "the material world"; and "the features and products of the earth itself, as contrasted with those of human civilization" (p. 1900).[3]

Building upon this array, Gary Snyder (1990) provides a revealing reflection on the word nature. It can refer to "'the outdoors'—the physical world including all living things" (p. 8). Nature often connotes that which is "other-than-human" (p. 8). Snyder then quotes the *OED* regarding "the material world" and adds that this includes "the products of human action" (p. 8). In some versions of this encompassing meaning, we could claim that "*everything* is natural" (p. 8). This would include, say, megacities, industrial toxins, nuclear weapons, the Holocaust, and global warming. Snyder says that he prefers the following meaning for nature:

"The physical universe and all its properties" (p. 9). Imagining *everything* to be natural reminds us of the all-embracing, all-permeating quality of nature. And it dissolves the core dissociative fantasy that terribly afflicts us today, namely, the supposed disconnection of humankind from the rest of nature. But it can also impede our critical discernment and ethical engagement. Living in an abundantly diverse world is very different from living in one that is being plundered. "When an ecosystem is fully functioning, all the members are present at the assembly" (Snyder, 1990, p. 12). But far too many are being banished from their rightful place in the assembly: nonhuman beings and presences, people of color, the poor, to name just a few. It is crucial that we discriminate between sustainable actions that join with what is "natural" and others that go against it.

Snyder addresses such concerns by discussing the word "wild." Scholars trace its origins to the Old English *wilde* and *wyld*. In even more ancient tongues, wilderness may have come from wild-deer-ness. All of these wild words are linked with kindred ones, including "will." The latter helps us appreciate a core point, namely, that *wild nature has a kind of will or mind of its own, infinitely beyond our efforts to master and dominate it.* The OED (1971) provides various definitions of wild: "living in a state of nature"; "not tame, not domesticated"; "not cultivated"; "uninhabited; hence, waste, desert, desolate"; "uncivilized, savage; uncultured"; "resisting control or restraint, unruly"; "self-willed"; "passionately excited or desirous"; "fierce, savage, ferocious; furious, violent, destructive, cruel" (pp. 3776–3777). Pondering these characterizations, Snyder observes that "wild" tends to be defined by what it is *not*, according to a Euro-centered perspective. I would also point out that these cultural constructions come from a stance that separates humans from the rest of nature; that privileges control, reason, and submission to authority; and that devalues humans' lively, felt, passionate, embodied engagement along with the spontaneously free functioning of the natural world. Wild nature certainly precedes and exceeds human will and control. We humans often detest this basic condition of our existence, as if it were an indignity, and we react by treating nature in demeaning and violent ways. In a countercultural move, Snyder (1990) asks us to ponder that which is wild from an affirmative perspective:

> Of animals—free agents, each with its own endowment, living within natural systems. . . . Of land—a place where the original and potential vegetation and fauna are intact

and in full interaction and the landforms are entirely the result of nonhuman forces. . . . Of societies— . . . Societies whose economic system is in a close and sustainable relation to the local ecosystem. . . . Of behavior—fiercely resisting any oppression, confinement, or exploitation. . . . Expressive, physical, openly sexual, ecstatic. (pp. 9–10)

Continuing, Snyder points out that these appreciative views of the wild

come very close to being how the Chinese define the term *Dao*, the *way* of Great Nature: eluding analysis, beyond categories, self-organizing, self-informing, playful, surprising, impermanent, insubstantial, independent, complete, orderly, unmediated, freely manifesting, self-authenticating, self-willed, complex, quite simple. . . . In some cases we might call it sacred. It is not far from the Buddhist term *Dharma*. (p. 10)

I will draw from nearly all the preceding significations, but mostly I mean the following overlapping and interrelated faces of nature. The numbering does not indicate priority.

1. *Nature as* the animals, plants, fungi, viruses, bacteria, and elemental presences of an eco-community, along with their dynamic, participatory, conversational, inter-responsive functioning. Sometimes this will refer to the nonhuman world. Sometimes it will include human beings, culture, and society.

2. *Nature as* human nature: nature as it takes form and functions in an individual, in our relations with others, and in human culture. Human nature can include our biophysiology; genetics; instincts; sensory capacities; embodied awareness; sexuality; aggression and self-assertiveness; meaning-making abilities; feeling; thinking; language; culture; experiential awareness; creativity; intuition; death awareness; understanding, compassion, love, justice; kinship with the more-than-human world; and the inter-responsive structure, functioning, and ethical responsibility of our (co)existence. Significantly, it is

part of human nature to discover our participatory role in relation with the larger ecological and cultural communities. By designating these capacities as natural, I am not saying they are uninfluenced by culture. Ecopsychology challenges the old nature/culture binary split, and ecologists have demonstrated that culture is not limited to humankind. Think of the complex sociocultural organization of chimpanzee and Orca whale communities. Social learning plays a major role in individuals' development regarding relational interaction, hunting, nest building, group dialect, migration, and so much more. Elders teach their young about how to live well with each other in their particular home bioregion. Thus, many nonhuman animals are profoundly cultural beings. Conversely, *nature encompasses human culture.* "Civilization is part of nature" (Snyder, 1990, pp. 181–182). Almost any human quality can be expressed in a natural way, say by coming forth in consonance with the context-dependent needs of the particular individuals involved and of the whole community. *It is in our human nature to act with care for the world of nature.* But any human quality can also be distorted into unnatural, anti-natural, pathological, and pathogenic forms. Humans' presumed separation from and exploitation of the nonhuman world are not natural in the way I mean it here. Neither is global warming, racism, genocide, nuclear war, or the human-generated mass extinction of species.

3. *Nature as* a convivial, inter-responsive, conversational, participatory ecological system: holistic, indivisible, dynamic, animate, sentient, sapient, loving, integrated, harmonious.

4. *Nature as* the whole earth and all-embracing cosmos in their integrated, wise, loving, dynamic, inter-responsive functioning. Humans are included here, of course.

5. *Nature as* our home: the bioregion wherein we dwell, the place where we are engaged in close contact with our intimates, the place that supports our well-being (or

not, depending on circumstances). Note that *eco-* comes from the Greek *oikos*: home, house, dwelling place.

6. *Nature as* our community: the shared, participatory, socio-cultural, ecological fellowship of all beings and presences in a local bioregion and beyond.

7. *Nature as* the deep way, order, and coherent functioning of life or being or reality; the essential, inherent way things are and are with each other. Humans can consciously live in consonance with this way. And we can turn away from it or lose touch with it, as in the cases of individual narcissism and collective anthropocentrism.

8. *Nature as* a provisional name for that which is ultimately unnamable and unfathomable—the one great, seamless, indivisible, nondual, all-inclusive, all-permeating, participatory mystery in its complete, integrated, wise, loving, dynamic functioning: life, being, reality, God, the Dao, buddha-nature, the cosmos (by whatever name). Nothing can be separate from, outside of, excluded from, or other than this version of nature. In this specific sense, nothing is unnatural.

9. *Nature as* our self: our true self, deep self, real self, no-self, true nature, essential nature, no-nature (to use the language of mystics across various spiritual traditions). We can also call this our transpersonal self or ecological self.

10. *Nature as* our conversational partner: friend, companion, lover, mother, father, mentor, stranger, adversary, therapist, nurse, patient, benefactor (be they human or other than human).

Notice that one popular phrase is missing from the list: "the environment." When people ask if I am an "environmentalist" or "environmental activist," I heartily answer, "Yes!" But if things deepen into a real conversation, I go on to say that I am not fond of the term because *environ* means to surround, encircle, or encompass. The connotations are implicitly dualistic or separatist, as in "I am over here and nature is over there." The term also suggests that nature is a mere backdrop for human activities. And it obscures the crucial *interrelationship* transpiring between humans and the rest of nature. These views are seriously misleading, a symptom of our lost intimacy with the rest of the natural world. Nature does encompass every individual and society, no doubt. Yet nature also permeates us, comprises us, *is* us (and everyone else).

Similarly, I will use phrases such as "humankind's relationship with the natural world." It would be awkward, but more accurate, to say nature in human form in relationship with nonhuman nature. That is, *while humans are different from the rest of nature in significant ways, we certainly are never separate from it.* We are always involved with the natural world, indivisibly so even if unconsciously so: life keeps us breathing, we contend with a virus, we eat an apple, we build a skyscraper, we seek shelter in a hurricane, we enjoy the sweet scent of a flower. Further, from a transpersonal perspective, each of us and the whole human species is a distinctive expression of and co-creative participant in the animate earth. As etymology discloses, *a human is a being of the humus,* the earthy soil. You are nature coming forth as you. Your life is one way the earth is continuing to be and become itself.

## Research Method and Evidence:
## Hermeneutic Phenomenology

One of my basic commitments is that the findings in this study be based upon lived experience, upon evidence that readers can consider for themselves. My experientially grounded data have been drawn from various sources: testimony from ordinary citizens, psychologists, spiritual/mystical/contemplative teachers, philosophers, poets, and nature writers; testimony from participants in empirical phenomenological-hermeneutic research that I conducted; and descriptions of encounters that have occurred in my personal life. Such evidence is always offered to draw out its psychological significance. For example, I do not present poetry strictly as poetry, but as phenomenological data. When I highlight an aspect of our relations with nature, please consider how your personal experiences resonate with, contradict, or supplement the discussion. Our current eco(psycho)logical emergency is calling for a generative collaboration among engaged citizens around the world, including contributions from specialized disciplines. Here people often think of ecology, biology, technological fields, and environmental activism. Yet equally important are psychology, economics, education, politics, law, spirituality, and the arts. In my view, ecopsychology can make a distinctive contribution to an interdisciplinary, *psycho-cultural-spiritual "therapy"* on behalf of the truly great work of our era. This endeavor must address four synergistic dimensions: *personal experience, interpersonal relationships, the sociocultural world, and spiritual life.* Personal involvement is the primary source of all the benefits we gain from nature, and the experiential source of our care for the larger natural world. However, no one can flourish alone. Interpersonal support between friends, mentors, and other allies can make all the difference. This includes participation in small or large group initiatives like those sponsored by environmental activist organizations. Our work must also address systemic sociocultural values, structures, and forms of discourse that enhance or diminish the nature-human relationship. Economic, political, educational, and legal practices are crucial here. And whether we identify as religious or not, our spiritual life must be included in the great work.

Giving primacy to lived experience, the guiding approach of this book will be phenomenological and contemplative. Originally a distinctive movement in twentieth-century philosophy, phenomenology's innovative contributions have been influential in existential, humanistic, psychoanalytic, and transpersonal/contemplative psychotherapy; and in the growing field of qualitative research. To invoke the heart of this approach right away, phenomenology involves " 'wonder' in the face of the world" (p. xiii), as Maurice Merleau-Ponty (1962) attests. The aspiration is to discover/create vivid, subtle, complex understandings of a phenomenon as it is experienced in its common lifeworld context. It is easy to quickly "understand" something in a superficial way, without really letting it speak to us and teach us something new. We can all be lured into the complacency of thinking we "get it" because we have "been there and done that." Embracing the epistemological power of intimate attention, phenomenological inquiry is often initiated by contact with something that appears quite obvious and taken for granted. But *the significance of the obvious is rarely very obvious.* Thus, I will often point to common events and ask us to (re)consider them carefully.

Edmund Husserl (1970), the founder of phenomenological philosophy, emphasized that "we must go back to 'the things themselves'" (p. 252), back to the way things present themselves in direct lived experience. Notice the resonance with Bashō's (1966) contemplative guidance from the preface: "Go to the pine if you want to learn about the pine"

(p. 33). Martin Heidegger studied with Husserl, built upon his work, and eventually gave phenomenology a more sociocultural and linguistic focus. Yet he continued to stress the importance of careful attunement to lived experience. In an awkward locution that is worth pondering, Heidegger (1996) said that "phenomenology' means . . . to let what shows itself be seen from itself, just as it shows itself from itself" (p. 30).[4] Yet the meanings of another's expression are rarely easy to understand and never totally determinable. This is because complexity and subtlety pervade every significant expression; because all interpretation depends upon perspective and context, and there are always other perspectives and contexts; and because each newly developed understanding carries intimations of further significance. Therefore, Husserl stressed the importance of intentionally "bracketing" our conventional preconceptions and expectations—setting them aside as if in brackets, suspending their automatic meaning-bestowing effect (as much as possible)—so as to foster open seeing and understanding. To work phenomenologically is to be "a perpetual beginner" (Merleau-Ponty, 1962, p. xiv), taking nothing for granted and inquiring freshly each time. This phenomenological attitude is quite similar to meditative awareness. As the Zen teacher Shunryū Suzuki Rōshi (1970) declared, "The goal of practice is always to keep our beginner's mind. . . . If your mind is empty, it is always ready for anything; it is open to everything" (p. 21).

However, we are all affected by sedimented biases that come from our personal history, cultural conditioning, and native language. These preconceived views function largely unconsciously. Aware of this fact, *hermeneutic* versions of phenomenology were developed by philosophers such as Heidegger (1996) and Hans-Georg Gadamer (2011). The word hermeneutic is a scholarly term for the art and (human) science of interpreting qualitative data. It derives from the Greek god Hermes, whose task was to convey messages back and forth between the gods and human beings, translating them as skillfully as possible. Heidegger and Gadamer emphasized that there is no such thing as bias-free understanding. All interpretations are inevitably shaped by the interpreter's stance. The context-laden, culturally influenced, perspectival nature of perceiving and thinking is intrinsic to the very way we understand. Thus, *hermeneutic* phenomenology is oriented by the intentional practice of catching our prejudices (as best we can) and then *placing them not aside but right in front of us for critical reflection and revision*. It is not a matter of getting rid of our prejudices but working with them consciously.

The phenomenological attitude helps cleanse our "doors of perception," as William Blake (1988, p. 39) famously put it, thereby opening to the real alterity of the phenomenon. In a complementary manner, whatever we begin to understand needs to be held lightly and provisionally. Thus, phenomenology and hermeneutics are actually inseparable. I am sure that my preferences, privileges, and blind spots have shaped the interpretations in this book. It is an ongoing work for me to be aware of the good fortune built into my position as a White, male, middle-class university professor. A person of color or one who is economically impoverished would surely view aspects of their relationship with nature differently. For example, for calculated reasons, far more ecological degradation occurs in underprivileged communities.

A related point involves an implicit consent agreement with you as a reader. I hope you will be generous when I say "we," "us," and "our"—as in "our" great work of cultivating a mutually enhancing partnership with the natural world. Even when I say "I," the reference is usually to people in general. My intention is not to make totalizing statements that level out the diversity that comprises any collective "we." When a glorious eco-community is annihilated by mountaintop removal, I am not angry at "us" for the rapacious violence but at "them," coal corporation executives and the political-legal system. Still, I want to appeal to the most inclusive group of allies as "we" face "our" current crisis.

I would like to call your attention to one more characteristic of hermeneutic phenomenology. The work of interpretation has often been depicted as a *hermeneutic circle* or *spiral*. In presenting meaningful (and action-inspiring) stories about our relations with the rest of nature, I will show how particular constituents of the overall story are linked with each other and with the larger story as a whole. For example, two major themes will reappear in various versions throughout the book. (1) We will look critically at the suffering created by *our felt-sense of dualistic separation*: the fallacy that our self is really separate from others and the world, along with the felt-belief that we are merely sovereign, masterful, autonomous, self-sufficient, self-concerned subjects; and the associated fallacy that humankind is intrinsically separate from the rest of nature, with our supposedly exceptional species elevated to superiority and the natural world devalued and exploited. This fundamental—albeit normative—delusion of humankind generates great fear and greed. (2) We will explore *inter-responsive, interdependent, nondual (nonseparatist) alternatives to these dissociative fantasies*. This will involve an explication of *the inherently ethical structure and responsibility of human existence.* By way of a hermeneutic spiral, each time we (re)consider these matters, our previous analyses will be supplemented, deepened, and carried further. I trust the intentional repetition will be freshly creative, not redundant. Rather than settling for cognitive insight, I'm hoping to foster a vital way of knowing that we feel in our blood, bones, and heart, and that we bring into our daily relationships. After all, *knowledge should be embodied as new ways of being, understanding, and loving.* This is what I mean by a transformation of consciousness, one of ecopsychology's crucial tasks.

## The Emergence and Development of Ecopsychology

Before ecopsychology came onto the scene in the 1990s, there were only occasional psychological inquiries into the relationship between humans and the natural world. Without trying to be exhaustive, I would like to acknowledge a few significant examples. The most famous psychologist ever, Sigmund Freud, was critical of cultural and intrapsychic forces that exerted excessive control over the natural body-based drives and passions of the so-called "id." But he also inherited a modernist ethos of separation, domination, and exploitation regarding the natural world. Freud (2010) thus advocated for an "attack against nature and subjecting her to the human will" (p. 45). In contrast, in *Gestalt Therapy,* a 1951 text that founded a new humanistic psychotherapy, Paul Goodman and Fritz Perls presciently expressed concern that "there are disturbances that may be called neurotic that occur in the organism/natural-environment field, for instance . . . our contemporary disease of 'mastering' nature rather than living symbiotically" (Perls et al., 1951, p. 355). Paul Shepard, an ecologist with deep psychological insight, also did sustained work in this area. He stressed that "if man's environmental crisis signifies a crippled state of consciousness as much as it does damaged habitat, then that is perhaps where we should begin" (Shepard, 1973, p. xvi).

The field of "environmental psychology" began to emerge in the 1960s, with an interest in how contact with nature contributes to the psychological health of humans. Rachel and Stephen Kaplan (1989; 1998) are notable researchers in this field, with a series of influential publications focusing on the restorative benefits of experiences with the natural world. The word "ecopsychology" (and the interdisciplinary field by the same name) were originated by the cultural historian and countercultural critic Theodore Roszak. He was chief editor of *Ecopsychology: Restoring the Earth, Healing the Mind* (Roszak et al., 1995), a landmark anthology that made our relations with nature a respected theme of psychological research and psychotherapeutic inquiry. Roszak (1995) was one of the first to emphasize that "*ecology needs psychology, psychology needs ecology. The context for defining sanity in our time has reached planetary magnitude*" (p. 5). Andy Fisher's *Radical Ecopsychology* (2013), with its insightful integration of theoretical and clinical perspectives, helped carry the field further. As Fisher says, "Ecopsychologists argue that genuine sanity is grounded in the reality of the natural world; that the ecological crisis signifies a pathological break from this reality; and that the route out of our crisis must therefore involve, among other things, a psychological reconciliation with the living earth" (p. xiii). In a series of profoundly illuminating works, the psychotherapist and ecopsychologist Jeff Beyer (1999) presented an in-depth, nondual phenomenology of "experiencing the self as being part of nature" (p. 5). "Why are we apparently so willing to push it to the very edge of catastrophe? . . . Perhaps we are in denial about being 'in' the world. . . . The central, most fundamental, and most pathogenic problem in our relating with nature is that we like to think of ourselves as being 'apart from it' rather than as being 'a part of it'" (Beyer, 2014, p. 199). Thankfully, as we will see, scholars from disciplines other than psychology have also made major contributions to ecopsychology. A particularly noteworthy text is Warwick Fox's (1990) *Toward a Transpersonal Ecology*. Building upon Arne Naess' "deep ecology," Fox articulates a transpersonal foundation for ecophilosophy. While I will not draw explicitly from the deep ecologists, their keen insights are thoroughly consonant with our present work.

## Transpersonal (Eco)Psychology and Contemplative/Mystical Spirituality

Advancing a *transpersonal* and *contemplative* approach to ecopsychology is the most distinctive contribution of this book. Transpersonal psychology is a subfield of psychology devoted to understanding experiences, modes of consciousness, senses of self, and ways of relating with others that go beyond (*trans-*) our personal, ego-centered identity and ways of being. Transpersonal psychology is sometimes called spiritual or contemplative psychology, since the phenomena it studies have traditionally been associated with religion and spirituality. The whole discipline of psychology has a deep (if often disavowed) connection with spirituality and with wild nature as well. The very word psyche comes to us by way of the Greek *psykhe*, and this ancient word gathers a significant collection of interrelated connotations: breath, life, soul, spirit, mind, animating spirit. As we will show, the psychological, spiritual, and ecological dimensions of existence are intertwined, interacting with one another in mutually creative ways.

The field of transpersonal psychology originated in the work of humanistic psychologists such as Abraham Maslow and others in the late 1960s. Maslow (1968) emphasized that "without the transcendent and the transpersonal, we get sick, violent, nihilistic, or else hopeless and apathetic" (p. iv). And he often connected this sensibility with the natural world. In the years that followed, transpersonal psychology grew through the contributions of theorists such as Stanislav Grof, Jean Houston, Ken Wilber, Stanley Krippner, Roger Walsh, Frances Vaughn, John Welwood, Michael Washburn, and Jorge Ferrer. Transpersonal psychologists are especially interested in situated experiences and stable modes of consciousness wherein we realize that our self is not limited to a conventional, skin-bounded, sovereign, supposedly separate self (or ego).

Because psychology is such a well-known field today we easily forget that it only became a distinct research and therapeutic discipline in the second half of the nineteenth century. Throughout most of history, the deepest psychological inquiry has been conducted by the mystics and sages from the world's spiritual and philosophical traditions. Indeed, I see *the contemplative/mystical schools of each religion as indigenous psychologies*, each one carrying wisdom and methods of inquiry that have been cultivated across millennia. This compares with only 150 years for modern psychology. On the other hand, there now exists a large body of psychological knowledge that was unknown to the spiritual traditions. I will endeavor to draw out the psychospiritual insights of contemplative/mystical/transpersonal spirituality and make these relevant for our everyday relations with the natural world. The mystics are renowned for not being satisfied with secondhand, experience-distant, conceptual knowledge about the depths of life. Hearsay regarding the great matters of life and death and love were not sufficient. Rather, they crafted *experiential* practices of personal inquiry into these depths, practices that helped people bear pain, alleviate suffering, and sponsor well-being. They showed how meditative attunement to our direct experience disrupts the fear-filled dream—nightmare!—of our self-absorbed existence, thereby fostering real awareness, understanding, compassion, love, and justice. These capacities comprise the ethical heart of being human, and they can help remedy the dualistic dissociations now afflicting our lives: humankind over nature, self over others, mind over body, my tribe over others', and so forth.

Our imperiled earth is imploring us to surpass such supposed splits for our own well-being and that of the rest of nature. As the book's title suggests, this is truly a wild and sacred call. Nature is infinitely deeper, subtler, and freer than even our best understanding and gesture of care, much less our self-centered, human-centered efforts at mastery and control. This is the wildness of earth's sacred summons. In encountering that which is sacred, we open to infinitely precious and powerful dimensions of other people, the natural world, and life itself. These are dimensions of depth and wholeness that draw us beyond our supposedly separate and self-preoccupied ego, thereby fostering loving responses to others in accordance with their unique preciousness and ethical appeal. This approach contests the classic opposition of sacred and secular. A sacramental sense is not dependent upon *what* we are encountering, *but upon the depth of consciousness we bring into the contact.* Still, nature is one of the most auspicious circumstances for the sacred to be revealed. Others include love, death, sexuality, beauty, embodied engagement, art, music, pain and suffering, and spirituality.

In light of all these issues, a contemplative, transpersonal, psychospiritual approach to ecopsychology is especially valuable. The various etymologies of "religion" are telling in this regard. Religion as *re- + ligare*, to *bind fast or bind again* (what *appears* to be separate); to *unite* or *make a bond* (between humans and God, yet also humans and the rest of nature); to *bandage* (our dissociative wounds); to *place an obligation upon* (to answer the other's call). Also, religion as *religiens*, meaning to *care*, in contrast with *negligens*, to neglect. And religion as *re- + legere*, to *read again* (as in rereading the messages nature is sending us). Relatedly, mystical or contemplative spirituality is often called yoga. Yoga is popularly thought of as a physical exercise, but most deeply it means union—as in the English word "yoke." Yoga is a process of consciously uniting mind and body, self and other, self and nature, self and God (or life or the Dao or the great way). More precisely, we realize these were never really separate in the first place. Hence, *ecopsychology is a kind of nature yoga*, appreciating that the union is not just with the biological world but with nature as the depths of being.

We can clarify our use of three more key words: "meditation," "contemplation," and "mystic." What is called meditation in popular parlance and in Asian spirituality is called contemplation or contemplative prayer in the Christian mystical tradition. For our purposes, these words will be used as synonyms. Also, mystic, contemplative, and meditative practitioner will function interchangeably. In all cases I am referring to someone who devotes their existence to conscious experiential contact with the infinite depths of life; to communion with and identification *as* these very depths; and to compassionate, loving service of those depths by way of serving others day by day. For those who are religiously inclined (as most but not all mystics are), this depth dimension might be called God or the Dao or buddha-nature. In practice, I am talking about the holy depths that touch us, say, in the face of another person, a nonhuman being or presence, a civic concern in our community, or the stirring voice of our authentic self.

The English word mystic derives from the Old French *mystique*, mystery, and further back from the Greek *mystikos*, secret, connected with the religious mystery schools. However, in the present work, *the mystery intimated in the word mystic has to do with the ever-present and ever-available heart of life.* I am concerned that the sense of secrecy suggests that the mystical or contemplative life is exclusionary, reserved only for a few elite people. A related concern is that the mystical path is sometimes associated with a dualistic, ascetic, world-denying, body-denigrating, otherworldly spirituality. Some mystics have adopted such a dissociative stance. Across traditions, however, most of the esteemed contemplatives emphasize that mystical awareness is neither extraordinary or exclusionary, and that its authentic forms are profoundly world affirming rather than world denying. "Mystical union is not an experience of the extraordinary, it is a new vision of the ordinary" (Sells, 1994, p. 202).

Listening for the truth held in the words mystic and mystery, I would say that the depths of life and nature are indeed obscured when met through our conventional self-sense, consciousness, and way of being. Yet, when these contracted modes are surrendered, we can welcome and realize our identification with the very depths as they are coming forth right here and right now. "The moment in which the transcendent reveals itself as the immanent is the moment of mystical union" (Sells, 1994, p. 212), that is to say, reveals itself via direct experience. There will always be mystery. Such is the case before, after, or without any (so-called) mystical realizations. Yet, as our very birthright, conscious mystical awareness is potentially accessible in every moment. And it can radically transform our relations with the natural world. If the mystical life is a secret, it is one we keep from our self, a truth our superficial ego unwittingly obscures. If the mystical life is a secret, it is really an *open secret*.

Inspired by the mystics' *experiential* ethos—and this is an earnest invitation to readers—I am not content with merely writing *about* our relationship with the rest of nature. My hope is to create conditions for lived discoveries that sponsor a true metamorphosis in our way of relating.

## Spontaneous Mystical Experience and Formal Contemplative Practice

A mutually generative alliance between the world's spiritual/wisdom traditions and Euro-American psychology has been possible only in the last several decades. Never before in human history has the expertise of each come into dialogue with that of the other. This means that transpersonal (eco)psychology holds immense potential for understanding, healing, growth, transformation, and liberation. Transpersonal psychologists appreciate both serendipitous spiritual experiences and formal meditative practices. Most deeply, the preeminent "practice" is our inter-responsive engagement in everyday life. The world is our real *zendō* (or meditation hall). Indeed, *intimate involvement with nature was probably the original form of meditation.* Imagine, in ancient days, listening sensitively to a bird's call, maybe for pure pleasure, maybe to discern what's going on in the forest. Or think of a hunter whose survival depends upon open, patient, still, silent attention. Or someone being drawn into reverie by the flames of a campfire.

Contemplative contact with the natural world was crucially important in the origin of today's major religious traditions. In one famous case, as the story goes, Moses is far out in the desert wilderness when he encounters a bush blazing with fire but not being consumed. Pausing, he beholds this intense sight and realizes that the burning bush is the very presencing of God. In the form of the fiery bush, God calls to him: "Moses, Moses!" And Moses responds: "Here I am! (*Hineni!*)" (Exodus 3). (When the depths of life are calling upon us, "Here I am!" is an exquisite initial response, both contemplative and ethical at the same time.) We can sense Moses' open, vivid contact with the flaming face of the divine. Inseparably, let us appreciate that he is meeting an ordinary bush. Yet, in contrast to most encounters, Moses allows the depths of nature to speak to his depths. Thereby the bush becomes hallowed. The inherently ethical quality of our (co)existence is intimated in this encounter, because "Here I am!" really means "Please tell me what I can do for you." And the message Moses receives is profound: God says, "The place on which you are standing is holy ground." This event occurred in a location many would deem a desolate wasteland. Yet every place may be hallowed when met with open awareness.

## Placing Powerfully Charged Words Context:
## Nature, Buddha-Nature, God, Being, Life

I welcome the mystics as mentors because they have been the experts in the transpersonal realm for millennia. Therefore, I heartily—but cautiously—work with several time-honored spiritual words. Using these in a scholarly context deserves some contextual commentary, however. "God" is the prime example, as it tends to carry complex, conflictual, emotional baggage. When exploring the writings of Christian mystics, I work with this classic word because it was central in their experience. Today, though, the word God is often tossed around so casually that it becomes banal; or, conversely, it is automatically and presumptively dismissed without a real consideration of its evocative potential. These reactions mirror each other, both being largely devoid of reflection, thereby foreclosing the life-enhancing possibilities held in this word. God is among countless ancient names that have been bestowed on the one sacred, nondual, all-inclusive, all-pervading, dynamic, participatory mystery. Without claiming that the following are identical, there are many alternative *names for the great unnamable*: nature, buddha-nature, the Dao, the way, the beloved, being, spirit, energy, reality, the one, the cosmos, heart, light, love, life. At this point in my life, most classical spiritual or philosophical names work very well for me. *But I am happy with traditional renderings only after critically reinterpreting them.* My inquiries—both scholarly and experiential—into phenomenology, psychoanalysis, transpersonal psychology, Zen Buddhism, and Christian mysticism have been crucial here. Yet I understand that spiritual language does not suit many people today. Significant translation is often required for words like God to resonate authentically. Be assured, spiritual language is not necessary for the journey we are taking together in this book.

Mystics have long held that it is impossible to fully conceptualize what God (or the Dao or ultimate reality) means or is. Joseph Campbell emphasizes that we must "realize that the word God is metaphorical of a mystery and the mystery is absolutely beyond all human comprehension" (Abrams, 1987). And as Laozi famously tells us, "The Tao that can be told is not the eternal Tao [Dao]" (Mitchell, 1988, p. 3).[5] Still, we can appreciate the fact that the old master's teaching comes to us in a text, a medium that brings the Dao into words in order to bring readers into conscious consonance with the Dao. The unsayable actually calls to be said—reverently, tentatively, provisionally, strategically—so as to be more consciously lived, with understanding and love. Thus the ancient philosopher Plotinus (205–270 CE) proposes "the one" as a felicitous name for the unnamable ultimate reality. But in doing so he honors the intrinsic aporia we encounter when endeavoring to say what cannot really be said. From Greek roots, aporia means not porous. It connotes the doubt, perplexity, and agony of facing an apparently insoluble impasse, here the impossibility of saying what "the one" is. As Plotinus confesses, "We find ourselves in an aporia, in agony over how to speak. We speak about the unsayable; wishing to signify as best we can, we name it. If the one is to be taken as a positing, name, and referent, we would express ourselves more clearly if we did not speak its name at all. We speak it so we can begin our search" (Sells, 1994, pp. 16–17). Plotinus' last remark is crucial for our purposes. I join the mystics in invoking various names for the great mystery. However, I do this not to specify any definite referent, but to begin (ever again) a search for experiential discovery and further dialogue. Such words are offered, taken back, said differently, supplemented in a reverent, tentative, provisional, strategic way—all in hopes of deepening our explorations, fostering transformation, and carrying the conversation further.

Poets and mystics—often one and the same—are the best at this awesome linguistic and psychospiritual venture. As Shakespeare avows, "The poet's eye . . . / Doth glance from heaven to Earth, from Earth to heaven. / And as imagination bodies forth / The forms of things unknown, the poet's pen / Turns them to shapes and gives to airy nothing / A local habitation and name" (A Midsummer Night's Dream, act 5, scene 1). The core aporia is the simultaneous impossibility and urgent necessity of speaking (of) the mysterious heart of life. I certainly don't have the great bard's gifts. Nonetheless, the infinite sacred depths of nature need to be honored, to be given "a local habitation and name," even (or especially) because they are subtle like air, really nothing at all—no substantial, isolated, or fixed thing—and ultimately unknowable (conceptually). Yet they are experientially accessible. That is why I draw gratefully from poets and mystics, the preeminent experts in articulating the ineffable. Yet to meet them eye to eye, heart to heart, we need to release our habitual stance and drop into our own version of the consciousness from which they speak, welcoming their words via a kind of *lectio divina* (contemplative reading).

To illustrate, consider the word "God." (If this rubs you the wrong way, please substitute another word such as life, being, reality, the great way, the Dao, or the cosmos.) Adopting one strategy, we can use language to say what God is *not*. Alternately, we can offer words for what God is *like*, metaphorically, analogously. Best of all, we can *consciously realize* our inherent union with the great mystery, realizing too our supreme identity as a seamless and responsible manifestation of this infinitely deep reality. This experiential way is the preeminent one. But all three are complementary. Adopting a so-called apophatic approach, a *via negativa*, some mystics have cultivated the linguistic practice of pointing out what God is not: not this, not that, not any limited thing that can be defined or named. Sometimes it is said, startlingly, that God is nothing. In other words, God is no thing, certainly not any objective, reifiable, fixed thing or entity. Sometimes God is called the unsayable, unnamable, inconceivable, unqualifiable, formless, unborn, undying, unbounded, infinite. All of these negations aim to subvert the lure of idolatry: our reductive, complacent, or anxious inclination to turn God into some reified thing we presume to grasp and understand conceptually. In this spirit, Saint John of the Cross invokes "I-don't-know-what" when alluding to God (1991, p. 472). Mystics have also cultivated a complementary cataphatic strategy, a *via positiva*, a way of tentatively, provisionally, strategically making affirmations concerning God or life or the great mystery. They have experimented with language that explores something—not really a "thing"—that can never fully be languaged, a reality that addresses us and calls to be spoken (so as to be realized experientially, listened to, spoken with, identified with, and responsibly served). Here is one of the most beautiful cataphatic expressions: "God is love" (1 John 4:8). It is also said that God is life, peace, truth, justice, awareness, spaciousness, freedom, being, reality, the cosmos, mystery, the beloved, and on and on. Concerned that provisional affirmations will solidify into fixed notions to which we become attached, contemplative writers often say something and then unsay it, take it back, supplement it with alternative sayings. "I pray to God to make me free of God" (p. 424), as Meister Eckhart (2009) humbly says. Similarly, Zen master Linji (Japanese: Rinzai) declared: "If you meet a buddha, kill the buddha" (Watson, 1993, p. 52).[6] Regarding the word God in the present study, perhaps the most general affirmation I could make is to say that I am pointing to the infinite, all-permeating, dynamic heart of life, ever mysterious yet ever present, transcending every thing yet always—immanently, nondually—taking form in and as the particular beings, presences, and inter-responsive events that are transpiring here and now (and everywhere and everywhen). Please know that this includes you and me and elk and islands. The word buddha will serve similarly. But this is not limited to a single person who woke up to his true nature 2,500 years ago in India, Shākyamuni Buddha. Rather, buddha is an evocation of the intrinsically awake, alive, loving presencing of life itself—infinite open awareness saturated with love. At times the word "nature" will serve in essentially the same way.

The word God is used (and often misused) to mean vastly different things. Many of these are tragically destructive, as when a terrorist believes they are authorized to kill in the name of "God." A related danger involves the (largely unconscious) assumption that one knows what the word "God" means or refers to, or even the assumption that there can be some objective delimited meaning or reference in this unique case. This is a fantasy—idolatry, in religious terms—and it leads to naïve presumptiveness at best and violence at worst. Although the mystics I cite often speak of God or point to God appearing in the natural world, I want to acknowledge that I cannot really say what God means. But I do know what it cannot mean, at least in any spiritually mature way. God cannot justify killing those who see the world differently from "us," or exploiting those less privileged, or desecrating nature's beings and presences. And God cannot be reduced to a figure like Santa Claus (or B. F. Skinner conditioning rats or pigeons in a lab): a White male authority who observes us from a distance, discerns who is "naughty or nice," and intervenes with rewards or punishments. If someone were to assert that they "do not believe in God" while referring to such a conception of God, I would reply that I do not believe in *that* "God" either. That is the immature (notion of) "God" that Nietzsche and Freud cogently critiqued. And that is certainly not what the mystics in this book are pointing to.

By whatever name, the lived reality celebrated by the mystics is an existential given, one that is accessible and pertinent for everyone regardless of religious affiliation or nonaffiliation. Since transpersonal psychology involves a mutually informative—indeed, transformative—conversation with the world's spiritual traditions, I have given myself the liberty of using traditional spiritual language where it seems apt. But not without misgivings. Therefore, beginning right now, I will present the word "God" in an alternative form: G-d. I am taking a cue from the Jewish practice of pointing to G-d by way of the written tetragrammaton ("four letters"): YHWH. I adopt this strategy because, *at best*, the word G-d is charged with evocative, revelatory, transformative power—power that is most likely released when we pause humbly and receptively upon hearing such a revered word. Herein, we appreciate that no concept of "God" is G-d, even beautiful ones like love and life. To honor the unfathomable mystery, however, while bringing it down to earth and making it experience-near for those for whom religious language fails, *I often find it helpful to speak of "life" in place of G-d* (or the Dao or buddha-nature). By way of this translation we may intuitively sense into the depths of these ancient yet still timely words. By life I do not mean mere biology. Nor life as opposed to or excluding death. Rather, it is more like what is conveyed by phrases such as "This is what life is sending my way." We all have a sense of what this means, even if we cannot define it. This discussion is meant to encourage readers to make their own translations or substitutions. When the text says G-d or the Dao, you could try replacing it with "life" (or being or reality or your own preferred word).

I often opt for "life" because I find this word *experientially accessible*, grounded in our ordinary shared world.[7] Still, let me acknowledge that I cannot say what this life is, just as no one can ever really say what G-d is. After all, G-d is certainly not a "what," not a delimited thing. Nor is life. Nor is nature. Yet, with the mystics, I am reaching toward an *experiential realization and shift of consciousness* that has a guiding influence on our daily (co)existence. In his book *Mystics and Zen Masters*, Thomas Merton (1967) offers an intriguing commentary on Laozi's *Dao De Jing*. He says that the "*Tao* which is unknown and unable to be named authorizes us to find here something that corresponds with our notion of God" (p. 72). Continuing, he approvingly cites a Chinese translation of the Gospel of John. The text's most revered lines are usually rendered like this: "In the beginning was the Word [*Logos*], and the Word was with God, and the Word was God. . . . The Word became flesh" (John 1:1). As a Christian mystic, Merton dares to celebrate this alternative translation:

"In the beginning was Tao, and Tao was with God, and Tao was God" (p. 72). He then challenges us to appreciate that "If there is a correct answer to the question, 'What is the Tao?' it is: 'I don't know'" (p. 73).

Not coincidentally, the very same thing could be said about our "true nature," "essential nature," "true self," or "real self" (to cite common ways the mystics put it). Legend has it that an Indian monk, Bodhidharma, brought Buddhism to China in the fifth or sixth century where it blended with Daoism to become Chán (Zen). In an earnest conversation regarding the heart of Buddhism, Emperor Wu asked Bodhidharma, "Who is facing me?" (In other words, who are you most deeply?) And Bodhidharma replied, "I don't know" (Cleary & Cleary, 2005, p. 1). Yet, as Zen master Jizo once avowed, "Not knowing is the most intimate" (Wick, 2005, p. 63). All these kindred claims come from the contemplative appreciation that we cannot know *conceptually* what G-d or the Dao or our true self is. Nor can we put this fully into words. Anything we think or say that G-d or the Dao or our real self is, that is not it. *Nonetheless, by way of contemplative awareness, we can know this great mystery by consciously being it—by realizing that we (and all others) are a distinctive expression of that unnamable reality and by living accordingly. And precisely the same is true for "nature."* Therefore, I would like to propose that the following acknowledgment serve as a humbling touchstone for ecopsychology. "But we do not easily *know* nature, or even know ourselves. Whatever it actually is, it will not fulfill our conceptions or assumptions. It will dodge our expectations and theoretical models. There is no single or set 'nature' either as 'the natural world' or 'the nature of things.' The greatest respect we can pay nature is not to trap it, but to acknowledge that it eludes us and that our own nature is also fluid, open, and conditional" (Snyder, 1992, p. v).

## Contemplating Nature, Being Nature, Loving Nature

We have now spiraled hermeneutically—*back and ahead*—to our core focus. My aim is to offer some perspectives that will help foster the mutual well-being of humans and the rest of the natural world. Of course, "nature" has to be central. Yet I must acknowledge something that may sound strange in such a book: *Honestly, I do not know what nature is.* Nonetheless, this much is clear, although my clarity ends in mystery and awe: I am clear that my singular body-mind is a dynamic mode of and creative participant in something infinitely deep, subtle, and wild; a source immanently inseparable from, comprising, and yet transcending every situated encounter; "something" that is certainly not a thing but in and through and as which all particular things, beings, presences, and encounters arise, interact, and pass away. It does not really matter whether I call this nature, buddha-nature, G-d, the Dao, being, my true self, or life. That is because the "clarity" I mentioned is not some fact that I cognize conceptually, from a distance. Rather, it is an intimate, experiential, nondual, intuition that springs forth as an ethical sensibility, guiding my way of living and responding to others. This includes writing this very book, one small contribution to the great but precarious turning of consciousness and culture now underway.

*Nature. I really do not know what this wild and sacred mystery is. But I do know that I am it, just as all others truly are. And I know that I love it. And I know that I am being called to make that love tangible as responsive, devoted, engaged service.*

Chapter One

# Seeing Those Peach Blossoms
# Changed My Life

## Keeping Joy, Wonder, and Gratitude Alive in Our Heart

Be still and know . . .

—Psalm 46:10

We have a longing for coming home to the sacredness of our belonging to the living body of Earth and the joy of serving that at every step.

—Joanna Macy (Jamail, 2020)

And for me, the promise that comes up is the promise to love this planet. To love it all. To love it like my kin, because it is my kin. . . . That's the mystical promise.

—Nora, Christian contemplative and research participant

### Overture

Our first ecopsychological responsibility is to step outside and let ourselves be touched by nature's sacred beauty, wonder, wisdom, and love. Such experience is intrinsically nourishing, while also being the primary source of healing, gratitude, and loving care for the natural world. When we open ourselves for intimate contact, nature's depths will flow through us and change how we respond to other people and the rest of the natural world. In this way, our relational responses become more fitting and mutually enhancing for all involved. And when it comes down to it, *everyone is always involved.*

## Stop, See, and Love

Once upon a time a man was walking in the mountains. Turning around a bend, a blossoming peach tree shined forth in all its splendor. His life was changed on the spot. "Some thirty years I searched for a master swordsman. / How many times leaves fell, how many times branches burst into bud. / But from the instant I saw the peach flowers blooming, / Now no more doubts, just this!" (see Dōgen, 2012, p. 88; Miura & Fuller Sasaki, 1966, p. 292).[1] The man is Lingyun, a ninth-century Chinese poet who later became a Zen teacher. His poem commemorates an event of awakening, of seeing into and realizing his—our!—essential nature. Lingyun's spiritual quest had already spanned decades. Meditation practice had ripened his sensitivities. Then, like a sharp sword (as enlightening as any Zen master's teaching), the glowing blossoms cut through any lingering confusion, fear, and doubt, revealing "just this!" Astonished, he realizes that *this* is what he had been searching for all those years.

The expression "once upon a time," so familiar from countless childhood tales, has long held a cherished place in English literature. At best it serves as a kind of incantation for altering our conventional consciousness. The phrase intimates that events like those that are about to unfold in the story are archetypal human realities, core existential experiences that recur across eras and cultures. Poignantly, the classic opening line encourages us to appreciate that such events are actually transpiring in our very own life. Once upon a time really means right here and now. Lingyun's poem touches us across twelve centuries because such transformative events are not limited to any special time or place. Nor are they reserved for any (presumably) special people, Zen masters or otherwise. Quite the contrary. I trust that each of us has been blessed with similar encounters. Please substitute your own treasured versions: sunlight glistening like diamonds on a lake; the helping hand of a friend, providing assistance and opening your heart; tasting life itself when orange juice meets your tongue; your beloved caressing your naked body; the sensation of holding a handmade ceramic cup; a child dangling from a tree branch, laughing with delight; a vast mountain vista, leaving you feeling tiny, or infinite, or altogether gone.

Such are the common blessings of our (co)existence, although we often pass them by unnoticed or underappreciated. Regarding these initiatory moments of realized holiness, Martin Buber (1965) laments, "It is like this every day, only we are not there every day. . . . For the most part we have turned off our receivers" (p. 11). One key aspect of living well involves making fresh conscious contact with what seems obvious, welcoming solicitations from the generally taken-for-granted world. According to Zen lore, the Buddha silently presented a flower to a large assembly. A single student smiled an awakening smile, realizing that the little flower actualized the intrinsically radiant, wakeful heart of reality. As the story goes, this was the initial transmission of the dharma—the great way or truth, the essential nature of everyone and everything—from Shākyamuni Buddha to his disciple, Mahākāśyapa.[2] Psychotherapists also understand the revelatory power of dwelling with apparently obvious expressions. Upon catching a slip of the tongue or unexpected emotion in a casual phrase from a patient, a therapist might remark, "Listen to what you just said!" The world calls out to each of us, no doubt. But out of habit, convention, or defense, the richness of our experience often slips away. "In order to see the world . . . we must break our familiar acceptance of it" (Merleau-Ponty, 1962, p. xiv). Both phenomenology and contemplative practice begin by attending to what is obvious and evident—where else could we begin?—and then endeavor to disclose implicit meanings held latently therein. Such a sensibility helps us appreciate the untold depth, significance, preciousness, and even holiness of ordinary things and encounters.

It is so easy to quickly bypass the depths of life—peach blossoms, a tear in our beloved's eye, the silence of a clear winter night—as we busily rush to complete one task after another, whether authentic or insignificant. The dominant culture, with its obsession over profit (for a privileged few) and progress (narrowly defined), pushes us to move ever faster and faster. Rarely do we avail ourselves of the opportunity to drop out of the demands of the clock (and the market), and drop into the exquisite abundance of the present moment—both in its gifts to us and its requests of us. The fact that we usually live time only in this way is one of the great afflictions of our lives. Once I was not recovering well after spraining my ankle playing basketball, so I called my doctor to see if anything more than rest and ice could help. "Yes," she said, "there are some ways to speed the healing process." Or that is what she consciously meant to say. But this is what she really said: *"There are some ways to heal the speeding process."* Following an evocative silence, we both chuckled uneasily, anxiously aware of this peril: in today's world, our lives are pervaded (or invaded) with speeding processes. Driven largely by our business-as-usual worship of capitalism and consumerism—the collective secular religion into which we have all been thrown—such conventional speediness leaves us confused, anxious, depressed, irritable, or otherwise ill, while amplifying the destruction of the natural world. As I said to my doctor, healing the speeding processes is one of the most crucial challenges of contemporary culture.

I would like to highlight the relevance of formal meditation practice—and, by extension, *a meditative sensibility in daily life*—for opening us to a more intimate, sacramental involvement with the natural world. A famous contemplative text encourages us: "Be still and know . . ." (Psalm 46:10). I call the psalm contemplative because it conveys the spirit of meditation practice. More precisely, it celebrates two of three interrelated dimensions of meditation: stopping and knowing. The third and most crucial dimension is loving—that is, bringing our deep knowing into responsive and responsible action. Suspending our habitual busyness, being still, silent, peaceful, and relaxed: this is typically what comes to mind when people think of meditation. While stopping (being still) is only the first step, it is an important one. Our fast-paced culture makes it difficult to pause such that we can really understand and offer a loving response. Therefore, meditation begins by intentionally interrupting the momentum of our conventional existence, worldview, and supposedly separate sense of self.

There are many types of contemplative practice, but most involve the core sensibility of allowing oneself to be present, open, and in intimate conscious contact with every experience that arises. My Zen teacher, Bruce Sōun Harris Rōshi, has a marvelous phrase for this: "uncontrived naturalness" (personal communication, November 10, 2018).[3] This means continuously consenting to and confiding myself into the sheer presencing of each moment—like those radiant peach blossoms. This includes surrendering the habitual activity of clinging to pleasurable experiences or avoiding painful ones. In many traditions, this eventually consists of not actively directing attention to any particular object of focus (such as the breath) and instead surrendering into vast open awareness. "Relaxing into stillness" and "releasing into openness," as Harris Rōshi says (personal communication). Yet the crucial message of the psalm is not stillness, but knowing. In other words, stopping and surrendering allows us to see more clearly and deeply than we usually do. All real discovery happens beyond our willful capacity to manufacture or control it. It is a gift of life. Nonetheless, we can consciously create favorable conditions for revelation, for there to be an upwelling of clarity and energy from the very heart of being. Specifically, we have some choice about two contemplative attitudes: stopping and surrendering. Life's depths still may not be disclosed, but it is certain that they will not if we cling to our habitual ways and resist the spontaneous overture of our present experience.

And what do we know when we slow down, release into the presencing moment, and see clearly? First of all, we realize that we are not separate. The feeling of being a detached subject observing objective life from a distance falls away. In seeing from our depths—beyond ego, beyond separation—we are moved by the other's depths. We become conscious that we have already been contacted by the very depths of life, summoned and moved prior to our freedom and consent, with those true depths appearing as a particular other right there before me. Alternately, but with a little translation it comes to the same thing, the psalm offers a classic view of what we know when seeing deeply: we know G-d. The entire psalm continues: "Be still and know that I am G-d." For our present purposes, we could rename the final often-fraught word and say: the infinite, mysterious, precious, sacred depths of life, which—upon stopping and seeing clearly—we realize to be no other than a friend in the hospital, no other than a forest asking us to resist the impending clear-cut. You see, this brings us to the heart of the matter. In meditation and daily life, the real point of being still and seeing is to respond lovingly. Strictly speaking, it is not actually a linear process. *Being, knowing, and loving are actualized as one.*

The true aspiration of meditation is not merely to sponsor clear seeing in a formal practice period, but to integrate that consciousness into our everyday way of being. In the unfolding of any encounter, everything begins by letting myself realize vividly what is actually happening right now: someone is making contact with me, in fact asking something of me. Thus Allen Ginsberg shares an invitation, one that is far more subtle than first appears: "Notice what you notice" (in Gach, 1998, p. 198). In stopping to embrace this moment's relational touch, we often forget about clock time. That is not the only kind of time, after all, and we do not have to let it tyrannize us. The afflictive speeding processes can surely be healed. In any instance we can open into what the mystics call the eternal now, the infinite fullness of each presencing event, wherein nothing is lacking. The great thirteenth-century Zen master Eihei Dōgen (2012) points out that time is not just a quantity of hours or years that we have. *Time is what we are.* When we see deeply into any moment—joyful, painful, or neutral—we can honestly say: For the time being, *this is the time of my life.* An existential question follows naturally: How shall I live this time? And this existential question is inherently coexistential: Shall I live not just for myself, but in the service of *all* my relations in this shared earth community, both human and otherwise?

Two common examples involving our relations with nature may help illustrate the phenomenological-contemplative sensibility that I am celebrating. For instance, when I am a little less self-preoccupied than usual and a little more attuned, when I am not lost in a time-crush rush to finish some project, the ordinary and obvious can open and reveal infinite depths. My wife or daughter or son only have to walk into the room, and their very presence gives rise to a warm vibration in my heart, an upwelling of love and gratitude. Sometimes they see me smiling and ask why. In those moments, I can only say: "You! Just you being here. Just you being yourself. That's all." *And that's everything!* You may wonder how this example depicts our "relations with nature." Well, interactions between people are natural, yes? The presumed divisions of humans and nature, culture and nature need to be deconstructed again and again.

In another circumstance, contemplating the wild salmon on my plate, I realize that with each bite the flesh of the fish is becoming my very flesh, mind, and heart. And I remember that this nourishing food was once a sentient being, a magnificent fish that swam—amazingly!—from the river to the ocean then back up the river, that fed and mated and played with its fellows in ways different from but akin to my own. I feel the intrinsic value of this other animal's life, and know my life depends upon the life and death of other living beings. No wonder humans have long appreciated the sacramental quality of receiving a meal! For such gifts, I say thank you to the salmon, thank you to the earth, thank you to the cook.

But it is hard to let such significance sink in when we are insulated from direct contact with the natural world. Over the years I have asked many a child where hamburger comes from. I am sorry to report that kids mostly say the supermarket or McDonald's. There is little place for empathy, gratitude, and care when we think in this way. Naturally, we draw nourishment from the rest of the world: eating the flesh of plants and (perhaps) animals, harvesting the body of the earth for our homes and work sites, sharing the spaces and places and energies of the larger natural world. The vexing problem is that we do this mostly unconsciously and with uncritical entitlement, feeling little appreciation for what we are doing to the kindred participants who grace our world and sustain our existence. Life carries on dependent upon the life and the death of other life. There is a tragic dimension of this, since it means the death of beings whose life is precious. But there is also glory in the fact that life is comprised of a grand mutual interchange of existence. The natural response is great gratitude and care.

Every day we live on the life and death of others. This would be horrifying if not for the existential truth that this is simply how our shared life is necessarily structured. There is no other way. What really matters is the quality of consciousness we bring to eating (or to any other form of relating with the natural world). Do we treat nature as merely an "it," a thing to be exploited? Or do we meet nature as a Thou, a deep and hallowed presence that calls upon us in our depths? Do we take nature's gifts for granted, in a self-entitled way? Or feel grateful to be participating in life's grand giveaway? Most basically, "we must try to live without causing unnecessary harm, not just to fellow humans but to all beings. We must try not to be stingy, or to exploit others. There will be enough pain in the world as it is" (Snyder, 1990, p. 4). When aware that we are involved in this sacred compact with the other-than-human community, we tend to respond more sensitively with all our relations. Supported by life-enhancing interactions like the ones I just described—nourished by tasty food and by my sweet family—I naturally go on to offer what I can to this splendid world. I also do my best with the fiercer things sent my way in the course of existence: pain, suffering, death, loss, trauma, oppression, injustice, desecration of the natural world, and on and on. These too are life coming to meet me.

## Benefits of Conscious Contact with the Natural World: A Brief Survey

Extensive research has demonstrated something that has been completely evident until recent times: conscious involvement with the natural world enhances human well-being. Interacting with nature includes the following physiological benefits: boosts the immune system; reduces inflammation;

lowers blood pressure; improves sleep; fosters cardiac health; lowers cholesterol levels; enhances physio-motor coordination; reduces obesity; mitigates respiratory disorders; lowers chronic disease risk; accelerates recovery from surgery and illness; and provides sources of medicines, many yet to be discovered. Sociocultural and economic benefits: serves as the source of all our food; provides raw materials used for building and the production of artifacts; enhances the health and productivity of the workforce; lowers crime rates; increases job satisfaction; provides gathering spaces. Psychological and spiritual benefits: elevates mood; fosters positive outlook; reduces stress; raises energy levels; induces emotional healing and restoration; reduces aggression and anger; improves focus and concentration; enhances sensory perception; improves memory; restores mental energy and clarity; restores capacities for directed attention; improves academic performance; increases creativity; improves self-esteem; enhances resilience; mitigates symptoms of psychological disorders such as attention deficit hyperactivity disorder, posttraumatic stress disorder, anxiety disorders, depression, and Alzheimer's; fosters enjoyment of beauty; enhances social relations; enhances care and service to others beyond one's self-centered concerns; fosters a sense of meaning and purpose; diminishes biophobia; fosters care for the beings and presences of the natural world; sponsors transpersonal realization and self-transformation; and enhances spiritual well-being. Even when such benefits are not cited explicitly, they will be informing our explorations. Indeed, an extensive survey of the research literature recently made a cogent case for "nature relatedness" being a "basic human psychological need" (Baxter & Pelletier, 2019).

The growing array of research is quite compelling. So is testimony from lived experience. In our ecopsychology courses at Duquesne University, I require students to go out and make contact with the natural world at the same place for at least 45 minutes each week. They are to attend carefully to the way things are at their site and how it is for them to be there, then journal about their experiences. On a cold February day, one student remarked: "Nature kicked SAD's ass today!" If only more people knew of nature's therapy for Seasonal Affective Disorder!

## Savoring Joy, Wonder, and Gratitude

The examples I have shared in this chapter have to do with pleasure and beauty. This is an intentional choice, but I understand that it may raise concerns given the rampant ravaging of nature now taking place. Our hearts feel like they are breaking when forests are destroyed for profit; a crumb-seeking pigeon is wantonly kicked off the sidewalk "just for fun"; earth's climate, chemistry, community, and consciousness are disrupted with disastrous consequences, mostly for money for merely a privileged few. I promise that this book will not turn away from the destruction, pain, and loss that are plaguing the earth today. As Thomas Hardy (2001) knew, "If way to the Better there be, it exacts a full look at the Worst" (p. 168). But the complement is equally true: *to face the worst we need to keep the best alive in our hearts.* Every day we are confronted with bad news about ecological ills that are beyond our immediate control. For this very reason, it is crucial to stay in touch with our gratitude for nature's awesome beauty, wonder, and mystery. Otherwise we are liable to be overwhelmed by the pain we inevitably suffer when attuned to the plight of earth under assault.

Earth's beauty is abundantly evident and revitalizing. To create sustainable alternatives to the eco(psycho)logical catastrophes afflicting our world, we have to find ways to foster *pleasurable experiential contact* with nature. This can be as simple as drinking fresh, clean water; savoring the sweet scent of a lilac; pausing before a giant orange harvest moon; feeling life coursing through our body. As Rilke (1989) reverently attests, "Earth, my dearest . . . you no longer / need your springtimes to win me over—one of them, / ah, even one, is already too much for my blood" (p. 203). For the time being, a single encounter may be all it takes. Yet consistent contact allows the significance of our relationship with nature to settle into our body, mind, and heart; to really transform our ongoing consciousness and sense of self; to guide us along the way. Recurring engagement is required to cultivate a real friendship between people, and so also between humans and the natural world. I am sure Rilke relished many a spring, with flowers blooming and birds returning, before those exquisite lines could flow through his heart and pen. Staying in touch with the gratitude we feel in such experiences, our hope, courage, and resiliency are bolstered to face the traumas we are bound to undergo when we care about the natural world. Cherishing the joy that nature bestows, we step forth in the service of all our relations. Holding these encounters in our heart, they simultaneously hold us.

Sparrow song! Garden tomato! Thunderclap! Something much deeper than pleasure is going on in these experiences. In awakening to the sheer presencing of nature, we are touched by something profoundly deep and precious. We can sense our creative involvement in a great dynamic life that is unfathomably ancient and completely fresh. Don't get me wrong: pleasure is wonderful and I'm all for it! Yet further, the animate earth's expressivity can lead to (co)existential and ethical realizations. As a real mentor, the natural world shows us that we can never really be separate from others. And an ethical overture is presented in such encounters, an appeal to respond otherwise than our self-interested individualism inclines us to do. The joy we feel in being with others draws forth real care, compassion, love, justice, and engaged service. Another's suffering can sponsor loving care as well, but that is a story for a different chapter.

Let us listen to Mary Oliver (2004), a poet whose work flows from intimate contact with nature. Hearkening the core ethical-relational summons that such contact bears, basic questions arise: "What does it mean . . . that the earth is so beautiful? And what shall I do about it? What is the gift that I should bring into the world?" (p. 9). Nature ceaselessly sends precious gifts, and each one simultaneously presents us with an appeal to share our distinctive gifts in reply. This call-and-response process functions quite differently from a calculated, instrumental, economic deal: "I'll give you something but only because I will get something back from you." Rather, when touched intimately by what nature bestows, our genuine care emerges freely.

## Love of Life, Love of Nature

In our relationship with nature, just as with other people, conscious contact is the primary source of wise compassionate action. Ethical standards and laws regarding the environment have an important place, and they need to be strengthened. Nonhuman beings and presences surely need to be granted formal legal and ethical rights. Ultimately, though, we are best guided not by the mandates of external authority but by conscious attunement to our direct lived experience. However, we have been thrown into a dangerous situation in this regard. The human-centered values and lifestyles of today's capitalist-techno-corporate culture are actively removing us from aware contact with the natural world. Social, economic, and political practices are driving species to extinction, diminishing biodiversity, and destroying habitat at rates unprecedented in earth's history. These forces are obliterating many of our relational partners, foreclosing countless opportunities for enlivening encounters in the community of nature. These circumstances are creating yet another unprecedented concern: "nature-deficit disorder" (Louv, 2008). Unwittingly, we have fallen into sociocultural practices that afford less and less interaction with the natural world. Increasingly our attention is focused only on human projects and artifacts, whether we are busily occupied with our jobs or tuned into screens; whether our kids are rushing from school to piano lessons to soccer to the gym to a job, or being captivated by a video game. This scenario depicts normal everyday life for many of us. But it is actually quite insane because we are depriving ourselves and our children of a crucial constituent of human well-being: namely, nourishing involvement with the rest of nature.

In contrast to this pernicious trend, for *hundreds of millennia (!)* we human animals have coevolved in close conscious rapport with earth's wildly diverse animals and plants, and with other natural presences such as mountains, rivers, air, and the bountifully fertile earth. These were— and those remaining still are—the neighbors with whom we co-created a supportive community, day by day, generation by generation. Some could kill us, some could enliven us, and all could teach us. Each and every one offered distinctive contributions to the flourishing of our local bioregion, including the health of us humans. The renowned biologist Edward O. Wilson implores us to understand that "for more than 99 percent of human history people have lived in hunter-gatherer bands totally and intimately involved with other organisms. . . . In short, the brain evolved in a biocentric world, not a machine-regulated world" (Kellert & Wilson, 1993, p. 32). Human flourishing has always been contingent upon engagement with our more-than-human companions. In the 1960s the psychoanalyst Erich Fromm began celebrating a core human sensibility that he named biophilia. "Biophilia is the passionate love of life and of all that is alive" (Fromm, 1964, p. 406). Eventually Wilson's (1984) research brought this phenomenon to popular attention. In his words, biophilia is "the innately emotional affiliation of human beings to other organisms. Innate means hereditary and hence part of ultimate human nature" (p. 3). A convivial relationship with the more-than-human world is intrinsic to our very nature. The term biophilia combines two Greek words that are very old but quite familiar, one connoting love, affection, fondness, attraction; and the other connoting life and living. Our ancient *philia* for the *bios*, our love for the living world, is still present, albeit obscured. When asked to describe their ideal places to live, people strongly prefer sites populated with natural elements: an open, expansive view with access to the local ecosphere; a variety of plants and animals; fresh air; bodies of water such as lakes, rivers, oceans, and so forth (Kellert & Wilson, 1993).

## Joy as the Seed of Transpersonal Realization and Ethical Action

People have long venerated our communion with the natural world as a hallowed relationship, so far back in time and so deep in our psyche does it go. Our biophilic desire for conscious engagement with the rest of nature is so essential to being human that I think of it as a sacred yearning, a "holy longing" (to borrow Goethe's wonderful phrase) (Bly, 1980, p. 70). Recall times you've watched a wild animal going about its life: say, a common squirrel leaping from branch to branch, a bee alighting on a flower; or, more rarely, a bear walking in the distance, a snake slithering up a tree toward a bird's nest. Such encounters may give rise to wonder, fear, joy, or other intense feelings. Whatever the case, we surely feel a powerful allure. We are pulled out of our self-enclosed bubble, pulled into the encounter brought alive by it. In my view, there are three complementary ways that our longing for intimacy with nature is imbued with a holy or sacred quality. First, we yearn for conscious contact with the wild otherness of nonhuman beings and presences, for involvement with something different from ourselves (yet still akin to us). Second, we yearn to release ourselves into something infinitely deeper than our supposedly separate self. Indeed, the natural world is one of the most accessible contexts wherein we can become conscious of an essential reality: namely, that we are manifestations of a transpersonal mystery that precedes and exceeds and comprises our individual existence. Third, this yearning helps us actualize the most revered human capacity of all: responding to others with compassion and love.

"We have a longing for coming home to the sacredness of our belonging to the living body of Earth and the joy of serving that at every step," as Joanna Macy says (Jamail, 2020). This is for our own well-being, yet so too for others. For without the health of others we and our dear ones will inevitably be impoverished, since we are never actually disconnected from each other. In this way, a holy responsibility comes hand in hand with our holy yearning. Health, holy, whole, healing: these all derive from an Old English word, *hælan*, which carries the sense of wholeness and making whole. We can never feel whole while taking ourselves to be self-sufficient subjects cut off from others and the rest of nature. From that habitual stance, we will always sense something is lacking, although we rarely know what that is. A core human yearning is for wholeness, and one aspect of this is a desire to include and be included by the whole of life. This holy desire is also, inseparably, a desire *of* the whole, a desire mysteriously conveyed by the whole of life. The sheer presencing of nature's splendor, beauty, and intelligence draws us into intimate contact. Such deep qualities speak to our own depths, appealing to us for sustained connection and loving responsiveness. Thus we could say that *the natural world is sending us a holy summons that joins perfectly with our holy longing*. Here we can sense earth's desire that we awaken from the fantasy of being merely a separate, self-concerned species or ego.

In Ken Burns' film and companion book *The National Parks*, we are privileged to hear from Shelton Johnson. Of African American, Cherokee, and Seminole heritage, Johnson grew up in the city yet fell in love with the natural world during a visit to Yellowstone. Years later he became a park ranger there. One day Johnson was delivering mail on a snowmobile across a snow-covered valley, at 60 degrees below zero! When a herd of bison blocked his path, he stopped, turned off his vehicle in favor of silent attunement, and was awed by what unfolded:

> The bison, as they breathed, their exhalation would seem to crystallize in the air around them. . . . And they just moved their heads and were looking at me. . . . It was one of those moments when you get pulled outside of yourself into the environment around you. I felt like I was just with the breath of the bison as they were exhaling and I was exhaling, and they were inhaling, and it was all kind of flowing together. (Duncan, 2009, p. 131)

Here Johnson was drawn out of his small conventional self and into truly intimate contact. He became aware of the buffalo in vivid detail, and aware too that he was involved "in the presence of everything around me" (p. 131). Eventually, inhaling and exhaling with one another, it seems there was no separate park ranger nor any separate buffalo, only an event of deep communion with everything "flowing together." "A sense of something that's greater than yourself, a way of being that's greater than yourself" (p. 128).

It is significant that Johnson invoked *a way of being* greater than ourselves. Ecopsychology is not only interested in momentary depthful encounters with the natural world—"peak-experiences" in Maslow's phrase (1968, 1971). (It is no accident that this metaphor derives from nature.) Such fleeting experiences are significant, but not in isolation. By disclosing the depths of self, world, and their interrelationship, they show us possibilities that go beyond our habitual sense of things; and they help us internalize and integrate these depths in stable, ongoing ways. In the wake of each transient event, we are given the opportunity to transmute fleeting "altered states" of consciousness into more stable "altered traits of character," in Huston Smith's formulation (Snell, 1977, p. 43). Our consciousness, self-sense, worldview, ethos, and way of being-with-others are transformed. Johnson thus went on to devote his life to bringing people into contact with the natural world, thereby serving nature in the process. He is especially involved in fostering that connection for Black people. As Johnson lamented, "One of the great losses to African culture from slavery was the loss of kinship with the earth" (Fimrite, 2009).

## This Is It!

Annie Dillard's (1974) Pulitzer Prize–winning book *Pilgrim at Tinker Creek* is a beautiful inquiry into the sacramental depths of our relationship with nature. When writing of her daily pilgrimages, Dillard was living in the Blue Ridge (Appalachian) mountains. They are so named because they appear bluish when seen from a distance. Scientists say that this is due to the way that sunlight filters through a haze of terpenes, bioactive organic compounds that trees release through their leaves and needles. More to the point, our eyes and heart say, "Ahh! Those glorious ridges are blue!" Terpenes are absorbed via our lungs and skin when we walk in the woods, vividly demonstrating our inseparability from the rest of nature. Those molecules—previously constituents of the bodies of trees—become integrated as constituents of our body and serve to boost our immune system (Arvay, 2018, pp. 5–27). Staying close to lived experience, we say, "Yes, it feels so good to be in the forest!"

Dillard's writing makes it clear that her neighborhood eco-community was in her blood in ways that go far deeper than biochemistry. As in the following story, she often shares her delight in being touched by the ordinary natural world's brilliant self-presentation.

> One day I was walking along Tinker Creek thinking of nothing at all and I saw the tree with lights in it. I saw the backyard cedar where the mourning doves roosted charged and transfigured, each cell buzzing with flame. I stood on the grass with lights in it, grass that was wholly fire . . . It was less like seeing than being seen for the first time. The flood of fire abated, but I'm still spending the power. Gradually the lights went out in the cedar, the colors died, the cells unflamed and disappeared. I was still ringing. I had been my whole life a bell, and never knew it until at that moment I was lifted and struck. (Dillard, 1974, pp. 33–34)

I trust Dillard had passed by this "backyard" cedar hundreds of times. But in this instance, through some blessed confluence of open receptivity and grace, she found herself face-to-face with a familiar tree flaming like Moses' burning bush. I have not talked with Moses or Dillard, so I don't really know, but I doubt that what they saw looked much like an actual fire. Rather, I imagine that they realized that the natural world, just by being itself, was shining vividly—dynamically alive, vibrantly beckoning, and touching their heart. In serendipitous encounters, they were moved by one ordinary plant, not as a mere material object but as an animate, sacred, fiery presence. Dillard was given a visionary glimpse of the luminous life of a rooted-and-leafing being; and so too of her own life. It was not only that she saw deeply into the cedar's glowing depths, but that she knew she was being seen by the tree, that her depths were being contacted and summoned forth. Struck by the radiant presencing of the cedar, she discovered essential dimensions of herself that were previously unknown, like a bell that realizes ringing to be its true nature. She and the world were transformed together, indivisibly so.

On another occasion Dillard tells of stopping at a remote gas station in the foothills of Appalachia. She talks with an attendant, gets a cup of coffee, and sits down outside. Petting a beagle pup that came to make her acquaintance, she gazes out on the expansive field of nature.

Before me extends a low hill trembling in yellow brome, and behind the hill, filling the sky, rises an enormous mountain ridge, forested, alive and awesome with brilliant blown lights. I have never seen anything so tremulous and alive. . . .

My hand works automatically over the puppy's fur, following the line of hair under his ears, down his neck, inside his forelegs, along his hot-skinned belly.

Shadows lope along the mountain's rumpled flanks. . . . The air cools; the puppy's skin is hot. I am more alive than all the world.

*This is it, I think, this is it, right now,* the present, this empty gas station, here, this western wind, this tang of coffee on the tongue, and I am patting the puppy, I am watching the mountain. (1974, pp. 78–79, italics added)

Encounters with the everyday-yet-marvelous natural world can arrive with great intensity, like the tree with lights. More often they are subtle, like petting the puppy and meeting the mountains. In either case, their special vividness will inevitably fade. Still, at best, they leave us changed, usually in small ways and occasionally profoundly.

The natural world is among the most privileged contexts for the spontaneous emergence of revelatory, healing, transformative experience: the depths of the world coming forth to meet our own depths—truly an auspicious coupling! As noted earlier, mystics and poets often deem such encounters to be manifestations of the sacred, the holy, or the divine. Whether couched in spiritual language or not, we may realize: *This is it! This is how it is!* As Dillard (1974) attests, "Seeing the tree with lights in it was an experience vastly different in quality and import from patting the puppy. . . . But on both occasions I thought, with rising exultation, *this is it,* this is it; praise the lord; praise the land" (p. 80, italics added). "Just this!" as Lingyun exclaimed. "This" refers to the sheer vivid suchness, presencing, or how-it-isness of whatever is transpiring right here and now. But the "it" of "this is it!"—what is that? This is one of life's core psychospiritual questions. When Dillard or Lingyun declare, "This is it!," they are trying to honor the ineffable depths that came through so vividly in their revelatory experience. Afterward they might elaborate with remarks like: "*This* is the heart of life!"; "*This* is the sacred depth I've been yearning for"; "*This* is who I am, really, beyond any presumption of being a separate self!"; "*This* is what others and the world really are!"; "*This* is the very point of my existence, this is what I am in this life *for*, ever responsively and responsibly!" The mystics insist that we cannot really say what "it" is (although our very saying is one form "it" takes). Still, it is important that we venture to do so. Our saying can help us realize it more fully, help us live in accordance with its reality, help us offer our distinctive gift to its local flourishing. Honestly, this whole book is an endeavor in such saying.

Like all contemplative teachers, Thomas Merton tried to say "it"— the heart of this great matter of life and death and love—and to disclose and live and serve "it" again and again. A twentieth-century Trappist monk, mystic, spiritual mentor, poet, social critic, and gifted author, Merton played a key role in introducing Christian meditation to the lay public. Working for civil rights and racial justice in the 1950s and '60s and for peace during the Vietnam War, he cogently demonstrated the deep connection between contemplative spirituality and social/ecological justice. Merton loved being in nature. Had his life not been cut short so tragically I am sure that ecospirituality would have become even more prominent in his work.[4] Fortunately his writings live on, and through them we can get a sense of how the natural world appears when seen through contemplative eyes. Consider this exquisite 1958 entry in his personal journal:

> Beauty of the sunlight falling on a tall vase of red and white carnations and green leaves on the altar in the novitiate chapel. The light and shade of the red, especially the darkness in the fresh crinkled flower and the light warm red around the darkness, the same color as blood but not "red as blood," utterly unlike blood. Red as a carnation. [Red as *this particular carnation* I would say, and I trust Merton would agree.] This flower, this light, this moment, this silence = *Dominus est* [G-d is! Or, this is G-d!], eternity! (Merton, 1996, p. 164)

On the surface, this is such a common experience. Just flowers. "Only that," as Merton (1968a, p. 146) said, commenting on the same encounter. Really, just this! Yet, *this is it!* Clearly, Merton is moved by the sheer presencing of the red and white carnations. He realizes that the flowers go infinitely deep, sacramentally so, since—as he affirms—his contact with the carnations is no other than contact with G-d. He awakens to G-d in and as one single, tangible incarnation of nature; awakens to nature as one single, tangible incarnation of G-d: carnations-sunlight-silence-present moment-eternal moment = "This is G-d!"

This eco-psycho-spiritual event is a wonderful example of transpersonal realization. The carnations' divine depths intertwine with and call upon Merton's divine depths—two depths that are ultimately one. An instant of sensuous contact suddenly becomes hallowed, transmitting a truth that is at once profoundly spiritual and completely ordinary. Contemplating Lingyun's or Merton's or Dillard's experience, we see something mysterious happening, something very different than a conventional (supposedly) separate subject encountering a (supposedly) separate object in the natural world, something usually eclipsed by our ego-centered ways. Staying with Merton, those red and white carnations *both were and were not* simple flowers. I trust he would have felt an affinity with these words of an ancient Zen master: "Before I had studied Zen for thirty years, I saw mountains as mountains, and rivers as rivers. When I arrived at a more intimate knowledge, I came to the point where I saw that mountains are not mountains, and rivers are not rivers. But now that I have got its very substance I am at rest. For it's just that I see mountains once again as mountains, and rivers once again as rivers" (Watts, 1957, p. 126, translation slightly altered). There is another world: the very depths of our everyday world. Merton encounters carnations and is touched by G-d. Lingyun sees peach blossoms and is awakened to his (our) true buddha-nature. Dillard strokes a puppy and realizes *this is it!*

## The Sacred Depths of the Obvious and Ordinary

In attending closely to lived experience, a phenomenological approach has been guiding our work in this chapter. So too in the following example from the research study I mentioned in the preface. "Nora's" eloquent account is based upon her contact with the elemental forces of nature on a small island off the coast of Ireland:

> I would get up in the morning. I would go out and I would first make my way to the sea. I would sit on the rocks and I would try to find a place where I wouldn't be literally blown away. I would love the feeling of that wind going through every single cell. Freezing, really freezing sometimes. . . . I love the feeling in my body of all of that, of the cold, of the

fierce, the ferocity of the elements. . . . The most intense and the most dramatic was to spend days from sunrise to really moon rise or a star rise, out in the natural world and you know having your mind fall away. . . . I got a new life. I discovered my true nature. I really did. You know, discovering your true face before you were born. I got a true glimpse of it in a cow; in the natural world; in the rain. In everything. . . . To me, it was to recover or to renew my covenant with the natural world. . . . In those moments, in those sacramental moments of being present and really being present and in a sense understanding what human presence could be to the natural world: That we are in some sense the celebrants of this, that we *are* this, we *are* these elements, conscious of themselves. . . . We *are* this breathing, mindful, kind of poetic mind of this earth. . . . I feel called to in a sense be a priest or priestess of this natural world, in the sense of celebrating it. Not consecrating it. It is consecrated. Of celebrating. . . . It is to do this profound bow toward everything. And for me, the promise that comes up is the promise to love this planet. To love it all. To love it like my kin, because it is my kin. . . . That's the mystical promise.

Nora's testimony reminds us that such intimate contact with nature is our birthright as sentient participants in earth's dynamic fellowship of being. And, preeminently, it is our ongoing privilege and responsibility. Nora is a person much like you and me, responding as best she can in this splendid but troubled world. She extols several constituents that are commonly involved in such sensitively attuned encounters: (1) vibrantly *embodied sensuous* relational contact ("I love the feeling in my body of all of that"); (2) *wonder and awe* ("sacramental moments," "really being present," "celebrants of this"); (3) *surrendering* her preestablished concepts, willful activity, and ego-centered sense of self ("having your mind fall away"), thereby leaving her open, vulnerable, and receptive; (4) a transformative revelation of her *"true nature," her essential being, true self, transpersonal self* ("I got a new life. I discovered my true nature. . . . We *are* this breathing, mindful, kind of poetic mind of this earth"); (5) a vivid sense of nature's *holy or sacred depths* ("It is consecrated"); (6) *gratitude* for the "sacramental" quality of her experience ("to do this profound bow"); and, most importantly, (7) a revitalization of her *loving, compassionate devotion to serve* this earth, which is not other than her "true nature" and her intimate "kin" ("That's the mystical promise"—"To love it all.") These also appear in Lingyun, Dillard, and Merton's stories, at least implicitly.

In all these encounters, what mattered were not the qualities of the world alone. Rather, it was *how* each person welcomed them, the consciousness through which they perceived. As Georgia O'Keeffe (1939) once observed, "Everyone has many associations with a flower—the idea of flowers. . . . Still—in a way—nobody sees a flower—really—it is so small—we haven't time—and to see takes time, like to have a friend takes time" (n.p., para. 1). Flowers, winds, trees, vibrant bodily sensations: beautiful, pleasurable solicitations are sent our way quite frequently. We are rarely moved as deeply as our contemplative allies in this chapter, but we could be! Pondering this rueful fact, why do we often bypass the sacred quality of our day-by-day encounters with nature? I believe we often miss the treasures of ordinary life because we are confused in a fundamental way. We take our self to be a sovereign separate subject, and this core misunderstanding generates a haunting feeling that operates in the background of our awareness: a chronically compelling sense of fear and greed subtly colors our perceptions, desires, and (inter)actions. And a pervasive cultural confusion interacts perniciously with this individual confusion. That is, modern society induces us to believe that we humans are disconnected from and elevated above the rest of nature. These reciprocal sources of confusion impede our ability to welcome the overtures life sends our way.

However, in *every* presencing moment, we can make a radical turn and open directly to the deepest nature of life. Precious, sacred experiences come into being *contingent upon mystery*, through a dynamic confluence of circumstances that are infinitely beyond our control. We cannot willfully manufacture nor master them. Nonetheless, we can help ourselves be receptive to their emergence by intentionally placing ourselves in the flow of their grace. Thus, by way of our relative freedom and agency, we can cultivate an open, attentive, attuned, accepting heart and mind. This is a core relational/ethical awareness practice, one that we would do well to nurture over a whole lifetime. But it also involves a daring willingness to confide ourselves into the sheer presencing of now. *Prior to our conscious intention and consent*, the beauty and suffering of the world beseeches us. Beyond our wishes or expectations, life sends us questions, invitations, challenges, and requests. Yet we can consciously hearken such appeals, pausing and confiding ourselves compassionately into the pure unbidden arrival of this moment. Zen master Soko Morinaga Rōshi once put it beautifully: "The point of Zen is to release the inherent warmth of the human heart" (Bruce Harris, personal communication, April 30, 2019). This is the real ethos of a contemplative or mystical sensibility.

I am curious what came to mind earlier when I encouraged you to remember your enjoyable encounters with nature. Perhaps, then and there, you were taken right to the heart of this one great matter, the ultimate concern of life and death and love in this shared earth community. Instantaneously, such events can spring forth with blessed lucidity. And yet our realizations can be so ephemeral, yes? Today's demanding speedy existence induces us to dismiss the significance of what we know deeply in those heartfelt moments. In large part, the aspiration of this book is to help us *sustain trust in what we realize vividly in those sacramental encounters; and to live accordingly, in loving response to others. It only takes a single instant, and a lifetime of relationally involved practice.*

## *This (!)* Is the Perfect Gateway

By way of the stories in this chapter I am approaching a basic (co) existential condition, one that instills hope in these perilous times. That is, *there is a core call-and-response structure at the heart of our shared life: nature's holy depths continuously send forth a holy summons; correlatively, a holy longing always lives latently in our heart. When these meet, our holy responsibility rises up spontaneously.* It is truly exquisite when these primordial forces intertwine, become conscious, give birth to something fresh and new—perhaps an awakening, a poem, some seeds for the birds, or ecological activism. Nature keeps sending us a deep, wild, sacred, ethical call. The appeal of any being or presence can turn into a gateway. It only takes one moment (now), one place (here). Granted, this is a special moment (even if completely ordinary), a time out of time, transpiring at the intersection of this time and eternity, the only possible moment for the time being. And it is a special place (even if completely common), transpiring at the intersection of this spot and infinity, the only possible place right here.

Any encounter can serve as a gate. But we might ask, a gateway to what? I will venture this: an ever-open gate to our true nature, and most crucially to a fitting response to the summons life is sending in the present moment. This may be the song of a full-flowing creek after a rainstorm, a local park defaced with litter, a mother fox and her pups across the twilight meadow, a friend striving to resist a corporation polluting our city's air, midnight silence in deep winter. The fact of the call is undeniable. I might choose to turn away (which itself is a response). But *I cannot not be called: that is the structure of our very (co)existence.* At best I make the equivalent of Nora's bow, acknowledging the unique one before me and responding accordingly. To the preceding overtures: smiling, I let my ears and heart be filled with creek song; dismayed, I pick up the litter; I stand still and let the foxes move on as they will; I join my friend in challenging the offending companies and local politicians; I disappear into the dark infinite silence.

Rising up from one bow after another, I am called to a life of continuous practice with all my relations, indeed *in service of all my earthly companions.* The depths of the animate world come unbidden and intertwine (at best) with my own depths. Every single encounter opens a gate to wakeful intimacy and loving service. Zen deems this a "gateless gate" because *there never is any real barrier to realization, love, and compassion.* But we do have to realize the gate is open and find a way to walk through it. My practice is to stay in touch with the particular being or presence who shows up and calls upon me. *My very life is this ordinary inter-responsiveness.* Caring contact with others *is* my essential nature, my—*our*—deeper self (or self-in-relation). In this too-abstract paragraph, I am stretching toward some crucial implications that are given in our encounters with the natural world. Taking a different approach, I could simply point to lightning! your lover's kiss! red maple leaf! I trust you know what I mean, at least intuitively, in your body, in your heart (even if the conceptual details are not yet developed at this stage of our study). Even better: please set this book down, step outside, look, listen, smell, taste, touch, and let yourself be touched—really savoring the presence of the one splendid life we all share . . .

Chapter Two

# The Ghost Bird's Haunting Cry

## Letting Our Heart Break . . . Open

The extinction of a species, each one a pilgrim of four billion years of evolution, is an irreversible loss. . . . Hundreds of millions of years might elapse before the equivalent of a whale or an elephant is seen again, if ever.

—Gary Snyder (1990, pp. 176–177)

One of the penalties of an ecological education is that one lives alone in a world of wounds.

—Aldo Leopold (1993, p. 165)

Kent kent, kent, kent kent . . .

—The voice of an Ivory-billed Woodpecker

## Overture

We are currently suffering the sixth mass extinction of species in earth's history. Extinction is a natural phenomenon. But today's trauma of massive extinction is unprecedented because it is primarily caused by a single species, us humans. Our nonhuman companions are beautiful, intelligent, and irreplaceable. Grieving our ever-lasting annihilation of them must be a key ingredient in the transformative work of ecopsychology. There

55

is real wisdom and love in our heartbreak. These can guide us through and beyond our destructive ways.

## We Are Annihilating Other Beings: Bearing Grief in Traumatic Times

Sometimes nature seizes our attention with powerful intensity, like the Irish gales for Nora in the last chapter, or like the disastrous storms sponsored by global warming. More commonly, nature's gifts come to us subtly: we are graced with a sparkling icicle, sweet juicy watermelon, timely encouragement from a trusted colleague, a delicate crescent moon. When we are open enough to notice, these experiences can become true epiphanies. We realize that we are blessed to be involved in—and indeed expressions of—a mysterious life that goes infinitely deeper than our conventional presumptions, preoccupations, and self-sense. Herein, gratitude and responsibility arise together. It does not take the Amazon rainforest or a critically endangered gorilla to awaken this ethical sensibility. I agree with Buber that our central (co)existential responsibility is to "hallow" all of life, to welcome all other beings or presences as a holy Thou.

But with earth under assault, the next meeting might well be a harrowing one. I recently learned about an increasingly common method used for undersea oil and gas exploration (Brune, 2015; "Seismic surveys," 2015). Arrays of powerful air guns are dragged behind boats in order to emit extremely loud (over 200 dB) sound bursts every 10 to 15 seconds for weeks or months in a row. These explosive sounds radiate in every direction for up to a thousand miles, injuring countless animals in the process. Sometimes they are killed outright by the blasts. More commonly they are deafened or driven away from favored habitats. Whales, dolphins, and sea turtles are especially vulnerable. The North Atlantic right whale is one of the world's most endangered animals, and the air guns could drive this species into extinction. To put this into an experiential context, these blasts force animals to "endure a noise *100 times louder than a jet engine*. Every ten seconds. For weeks at a time. . . . That's like standing next to 100 planes taking off at the same time, 8,000 times a day" (Brune, 2015).

Long ago Aldo Leopold (1993) acknowledged that with ecological sensitivity comes the anguishing awareness that we are living in a "world of wounds" (p. 165). It is immensely distressing to realize the magnitude of humankind's violence against the beings and presences of nature, and thus, inseparably, the violence against ourselves, our children, and strangers' children around the world (and even those not yet born), because all of these precious ones are dependent upon nature's well-being. Given these circumstances; given the ravages of interpersonal wounds, sociocultural oppression, injustice, and violence; given the existential tribulations of injury, illness, aging, loss, and death, a surplus of pain is often thrust upon us. At best we do what we can to prevent unnecessary suffering and to assuage the suffering that is already here and arising anew. Often, however, we are excessively preoccupied with avoiding pain, even ordinary discomfort. We lose touch with the fact that these experiences are an intrinsic part of life, and that they can be meaningful pointers to living well. Most basically, pain is a message for us to pay attention and respond accordingly. *And a fitting response depends upon a fitting interpretation of the pain.* When we slice our finger instead of the bagel, things are quite clear. We stop cutting and take care of the injury. It is far more challenging to understand the meanings of emotional pain. We tend to forget that pain arises in diverse forms—biological, psychological, sociocultural, spiritual—and in quite diverse circumstances. Because we have all been hurt, and many of us egregiously so, we are *inclined to react to all pain as if it were a signal of danger.* It then appears as something that needs to be avoided or banished. But we thereby preclude our ability to make sense of a particular event of distress. One of the greatest impediments to understanding, healing, and growth is our automatic flight from pain and discomfort. It is part of our nature to move away from pain. But human nature also includes the capacity to mediate our habitual reactions.

I am especially concerned with how we handle our heartbreaking anguish over humankind's plundering of the natural world. Feeling sadness and grief over real losses, feeling angry over real injustices, feeling frightened about our future and that of generations to come: these are truly wise, compassionate responses, ones we would do well to honor by way of our own courage and the support of others. Pain's fierce intensity can be too much to bear at times, and we may need to push it away for a while. However, rather than a temporary reprieve, defensive avoidance often becomes sedimented into a habitual stance. To be sure, it is hard to bear the anguish we feel once we become aware of our perilous situation. It is easier, temporarily, to tranquilize ourselves with the fantasy that business as usual is satisfactory or even praiseworthy. Nonetheless, we actually intensify our eco(psycho)logical suffering by repressing realities that feel unbearable, since the pathogenic conditions become further consolidated and the pathological symptoms resurge with extra force. As Freud and Jung demonstrated a century ago, anything we push out of our awareness will inevitably return in symptomatic form. What Freud (1957) aptly called the "return of the repressed" (pp. 141–158) is evident in our relations with the rest of nature. When we repress our inherent intimacy with nature or deny the painful fact of ecological destruction, then these supposedly banished realities return to haunt our personal and sociocultural lives. When we repress the reality of global warming, then that malady is amplified. The natural world continues to be destroyed and we are left with a psychospiritual malaise that we feel but do not understand. Still, psychotherapists and spiritual teachers have shown that we can uncover that which has been repressed, welcome the whole range of our experience, excluding nothing, and craft more life-enhancing responses.

Whether we shirk or embrace our responsibility (and response-ability), the calamitous circumstances keep calling—and calling *upon*—us. But we do far better when we face things consciously and collaboratively. With sufficient support (from other people, from society, from nature), we may address the suffering—earth's and ours, together—and create healing pathways through. While staying in touch with the heartening encounters from the previous chapter, let us turn toward what we often turn away from: the grief, guilt, despair, and anger we feel when confronted by our eco(psycho)logical crisis. As humans strive for security, convenience, and monetary profit, the climate is being disrupted; forests clear-cut; topsoil depleted; wetlands drained; toxins spewed into the air and waters; species driven extinct at an unprecedented rate; the world overpopulated with humans; food and water becoming scarce; and precious animals, plants, mountains, and rivers lost, needlessly and heedlessly. Correlatively, alienation from the shared earth community means alienation from our full humanity.

In the next chapter we will see that *in desecrating the earth we impoverish ourselves*. For now, we will focus on the grievous losses occurring in the more-than-human world. As psychotherapists know, when we allow painful symptoms to teach us about their nature and source, they can guide us toward an alternative way. Today's mass extinction of species is a key case in point. Lamentably, we could focus on any issue from the preceding list. But the root malady will persist if we only address symptoms in isolation. All ecological concerns are intertwined because all are driven by a radical disturbance of human consciousness, culture, and relationship. In the present chapter, human-generated mass extinction will exemplify this larger crisis of alienation.

"The one process now going on that will take millions of years to correct is the loss of genetic and species diversity by the destruction of natural habitats. This is the folly our descendants are least likely to forgive us" (Wilson, 1984, p. 121). This is a biological disaster. Inseparably, it is a psychological, sociocultural, and spiritual disaster because humans are inherently relational beings and we are losing a multitude of precious partners in the shared earth community. Likewise, the surviving animals and plants are losing their longtime relational companions. Ecology is the science of interrelationships within an eco-community: relationships between organisms, and between those organisms and the larger field of elemental presences (air, earth, fire, water). Today, the *logos* of our *ecos* is being disrupted, the deep order of our home dwelling places and communal (co)existence is under assault. As life's relational rapport becomes less diverse, everyone's health is diminished.

## Hearkening the Ghost Bird's Call

In spring 1987, the esteemed ornithologist Dr. Jerome Jackson was searching a swampy forest in Mississippi for a mysterious bird most experts thought was surely extinct: the Ivory-billed Woodpecker (Jackson, 2004, p. 181; Tremblay, 2002). Museum specimens showed it to be the third largest woodpecker in the world and the largest in North America: 16–20 ounces, 18–20 inches tall, with an enormous wingspan of 30–31 inches. Its deep black and white feathers, brilliant yellow eye, intense red crest (on the male), and great ivory-colored bill are strikingly beautiful. Resembling the magnificent pileated woodpeckers who live near many of us, but even larger, the ivorybill appears wondrously ancient in old photographs and recent paintings. When flying, the bird's appearance vividly conjures the evolutionary link with dinosaurs.

The ivorybill was known as the "Lord God Bird" because folks would exclaim "Lord God what a bird!" upon encountering one, so truly grand and awe-inspiring it was. As a rare and precious being that evoked people's spiritual sensibilities, the ivorybill has also been called the

"Holy Grail Bird" and the "Ghost Bird." Sadly, with nearly all its habitat destroyed and no authenticated sightings occurring in the United States since 1944, ornithologists feared that the ivorybill was extinct, another grievous loss among countless losses in the calamitous, human-generated mass extinction of species taking place. Nonetheless, Jackson and his graduate student hoped that a remnant population had survived. Their extensive search included systematically playing a 1935 recording of an ivorybill's call, and one morning they heard a reply in the distance: a nasal-like "kent kent, kent, kent kent" (suggesting a large nuthatch or a child's tin trumpet). They were thrilled that an ivorybill might still be alive, and nearby! As the tape played, the bird continued to respond, coming closer and closer. But then it stopped. Jackson and his student hurried toward the sound, but could not find its source. They never saw an ivorybill, not that day nor in two years of devoted searching.

This may have been an Ivory-billed Woodpecker responding to what it thought was a fellow member of its own species. Indeed, what if it was the last surviving ivorybill on earth? Imagine this marvelous bird, which naturally exists in close social groups, living alone for years and finally hearing the call of its kin. Then, drawn powerfully, primordially by the sound, being terribly stunned to find that it came from a group of humans. Can we develop some sense of what this experience might be? What if you were the last human being on earth? What if—due to nuclear war sparked by global warming, let us say—all your family and friends had died, and you were left alone? What if you had gone for years without any contact with your fellow humans? What if your home neighborhood had also been ravaged? And after nearly giving up hope, what if you heard another human voice calling out in the distance? Then, with body-mind-heart drawn to the call, you discover that it is not a real person at all, but only an old audio recording. You are still alone, and will be until you die. And with your death the whole human species dies, forever, never to exist again.

This imaginary scenario would be catastrophic. But so is the actual and escalating demise of countless kindred species. Consider just a few of the most well-loved species that are now endangered: monarch butterfly, mountain gorilla, Sumatran tiger, Florida panther, African baobab tree, humpback whale, bluefin tuna, giant panda, and Asian elephant. With over 30 species being killed off every single day, something like the ivorybills' tragedy is recurring hour after hour. Ecologists warn that we are in the midst of the sixth mass extinction of species in earth's existence

(Kolbert, 2014). We know that all living beings must die, and that entire species do go extinct due to normal ecological processes. There have also been occasional phases of naturally generated mass extinction. The most famous involved the disappearance of the dinosaurs, about 65 million years ago. However, the present mass extinction is unique in that the destruction is being caused primarily by a single species (human beings) and culture (Euro-American techno-corporate-consumerist culture now spreading around the earth). Today we are killing off animals and plants faster than ever before. The immediate anthropocentric culprits are habitat destruction, overpopulation, pollution, invasive species, overharvesting, and climate breakdown. Less immediately but more perniciously, mass extinction and all of its proximate causes are symptoms of an underlying crisis, a fundamental confusion about who we are and about our place in the world. The root cause is a dissociative belief that we are separate from each other and from the rest of nature, and the linked fantasy that our health can be independent from the health (or illness) of the natural world. This means that *our ecological crisis is not primarily biological, but is driven by a derangement of consciousness and culture*. Far from being unavoidable (like the asteroid strike and volcanic activity that led to the dinosaurs' demise), the mass extinction of our era is contingent and optional. Because our self-sense, cultural values, and ways of relating are constructed, they can be deconstructed and reconstructed differently.

Through my solemn tribute to the Ivory-billed Woodpecker, I also want to honor all the wildly marvelous beings who have been driven extinct or are now precariously close to perishing. The wooly mammoth and sabertooth cat have long been absent from this earth. Passenger pigeons went from "billions to none" in less than a century ("From billions," 2015). The Chinese river dolphin (or Baiji), a beautiful freshwater mammal revered in folklore as the "Goddess of the Yangtze," is almost certainly gone. The glorious monarch butterfly is now officially endangered, its population having declined 90 percent in a mere 20 years. Honeybees and other insects are vanishing rapidly. Many fruits and vegetables are now lacking essential pollinators. Marine communities are collapsing too due to commercial overharvesting. Atlantic cod are a prime example, even though people in the seventeenth century said they were "so abundant then that you could almost walk across the ocean on their backs" ("Atlantic cod," 2014). The Galapagos tortoises that so fascinated Charles Darwin are now endangered after an ancestry that spans 220 million years! Coral reefs are under assault across the planet. Countless unknown plants are going extinct every week, each previously playing a significant role in its local eco-community, each a potential source of food or medicine. Sadly, it is impossible to name all those who are at risk. Yet let us not fail to acknowledge our closest living relative, the chimpanzee. These kindred beings, with whom we share about 99 percent of the same DNA, are extinct in much of their native range and endangered in the rest. Perhaps you feel an affinity with one of the species I mentioned, or another vulnerable one? The gravity of the crisis is demonstrated in a recent study that found that "current extinction rates are 1,000 times higher than the natural background and future rates of extinction are likely to be 10,000 higher" (De Vos et al., 2015, p. 460). Of all known species, 31,000 (or 27%) are in danger of extinction, including 25 percent of all mammals, 41 percent of amphibians, 34 percent of conifers, and 14 percent of birds (IUCN, 2020). And these alarming rates are rising. One half of all extant species will be vanquished by the end of this century!

Nature is immensely abundant and resilient. But the shocking annihilation of the passenger pigeon during the nineteenth and early twentieth centuries should serve as a cautionary tale (Greenberg, 2014). This sleek blue-gray-and-orange bird lived in deciduous forests across the eastern United States. In the early 1800s John James Audubon "watched a flock pass overhead for three days and estimated that at times more than 300 million pigeons flew by him each hour. Nesting colonies several miles wide could reach a length of *forty miles*" (Erlich et al., 1988, p. 273). The sky would actually darken as they passed, their astounding numbers blocking the sun. Pigeons had long served as tasty food for Native Americans, who were careful not to kill them while they were nesting nor take too many at a time. This was in contrast with White settlers unfamiliar with the balance of the local ecosystem, and also caught up in a burgeoning capitalist system radically different from the gift economy that had forever sustained indigenous communities. Not fully knowing what they were doing, market hunters massively overharvested the birds, leading to their total extinction. Largely due to their excessive slaughter, Congress enacted the Lacey Act in 1900, the nation's first law protecting wildlife. The last known passenger pigeon, a captive bird named Martha, died in the Cincinnati Zoo in 1914. Four years later, what was probably the sole surviving member of North America's only native parrot species perished in the same zoo: the glorious, multicolored Carolina parakeet. When such marvelous beings are extinguished, their living presence can no longer speak to us. However, their "ghosts" still haunt us. And we can grieve and make reparations.

## Empathy with Our Kindred Companions

When we do the math, on average, it turns out that at least one species is going extinct every single hour. Who are we losing while you are reading this chapter? I ask this poignantly because I believe it is crucial for us to actually feel and grieve the loss of our kindred species. We need to know this tragic reality not merely cognitively but in an embodied, heartfelt way. Some might contest this approach, including my imaginative reversal of Dr. Jackson's ivorybill search. They might claim that my notions are "anthropomorphic," that I am misleading readers by attributing human characteristics to nonhuman beings. I take these concerns seriously. If even our most intimate friends are infinitely beyond our best conceptions about them—which they truly are—then what about all those wildly different four-legged, winged, finned, and rooted ones? As the wolf expert Barry Lopez (1978, p. 4) acknowledges, "No one—not biologists, not Eskimos, not backwoods hunters, not naturalist writers—knows why wolves do what they do" (p. 4). We should never presume to definitively comprehend the experience of other beings. When we uncritically follow our preconceptions and fail to attend carefully, we obscure the real alterity of the other-than-human world. And our actions become narcissistic and imperialistic.

But it is also narcissistic to imagine that we can sever ourselves from the rest of nature, to believe that our experience is totally different from that of our fellow companions. We are natural beings, after all, distinctive yet inextricable expressions of the whole integral earth. Personal experience and formal research should help us discover our existential similarities with the rest of nature as well as our differences. Aware that my understanding is always shaped by my situated humanity and perspective, and never presuming to fully understand any other being, I still trust that my shared animality and embodied relational resonance allow some felt, intuitive, and imaginative appreciation of others' experience. And such empathic connection can grow into caring action. When our family dogs cool off in a creek on a sweltering day, sometimes I too step over and splash my face. When I see documentary scenes of a lion cub cuddling close with its mother, I recall many sweet times that my kids snuggled in with me. And just few days ago, as I reached into a trail-side bramble to gather some blackberries, I noticed that someone had arrived before me with the same idea, someone wildly different and yet still akin to me: a daddy longlegs had her mouth on a droplet emerging from a dark plump berry, apparently enjoying a juicy snack. Detached observation can be valuable in specific scientific contexts, but not in our everyday relations. Empathic contact with the beings of nature surely serves them and us much better. Be assured, I am not talking about the kind of anthropomorphism we see in Disney movies. Further, let us not be confused, the real danger is not anthropo*morphism* but anthropocen-*trism*: uncritically enacting values that serve humankind exclusively or, even more narrowly, only those few with power, privilege, and money.

When held tentatively and revised as an encounter unfolds, so-called "anthropomorphism"—resonant, responsive understanding and compassion—can be an *experiential* source of life-enhancing contact with our nonhuman fellows. Perhaps we should even rename it zoomorphism, grounding our felt-attunement in forms of shared animal sensibility. All the while we can guard against naïve, self-centered anthropomorphism and mount a fierce critique of human elitism. Better than egocentrism, anthropocentrism, and corporate-centrism, better even than biocen-trism—indeed, better than any limited and exclusionary *–ism*—we humans can come to cultivate an all-inclusive ecocentrism: that is, devotion to a shared (co)existence centered consciously in the present relational encounter, transpiring within the open, interdependent community of the local and global ecosphere, including but not limited to human society and culture. This center is always freshly renewed right here and now, in each moment's meeting. We will explore this ecocentric ethos in later chapters.

## The Earth Is the Real Therapist

We are all being afflicted by a dissociative severance in the nature-hu-man relationship. Yet we know ruptures in connection can be repaired, relationships renewed and carried further. Such healing necessarily takes place in loving partnerships in daily life and in the work of psy-chotherapy. In psychotherapy—and also between intimate friends and lovers—a crucial source of transformation is the relational process of "rupture and repair," that is, the capacity of the patient and therapist to collaborate in acknowledging, bearing, and growing from the pain of occasional but inevitable breaks in the therapeutic alliance (Safran & Muran, 2000). Wise psychotherapists appreciate that they must openly accept responsibility for their contribution to every rift with a patient, humbly acknowledging the pain generated by their mistaken actions and empathic failures. (Wise therapists also know that transformation comes not through their power alone nor the patient's, but through the mystery of their engaged partnership.) Likewise, we humans are responsible for ameliorating today's severe breach with the rest of nature. Seen in this way, the natural world is like a traumatized patient and humankind a psychotherapist. A core human responsibility now is to provide the best therapeutic service we can muster.

Yet when we ponder who is wounded and who is the agent of healing, things are not unidirectional. In the great work we are being called to do, there is a danger of unwittingly replicating the dynamic that is sustaining our mutual affliction: namely, placing humankind above the rest of nature and presuming that we are the masterful ones. Something important is missing when we locate the suffering only in the natural world and see ourselves as the exclusive source of healing. In confusion, fear, greed, and alienation from the rest of nature, we humans are surely wounded. And this drives us to wound others, human and otherwise. Alternatively, in a fruitful circle, we can open ourselves for nature's healing ministrations and go on to offer our best care for the more-than-human world. Nature ever precedes, exceeds, and permeates our being. This means that our skillful responses can only grow from creatively welcoming the gifts of the great wide earth. Nature is the real therapist. Without contradiction, as an essential aspect of our human nature, each of us is irreplaceably responsible.

Nora's encounters with the natural world (as in chapter 1) sponsored engaged devotion to nature's well-being (as in the preface). Yet Nora also raises a subtle quandary and points to a deeper source of healing:

> You know that whole thing, Will, about nursing the earth—
> there is a part of me that has to be really careful . . . I am
> not the nurse of the earth even though I must nurse the
> earth in some ways. The earth is *the* nurse. She is the great
> mother. She nurses everything and everyone. Again, that
> ambivalence, that tension, the paradox, of wanting to nurse
> the earth back to being the nurse, and not appropriating that

for ourselves. . . . The earth itself will not prosper or function, without the consent of the human and the support and the aid of the human.

The natural world is urgently calling for our conscious care. Yet, if we place humankind first and presume we alone are the wise ones who know how to nurse the earth to health, then we remain captivated by the anthropocentric stance that originally created our shared suffering.

The challenge resembles one that often comes up when people of privilege and power—usually White—genuinely want to offer assistance to those who are oppressed, but err in trying to seize the lead rather than listening and learning. This dynamic occurred in the 1960s civil rights movement in the United States, in the recent Black Lives Matter antiracism and racial justice initiatives, and in justice movements of indigenous peoples around the world. Activists of color and indigenous heritage have often embraced a cautionary maxim: "If you have come to help me, you are wasting your time. If you have come because your liberation is bound up with mine, then let us work together" (see "Lilla Watson," n.d.). This quote is often attributed to Lilla Watson, an indigenous Australian (Murri) elder, visual artist, scholar, and activist. Apparently it emerged collaboratively among Aboriginal activists in the 1970s. They were striving to find constructive ways to work with White people who had earnestly reached out to help, but in an unwittingly insensitive way. Many of the Whites had little prior relationship with or understanding of the indigenous people, so they needed much mentoring before being able to join constructively in the work. Similarly, we all can learn to attend more carefully to the voice of the earth, for our liberation is surely bound up with liberation of the larger natural world.

Much of ecopsychological practice involves (re)learning to hearken meaningful messages being conveyed by the more-than-human natural world: to listen to blue jays squawking and realize that a hawk just snatched away their young chick; to listen to global warming and realize that our addiction to economic expansion and fossil fuel is debasing the lives of our children and their children and generations to come. Throughout human history we have been sensitive to such communications that are always being sent our way. But as cultural changes in the modern era took us away from conscious intimate contact with the natural world, we increasingly lost that crucial capacity. Now, as a *countercultural and counter-consciousness alternative*, we are understanding (anew) that life's wisdom is located not primarily in *Homo sapiens*—humans who are "wise" (at times)—but in the sentient, sapient earth. Appreciating this, we see that nature always comes first and we take our cues from there. Thereby we welcome nature as a real mentor, therapist, nurse, healer, and guide.

Perhaps you heard that researchers recently discovered the "missing link" between the great apes and deeply conscious civilized beings? That species, it turns out, is *Homo sapiens*! This is a (darkly serious) joke, and one that comes with an apology to the great apes (with their marvelous consciousness and culture). I share it because we need to be humbled by some gentle (and sometimes stronger) shocks. In moments of despair or rage over our hubris, I find it helpful to remember that we humans are members of a very young species. To develop their own way of living well, youngsters need time and ongoing support from their elders. When the 4.5 billion–year history of earth is rendered as 24 hours, human beings only arrived on the scene 77 seconds before midnight! Even in our youth, we are primarily an intelligent, creative, compassionate, loving species. This is true even in the midst of our rampant confusion, fear, and dissociative violence. In these challenging times, it is important to realize that our elders are ready to help us. I am referring to those who have dwelt here far longer than humankind: most of earth's other species, all of its elemental presences, and indeed the whole earth ecosystem in its coherent, indivisible, dynamic, inter-responsive functioning.

## Wisdom and Love in Heartbreak: Our Hearts Are Breaking . . . Open . . . for Others

Today's eco(psycho)logical maladies are heartbreaking. Much that has been lost is not replaceable, and much that will be lost in the near future is unavoidable. Given the decrease in conscious contact with nature and the increase in corporate power, things are likely to get worse. Yet we can also embrace our era as a crucial revolutionary and evolutionary phase. Wise observers often say that crises present us with both danger and opportunity, and that is certainly the case now. In this time, our time, our only and ever precious time, we and the rest of earth need a radical psychological-cultural-spiritual transformation. Like other key turning points in history, we are challenged with the task of reconstructing what it means to be human, which is to say: to be human-with-others-and-for-others, in the service not just of ourselves but of other people and our nonhuman partners in the natural world. Depending on our perspective we might deem this a developmental emergence, a sociocultural revolution, or a spiritual awakening. All of these are complementary dimensions of a multifaceted process of ethical/interrelational transformation. But can we actually do this when faced with the fierce momentum of society's reigning ideology, especially the structures of corporate capitalism, technological captivation, media entrancement, compulsive consumerism, and nature-deficit disorder? Is it possible to break free to any significant extent? There is no way to know in advance. The "great turning" (Macy & Brown, 2014) and "the great work" (Berry, 1999) must transpire together. *Our time and our calling are one and the same.* We can only begin here and now, with engaged hope, faith, courage, and devotion, right in the midst of this vexing age—vulnerably daring to venture a reply to earth's ethical cry. Not knowing quite what we need to do, and without any guarantee regarding the fruits of our efforts, we listen as deeply as we can, offer the best response we can muster (for the time being), attend to what happens, and then respond again and again.

Things are precarious, but there are some heartening signs. At least one living Ivory-billed Woodpecker was discovered in the swamps of Arkansas! A sighting by a kayaker led to a systematic field investigation by the Cornell Lab of Ornithology and the Nature Conservancy. Experts encountered this magnificent bird on at least seven occasions and recorded one video that appeared to be an ivorybill (Fitzpatrick et al., 2005; Gallagher, 2005; "Search for the Ivory-billed Woodpecker," 2015). While occasional possible sightings continue to this day, no one has been able to make a photograph or video that definitively verifies the bird's existence. Yet, in a heartening development, they are getting close. After the US Fish and Wildlife service proposed in 2021 that the ivorybill be removed from the endangered species list and declared extinct, researchers with the National Aviary in Pittsburgh presented extensive evidence of its ongoing survival in Louisiana (Latta et al., 2022). Whatever its liminal status, the "ghost bird" continues to haunt us with its presence-in-absence.

Today most people have a basic cognitive conception of the extinction of species. We can provide a dictionary-like definition. Yet it is difficult to really appreciate what it means that we are killing off these beings forever. The reality is so heartbreaking that we often keep ourselves from being affected by it. We know *about* extinction, but when this intellectual notion is split off from its emotional import, we do not know in a way that really makes a difference. There are powerful psychodynamic reasons that we avoid the affective significance of extinction. It can be overwhelming to realize that we are annihilating entire lineages of beings, each with their own marvelous ways. Further, our nature-estranged culture conditions us to believe that these losses do not matter. And nature-deficit disorder has truly pernicious consequences. When awareness of nature is absent from our daily lives, care for the rest of nature is absent as well. To convey a sense of how severely we can be affected by lack of conscious contact with nature, let me share a small story. One spring my family decided to welcome another member into our pack, that is, by adopting a second dog. When we first met the puppy we noticed how the small rescue center was surrounded by parking lots and roads, cut off from the more-than-human world. The adorable pup was subdued, but we still sensed his lively, intelligent, wakeful presence and readily adopted him. Honoring these qualities, we named him Bodhi, meaning awake—from the same Sanskrit root as buddha. Upon arriving at our home in the woods after a long drive, we assumed Bodhi would enjoy getting out of the car and into the natural world. So we were surprised to see him cowering with fear upon touching the grass and encountering trees and open sky. Then it occurred to me: the little fellow was suffering from nature-deficit disorder! After living his first three months indoors, the natural space actually frightened him. But I am happy to share some encouraging news. With gentle support from my family, including our older dog in her great kindness, wisdom, and patience, and with repeated trips outside to play and pee, Bodhi soon fell in love with the surrounding eco-community. We could see the natural world waking him up, thus helping him live up to his name. Then he was really home, in more ways than one.

We humans can come home too. But we sure have plenty of work to do. A friend of mine expressed dismay that millions of dollars were spent to preserve the Ivory-billed Woodpecker's habitat. He asked sincerely, "What about all the human needs that could be addressed instead?" Given the immensity of human suffering around the world, this is a question many concerned citizens pose when ecological issues are raised. However, such questions presume that human well-being can be isolated from that of the natural world. When I shared this story with another friend, the Buddhist social critic and Zen teacher David Loy, he responded poignantly: "The real issue is not whether millions are being spent to preserve [the ivorybills'] habitat, but that billions are being spent to destroy such habitats" (personal communication, November 23, 2005).

Fortunately, in a variety of forums, we humans are consciously holding these painful realities in our hearts and minds, and thereby crafting therapeutic responses. The "ghost bird" may still be gracing our world, calling to us in its presence/absence. But this uniquely breathtaking experience is hanging in the balance. We almost extinguished the bald eagle, peregrine falcon, gray wolf, American bison, and countless others, known and unknown. Unknown by us, that is, but certainly known by their fellow participants in their local eco-community. As with the ivorybill, by sharing stories of both delight and distress, we support greater intimacy and responsibility in the shared earth community. These exchanges may occur across a campfire or café table, in living rooms or classrooms, in wilderness treks or activist initiatives, in psychotherapy offices or corporate offices, in art and literature, in emails to political representatives and in scholarly work like the present book.

To feel sad and angry when we witness the annihilation of wild beings and presences means that the appeals of the natural world are getting through to us. Since we humans are a distinctive mode of nature, our heartbreak is a way that nature—by way of human nature—is listening and responding to its own deepest needs. *Feeling and trusting our heartbreak is truly a manifestation of health, sanity, wisdom, and love.* It is evidence that our open, exposed, vulnerably sensitive hearts are working just as they should; that we are alive, caring, and touched by earth's suffering; and that we are consenting to be moved by this ethical cry, responding as best we can to the fear-filled confusion that is creating such horrors. *Our hearts breaking for others reveals that we are only illusorily divorced from the natural world in the first place.* And truly, it is not exactly that our hearts are breaking. Rather, in letting ourselves be moved by the suffering of our fellow beings, we soften the surplus defensiveness by which we keep ourselves overprotected. Our conventional self-sense is usually held tightly as if our lives depended on it. But now this self and its habitual way of being are *breaking open*—open *to* intimate contact and open *for* understanding, compassionate, loving, and just responses. Sometimes our defenses are forcefully broken through when we are confronted with nature's plight. We shudder upon seeing pelicans crudely smothered with oil sludge in British Petroleum's Gulf oil disaster; dolphins' writhing-before-dying in Japan's authorized slaughter; emaciated polar bears on melting ice sheets; animals suffering and being killed in lab experiments. Other times our defenses are gently dissolved or freely released, as when a sunflower blooms in our garden or a rabbit scampers through our yard. In attending to the natural world we discover immense beauty, wisdom, and pain. Each in its own way solicits our loving care.

These are dangerous times, but that is not the end of the story. Crises can call forth the worst of ourselves but also the best, avoidance and avarice and violence, or understanding and compassion and generosity. Heeding the lessons of psychotherapy, we can be heartened in knowing that *breakdown can be a prelude to breakthrough*. In opening our embodied heart and mind, in letting rampant extinctions touch us deeply, death may give rise to loving care. Authentic love of nature is no sentimental feeling, wishful fantasy, or abstract ideal. It involves conscious collaborative action in the face of earth's infinite splendor and its wanton desecration.

## Death and Love

Love and death—extinction does evoke both—are perhaps the most life-altering experiences of all, the ones most likely to foster real awakening and transformation. This was certainly the case with Aldo Leopold, twentieth-century leader in the fields of ecology and environmental ethics. Leopold confessed that when he and his hunting companions were young they would never consider bypassing a chance to kill a wolf. One day, upon finding a mother wolf playing with her pups, they unthinkingly barraged the pack with gunfire:

> We reached the old wolf in time to watch a fierce green fire dying in her eyes. I realized then, and have known ever since, that there was something new to me in those eyes—something known only to her and to the mountain. . . . I thought that because fewer wolves meant more deer, that no wolves would mean hunters' paradise. But after seeing the green fire die, I sensed that neither the wolf nor the mountain agreed with such a view. (Leopold, 1949, pp. 129–130)

The young Leopold was a conventional hunter with a typically human-centered identity and ethos. Yet his encounter with the wolf initiated a true psychospiritual transformation. Contrary to the dominant ideology of his (and our) era, he allowed the experience to resonate so deeply as to change his life. Afterward Leopold lived by way of what he called an "ecological conscience" (p. 207) and a "land ethic" (p. 204): "The land ethic simply enlarges the boundaries of the community to include soils, waters, plants, and animals, or collectively: the land. . . . In short, a land ethic changes the role of *Homo sapiens* from a conqueror of the land-community to plain member and citizen of it" (p. 204). Seeing the wolf die took Leopold directly to the crucial point: "A thing is right when it tends to preserve the integrity, stability, and beauty of the biotic community. It is wrong when it tends otherwise" (pp. 224–225). Strangely, although our existence can never really be human-centered—we cannot even exist without gifts from sources beyond our supposedly independent self and species—our society will keep trying to make it so until we awaken to our place in nature's conversational fellowship of being. According to Leopold, the ecological crisis requires that we learn "to think like a mountain" (p. 132). This begins with listening-seeing-feeling like a human, *yet a renewed human*, one whose heart has opened; who is attuned to nature's beings and presences, in all their glory and suffering; who appreciates our intrinsic communion with the rest of the great wise animate earth.

For real healing to occur, an extreme encounter like Leopold's is not necessary. Wild nature is omnipresent. We just have to start where we are, becoming aware of what is happening all around us and within us. Once, when visitors from Germany directed my attention to "that amazing bird!," I was disappointed to tell them, "It's just a cardinal." But their excitement resounded enough to awaken me from my habitual trance. Getting me in touch for a fresh look at my familiar red-feathered neighbor, my guests helped me realize again what beautiful beings cardinals are. Yes indeed, what an amazing bird! Leopold was touched deeply by a mother wolf as she was dying. Friends helped me see that ordinary cardinals are truly extraordinary. Sensitive parents are initiating children into a life of intimacy with nature. And at least one living ivorybill was—is?!—eking out an existence on the edge of extinction in those remote southern swamps. How marvelous! It is true that we are in the midst of a complex ecological-psychological-cultural-spiritual crisis. It is true that we tend to be dreadfully alienated from our inherent intimacy with the natural world. It is heartbreakingly true that entire species are being killed off, ecosystems vanquished, relationships annihilated. And with capitalism, techno-idolatry, and consumerism functioning as a kind of new religion, it is true that we are confused about who we are, what nature is, what really matters, and what we are here to do in this one life we share. However, whether in searching for the ivorybill or in crafting an international response to the climate crisis, we can deconstruct our wayward ways and reconstruct healthy alternatives.

Wisdom and love live within our heartbreak. Yet what immense grief we are being summoned to bear, what profound work we are being called to do. *Another unique species just vanished at human hands, never to grace our lives again.* I don't know which one was killed off, but whoever it was they are irreplaceable. The world has been forever debased by their demise. A poignant lesson from the Buddhist teacher Achaan Chah is directly pertinent here: "If you haven't cried a number of times, your meditation hasn't really begun" (Kornfield, 1993, p. 40). In our relations with the rest of nature, if we have not cried deeply we have not let the harrowing truth of our shared plight really sink into our heart and mind.

> it's 3:23 in the morning
> and I'm awake
> because my great, great, grandchildren
> won't let me sleep.
> My great, great, grandchildren
> ask me in dreams
> what did you do while the planet was plundered?
> what did you do when the earth was unraveling?
> surely you did something
> when the seasons started failing
> as the mammals, reptiles and birds were all dying?
> did you fill the streets with protest
> when democracy was stolen?
> what did you do
> once
> you
> knew? (Dellinger, 2011, p. 1)

Chapter Three

# All Real Living Is Meeting

## Losing Nature, Losing Our Humanity

The most dangerous idea in the world is that humans are separate from the rest of nature.

—Robert Michael Pyle (2005, p. 69)

There is no I taken in itself. . . . All real living is meeting.

—Martin Buber (1958, pp. 4, 11)

i am through you so i

—E. E. Cummings (Firmage, 1994, p. 537)

## Overture

We humans are inherently inter-responsive beings, not separate, skin-bounded, self-sufficient, sovereign subjects. Our relationship with the wildly glorious beings and presences of the natural world is a real relationship, one that is crucial for our well-being and that of the rest of nature. When this relationship is destroyed—say, by mass extinction or nature-deficit disorder—then we lose something precious and essential at the heart of being human.

## When Nature Suffers, Humans Suffer:
## Global Warming and Other Maladies

Our experiential alienation from and pervasive plundering of the earth is perhaps the greatest existential challenge humankind has ever faced. In 2020, over 250 scientists and scholars from 30 different countries issued a grave warning: "researchers in many areas consider societal collapse a credible scenario this century" if policymakers continue avoiding our climate emergency and other ecological maladies ("Warning on climate," 2020). An assault on humankind comes inevitably with an assault on nature. The consequences are especially severe for the poor, for people of color, and for children. The detrimental effects on our physical health and material well-being tend to garner our attention. That is where we will begin in this chapter. But then I will turn our attention to something far less obvious but even more perilous: the *psychospiritual trauma* created by the lack of conscious contact with nature, by the loss of our nonhuman relational partners, and by the other stressors connected with ecological destruction. All of these traumatic effects flow from a common source: the fantasy that humankind is intrinsically separate from, elevated above, and entitled to exploit the natural world. The ecologist Robert Michael Pyle (2005) puts it powerfully: "The most dangerous idea in the world is that humans are separate from the rest of nature. The greatest enormities against the Earth stem from such delusions, just as us-and-them thinking justifies our inhumanity toward one another" (p. 69). If it's their wish, a married couple can surely get a divorce. However, our hubris-filled fantasies notwithstanding, we absolutely cannot get a divorce from the natural world. Fortunately, a countercultural and counter-consciousness movement is growing, a great turning oriented by our intrinsic insepa- rability from and ethical involvement with our kindred fellows in the holistic earth community.

Because people are dying and economies and lifestyles are being disrupted, global warming and climate disruption are finally drawing serious attention (yet still not enough serious action). Deadly storms, floods, and wildfires are escalating in frequency and force. Draughts are compromising the supply of food and water. Rising sea levels threaten the very existence of coastal cities and towns. People are being forced to emigrate from their homelands. Wars are breaking out over food and water shortages and rising social stress due to climate refugees. Illnesses transmitted from nonhuman animals to human animals are growing more common: COVID-19, Lyme disease, monkeypox, West Nile virus, Zika virus, and malaria, among others. Polluted environments are exacerbating asthma, heart disease, stroke, lung cancer, and hormonal imbalances. Bee colonies are collapsing due to the wanton misuse of toxic chemicals. Fruit and vegetable crops are left without sufficient pollinators, thrusting us to the precipice of a disastrous food crisis. Countless life-saving medicines will never be discovered due to the extinction of plants. The American Psychological Association has expressed concern about climate-related increases in anxiety, depression, posttraumatic stress, drug abuse, suicide, interpersonal and intergroup violence, helplessness, hopelessness, and grief (Clayton et al., 2017).

In a landmark event, the United Nations' Intergovernmental Panel on Climate Change (IPCC, 2018a, 2018b) issued a major report in 2018. Ninety-one scientists from 40 countries collaborated on the project, which involved an analysis of over 6,000 scientific studies. Their findings were so ominous that shock waves were felt around the world. At the present (turning) point in history, human activity has already raised earth's mean surface temperature approximately 1° C above preindustrial levels. The researchers stated with "high confidence" that increases will reach 1.5° between 2030 and 2052 if we continue with business as usual (p. 6). The report's key finding, stated bluntly, is that global warming will be catastrophic if the increase is kept below 1.5° C by midcentury, and ultra-catastrophic if it goes above that. *The very best-case scenario will result in massive destruction, suffering, and death.* But to achieve even that dire outcome will "require rapid, far-reaching and unprecedented changes in all aspects of society" (IPCC, 2018b). Let us pause for a moment and let this urgent assessment sink in.

Massive climate change could displace up to 200 million people worldwide by 2050. People in poverty, and villages that depend upon subsistence fishing, will suffer the most. Major population centers will also be afflicted: New York, Boston, Miami, San Francisco, New Orleans, Mumbai, Bangkok, Shanghai, Hong Kong. Yet this is not merely a future problem. Disastrous effects are being felt right now. An important case involves the Isle de Jean Charles in Louisiana, a thin marshy strip of land in bayou country. For generations, the thriving community has predominantly been comprised of members of the indigenous Biloxi-Chitimacha-Choctaw tribe. By way of fishing, hunting, and trapping, they have long flourished in this beautiful place. But Louisiana is losing an area the size of a football field every 90 minutes, day after day. The people of Isle de Jean Charles have become the first climate refugees in the United States. As resident Chantel Comardelle says, "Once our island goes, the core of our tribe is lost. . . . We've lost our whole culture. . . . Water was our life and now it's almost our enemy because it is driving us out. . . . It's our life and our death" (Van Houten, 2016). In a tragic irony, the island is located in Terrebonne Parish—French for "good earth." But now that good earth is vanishing.

The climate emergency (and larger ecological crisis) is a symptom of our pathological and pathogenic estrangement from the rest of nature. It demonstrates the unanticipated consequences—the shadow side—of our efforts to master and control nature by technological means. Thus far there have been three major responses: (1) denial, avoidance, and repression: continuing on with business as usual; (2) adaptation: trying to survive and prosper in a warmer world; and (3) mitigation: limiting the extent of future warming by reducing the release of greenhouse gases into the atmosphere. Adaptation and mitigation certainly play important roles in this perilous time. Yet a more radical alternative is called for, namely (4) transformation: a deep metamorphosis in our consciousness, self-sense, society/culture, and ethical relations.

Unfortunately, response 1 has been predominant for decades. But denial, avoidance, and repression can only work as a short-term tactic for surviving unbearable pain. When such defensive responses become sedimented into stable ways of being, then whatever we have repressed or avoided will resurface in even more painful, symptomatic forms. Many in power are still opting for avoidance, not out of pain but of greed. Donald Trump has long held tightly to public proclamations of denial: "Global warming is a total, and very expensive, hoax!" (Beckwith, 2017). As president he withdrew the United States from the international Paris Climate Agreement. And he installed Scott Pruitt as head of the Environmental Protection Agency after the latter received over $200,000 from the fossil fuel industry when campaigning to be Oklahoma's attorney general, a role in which he sued the EPA 14 times. Unconscionable denials by politicians and corporate executives do not eliminate the possibility—surely the case to some extent—that they are well aware that human-generated global warming is real and that the status quo is terribly dangerous (yet quite lucrative for themselves and others who are already wealthy). Exxon's nefarious cover up of the scientific evidence is now well known (Hall, 2015).

## Humans Are Relational Beings and
## We Are Losing Our Relationships

I just described an array of critical concerns. I could have raised countless others, since the media report more bad news every day. Yet there is an even deeper issue the media rarely mention. That is, *we are suffering from a foundational psychological and spiritual malady, one that underlies all the alarming problems discussed so far. Namely, we are terribly confused about who we are; and this leaves us afraid and disoriented in our relations with others.* Two interwoven fantasies are involved here: the notion that each of us is a separate, sovereign, self-sufficient, ego-centered subject; and the notion that the human species is separate from, superior to, elevated above, and entitled to dominate the rest of nature. Together these felt-beliefs comprise a *fundamental delusion of modern humanity.* Conscious convivial contact with the natural world is a core constituent of human nature. Relational rapport, not just with people but with others in the local eco-community, has been the basic guiding circumstance of our lives for over 300,000 years, since the emergence of *Homo sapiens.* We could even say for two million years, since *Homo habilis* and earlier human ancestors came into being. Millions of years of interdependent, inter-responsive existence have certainly shaped who we are in deeply enduring ways, not just biologically but psychologically. Further, relationships have been crucial not only from the beginning of our species, but also from the beginning of everyone's life, in our connections with caregivers, and most significantly, from *the continuously arising beginning of every present encounter.* A call-and-response dynamic is built into the very essence of being human, comprising the intrinsic ethical-ontological structure of our (co)existence. The quality of our responsiveness with each other is the most important facilitator of well-being. We become who we are, others become who they are, through inter-responsive engagement. Because humans are inherently relational beings, and we are rapidly vanquishing countless nonhuman companions that have forever blessed our lives, we are colluding in our own impoverishment. In E. O. Wilson's (1984) cogent assessment, "We are human in good part because of the particular way we affiliate with other organisms. They are the matrix in which the human mind originated and is permanently rooted" (p. 139). *In losing our relations with the natural world, we are losing much of what it means to be human. We are abdicating something essential, sacred, and precious at the very heart of being human.* The psychological consequences of these harrowing losses are barely understood.

Appreciating the inter-responsive structure and functioning of human (co)existence is a key for ecopsychology. (By structure I mean the coherent way our life is comprised. By functioning, I mean its dynamic interplay.) To illustrate this, I will present several brief "parables" and then explicate them by way of Buddhist, psychoanalytic, and phenomenological psychology. Like cairns placed along a trail, the parables will serve as pointers toward further exploration. These examples, from the cradle to the grave, provide initial evidence that nondual, participatory *responsiveness*—and ultimately *responsibility*—are quintessential in being human.

*Parable One*: Martin Luther King Jr. delivered a "Christmas Sermon on Peace" in December 1967, just over three months before being assassinated in a heinous racist attack. Anguished by the violence of racial injustice at home and the war in Vietnam, he made an eloquent appeal for an alternative path. His beautiful challenge is directly applicable to our relations with nature:

> Now let me suggest first that if we are to have peace on earth, our loyalties must . . . transcend our race, our tribe, our class, and our nation [and our species, not to mention our individual self]; and this means we must develop a world perspective. No individual can live alone, no nation can live alone, and as long as we try, the more we are going to have war in this world. . . . We must either learn to live together as brothers or we are all going to perish as fools.
>
> Yes, as nations and individuals, we are interdependent. . . . It really boils down to this: that all life is interrelated. We are all caught in an inescapable network of mutuality, tied into a single garment of destiny. Whatever affects one directly, affects all indirectly. We are made to live together because of the interrelated structure of reality. Did you ever stop to think that you can't leave for your job in the morning without being dependent on most of the world? You get up in the morning and go to the bathroom and reach for the sponge, and that's handed to you by a Pacific islander. You reach for a bar of soap, and that's given to you by the hands of a Frenchman. And then you go to the kitchen to drink

your coffee for the morning, and that's poured into your cup by a South American. And maybe you want tea: that's poured into your cup by a Chinese. Or maybe you're desirous of having cocoa for breakfast, and that's poured into your cup by a West African. And then you reach for your toast, and that's given to you at the hands of an English-speaking farmer, not to mention the baker. And before you're finished eating breakfast in the morning, you've depended on more than half of the entire world. This is the way our universe is structured, this is its interrelated quality. We aren't going to have peace on earth until we recognize this basic fact of the interrelated structure of all reality. (King, 1986, pp. 253–254)

*Parable Two*: Ecologists teach us that nature works in the same interdependent, inter-responsive way. The discipline of ecology is oriented by one core fact: *every ecosphere is structured by and functions through an indivisible, dynamic, communal network of life-giving interrelationships*. The whole eco-community brings individual participants into being and furthers their (co)existence, while the participants and their interactions bring the whole community into being.

*Parable Three*: Our close evolutionary ancestor, *Homo erectus*, dates from 1.9 million to 70,000 years ago. The species was so named because fossils indicate a shift from a posture adapted for a life in trees to one oriented for walking upright in relation with the expansive eco-community of the African savanna. When one's survival depends on seeing a lion lurking over in the grasses, it is good to be able to stand upright with open receptive senses. Further, moving on two legs frees our hands to grasp things, make tools, and creatively interact with the beckoning world. Thereby, we also open our vulnerable yet sensitive heart to the relational appeals of a nourishing and threatening world. In countless ways our physical body has been reshaped over eons in accordance with the soliciting calls of the animate earth. And so too our mind and heart. We and our nonhuman companions have coevolved responsively in concert with one another.

*Parable Four*: "There is no such thing as a baby." This strange assertion was made by D. W. Winnicott. Stranger still is that he took this position even though, or more truly *because*, he was a pediatrician, psychoanalyst, and expert in child development. Winnicott's declaration is startling, but he did go on to clarify: "I once risked the remark, 'There is no such thing as a baby'—meaning that if you set out to describe a baby, you will find you are describing *a baby and someone*. A baby cannot exist alone, but is essentially part of a relationship" (Winnicott, 1987, p. 88). Truly, our inter-responsive contact with others is an essential part of the nature of what it is to be human. Being human *is* being-in-relation-with-others.

*Parable Five*: An interviewer once asked Sigmund Freud what "normal" humans should be able to do well. Since health and normality are not the same, let me rephrase things while honoring the intent of the original question: "What are the key qualities of psychological health and well-being?" The interviewer probably expected a profound and complex answer from the world's most renowned psychologist. Freud did give a profound response, yet one that was beautifully simple: "to love and to work" (Freud, in Erikson, 1980, p. 102). Decades earlier, Leo Tolstoy expressed the same sentiment: "It's possible to live perfectly on earth if one is able to work and to love" (Christian, 1978, p. 70). Two wise fellows, two kindred celebrations of love.

*Parable Six*: Intersubjective responsiveness is built into the neurological structure of our body. Cognitive scientists have shown that our brain is "wired to connect" with others (Goleman, 2006, p. 4). "Our mirror neurons fire as we watch someone else . . . so that a portion of the pattern of neuronal firing in our brain mimics theirs. . . . Mirror neurons make emotions contagious, letting the feelings we witness flow through us, helping us get in synch" (p. 42).

*Parable Seven*: The COVID-19 pandemic—transpiring as I am completing this book—is fiercely subverting the delusion that we are separate selves living independently from other people and the rest of nature. Apparently bats spread the virus to humans, with habitat destruction and human habitation driving them into more frequent contact with people. And we are spreading it to each other (and to other primates in zoos and deer in the wild). Often unaware that we carry the coronavirus, we infect others and others infect us. And infections flow on in a contagious cascade. Biologically, psychologically, culturally: when the world is ill, we are all ill. Yet embracing our interdependence is also helping us manage this terrible plague. Folks are naturally assisting their fellows: a dear elder in a nursing home who could benefit from a phone call, a child past ready for a reassuring hug, a village that needs more vaccines. Far more powerful than any virus, each gesture of loving-kindness radiates ripples of compassion.

*Parable Eight*: I would like to tap into the universal fear of dying. But I also hope to tap into *something that goes deeper than death*. If you are willing, please imagine a scene at your own deathbed . . . Let's say that you know you only have a few days yet to live. In this precious liminal time people tend to review their lives and connect with people they truly care about. Although power, fame, money, possessions, pleasure, and security may have been enticing in other circumstances, such things surely do not hold sway when we are poised at the edge of imminent death. Pondering what has mattered most in their lives, people turn to love. "Did I live well?" morphs quickly into "Did I love well?" "Was I well loved?" "Let me be with those dear to me."[1] It is often claimed that we must die alone, and I understand the element of truth in this. Nonetheless, primarily, people approach death with beloved companions in their heart and if possible in their arms. *Truly, love is deeper than death.*

*Parable Nine*: "Who am I?" This core existential question has been pondered across the ages. Our answers implicitly guide how we live. Yet the question of one's identity soon moves us beyond our supposedly independent self and into an appreciation of our interpersonal connections. Being a parent or spouse is an intersubjective mode of existence, far more than a self-assured, individualistic one. One can only be a teacher in relation with students, a gardener in relation with plants, soil, sun, and rain. No specific quality can ever totally define us, but when describing our self we inevitably speak of our involvement with others. *When asked who we are, those we love are included inseparably.*

*Parable Ten*: Thoroughly in the spirit of all these interresponsive "parables," the following passages are so beautifully revealing that I will share them with little commentary.

"I am, because we are; and since we are, therefore I am" (Mbiti, 1969, p. 106). This African proverb honors an intrinsically interrelational sense of self, a hallmark of the ubuntu worldview.

*Mitákuye Oyás'in*. "All my relations" or "all are related." This sacred prayer from the Lakota Sioux celebrates the participatory communion and harmony of all beings and presences.

"No man is an island, entire of itself; every man is a piece of the continent, a part of the main. . . . Any man's death diminishes me, I am involved in mankind, and therefore never send to know for whom the bell tolls; it tolls for thee" (Donne, 1999, p. 103). This wise teaching from John Donne is widely revered. Sadly, its experiential ethical significance is widely ignored.

"i am through you so I" (Firmage, 1994, p. 537). This is a line from E. E. Cummings. What if we let it live in us as a transformative incantation and guide in our daily living?

*Parable Eleven*: Guided by the Zen teacher Thich Nhat Hanh, let us pause and contemplate an ordinary blank piece of paper. Please find one now if you can. Looking deeply

> you will see clearly that there is a cloud floating in this sheet of paper. Without a cloud, there could be no rain; without rain, the trees cannot grow; and without trees, we cannot make paper. The cloud is essential for the paper to exist. If the cloud is not here, the sheet of paper cannot be here either. So we can say that the cloud and the paper *inter-are*. . . . If we look into this sheet of paper even more deeply, we can see the sunshine in it. If sunshine is not there, the forest cannot grow. . . . And if we continue to look, we can see the logger who cut the tree . . . and the logger's father and mother. . . . You cannot point out one thing that is not here—time, space, the earth, the rain, the minerals in the soil, the sunshine, the cloud, the river, the heat. Everything co-exists with this sheet of paper. . . . "To be" is to inter-be. You cannot just *be* by yourself alone. You have to inter-be with every other thing. (Nhat Hanh, 1988, pp. 3–4)

## Buddhist Psychology and the Interdependent Co-arising of Everyone's Existence

As you may have noticed, the first and last parables are essentially the same, even though Dr. King is oriented by a Christian perspective and Nhat Hanh a Buddhist one. The latter's passage is from a commentary on the *Prajñāpāramitā Heart Sūtra*, a core text of Māhāyana Buddhism. (*Prajñāpāramitā* means the heart or essence of understanding, the deepest wisdom.) Nhat Hanh's poetic words are an evocative presentation of five intertwined concepts—*experiences*—from Buddhist philosophy/psychology/ practice: "emptiness," "no-self," the "interdependent co-arising of all phenomena," "impermanence," and "nonduality." When contemplated together, they provide a vivid illustration of our inherently inter-responsive nature. In its most renowned teaching, the *Heart Sūtra* declares: form is emptiness, emptiness is form, form is not other than emptiness, emptiness is not other than form. "Form" refers to each particular being, presence, experience, encounter, or event in the phenomenal world. Regarding "emptiness," Zen and Tibetan Buddhism attest that this is our essential nature and the essential nature of all that is. But because it sounds nihilistic, emptiness is often misunderstood. Yet Nhat Hanh (1988) clarifies things: "emptiness" means being "empty of a separate, independent existence" (p. 10). A person, a laugh, a chess move, a fern, a tiger, even a grain of sand: every distinct form is empty of any isolated, self-encapsulated, self-sufficient reality. Like the paper we considered a moment ago, far from being isolated and self-existent, every individual form comes into being, is comprised of, and continues to (co)exist by way of influences it receives in connection with other forms. This is true of sheets of paper, but more dynamically so in human beings. My life is possible only thanks to the gifts all my relations have shared with me over the years, including the overture of my relational partner in the present moment. Gathering these bountiful influences across time and space, and inflecting them in my own unique way right here and now, my very self emerges into being (inter)responsively and ever anew. Like Nhat Hanh (1988) says, "Empty of a separate self means full of everything" (p. 10). This wondrous sense of relationality and plenitude is not present in the English word "emptiness." But the Japanese word translated (rather misleadingly) as emptiness is *shūnyatā*, which carries two complementary connotations: vast all-inclusive openness, like a clear blue sky that welcomes every passing bird, plane, or kite; and abundant fullness, like in pregnancy. Nhat Hanh's example illustrates this perfectly: clouds, rain, trees, people, and more, all there in one sheet of paper. Yet so does an ordinary ecosystem, holistically inclusive and comprised of dynamically interconnected participants. So too the indivisibly inter-responsive functioning of our everyday life. The *lived experience* of so-called "emptiness" is one of boundless openness and intimate nondual communion.

These views help us appreciate the (co)existential reality that Buddhism refers to as "no-self" (*anattā*, Pali; *anātman*, Sanskrit). Buddhism certainly does not contest the obvious fact that each of us is a distinct individual, or that aspects of the world appear as distinct things. Rather, in consonance with emptiness, no-self simply (and profoundly) points to the truth that there is *never a separate self: no substantial, independent, permanent, reified, nonrelational entity. Nor is there ever really a separate, objectified world*. The "nonduality" of subject and object does not deny that two or more different participants are involved in a situated encounter, only that none actually abide by themselves, independent from each other or from a seamless dynamic field of interrelationships. Not accidentally, wise ones from other traditions agree. As Martin Buber (1958) says, "There is no *I* taken in itself, but only the *I* of the primary word *I-Thou* and the *I* of the primary word *I-It*" (p. 4). Further, appreciating the "truth of no-self, is to realize that the boundaries between inside and outside, yourself and the surroundings, are permeable, and that the air and water of this neighborhood, this valley, is also inextricably part of your being" (Snyder, in Gonnerman, 2015, p. 279). Indeed, when we look carefully we realize that every single self implicitly gathers and is constituted by its history of relational influences, including (especially) those of the present moment. To use non-Buddhist language, *every self is a self-in-relation-with-others*. Even a hermit in the forest (co)exists in responsive involvement with a whole network of participants: animals, plants, water, weather, and so on. Nhat Hanh coined the term "interbeing" (p. 3) to celebrate this inter-responsive character of life. Contemplative experiences can bring it vividly to awareness, but so can careful attunement to our everyday life. The being of others imbues our being, and vice versa. The local river—healthy or unhealthy—is a dimension of our very self. Our actions—loving or ignorant—are a dimension of the river's being. The boundaries between self and world are intrinsically permeable.

These explorations bring us to yet another major relational experience: the *interdependent co-arising (or dependent co-origination)* of all phenomena. In Sanskrit, this is called *pratītya-samutpāda*: "in dependence, things rise up" (Nhat Hanh, 1998, p. 221). While sustaining our irreplaceable uniqueness, each of us is an expression of and creative participant in an infinitely deep community (*sangha*) or inter-responsive field. Our indivisible involvement in this dynamic communal network actually comprises our being and the being of others. Given such continually creative interactive participation, no thing or person abides statically or in isolation. Thus the Buddhist celebration of impermanence (*annica; anitya*). Invoking life's interdependent co-arising, the Buddha avowed: "This comes to be, because that comes to be. This ceases to be, because that ceases to be" (Nhat Hanh, 1998, p. 221). Bashō gives us a feel for this: "Dusk / dims the hawk's eyes / and the quail starts chirping" (Hass, 1994, p. 30). The darkening meadow, the hawk's seeing, and the quail's chirping are each there, while seamlessly arising as one. Bashō is there as well, with reverence for the dance of prey and predator—for the quail (safer now) and for the hawk (hungrier now).

The Dalai Lama points out that the "two truths—dependent co-origination and emptiness—are taught as two perspectives on the same reality" (Garfield, 1995, p. 305). The key issue is that our true nature—call it buddha-nature, emptiness, the dharma—is no other than our everyday relational life, the inter-responsive co-arising, coexisting, and co-creating of all phenomena. And our true nature comes to fruition when we live these relationships with awareness and love. The Buddha put it clearly: "One who sees dependent origination sees the Dhamma; one who sees the Dhamma sees dependent origination" (Bodhi, 1995, p. 283). *Dhamma* (Pali)—*dharma* (Sanskrit)—is a commonplace word and a special spiritual/philosophical one. It is often translated as Dao (Chinese). Sometimes it refers specifically to the teachings of Shākyamuni Buddha. More deeply, it means the great way (*dao*), the great truth, the "law" of the cosmos, the way things are, the harmonious structure and functioning of reality, our essential nature, the radiance of this essential nature. Dharma can also mean duty or responsibility. Significantly, it also refers to all the particular things and phenomena of everyday existence. As the Buddha suggests, when we awaken to the dharma we discover the inseparably inter-responsive nature of life. We meet others in all their beauty, intelligence, and suffering. Never severed from these fellows, human or otherwise, we feel those very qualities as our own. A loving reply follows spontaneously: celebrating others' glory, ministering to others' pain.

## A Paradigm Shift in Psychology: From Separation to Relationality

*None of us could even be, at all, without engaging in responsive relations with others.* Self and others, self and society, self and nature: all are completely free of any independent reified reality. This is the case intrinsically, but when we realize it consciously our life and relationships are enhanced. However, against all evidence, for much of the twentieth century the field of psychology supported separatist notions of identity and personal development. Eventually, however, things turned toward an interrelational sensibility. The history of psychoanalysis provides a good illustration of this evolution. Based upon his therapeutic work, Sigmund Freud knew that our connections with others are profoundly formative, whether for health or psychopathology. And he extolled human relationship by giving preeminence to our capacities for love and work. Nonetheless, he was strongly influenced by the dualistic notion—inherited from Descartes and others—that there is a radical separation of self and others, self and world, organism and environment. Freud held that we have a reservoir of biologically based psychic energy—"libido"—that seeks to be discharged in order to enhance pleasure and reduce pain. He posited that people were principally driven by hedonic urges to direct sexual and aggressive energy toward others; or when conflicted, to inhibit such a release. *This view gives primacy to a (presumably) detached individual who only secondarily comes into relationship*—with a mother, say, to satisfy a tension when hungry; or with a romantic partner, say, to satisfy a sexual drive.

But after Freud's death in 1939, a "relational" approach emerged as the most innovative and influential school in contemporary psychoanalysis.[2] Although physiological needs must be met, and we are inclined to seek pleasure and banish pain, analysts came to understand that humans are intrinsically relational beings who are *primarily motivated by the desire for close, loving, affectionate contact with others*. D. W. Winnicott, cited earlier, was a key figure in this movement. So was John Bowlby, whose research initiated the now burgeoning field of "attachment theory." Bowlby (1969, 1979) was disturbed by the trauma suffered by children who had lost their parents during World War II. In studying these relational ruptures, Bowlby came to appreciate that loving contact with others is crucial not only in our earliest development but across the entire lifespan: "attachment behaviour is held to characterize human beings from the cradle to the grave" (1979, p. 129).[3] Nonetheless, in psychological theory and popular culture at the time, a particular type of self was still imagined as the hallmark of maturity and health. This self was thought to be intrinsically separate from others and the world: sovereign, independent, firmly bounded, autonomous, self-sufficient, rational, and masterful. Qualities such as *inter*dependence, close attachment, relational sensitivity, empathic attunement, and responsive care for others were downplayed or even pathologized. It is no accident that the latter have traditionally been associated with women, whereas the former have been linked more with men. Even today the developmental path through the life span is often envisioned as follows: one (presumably) moves from absolute helplessness and dependence in infancy; to relative but diminishing dependence in childhood (with the growing ability to use language and exert agency); to independence, autonomy, self-sufficiency, and mastery in adolescence and adulthood. This conceptualization is consistent with the values of individual freedom and self-determination that have long been import-ant in modern Euro-American culture. Yet an *excessive* valorization of individualistic freedom is evident in some responses to the coronavirus plague. I heard one man remark, "If you get rid of individualism, you get rid of America." And one woman insisted, "It's my choice whether I wear a mask or not!" Of course, such exclusive self-interest ignores the fact that not wearing a mask not only puts her at risk but increases the probability she will infect others who might die or infect others. Yet contrary to this I-me-mine ethos, a kindly, other-centered view also emerged: "My mask is for you. Your mask is for me."

Beginning in the 1960s, the "self psychology" of Heinz Kohut helped psychoanalysis surpass its overemphasis on independence. In his words, "A move from dependence (symbiosis) to independence (autonomy) in the psychological sphere is no more possible, let alone desirable, than a corresponding move from a life dependent on oxygen to a life inde-pendent of it in the biological sphere" (Kohut, 1984, p. 46). Similarly, "relational-cultural theorists"—mostly female psychotherapists influenced by relational psychoanalysis, feminism, Buddhist psychology, and social justice theory—have emphasized the crucial importance of empathic, mutually supportive connections *across our entire life span.*

> Mainstream Western psychological theories tend to depict human development as a trajectory from dependence to independence. . . . In contrast, relational-cultural theory (RCT) is built on the premise that, throughout our life span, human beings grow through and toward connection. It holds that we need connection to flourish, even to stay alive, and isolation is a major source of suffering for people, at both a personal and cultural level. [And an ecological level.] Seeing connection as the primary ongoing organizer and source of motivation in people's lives transforms the work of socializa-tion into assisting our children to develop relational skills and elaborating the possibility for mutuality in relationships. It furthermore calls attention to the need to alter the socio-political forces of disconnection that create significant pain for people. (Jordan, 2010, p. 1)

Critiquing "the myth of the separate self" (Jordan, 2010, p. 2), relational-cultural theorists speak not only of self but of self-in-relation. Transpersonal psychologists also highlight our inter-responsive nature (Wilber, 1980, 2000b; Washburn, 1995). Wilber (2000b) shows how all individual agency is "agency-in-communion" with others (pp. 560–561, see also p. 49). Note that I am not critiquing each person's particular distinctiveness, nor the value of *relative* autonomy and agency. Creating a sense of our unique self, worldview, identity, and personal agency is a key developmental accomplishment. In part this involves the construction of self-boundaries that differentiate us from others (yet simultaneously unite us as well). But our capacities for self-direction are always situated in the larger context of responsive communion with others. To act as an assertive agent is to have already been supported by others and to be acting now as a self-in-relation-with-others. A phase of total dependency in infancy fosters increasing but *relative and relationally supported independence* in adolescence and young adulthood. This can grow into a conscious embrace of both our *relative autonomy and interdependence* throughout the rest of our life. Truly, authentic agency and self-assertiveness emerge by way of listening to the wild and sacred calls that are being sent to us from the depths of life, right here and now.

## Our Involvement with Nature Is a Real Relationship

Recall that Buber celebrates three different forms in which a true Thou may come to touch us: another person, G-d, and the natural world. But I-It relations tend to rule our lives these days. Buber's term "it" captures the dominant culture's reductionist, unseeing, unfeeling view of nature. Wouldn't you feel demeaned if someone referred to you as "it"? But we do this all the time with the beings and presences of nature: "Check out that hyacinth, *it* smells so wonderful!" The English language simply does not provide a pronoun that would honor a flower or tree as an intelligent expressive being. Viewing a tree, "I can assign it to a species . . . I can dissolve it into a number. . . . Throughout all this the tree remains my object" (Buber, 1970, pp. 57–58). In such a utilitarian encounter, we reduce the tree to a reified thing and exploit it for our own purposes. (Note the correlative reduction of self to an objectified, ego-centered, acquisitive subject.) This can be appropriate in certain circumstances, like when a biologist wants to identify a tree's species or a builder needs lumber to make a house. Yet Buber (1970) urges us to see more deeply: "It can also happen, if will and grace are joined, that as I contemplate the tree I am drawn into a relation, and the tree ceases to be an It" (pp. 58–59). Buber is describing an authentic I-Thou relationship, in this case with a partner who is rooted and leafing. But we do not have to take his word for it. Remember, say, your childhood involvement with a familiar tree: a real companion you climbed, hid in, dangled from. Or walk outdoors right now and be open to actually meeting a tree you usually pass by. I am inviting us to embrace the ever-present opportunity for intimate contact with the natural world. *Yet the primary invitation is from life itself, from the animate world that is always soliciting our response.*

Buber encourages us to realize that nature is sending us overtures as a true Thou, addressing us as an expression of the "eternal Thou"—his phrase for G-d. "What is greater for us than all enigmatic webs at the margins of being is the central actuality of an everyday hour on earth, with its streak of sunshine on a maple twig and an intimation of the eternal You [Thou]" (Buber, 1970, pp. 135–136). Crucially, an ethical imperative is presented in such encounters: "We . . . are resolved to tend with holy care the holy treasure of our actuality that has been given to us for this life" (pp. 136–137). That is the core point. Later I will show how *inter-responsiveness is our essence, our deepest calling, the path to fulfilling this calling, and the very fruition of our essence and calling.* Stated differently: *love is our nature-calling-path-fruition.*

Caring contact with the rest of nature has always been at the heart of being human. But today nature is often construed as a "lower" form of life, a mere material resource to exploit, or a backdrop for human activities. Common insults include calling someone "a birdbrain" or "a pig." Nazis referred to Jews as "rats." Regarding (his fantasy about) Central American immigrants, Donald Trump ranted, "You wouldn't believe how bad these people are. These aren't people, these are animals" (Davis, 2018). Along with inciting racist violence, Trump was perpetuating the presumed split between humankind and the rest of nature, with nature being denigrated and our own animality disavowed. The very notion that we are engaged in a real relationship with the natural world can appear bizarre to our (post)modern mind. This fact demonstrates the extremity of our dissociative estrangement from a (co)existential condition that has been completely obvious from time immemorial. One day a class of undergraduate students and I were discussing our connection with the natural world. A bright young woman spoke up and said, "I'm a city person. I don't have a relationship with nature." I was initially taken aback, since it is impossible to not have a relationship with nature (although we do often live it unconsciously). But this way of thinking is quite common. A dangerous belief lurks unwittingly in the student's view, a conviction that there is a real separation between humankind and nature. This leads to the foolishness of trying to live well without regard for the health of the larger earth community. This is doomed to fail, inevitably. As Gregory Bateson (1972) remarked, "The unit of survival is *organism* plus *environment*. We are learning by bitter experience that the organism that destroys its environment destroys itself" (p. 483).

*Our daily life is an ongoing, call-and-response conversation. How well we relate is always in question, but we cannot not relate with other people and the rest of nature.* Helping us "acknowledge . . . the human-nature relationship as a relationship" (p. 7) is actually one of ecopsychology's major tasks (Fisher, 2013, p. 7). Most everyone would agree that human existence depends upon a connection with the natural world. But this is not merely a piece of factual information requiring cognitive acknowledgment. Rather, it must be known experientially, realized deeply, and integrated into our spontaneous perception and relational responsivity. These are matters of the utmost practical importance. *Because we are relational beings, and we are destroying our relationships with our companions in the natural world; because real living involves truly meeting others, and we are not showing up for the meeting with our natural partners; because many of our nonhuman fellows are not even there to be met anymore because we have vanquished them; because these are the tragic conditions of contemporary existence, then the psychological consequences of such unprecedented changes are especially disastrous.* To provide healing pathways through this traumatic crisis, we must come to know—as clearly as we recognize our best friend walking into the room—that we are inherently interdependent, inter-responsive beings, not independent self-interested egos.

## Listening to Nature as a Conversational Partner

Enjoying the buzzing, whistling mating song of a black-throated green warbler—"zee zee zee zoo zee!"—but not yet able to see this beautiful bird, I move closer and the singing stops. When my body-mind becomes still, quiet, and unthreatening, the birdsong begins again. I listen to the warbler and the warbler listens to and watches me. The black-throated green speaks to me and I speak with him (via the meaningful gestural presencing of my movement and stillness). The warbler's singing imbues my being as my comportment imbues his being. It is an arbitrary abstraction to focus only on the bird or me in isolation. Of course, the black-throated green is not singing for me but for his mate, the mate who just flew to a nearby branch in order to eat a gnat, a gnat who was blown toward that tree by a breeze, a breeze that is the leading edge of a thunderstorm rolling over the distant hills, and on and on. These are real conversations.

Even ordinary perception is like a conversation, as revealed in the phenomenological work of Maurice Merleau-Ponty and David Abram. Usually we imagine that perceiving consists of an independently abiding subject becoming conscious of an independently abiding objective world. Yet such dualistic separation and reification are merely conceptual abstractions far removed from direct experience. When we attend closely to actual perceiving, we realize that it is an indivisibly intimate, inter-responsive, intertwining process. Far from existing as a detached self, in perceiving I am involved in an "ongoing interchange between my body and the entities that surround it. It is a sort of silent conversation that I carry on with things, a continuous dialogue that unfolds far below my verbal awareness" (Abram, 1996, pp. 52–53). Whenever we are touching something—like soft green moss—we can feel that we are simultaneously being touched by it. Even with "distal" senses like seeing or hearing, we can feel a subtle back-and-forth energetic flow transpiring between us and our relational partner. When we bring this into awareness, our responses harmonize better with the messages the world is sending our way.

Merleau-Ponty remarks that "the whole of nature is . . . our interlocutor in a sort of dialogue" (1962, p. 320); "the whole landscape is . . . but a variant of speech" (1968, p. 155). Meaningful speech implies intelligence, and we would do well to appreciate that nature really is speaking to us in its own wildly diverse, intelligent ways.

> For the largest part of our species' existence, humans have negotiated relationships with every aspect of the sensuous surroundings, exchanging possibilities with every flapping form, with each textured surface and shivering entity that we happened to focus upon. All could speak, articulating in gesture and whistle and sigh a shifting web of meanings that

we felt on our skin or inhaled through our nostrils or focused with our listening ears, and to which we've replied—whether with sounds, or through movements, or minute shifts of mood. (Abram, 1996, p. ix)

Many people would deem it preposterous that natural beings and presences are authentic others who are speaking to us and calling upon us. But not long ago, chillingly, cultural forces made it seem preposterous to many that Blacks and women could be welcomed as fellow subjects. We know that a major factor sustaining prejudice and oppression is lack of direct contact with people perceived as "other" than me and my tribe. Analogously, our relational contact with others in the natural community has been ruptured, leading to alienation and exploitation. To an exorbitant extent, our attention is dominated by human-oriented affairs and artifacts. Although normal now, this is a sadly deprived—even depraved!—state of affairs. It leaves us unfamiliar with the meaningful messages nature is sending our way—expressions of beauty, intelligence, and suffering. Our willingness to retune our consciousness to catch such communication is crucial for overcoming our ecocidal estrangement. Most of us are novices in this urgent endeavor.

The ecopsychologist Dorothy Cashore (2019) offers an inspiring story in this regard. She tells of her first encounter with the Jawbone-Butterbredt Area of Critical Environmental Concern in California's Mojave Desert. She came with her friend Darren who was intimately familiar with the place, having worked there for 16 months doing desert-restoration work. They had arrived at a remote location after dark and quickly set up their tent. Later Cashore was awakened from a deep sleep by Darren's excited voice outside the tent. When she crawled out to join him, he simply said: "Listen" (p. 2). She had not heard anything until he brought her attention to an initially indecipherable sound. But now, emerging through the desert's deep silence, there it was: "a single note: constant and concentrated, like the low-pitched droning of massive bees" (p. 2). Darren told her that this was the wind flowing through the mountains many miles away, wind they would only feel hours later. Knowing Dorothy well, it is not too much to say that her life was changed on the spot. "I had heard the same sound Darren heard, but whereas what I heard was so much mysterious noise, what he heard was a voice. We were both visitors to the place, but Darren had lived in close proximity to the colors, textures, and sounds, the charms and dangers of Jawbone. When the desert announced what was coming next, he was able to translate it" (pp. 6–7). This account comes from Cashore's exquisite PhD dissertation in clinical psychology at Duquesne University: "Listen for the Desert: An Ecopsychological Autoethnography" (Cashore, 2019). Her research was based upon 30 days of fieldwork in the Mojave Desert. I almost said 30 days "alone," because not a single human companion was there with her. Yet she was far from alone: she camped under the stars; interacted with animals, plants, terrain, sun, weather, and wide-open space; and contended with signs of unconscionable human intrusion and violence. I had the privilege of being her so-called dissertation "director," but the real director was the desert known affectionately as "Jawbone." The desert was her mentor, and she was a sensitive apprentice. I cherish this story because it demonstrates that we really can learn to welcome nature's wild and sacred voice. Cashore did not know how to listen to the desert until she devoted herself to becoming acquainted with the conversational companions who dwelt there. It took attentive care, practice, support from friends and teachers (human and otherwise), and a (counter)culture that valued this crucial venture. But she was transformed.

"Humans are tuned for relationship. The eyes, the skin, the tongue, ears, and nostrils—all are gates where our body receives the nourishment of otherness" (Abram, 1996, p. ix). Our human nature involves a holy longing for such interresponsive contact. Our own ego is not nearly enough. Nor is the exclusively human world. "The body asks for something other than . . . its relations with itself" (Merleau-Ponty, 2003, p. 225). But today we are mostly captivated by self-enclosed monologues with our own ideas or with human artifacts such as screens. Yet the rupture can be healed. Like Cashore, we can avail ourselves intimately in fresh new ways.

It is so easy to miss just how intimate such contact can actually be. Consider Merleau-Ponty's (1962) evocative words: "Every perception is a communication or a communion . . . a coition, so to speak, of our body with things" (p. 320). Not only does he insist that the world is communicating with us, but that perceptual contact is a kind of coitus, like making love, one of the most intimate experiences of all. It may be startling to consider perception as an event of lovemaking, our sentient sapient body interinvolved with the expressive and receptive body of the world. Yet such intercourse is occurring all the time (although usually as a prereflective process). "The look . . . envelops, palpates, espouses the visible things. As though it were in a relation of pre-established harmony with them" (Merleau-Ponty, 1968, p. 133). Espouse means "to marry." In truth, in every moment, there is an ongoing marriage taking place between ourselves and the depths of the world. Our great calling and task are to make this intimacy conscious, and respond in a way that is equal to its depths. Then we are truly making love.

## Loss of Nature, Loss of Humanity's Heart

"It is obvious," you might say, "that humans are relational beings." I agree wholeheartedly. However, with the destruction of the natural world and the insidious spread of nature-deficit disorder, our inextricable relationship with the natural world is far from obvious these days. We are depriving ourselves of inter-responsive engagements that have actually created and sustained what it is to be human across the ages. Our lives may never again be blessed by the Ivory-billed Woodpecker. In losing magical monarch butterflies and glorious coral reefs, in losing contact with wild ones that have always nourished our lives, the heart of being human is being impoverished. The science of ecology demonstrates that the natural world is a holistic, harmonious, interdependently co-arising community of relationships. But conversational interchanges become unbalanced when entire species are vanquished, habitat wiped out, and biodiversity diminished. Following the extirpation of wolves and mountain lions, deer populations are expanding excessively across the country while their food sources such as acorns and oak saplings are being depleted. Key participatory interactions are now missing. Fewer trees grow to maturity. No howls can be heard. Deer and rabbits need not be as alert as before. Their consciousness and behavior are changing. And so are ours.

We can readily see that when species die and relationships within a bioregion are lost, the health of the whole eco-community is diminished. It is past time to realize that humans are correspondingly impoverished. We are integral members of that community. Whatever afflicts our ecological neighborhood inevitably afflicts us. The natural world is a transpersonal dimension of our own being. When this essential dimension is destroyed, we humans are changed in a fundamental way. People were awakened by Winnicott's (1987) astonishing claim, "There is no such thing as a baby" (p. 88). Now we must come to realize that *there is no such thing as the human species.* Humankind can only coexist in interdependent responsivity with other species and with nature's elemental forces. No individual, no species can be alone.

The phenomenological psychiatrist R. D. Laing (1967) once offered this powerful critique: "the *ordinary* person is a shriveled, desiccated fragment of what a person can be" (p. 10). He was concerned that interpersonal and cultural forces were estranging people from the depths of their so-called "interior" being, say, from intimate contact with their feelings, thoughts, body, dreams, and desires. But his remark applies to our estrangement from the so-called "exterior" depths of our own being, from contact with our companions in the larger natural world.[4] In cutting ourselves off from the rest of nature, we become mere fragments of who we have always been and who we can become anew.

## Monologue with Ourselves over Dialogue with Others

Relationships can bring forth health or suffering, both for ourself and for others. Our well-being (or lack thereof) is interwoven with that of our family, friends, and the larger community/culture/society. The same happens with the natural world. A mutually enhancing relationship between people depends upon ongoing contact, engaged interaction, and inevitable rupture and repair at times. So too in our relationships with the rest of nature. But an insidious cycle is perpetuated by our self-centered, human-centered, dissociative alienation. *Lack of conscious contact with nature depletes our very self and our ways of being with others; confused and afraid, we further deplete the natural world; and this in turn depletes us even more.*

Since time immemorial, we have always been involved in conversations with the rest of nature. But now the conversation is changing acutely. Instead of a real dialogue, it is being turned into a self-absorbed anthropocentric monologue. Contemplate the vast difference between encountering the multiplicity of plants and animals in a healthy ecosystem as compared with the office cubicles, video meetings, and chemically controlled monoculture lawns so pervasive today. How many of us have walked through the woods with someone whose intimate knowledge of local plants and fungi reveals an astonishing diversity of edible foods? How many of us have experienced the pleasure of quenching our thirst with a luscious wild plum, much less enjoyed a meal of thrice-boiled milkweed buds?[5] The latter are delicious, by the way, tasting something like a combination of asparagus and artichoke! All too commonly our life is tyrannized by narrowly circumscribed, techno-corporate-consumerist culture fashioned for human convenience and profit for only a few. Our awareness and interactions are often dominated by things such as fast food, enticing superstores, brief texting, and skimming the surfaces of the internet. The diversity and depth of our relationships are dying. Increasingly we exist like Narcissus, relating only to our own reflection, to our own kind, to ever more of the same. When we lose the vivifying intensity of encountering nature as a truly different other—remember seeing that bear crossing the road, or that awesome waterfall?—we begin to subsist in a self-encapsulated, self-preoccupied world. Clinical psychologists have shown how people with narcissistic personality disorder treat others as an objectified extension of their own self—ignoring the real otherness of others—and primarily use others instrumentally to fulfill their own wishes. Similarly, today's dominant culture often converts the natural world into a utilitarian extension of humanity, using nature merely to fulfill human wishes. In place of multidimensional human-nature relationships we increasingly have one-dimensional human-human relationships. In the name of "progress" or "economic development," shopping malls replace forest ecosystems, mountaintop mining craters replace mountains-and-rivers eco-communities. *Rather than mutually enhancing (I-Thou) dialogues with nature we are creating mutually impoverishing monologues with ourselves.*

When Merleau-Ponty (1968) looked into the mystery of ordinary perception, he discovered a "strange adhesion" and "commerce" that transpires between perceiver and perceived (p. 139). This indivisible partnership functions like "two mirrors facing one another where two indefinite series of images set in one another arise which belong really to neither of the two surfaces, since each is only the rejoinder of the other, and which therefore form a couple, *a couple more real than either of them*" (p. 139, emphasis added). Here is the key point: *the relational couple and their dynamic coupling comprise the primary reality,* an inter-responsive process far more real than conceptual notions of a supposedly separate subject observing a supposedly separate, objective world. Buber (1958) implores us to see that "All real living is meeting" (p. 11). Not just living in any way, not just meeting in any way, but truly living by truly meeting. Since relational couplings are what is most "real"—are who we are, what nature is, what "real living" is—and since we are destroying our relationships as we annihilate species and abdicate contact with the natural world, then *we are diminishing our very self, diminishing nature's very being, and creating a void in lived reality.*

Instrumental I-It relationships are suitable at times, like interacting briefly with a store clerk. But when we habitually skim the surfaces of relationships, when we focus only on our self-serving wishes, when we rarely avail ourselves for I-Thou contact, then *we deprive ourselves and others of our full humanity.* Buber (1970) offers a stark warning: "And in all seriousness of truth, listen: without It a human being cannot live. But whoever lives only with that is not human" (p. 85). To be fully human we are obliged to open ourselves for intimate encounters, not only with other people but with the larger animate earth. *"If our experience is destroyed, our behavior will be destructive.* If our experience is destroyed, we have lost our own selves" (Laing, 1967, p. 12). Suffering a pandemic of biodiversity loss and nature-deficit disorder, our experience is being destroyed and our behavior is increasingly destructive.

With extinction, an important dimension of us dies with the other species' death, just as an important dimension of the integrated lifeworld dies. The distinctive relationship is gone forever, never to exist again. Neither we nor the world will ever be the same. "If we kill off the wild, then we are killing a part of our souls," as Jane Goodall (2016) starkly declares. Lack of daily conscious interaction with nature is another grave loss. "Human beings themselves are at risk—not just on some survival-of-civilization level but more basically on the level of heart and soul. We are in danger of losing our souls. We are ignorant of our own nature and confused about what it means to be a human being" (Snyder, 1990, pp. 177–178). Truly, "we are human only in contact, and conviviality, with what is not human" (Abram, 1996, p. ix). *When our relationships with nature are extinguished and convivial engagement is rare, we actually become less human.* What do we become instead? I shudder to think!

Having coevolved in intimate rapport with the rest of nature for hundreds of thousands of years, the natural world is an essential dimension of our very existence. Living in a society bent on dominating and often annihilating the natural world, how could we not feel that we are lacking, unreal, disconnected, deadened, empty, haunted by a sense that there must be more to life? Such lack makes us vulnerable to false solutions provided (for a monetary and psychospiritual price) by our corporate-consumerist culture, especially the disingenuous promise of acquiring material things. But such "solutions" never come close to touching our real needs, while intensifying our sense of lack and further destroying the natural world. As the animate earth is increasingly impoverished, we feel increasingly empty. Not understanding the source of our suffering, we compulsively attempt to fill our emptiness by consuming (ultimately unsatisfying) commodities that require further annihilation of nature for their production. Of course, our estrangement from the natural world is not the only source of our psychospiritual malaise. Given the extent of social oppression and injustice, intercultural conflict, interpersonal trauma, and existential pain in our lives, any single interpretation is too simplistic. But healing our dissociation from nature must be one part of a larger psychocultural therapeutic.

## Not Merely Change, but Impoverishment

Biodiversity fosters individual and communal well-being, much like other kinds of diversity do (cultural, racial, gender, ethnic, religious, etc.). This does not only mean the simple existence of a multiplicity of species. More importantly, it has to do with diverse forms of life responding with each other in a dynamic, integral, inter-responsive eco-community. Scientists are concerned about the depletion of the biological gene pool due to the massive extinction and extirpation of earth's glorious array of species. From an (eco)psychological perspective, I would like to emphasize an analogous peril: in losing so many of our interrelationships with nature we are depleting the relational "gene pool." Biodiversity and relational diversity are reciprocally enhancing. As we restore biodiversity we give each other more accessible and wide-ranging experiential opportunities. As we restore relational diversity, opening ourselves for participatory conversations with nonhuman nature, we enhance our own health. Being healthier, we respond with greater awareness, understanding, and loving care, thereby fostering greater biodiversity.

There is no doubt that the natural world will continue on in some way regardless of human actions. I find it consoling, at least in moments, to think in terms of vast spans of time. Nature was flourishing long before humans' destructive confusion began laying waste to it. Nature will eventually flourish long after our species vanishes. But, here and now, I am not at all interested in consolation. Humankind and the rest of nature are still going on today, but in a terribly depleted manner. There is no way for us to destroy the natural world without destroying essential dimensions of our own being. Conversely, we cannot help heal the natural world without healing ourselves and our culture. This must involve welcoming nature's gifts, gratefully, and letting nature work its healing magic on us.

Chapter Four

# The Dissociative Madness
# of Modernity's Shadow

## Constructing, Deconstructing, and Reconstructing Culture

If the world is made of stories, stories are not just stories. They teach us what is real, what is valuable, and what is possible.

—David Loy (2010, p. 3)

Natural science has . . . no other goal than to more firmly establish and extend the power and domination of men over nature.

—Francis Bacon (in Leiss, 1972, p. 48)

The fact that millions of people share the same mental pathology does not make these people sane.

—Erich Fromm (1955, p. 15)

## Overture

Along with all the benefits that came with the emergence of modern culture, there was an unanticipated shadow side: an intensification of humankind's felt sense of dissociation from the natural world. This set into motion a grave, fear-driven structure of alienation and oppression. Humans began to act as if they were separate from and superior to a devalued, desacralized natural world, and thereby entitled to dominate and exploit it. This was a radically new social construction of reality, one that has been afflicting humans and the rest of nature ever since. However, anything constructed can be deconstructed and reconstructed anew. Such collective, sociocultural transformation is a key component of the great work of ecopsychology.

## Stories of Separation and the Need for a Psycho-Spiritual-Cultural Therapy

Across all of humankind's extraordinary qualities, I believe there is one that marks us as unique among all other living beings. But it is not what people often think when we imagine ourselves as exceptional. Far from being a congenial quality, it generates great grief for ourselves and others. What makes us unique is not thought, language, culture, technology, or art. Rather, it is the fact that we are haunted by a felt-sense of being separate from each other and from the rest of the natural world. We humans like to think of ourselves as an elite species, not just different from our fellow species but elevated above, superior to, and entitled to exploit all the so-called "lower forms of life" (to cite a shameful expression of arrogance and contempt). This common condition is perplexing because it is obvious that no individual or species can ever exist alone. And yet the insidious feeling of separation lingers on.

A brief experiential check might be worthwhile, if you are willing to play along: Breathe in deeply, enjoying the vitalizing energy that comes with that breath. And then completely stop breathing . . . Forever, I mean! Of course, it is quickly evident that you cannot stop breathing for very long. Beyond your will and control, *you are soon being breathed* again by your natural body's inherent participation with the rest of the animate earth. We are sustained by the intercourse of our animal reflexes and the earth's air, thankfully so. We can never really be detached from the rest of nature. Nonetheless, the felt-belief that we are separate can also seem quite obvious. Is it not clear that I am over here, inside my skin-bounded body, and that you and the rest of the world are over there, outside, at a distance from me? Relatedly, given the genuinely awesome powers of human awareness, intelligence, and society, it is easy to understand how we can be lured into the grandiose fantasy that we really are the supreme species above all the rest on earth. How can we make sense of the uncanny fact that separation (duality) and nonseparation (inter-responsiveness, communion, nonduality) both appear to be true? To approach this vexing question, we will consider two major forces: (1) the collective sociocultural conditioning that has been dominant in Europe and North America, especially since the beginning of the modern era; and (2) the conventional construction of our sense of self in the course of personal psychological development, especially in modern Euro-American cultures. While each of these formative forces is significant in its own right, the confluence of the two is tremendously compelling. The present chapter focuses on the way culture and society operate to construct our sense of reality, particularly the belief in a real divorce between humans and the rest of nature. The next chapter explores the developmental construction of our supposedly separate self-sense.

The cultural anthropologist Richard Nelson (1983) makes a striking observation: "Probably no society has been so deeply alienated from the community of nature, has viewed the natural world from a greater distance of mind, has lapsed into a murkier comprehension of its connection with the sustaining environment" (p. 203). Thomas Berry (1999) concurs, highlighting the psychological dimension of our ecological crisis: "The deepest cause of the present devastation is found in a mode of consciousness that has established a radical discontinuity between the human and all other modes of being" (p. 4). Conceptually we understand we are always involved with nature, and yet a dreadful feeling of detachment still tends to lurk in the background of our awareness. Our lives are often driven—mostly unconsciously—by the avoidance and self-aggrandizement that arise as defensive reactions to the anxiousness that is inevitably present when we feel disconnected. Such separatist views have been affecting (and infecting) all of us from our early childhood experiences to this very day.

Fortunately, a collective psycho-cultural-spiritual therapy is emerging. We see a growing affiliation of diverse individuals, groups, organizations, and scholarly disciplines, all taking initiatives to foster the mutual flourishing of humans and the rest of nature. This truly is the great work of our era. As I have suggested, this therapeutic movement must attend to the personal, interpersonal, sociocultural, and spiritual dimensions of existence. The present chapter takes a sociocultural approach. The dysfunction of our dominant economic, political, and legal systems is menacing the earth. In a nature-debasing world, to transform conventional stories, values, structures, and practices of separation is deeply countercultural work. Here ecopsychology joins with liberation psychology, critical psychology, and other socially engaged initiatives.

One winter morning my wife and I were visiting Blackwater Falls, an impressively grand, 57-foot waterfall in the mountains of West Virginia. The night before it had snowed heavily, but when we arrived the sky was a deeply saturated blue. There was nary a cloud to be seen. The cold crisp air was crystal clear. This intensified the brilliant sunlight glistening on the white snow covering the surrounding spruce and hemlock trees. The falls were frozen, thick and still, and giant icicles hung all around. Our experience with this natural marvel was truly awe-inspiring. Touched by such beauty, I remember my body tingling with joy and my heart opening in gratitude. After about a half hour two other people walked up. They appeared to be middle-class White men, on the surface not so different from my wife and me. Immediately one man said to the other, "Hey, this looks like a Coors Light commercial." The friend instantly agreed. They stood there for a minute or so, and then left and drove away. My wife and I were startled by their remarks and rapid departure. Upon reflection, it occurred to me that these men had made an effort to trek outside to visit the falls on a cold winter day. They must have been yearning for contact with the natural world, otherwise they would not have come. This is a significant fact, one that harbors some hope. Nonetheless, as I see it, their way of construing the waterfall is a symptom of a severe systemic *psychocultural pathology*, one that they—and all of us—are immersed in prior to any free choice. Strictly speaking, their views would not warrant a clinical diagnosis of any type of psychological disorder. However, their perspective could be considered psychotic if it were not induced by a profound cultural confusion. Psychoses are the most extreme form of psychological disorder, with schizophrenia being the most common example. The APA *Dictionary of Psychology* defines a "psychotic disorder" as "any number of severe mental disorders, regardless of etiology, characterized by gross impairment in REALITY TESTING" (VandenBos, 2013, p. 475).[1] The way the visitors at the waterfall "tested" reality—that is, the way they determined the reality and meaning of their experience—was to compare their present encounter to a television commercial, giving preeminence to the commercial. A marketing executive's manipulative fantasy actually served as their point of reference for what was real. The man did not even say the Coors commercial was like the real Blackwater Falls. Putting it that way would at least have given primacy to a direct experience with the actual world of nature, while implicitly acknowledging the derivative quality of the television ad. Now, if one's very sense of reality is derived from a beer advertisement, isn't this evidence of gross impairment in reality testing? If not technically psychotic, it is certainly a manifestation of deep alienation and confusion. A real madness lurks here, as insane as any schizophrenic delusion and far more dangerous. The etiology of this insanity is a culture gone awry.

## Today's Normal State of Affairs Is Pathological and Pathogenic

*The basic beliefs harbored in these men's rather bizarre comments are completely consistent with those of normal, mainstream Euro-American society.* This fact is immensely disturbing. This waterfall example is relatively benign, but—make no mistake—the underlying cultural madness is malignant. "It is naively assumed that the fact that the majority of people share certain ideas or feelings proves the validity of these ideas and feelings. Nothing is further from the truth. Consensual validation as such has no bearing whatsoever on reason or mental health . . . . the fact that millions of people share the same mental pathology does not make these people sane" (Fromm, 1955, p. 14). Given today's ecologically exploitive conventions and their dire psychological implications, normality certainly does not imply health. Quite the opposite, and dangerously so. Today's status quo—driven by the delusional fantasy that we can be separate from nature and still live well—is pushing the earth to the brink of catastrophe. In truth, the catastrophe has already arrived. And business as usual is making matters worse. Even the most critically aware individuals and collective organizations are caught up in this basic sociocultural insanity. *A collection of intertwined dissociations* is generating the reciprocal suffering of humankind and the rest of nature: dissociation from the beings and presences of the natural world; from the depths of our self and our lived experience; from our bodily wisdom; from community; from genuine connection with each other, especially from those who appear different from our self or tribe; from the transpersonal or spiritual dimensions of life.

This insidious state of affairs is amplified by the dominance of capitalist economics in the political, social, and even psychospiritual spheres of our lives. Recent developments demonstrate with compelling force that corporate capitalism has become a kind of new religion, one bent on uncritical (and often violently destructive) self-expansion and aggrandizement. As Pope Francis (2015) declared in his landmark ecospiritual encyclical, "Whatever is fragile, like the environment, is defenseless before the interests of a deified market, which become the only rule" (p. 27). Today there can be little doubt that, for those wielding power, money for the few is far more important than wild nature and the plight of folks who are oppressed. Chillingly, the charity Oxfam recently reported that the world's eight richest people—all men, all White—have as much wealth as the poorer 50 percent of the earth's total population added together (Mullany, 2017). *Eight* privileged men over 3.6 billion other people, not to mention an inestimable number of our nonhuman companions. This is completely obscene, yet now all too common. "The condition of alienation, of being asleep, of being unconscious, of being out of one's mind, is the condition of normal man" (Laing, 1967, p. 12). *These days normal existence leaves all of us traumatized.* "Only by the most outrageous violation of ourselves have we achieved our capacity to live in relative adjustment to a civilization apparently driven to its own destruction" (p. 49). Conversely, in the contemporary world, *to feel maladjusted is often a sign of real sanity*, and an inspiration for countercultural resistance. Ecopsychology urges that we never let ourselves adjust to being estranged from nature.

Given the extremity of our eco(psycho)logical trauma, I appreciate Laing's powerful language. I readily acknowledge that I am angry about the rampant desecration of the natural world, and about the impoverishment of human existence that inevitably comes with it. Being angry can be part of a clear, compassionate, and creative response to the separation-and-domination ethos that pervades our culture. When wielded skillfully, my anger energizes me for actions that say "No!" to violence and "Yes!" to life-enhancing collaboration. Sometimes my anger sends me into a stance of judgment and blame toward corporations, political and legal systems, and even individuals. Some of the blame is justifiable. The assaults must be stopped and perpetrators must be held accountable. After all, "humankind" in general did not create this crisis. The major responsibility lies with wealthy societies captivated uncritically by the ideologies of individualism, materialism, corporatism, unlimited economic expansion, consumerism, technologism, and militarism. These intersecting social structures do not center on the interests of all humans (as the term anthropocentrism suggests), but mainly on the interests of those holding economic and political power and privilege. Strongly aggressive (but not violent) opposition is precisely what is called for in certain circumstances. Sometimes this is the most understanding and loving response for all those involved. However, borrowing insight from my work as a psychotherapist, I find it helpful to remember that most of the world's wounding forces are, at their root, maladaptive defensive responses to earlier wounds. People tend to hurt others (including the natural world) in a misguided effort to manage their own fear and suffering, or to protect themselves from further suffering. From this perspective, perpetrators of violence—individuals, institutions, structural systems—can be met with understanding and compassion as well as resistance. We certainly need to challenge unscrupulous corporations and their political allies, the unconscionable ways the advertising media manipulate us and our children, and our own self-absorbed estrangement from our local human community and the encompassing community of nature. But to be effective this critique must be tempered by psychological insight into the crisis, including a tender appreciation that the primary source of our maladies is not deliberate malice. Rather, emboldened by the psychocultural fantasy of sovereignty and control, we are bewildered about who we are and what nature is. *The egregious exploitation of earth comes not from evil people, but from confused and fear-filled ones who are caught up in powerful psychological-social-cultural-historical-economic-political structures.*

## The Social Construction of Our Relationship with Nature

Important issues are raised by the fact the other visitors perceived Blackwater Falls so differently from my wife and me. All four of us were at the same physical location looking at the same physical things. But in actual experience we never perceive mere physical objects, but meaningful presences in relation with ourselves. The *meaning* of experience is not given objectively in strict adequacy to a supposedly objective physiological stimulus. Instead, meaning is *co-constructed* through the lived relationship between our self and the world. How we perceive an other depends partly on their (relatively) "objective" or readily observable qualities. But, much more so, it depends upon the way our consciousness, desires, and present context blend with the beliefs, values, and self-sense we have internalized from our history of interpersonal relationships and sociocultural membership. We would do well to keep this key epistemological point in mind, because *how we treat the natural world depends on how we see it and what it means to us.* The same mountain appears very different to a backpacker, a timber company executive, two lovers, a mystic, and a white-tailed deer. The first might say that the mountain is a glorious animate community to be preserved for all. The second might claim it is a material resource that they are entitled to take for profit. The third pair might enjoy a sweetly romantic spot away from the watchful eyes of other people. The fourth might celebrate its holiness. And the fifth says something in deer language, expressing meanings mostly beyond our ken while enjoying the mountain as their home community. It can be startling to realize how influential this meaning-making process is, for good and ill. As William Blake (1988) says: "To the Eyes of a Miser a Guinea [gold coin] is more beautiful than the Sun. . . . The tree which moves some to tears of joy is in the Eyes of others only a Green thing that stands in the way. . . . Some Scarce see Nature at all. . . . As a man is So he Sees" (p. 702). Blake was a profoundly sensitive soul. It is easy to imagine him meeting a tree with an open heart and being filled with tears of joy by its sheer presencing. In vast contrast, I read recently about a man who illegally cut down a giant redwood to make it easier for him to park his car. Trying to justify his actions, he remarked, "My purpose for removing *my tree* was to gain access to my garage" (Rodriguez, 2016). I added the italics to stress the bizarre (but normative) presumption that we could own another living being. Apparently the magnificent tree was only a green thing that stood in the way. Our responses surely do flow from what we see: tears of joy, or rationalized violence.

Recall that these reflections began with the fact that Blackwater Falls was taken to be an imitation of a beer commercial. That event points to a pervasive process that carries liberating possibilities along with oppressive ones. I am referring to what is commonly called *the social or cultural construction of reality*.[2] This theoretical notion brings attention to the fact that the meaning of our spontaneous lived experience depends significantly upon our unconscious appropriation of the beliefs and values of our culture. An illuminating description comes from Carlos Castaneda, an anthropologist who apprenticed with an indigenous shaman in Mexico.

> The world of everyday life is not real, or out there, as we believe it is. . . . Reality, or the world we all know, is only a description [or interpretation]. . . . Everyone who comes into contact with a child is a teacher who incessantly describes the world to him, until the moment when the child is capable of perceiving the world as described. . . . From that moment

> on . . . the child is a *member* [of that particular cultural group]. . . . The reality of our day-to-day life consists of an endless flow of perceptual interpretations which we, the individuals who share a specific *membership*, have learned to make in common. (Castaneda, 1972, pp. 8–9)[3]

In our lived experience, the meaning of the world is created—to a significant extent—by a mostly unconscious process of cultural, societal, and interpersonal "transmission," "agreement," and "training." A culture's dominant paradigm—the shared story about the way things are—is "designed" to provide orientation for getting along well with each other and navigating the challenges of life. The scare quotes are meant to temper the agentic and reflective connotations of these terms. The cultural construction of meaning primarily takes place implicitly and prereflectively, far beyond the conscious control of any single individual or group.

As much as we rightly cherish our own perspective and individual agency, we humans see largely what our conventional culture (or subculture) directs us to see. (Thankfully, there is a crucial degree of freedom for critical/creative perception.) To cite a simple case, social convention in Britain prescribes that we drive on the left side of the road whereas in the United States we drive on the right. Now, the way each distinctive culture construes the natural world is not as arbitrary as this example, but there certainly is vast room for variation across eras and cultures. As Abram (1996) points out, "That which is regarded with the greatest awe and wonder by indigenous, oral cultures is, I suggest, none other than what we view as nature itself. The deeply mysterious powers and entities with whom the shaman enters into a rapport are ultimately the same forces—the same plants, animals, forests, and winds—that to literate, "civilized" Europeans are just so much scenery, the pleasant backdrop of our more pressing human concerns" (p. 9). Whenever a meaningful story, image, or idea about our self or the world is given to us by others—and we are relentlessly imbued with these—such a symbolic presentation comprises a particular *interpretation* of reality. This is the case whether the story is passed on collectively through the media, politicians, business interests, religious groups, educational institutions, and the dominant language; or interpersonally by parents or friends or teachers (who are themselves influenced by values from the larger culture); or by a complex mix of these. In infancy and childhood, such formative transmission occurs pervasively in our interactions with our caregivers (just as they themselves were shaped by messages from their caregivers). Both we and they are mostly unaware of this process. Throughout our lives we continue to receive messages about who we are and what should matter to us. This certainly includes various construals of the natural world. *As we identify (mostly prereflectively and uncritically) with the socially constructed meanings imbibed from our cultural milieu and intersubjective field, they turn into a part of our very self and increasingly constitute our taken-for-granted sense of what is real, true, good, and sacred.* Such culturally based interpretations do not merely describe things "as they are," but circumscribe, prescribe, and proscribe our answers to basic existential questions: Who am I? Who are others? What is the natural world? Insidiously, stories of separation are unconsciously guiding our practical responses to these core questions.

Let me make clear that I am *not* claiming that nature is socially constructed by humans. This stance would comprise a grandiose reenactment of the human-centered hubris we so urgently need to subvert and surrender. All meaning is dependent on context. Yet *the deepest context is nature itself*, appearing as our surrounding bioregion, the whole animate earth, the all-inclusive cosmos, and ultimately as the one great holistic mystery. Nature infinitely precedes and exceeds the meaning-bestowing powers of human culture and perception.

## The World Is Made of Relationships, and Relationships Are Guided by Stories

*Euro-American culture, preferring domination to diversity, is destroying the natural world.* Yet cultures are not univocal. Branches of this very culture created the Endangered Species Act, and it has made a huge difference. Whooping cranes are magnificent, being the tallest birds in North America. But their population had dwindled to a mere 48 when the law was enacted in 1973. Now there are over 600. Countercultural movements created the field of ecopsychology, and are now helping parents expose their children to the wonders of nature. Clearly, our world, self, and relationships co-arise interdependently with the socially constructed stories that orient (or disorient) our lives. In this time of great turning, we have a precious opportunity to develop alternative stories and associated ways of being together. However, because we are all swept up in the momentum of dominant views and values about the natural world, and the power structures that hold them in place, such transformation is hard won. Because these forces operate largely outside our awareness, to take a conscious stance toward their formative power requires ongoing critical-reflective work. Our instantaneous perception is prestructured by the normative narratives of our culture. For good and for ill and often some mix of both, the conventional stories, values, and language of a culture function like a lens embedded in our eyes, bending the relational solicitations of others in accordance with familiar, sedimented, taken for granted meanings. Here I am pointing to a distinctive form of unconscious psychic process. This is not the repressed unconscious that Freud cogently disclosed, wherein we push painful things out of our awareness. Rather, a culture's dominant beliefs—stories of separation, to take our prime example—are so pervasive and taken for granted that *they operate in us and on us without being noticed,* as a kind of systemic, sociocultural unconscious. "In a very real sense, our social conceptions have become individual perceptions" (Wilber, 1977, p. 218). These automatic uncritical perceptions largely predetermine how we treat others. Blackwater Falls appears as a beer commercial, so we quickly walk away. A great redwood appears as a mere obstacle to our self-centered wishes, so we cut it right down.

Indeed, "As a man is So he Sees" (Blake, 1988, p. 702). *Quite crucially, seeing and knowing are not merely epistemological matters but, indivisibly, ontological and ethical ones.* How I relate with others depends upon how I see them, and how I see them depends upon who I believe them, the world, and myself to be. Using philosophical language to stress the profound psychological implications, we could say that our lived ontology (i.e., the story of who am I, of what this world is) guides and is guided by our lived epistemology (i.e., the way I come to know and understand); and both guide and are guided by our ethical sensibility (i.e., how I respond to others, ultimately how well I love). *Being, knowing, and loving are intertwined and mutually generative, for good and for ill.* Making this interdependent (ontological-epistemological-ethical) structure more conscious can change how we live with others.

## Sociocultural Oppression and the Pathology of Separation

Sometimes explicitly but often implicitly, sometimes by way of particular people but often via the media or other sociocultural sources, we receive messages that condition us to believe: I am—or should be!—a separate, sovereign, self-sufficient, self-interested individual; humans are not nature, not animals; the exclusively human world is the real world, the only one that matters; the natural world is an insentient commodity to be used as we wish. Self/other and human/nature dissociations are the most basic and disorienting of all culturally constructed splits, and the ones that generate the most suffering. But similar forms of dissociation are linked with these foundational ones. Suffering under the spell of socially transmitted notions, we tend to identify with and privilege one side—my side, or that of my tribe—while disidentifying with, fearing, repressing, oppressing, and devaluing the other. This sponsors a misguided justification for dominating and exploiting those deemed "other"—humans over nature, self over others, "masters" over the enslaved, mind over body, males over females, Whites over people of color, heterosexuals over LGBTQ+ folks, wealthy over poor, my religion or country or group over others that appear different from me. These various forms of systemic oppression (and corresponding movements of resistance and liberation) intersect with one another. For example, ecofeminist work emphasizes the connection between the patriarchal exploitation of women and the anthropocentric—mostly, androcentric and economically privileged—exploitation of the natural world. As Karen Warren (1997) shows, *women are often disparagingly characterized as so-called "lower" animals in a culture that devalues (nonhuman) animals*: bitches, foxes, chicks, birdbrains, pussy-cats (not to mention the vulgar designation for vaginas), to cite just a few. And *nature is often characterized as feminine in a culture that devalues women*. No doubt, language, worldviews, social systems, and practical interactions are powerfully intertwined.

Similarly, oppression based upon race and class is also intricately linked with ecological degradation. Environmental racism is a severe systemic problem. A recent report revealed that "African Americans are exposed to 38 percent more polluted air than Caucasian Americans, and they are 75 percent more likely" to live in communities afflicted with environmental pollution (Fleischman & Franklin, 2017). The landmark 2018 United Nations study of climate change emphasized that "many of the impacts of warming . . . fall disproportionately on the poor and vulnerable" (IPCC, 2018a, p. 51). An illuminating metaphor is often used when addressing systemic injustice. If we imagine the sociocultural world as a river, racism and poverty are symptoms that become evident downstream. But their structural source is located far back upstream. Downstream, African Americans have higher rates of illness and mortality as compared with Whites. Systemic racism upstream is the major cause. And an even more fundamental cause can be located farther back upstream: fear-driven stories and practices of separation between Blacks and Whites. In a similar dynamic, downstream we are afflicted with symptoms of ecological degradation. But when we travel upstream to investigate the source, we again discover the fundamental delusion that humans could be detached from the rest of nature. The basic structure of suffering is shared across these various maladies: separation-elevation-devaluation-domination-exploitation. *Fantasies of severance initiate this poisonous flow.*

## Overview of the Dominant Construction of the Human-Nature Relationship

It is impossible for our species to actually be cut off from the rest of nature. But over the last five centuries we began acting as if we could thrive while destroying this intrinsic dimension of our being. If an individual were suffering such a confused process of self-severance, a psychotherapist would rightly be concerned that the person was undergoing a dissociative episode. Speaking clinically, dissociation is an unconscious defense mechanism wherein aspects of oneself that feel threatening—ideas, memories, feelings, urges, personality characteristics, and so on—are split off from one's conscious self and kept out of awareness. Analogously, modern culture fostered a dissociative fantasy that we are separate from the rest of nature. Thereby, a *culturally supported madness* spread through Europe and North America (and beyond), wreaking devastation in local bioregions and in the most intimate regions of our hearts and minds.

Because we have been under the influence of socially constructed stories of separation for several centuries, the beings and presences of nature now tend to appear to us only in the following ways: (1) *The natural world as nonexistent, out of our awareness, or merely the backdrop for more important human-focused activities.* "Some Scarce see Nature at all" (p. 702), as Blake (1988) lamented. It is not uncommon to hear remarks like this, shared during an early session of an undergraduate "Psychology and Nature" course: "Besides school and work, I just hang out with my friends. We mostly play video games or talk. *So nature really isn't part of my life.*" (2) *The natural world as a threat or danger.* When I was teaching at a rural college in the Appalachian Mountains, prospective students from a large city came to visit. We arranged a trip to a beautiful river nearby, but one young man anxiously said he did not want to go because he was worried that he would get "worms." (3) *The natural world as an impediment to our self-centered gratification.* A biologist told me that during his decade-long tenure in West Virginia's Division of Natural Resources only two injury incident reports were filed due to encounters with bears. One occurred when a black bear approached a man who was eating lunch at a picnic table in a state park. Feeling inconvenienced that his plans were so rudely interrupted, the man tried to swat the bear away like an annoying mosquito. As you can imagine, the bear swatted back! (The other incident occurred when a park ranger saw a bear, turned to move away, and bonked his brow on a tree branch.) (4) *The natural world as an insentient, nonsapient, material object to be exploited as a resource for human gratification and profit.* This is the most common and pernicious social construction of nature because it is being enacted not just individually but on a colossal scale by our techno-corporate-consumerist culture. In Leopold's (1949) prescient words, "We abuse land because we regard it as a commodity belonging to us" rather than "a community to which we belong" (p. viii). Herein, industry executives see only coal (and money) where a glorious mountain community thrived for eons, or only crude oil (and money) where a marvelous aquatic ecosystem flourished. Concerned with such symptomatic side-effects of modernity, Heidegger (1977b) warned of a growing pathology: "Man . . . exalts himself to the posture of lord of the earth" (p. 27). From this position of superiority, "the world changes into an object. . . . The earth itself can show itself only as the object of assault" (Heidegger, 1977b, p. 100). Such wanton imposition of human power is as grandiose as any clinical delusion, or, more maliciously in some instances, as sociopathic as the most exploitive con man.

All four construals are completely normal these days, to some extent because they each contain a partial truth, but mostly because we remain tyrannized by dissociative stories. Regarding the partial truths: (1) it (partly) makes sense that we humans would focus on human things; (2) the natural world is immensely powerful, and at times deadly dangerous; (3) natural forces can surely get in the way of preferred wishes and plans; and (4) our survival depends on the natural world giving us everything we eat and every material thing we use. However, immense suffering follows when these views predominate.

## Cultural-Historical Contexts for
## Our Supposed Divorce from Nature

The sources of our culturally constructed delusion of detachment go way back in history, spanning many cultures and eras.[4] While a detailed survey is beyond the scope of the present study, it is helpful to be aware of a few key influences. Joining many scholars who came before me I will emphasize how, beginning in the sixteenth and seventeenth centuries, the growth of modern Euro-American culture marked a major turning point in our alienation from the rest of nature. That is when the ethos of separation-superiority-devaluation-domination started to become a major culture force. But there were significant precursors. Ancient Greek culture, so crucial in shaping the Western worldview, often imagined humans as split off from and superior to the rest of nature. In Plato's *Phaedrus*, Socrates (ca. 469–399 BCE) and Phaedrus are walking and talking in the countryside when they eventually come upon a beautiful natural space. Socrates describes it as "a delightful resting place, with this tall, spreading plane, and a lovely shade from the high branches of the *agnos* [tree]. Now that it's in full flower, it will make the place ever so fragrant. And what a lovely stream" (Hamilton & Cairns 1973, p. 479). But then, quite tellingly, Socrates proclaims, "I'm a lover of learning, and trees and open country won't teach me anything, whereas men in the town do" (p. 479). Abram (1996) points out that this view "would have scant coherence within an indigenous hunting community, for the simple reason that such communities necessarily take their most profound teachings or instructions directly from the more-than-human earth" (p. 116). But for the Greek sage, all that is not human is stripped of intelligence. Our exalted species is left alone in a self-enclosed monologue.

Versions of the Judeo-Christian tradition have long supported the Western idea of humanity's severance from the rest of nature. In the Genesis myth—written by people expressing the culturally constructed values of the day—God elevates humankind to a sovereign position above the rest of nature and authorizes humans to master and rule over all nonhuman life: "God said to them, 'Be fruitful and multiply, and fill the earth and subdue it; and have dominion over the fish of the sea and over the birds of the air and over every living thing that moves upon the earth'" (Genesis 1:28). Resonating with the word domination, dominion is derived from the Latin *dominus*, meaning master or lord.

This is precisely the attitude that has plagued our relations with the rest of nature—as if we could be the lords of nature. In a classic article, historian Lynn White (1967) remarked that "Christianity is the most anthropocentric religion the world has seen" (p. 1205). "Christianity, in absolute contrast to ancient paganism and Asia's religions (except, perhaps, Zoroastrianism), not only established a dualism of man and nature but also insisted that it is God's will that man exploit nature for his proper ends" (p. 1205).

Apparently, even with these nature-demeaning influences, premodern Europeans still felt themselves to be inseparably involved with nature. The natural world was seen as an animate organism, a beneficent nurturing mother, and a sacred presence, while also being wild, dangerous, unruly, and uncontrollable (Merchant, 1980). In the words of Giambattista della Porta (1535–1615), an Italian philosopher, scientist, and alchemist: "The whole world is knit and bound within itself: for the world is a living creature . . . and the parts of it do couple together . . . by reason of their mutual love" (Merchant, 1980, p. 104). The ethical implications of this organic, interdependent perspective are apparent in another remark by Della Porta: "When one part suffers, the rest also suffer with it" (p. 104).

In contrast, as modern Euro-American culture emerged, people became enthralled with a social construction of reality that posited humans as elevated above the rest of nature; dissociated the spiritual from the realm of nature; devalued nonhuman animals, plants, and elemental presences; and thereby authorized the anthropocentric exploitation of the natural world. This paradigm shift involved a confluence of various sociocultural movements, most notably the growth of capitalist economics, the development of nation-states, population shifts from rural to urban areas, increasing reliance on printed texts, the scientific revolution, the Enlightenment, humanism, the decreasing efficacy of conventional religion, the political revolutions of American and French independence, and the industrial and technological revolutions.

## Shadow Maladies of Modernity: Separation, Elevation, Devaluation, Domination

We can appreciate that people's lives have been enhanced in many ways by the changes of the modern era. The hard-won benefits include the growth of critical reason; suspicion of the uncritical acceptance of traditional truths; the valuing of evidence in making truth claims; liberation from the oppressive dictates of powerful authorities and institutions (especially those of the church and state); the growth of democracy; the expansion of civil liberties; the empowerment of individuals, including legal rights, increased freedom, autonomy, independence, and agency; the empowerment of tyrannized groups (enslaved people, people of color, women, sexual minorities, those in poverty); empirical scientific research; technological innovation; improved physical health and medical care; widespread public education; and increased longevity. As it turns out, however, a dangerous shadow side came along with the significant accomplishments of the modern era. The United States' Declaration of Independence is one thing, but the fantasy that we could declare independence from the rest of nature is quite another. A healthy desire for relative security, autonomy, and power began to morph into a destructive stance of separation, elevation/ superiority, devaluation, domination, and exploitation. A trio of modern thinkers exemplify these eco-alienating beliefs and practices: Francis Bacon (1561–1626), English philosopher, lawyer, politician, and proto-scientist; René Descartes (1596–1650), French philosopher and mathematician; and Sigmund Freud (1856–1939), Austrian psychoanalyst. The following exposition is meant to illustrate a larger sociocultural movement that pulled us away from caring contact with the natural world.

Francis Bacon, often deemed the founder of the scientific method, asserted that "natural science has . . . no other goal than to more firmly establish and extend the power and domination of men over nature" (Bacon, quoted in Leiss, 1972, p. 48). Bacon boasted that science and technology have the "power to make radical changes, and shake her [nature] in the foundations" (p. 58). Linking the domination of nature with the domination of women, Bacon exhorted "man" to pursue a relentless "inquisition of nature" (p. 51), "to bind her to your service and make her your slave" (p. 55). Unabashedly, indeed proudly, Bacon promoted the supposed virtue of torturing (presumably feminine) nature just as so-called witches were tortured during the Inquisition. Wielding violently misogynistic language, he proclaimed, "You have but to follow and as it were hound nature in her wanderings. . . . Neither ought a man to make scruple of entering and penetrating into these holes and corners, when the inquisition of truth is his whole object" (Bacon, quoted in Merchant, 1980, p. 168). Chilling remarks, to be sure.

René Descartes, just 35 years younger than Bacon, enthusiastically bolstered the emerging modern worldview. Many people are familiar with

Descartes' (1637/1998) famous proclamation: "I think, therefore I am" (p. 18). Less well known is the fact that this stance is directly involved with his wish, expressed in the very same text, that science could give humans power to be the "masters and possessors of nature" (p. 35). Descartes presumed a radical separation of mind and body in individual existence, and a correlative separation of humankind and nature. He did not just differentiate two aspects of a unified whole, wherein mind and body or humans and the rest of nature are distinct but indivisible from each other. Rather, he created a hierarchical dissociation imbued with value judgments, essentially a prescription for the domination Bacon had advocated. Yet another justification for exploiting nature came when Descartes—like Galileo before and Newton after—began conceiving the local natural world (and indeed the whole universe) as a machine rather than a dynamic, animate, intelligent organism: "I do not recognize any difference between the machines made by craftsmen and the various bodies that nature alone composes" (Descartes, in Capra, 1983, p. 61).

Kirkpatrick Sale (1990) reports that earlier, in the medieval period,

> even with the best efforts of the Church, there still lingered in many places in Europe the common wisdom that gods and spirits inhabited the elements of nature—trees, certainly, streams and rivers, forests, rocks—or in some parts of the Church itself, that nature was sacred because God was immanent in all that He created. The task of rationalism, through science, was to show—no, better, to *prove*—that there was no sanctity about these aspects of nature, that they were not animate or purposeful or sensate, but rather nothing more than measurable combinations of chemical and mechanical properties, subject to scientific analysis, prediction, and manipulation. Being de-godded, they could thereby be capable of human use and control according to human whim and desire. (p. 40)

The way one treats an unfeeling material machine or a stockpile of dead matter is far different from the way one treats a sentient being who can suffer or a sacred presence animated by G-d. Thus, the ecofeminist scholar Carolyn Merchant (1995) emphasizes that "the [premodern] image of the earth as a living organism and nurturing mother served as a cultural constraint restricting the actions of human beings. . . . As long as the earth was considered to be alive and sensitive [and sacred], it could be considered a breach of human ethical behavior to carry out destructive acts against it" (p. 78). In vast contrast, views of the earth as inanimate and mechanistic "functioned as cultural sanctions for the denudation of nature" (Merchant, p. 77).

The modern era's cultivation of freedom and agency was much needed, but its excesses took a grave toll. Carried away by instrumental rationality and technological power, the shadow side of emancipatory "humanism" emerged as a dreadful dissociation between humans and the rest of nature. Driven by the idea of progressive mastery and control over wild nature, our conversational intimacy with the natural community was forcibly repressed—to our great detriment together with the rest of nature. Over time, a new array of socially constructed values began to reign: separation over communion; individuality over relationship and community; mastery and control over conversation and mutual negotiation; competition over collaboration; calculative rationality over embodied, felt awareness; material wealth for the few over psychospiritual wealth for all; greed over love and compassion; power over nature rather than power with nature; human wishes over the needs of the shared earth community. Max Weber (2004) famously described this cultural shift as a radical "disenchantment of the world" (p. 30).

A more recent authority, Sigmund Freud, followed this trend. His psychoanalytic insights have been crucial for so many of us doing depth-oriented work in psychology, psychotherapy, and related disciplines. By decentering the ego from its presumed position of psychic sovereignty and appreciating the depths of our bodily, affective, and sexual life, Freud's understanding of the unconscious challenged modernist assumptions about the masterful autonomy of the rational mind. He demonstrated that we suffer when we try to repress, dissociate, or overcontrol the nature within us. When our "superego" imposes excessive constraints on our sexual and aggressive urges, we become haunted by anxiousness and other neurotic symptoms. However, as an heir of Bacon and Descartes, and caught up in the industrialist zeitgeist of late modernity, Freud frequently demonized nonhuman nature. Mistakenly presuming that culture is separate from the natural world rather than an expression of it, Freud (2012) said of nature: "She kills us—coldly, cruelly, recklessly. . . . Indeed, the chief task of culture, its actual *raison d'être*, is to defend us against nature" (p. 81). In the modern era—*apparently for the first time in human history*—people began deploying a consequential metaphor: namely, that humankind must win a *war against nature*. The *conquest of nature* became another common trope. Freud (1961) thus advocated an "attack against nature and subjecting her to the human will" (p. 24). In the next sentence, with uncritical confidence in this drive to dominate (ostensibly feminine) nature, he asserted, "Then one is working with all for the good of all" (pp. 24–25). But when Freud invoked "the good of all," he certainly did not include *all of us*. The beings and presences of nature were conspicuously excluded. And we should be very clear: with our sense of "us," it is of crucial consequence whom we include or exclude. This is evidenced by genocidal atrocities (in colonial North America, Nazi Germany, Rwanda, and Bosnia); by individual and systemic racism; and by the extinction of species, obliteration of biodiversity, and habitat destruction across the earth.

The metaphors of war and conquest are quite revealing as we explore today's ravaging of the natural world. Thomas Merton (1995) insisted that "the root of war is fear" (p. 11). Some fear is natural and healthy. It helps us be attentive and respond skillfully when we are actually being threatened. But much of our fear is excessive, far out of proportion to the present reality. This surplus fear is the kind Merton is talking about, and the kind ecopsychology is addressing. I concur that the root of all war is fear, and I would add that *the root of all excessive fear is a misguided sense of separation*. The fantasy of humankind's disconnection from the rest of nature is the source of our catastrophic, unwinnable war against nature.

Everywhere Freud (2010) looked he saw "civilization and its discontents," as indicated by the title of one of his major cultural critiques. He believed humans were doomed to chronic unhappiness because society was intrinsically battling with nature—whether nature takes form as the forces of the larger natural world or, intrapsychically, as the instinctual forces of the "id" (or "the it," *das es* in Freud's German). According to the modern Euro-American view, the inevitable discontent of civilization is that nature is tremendously powerful and beyond our control. Ecopsychology agrees with the assertion that nature's forces are way beyond our control but insists that the source of civilization's discontent is that we strive to dominate the natural world anyway. The latter is a socially constructed option rather than an inevitability. In an alternative approach, humans can cultivate power and health *with the powers of nature* rather than insisting on wielding power *over and against nature*. It is truly bizarre to think we could be "masters and possessors of nature" (Descartes, 1998, p. 35). But I recently heard a weatherman exclaim, "It's snowing out of control today!" The absurd hubris of this remark would be humorous if its implicit, domination-driven worldview were not so disastrous. Nature is radically wild and deep and subtle, infinitely transcending our ego-centered or species-centered capacity to dominate it. The narcissistic fantasy that we are able to master the natural world is perhaps the most grandiose and pernicious delusion of all time.

## Contextualizing the Madness of Separation-Elevation-Devaluation-Domination

Nature-deficit disorder is an escalating concern today, but we can trace its emergence much further back. Most of Europe's forests had been cut down by the Middle Ages and populations began shifting to commercial cities. Consistent conscious involvement with the natural world was severely diminished. Bacon, Descartes, and Galileo lived their adult lives in cities, like most influential citizens of the era. Working-class people were also moving to urban areas, and this change was amplified as industrial capitalism expanded.

> By the sixteenth century . . . people were rapidly becoming nature-illiterate. . . . The leaders of these civilizations grew up with less and less personal knowledge of animal behavior and were no longer taught the intimate wide-ranging plant knowledge that had once been universal. . . . Then major blocks of citified mythology (Medieval Christianity and then the "Rise of Science") denied first soul, then consciousness, and finally even sentience to the natural world. (Snyder, 1990, p. 12)

Without close and regular encounters, the natural world appears far more threatening and empathically inaccessible than it actually is. Exploitation then follows.

A brief remark by Freud sheds further light on the modernist zeal for violent domination of the natural word. Acknowledging a basic existential fact, Freud (2012) says: "Life is hard to bear" (p. 81). No doubt, nature presents us with serious dangers. Life is terribly painful and even deadly at times—sharp as a knife, as the saying goes. The risk of death is always present, albeit mostly pushed to the background of our awareness. Nature deserves tremendous respect, because our existence is tenuous and we are ever vulnerable. An inopportune slip—from a cliff's edge or when meeting a poisonous mushroom—and we are gone. (As a naturalist once put it to me: There are old mushroom gatherers, and there are bold mushroom gatherers, but there are no old bold mushroom gatherers!) But even with no faulty slip, our life can suddenly be claimed by a hurricane, a cancer, or a plague (bubonic back then, coronavirus now). As the modern era unfolded, people were confronted with dangers far more severe than occasional attacks by wild animals: storms, floods, famines, droughts, and especially diseases. Authorities shaping the modern world were shaken by the terrible plagues that ravaged Europe and Asia from the fourteenth to seventeenth centuries. The "black death" killed as many as 200 million people, about 60 percent of the total population. "So lethal was the disease that cases were known of persons going to bed well and dying before they woke, of doctors catching the illness at a bedside and dying before the patient" (Tuchman, 1978, p. 92). The fatal source was not found until the late nineteenth century: bacteria carried by fleas who lived on rats. With massive death all around and no effective remedy, people truly believed, "This is the end of the world," as an observer put it at the time (Tuchman, p. 95). It is not surprising that people wished they could master the natural world.

Nonetheless, the respected rhetoric of modern thinkers pushed the domineering approach to extremes. Only one premodern understanding survived the change in worldview, the undeniable reality that nature is powerful, dangerous, disorderly, chaotic, and unruly. Defensively *overre-acting* to the latter, modern culture claimed—contrary to all previous history—that nature needed to be controlled by aggressive human intervention. Influential leaders conjured images of war, rape, torture by inquisitors, enslavement, and imperial conquest. Soon their vision was made into common reality by new technological means, all put into the service of an expanding capitalist-driven extractive economy. As Snyder (1990) points out, the leaders of modernity "not only didn't enjoy the possibility that the world is as sharp as the edge of a knife, they wanted to take that edge away from nature. Instead of making the world safer for humankind, the foolish tinkering with the powers of life and death by the occidental scientist-engineer-ruler put the whole planet on the brink of extinction" (p. 19). *In radical contrast, our sense of the sacred emerges when we see that—rather than a master species or sovereign ego—we are inextricable participants in an infinitely deep and holy mystery that precedes, exceeds, includes, and permeates us.* Efforts to separate and dominate inevitably fail because the goal is ultimately impossible. *In trying to master nature we are trying to master the great mystery, to control what is intrinsically beyond our control.* But the fierce momentum of this mad project continues to this very day. It is chilling that Bacon's preceding statements actually sound like a decree for rape. Four centuries later an article from *Psychology Today* asks, "Does raping the earth make us crazy?" (Simons, 2010). Tragically, the answer is a grievous "Yes!" And the insanity flows two ways. Raping the earth does in fact make us crazy, yet we rape the earth because we have already been entranced by "crazy" aspects of our culture.

To be clear, this is not a matter of mere abstract ideas a few privileged men came up with long ago. Over the centuries, the dissociative and domineering views of Bacon, Descartes, and others spread into the larger social milieu, significantly constituting *our shared felt-sense of what is real, true, and good.* By no choice of our own, each of us was born into a world dominated by stories of separation. This means that we have all been thrown into a culture that has gravely misconstrued the relationship between humans and the rest of nature. Similarly, all citizens of the United States have been thrown into a history characterized by traumatic separations from other people and from the rest of nature. In fact, *North American society was originally built on a series of massive movements of relational rupture.* European immigrants left their families, friends, community, and local natural world to come to the "new world." Africans were violently extricated into slavery, taken across the vast Atlantic to America, and required to live and work in bondage (if they were not killed first). Backed by military power, White settlers and politicians forced Native Americans away from their beloved homelands (if they were not killed first). Our conventional views of the natural world would be psychotic or sociopathic if not for the cultural-historical context sketched earlier. Recognizing the collective milieu that we have been thrust into, we can understand today's dominant construal of human-nature relations as *a culturally and historically situated insanity.*

## Eco(psycho)logical Maladies as a
## Collective Return of the Repressed

Charles Darwin famously demonstrated that humans are animals who have evolved through a process of natural selection. Another British naturalist, Alfred Russel Wallace, made the same discovery at the same time. The presentation of their joint papers on the theory of evolution in 1858 comprised a major turning point in humankind's self-understanding. But ever since they published their revolutionary research, humans have struggled to come to terms with the significance of the fact that we too are animals. Their findings marked a momentary *uncovering of a major species-wide repression*, a humble acknowledgment of our kinship with the rest of nature. But the public was shocked and resistant because this fact, which had been kept unconscious for centuries, threatened their favored self-sense. Even today, many still try to disavow our animality and elevate us above all other beings.

It seems that people in previous eras appreciated that we are animals, a particular variant of all our natural companions. Myths from around the world are populated with beings who are partly human and partly another animal (or a plant): centaurs, mermaids, angels, and so forth. The so-called "green man," whose face is comprised of leaves, shows up across cultures. A variety of humanlike beings serve as personifications of the natural world: the Greek goddess Gaia and the Native American Earth-mother, to name only two. While the Judeo-Christian creation myth depicts a process of human domination of the natural world, there are internal contradictions in the story. Genesis first tells us that humans were made from earth and air (breath). As the tale goes, "God formed man from the dust of the ground, and breathed into his nostrils the breath of life" (Genesis 2:7). "Dust of the ground" is an odd translation of the Hebrew *adamah*, which more directly means "earth" or "ground." The name Adam, derived from the same word, means human. It also means "formed from the earth." And, as mentioned earlier, the words "human" and "humus" are rooted in a Latin word meaning "earth." *Linguistically, as well as ontologically and ethically, human beings are earthlings.*

However, the awareness that we are animals became buried along the way. I believe this was an *intentionally motivated but largely unconscious process*, one that occurred due to the defensive forces of repression in the psychoanalytic sense. That is, we were once conscious of something that over time came to threaten our self-sense, tribe-sense, worldview, and security: namely, that we are animals akin to all the rest. Unable or unwilling to bear this fact, particularly the vulnerability and mortality that inevitably comes with it, we made a self-deceptive move to banish it from our awareness. But when something is repressed or dissociated it does not simply go away. (Short of organic brain damage, nothing really goes "away" in the psyche.) Whatever is repressed reappears in disguised and symbolic ways, primarily in pathological symptoms and patterns of relationship (but also in dreams and slips of the tongue). This is the "return of the repressed," a key phenomenon that Freud (1957, pp. 141–158) illuminated in his work. When we try to split off, deny, banish, or dominate any part of our existence it will live on to haunt us, inextricably influencing us in ways we are largely unaware of. Building on this insight, Jung (1959) developed the notion of the "shadow" to denote qualities of our self that are repressed because they conflict with and threaten our conscious self-concept, self-esteem, and self-security. Since they still remain part of our self, disavowed aspects inevitably follow us like a shadow. The repressed returns via symptoms such as anxiety, depression, rage, greed, obsessive control, and conflicts with others who remind us of our disowned (and then "projected") qualities.

A similar process came to be enacted collectively by modern Euro-American culture. Under the spell of modern stories of separation, we have tried to disavow crucial dimensions of our being, particularly our animality, our bodies, our death-awareness, and our identity with and inextricable involvement with the rest of nature. But because this is an impossible undertaking, the dissociative move generated an array of pathological shadow symptoms: mass extinction; habitat destruction; toxic environments; global warming and climate disruption; anxiety, depression, and emptiness associated with nature-deficit disorder; disconnection from our embodied vitality and intelligence; avarice and overconsumption; and anxious efforts at excessive mastery and control. Some of these symptoms appear more overtly ecological, some more overtly psychological, yet all involve both dimensions. *These eco(psycho)logical afflictions are a collective form of the return of the repressed.* This primary repression interacts with a second layer of repression wherein we avoid facing contemporary ecological crises. The claim that global warming is a hoax is a key example.

## The Power of Stories in (Re)constructing Our Culture, Self, and Relationships

Mightily formative stories of severance, propagated over generations, have placed humans and nonhumans alike in an impoverished world. Yet also—and still—we live in a world of splendor and awe. To surpass our separatist afflictions *we must create a better collective story*. "If you want to change the world, change the metaphor" (Joseph Campbell, in Moyers, 2009). The animate earth is calling for a truly transformative story that opens new experiences and relationships, one that frees us from the nightmare of dissociation and domination, one that sends us into conscious intimacy with and responsibility toward the rest of nature. Imagine the vast difference between humans having a "conversation" with nature instead of a "war." Or consider the fact that some scientists are saying we are now living in the "Anthropocene," a new geological era characterized by humankind's massive impact on earth's ecosystems, for ill and for good. This name is a well-intentioned effort to challenge humans to accept their irreplaceable responsibility for the well-being of our planet. However, it seems crudely obscene and grandiose to name an entire geologic era after ourselves, thereby placing the whole earth in the context of human society. This is a symptom of the very phenomenon the name is meant to critique. The "Ecozoic Era"—Thomas Berry's (1999) alternative—is far more apt because it places humankind in the deeper context of the shared earth community.

There are always openings for countercultural stories, metaphors, and ways of interrelating. Every conventional story is provisional and temporary because it is situated within the needs of a particular historical era and culture. This means that *all constructions contain hidden seeds of their own deconstruction, revision, and creative transformation*. If we understand that something is in fact culturally created, then we can ask how that particular construction serves us well, and how not; whom it serves and whom not; when and when not. But until we make that liberating epistemological discovery, the status quo appears to be the *necessary* way things really are. Ordinarily, "reality" seems so obvious and taken for granted that the issue of what is real does not even come up. When we are identified with the dominant culture, we hardly notice that pathogenic stories, images, and felt-beliefs of separation are filling our consciousness and driving our actions. In contrast, for those marginalized by the dominant culture, its maladies are painfully evident. Throughout this discussion, remember that the dominant worldview I am critiquing is the modern Western construal of the human-nature relationship. I am assuming that most everyone reading this book is significantly under the spell of this separatist paradigm, even those rightly rising up to challenge it. It is often said that we live within our primary culture's constructed realities like a fish lives in water. A fish (probably) does not recognize that she is swimming in water because water is simply the given medium of her existence. Similarly, we rarely recognize the stories by which we are living because these narratives are functioning as the (mostly) transparent medium of our lives. "We do not see our stories because we see through them: the world we experience as reality is constructed with them" (Loy, 2010, p. vii). Yet, to say we "rarely" recognize the stories shaping our lives implies that, with critical reflexivity and support from others, *we actually can recognize and revise them.* Throughout most of history people had little or no understanding that their own culture's worldview was a historically situated social creation, one that was somewhat arbitrary and open to change. It is quite an extraordinary thing that humans have now become aware of the fact that our typically taken-for-granted social realities are largely created, not simply given.

"The deepest crises experienced by any society are those moments of change when the story becomes inadequate for meeting the survival demands of a present situation" (Berry, 1988, p. xi). Regarding the Euro-American narrative of ceaselessly expanding "progress" through the technological domination of nature, "our supposed progress toward an ever-improving human situation is bringing us to wasteworld instead of wonderworld" (p. 17). Berry's (1999) wisdom again: "We need to reinvent the human *at the species level.* . . . Radical new cultural forms are needed. These new cultural forms would place the human within the dynamics of the planet rather than place the planet within the dynamics of the human" (p. 160). Scholar-activists like David Korten (2006) and Joanna Macy (Macy & Johnstone, 2012) have presented cogent evidence that a "great turning" of culture and consciousness is underway. Transformation of *personal consciousness* comprises a crucial ingredient in an overall psychocultural therapy. But given the oppressive forces of *systemic* dissociation and exploitation, individual change is not sufficient. If fish and their neighbors are sick because the water is polluted, treating single individuals—while acutely important—will not resolve the encompassing malady. The toxic water must be changed. *Consciousness and culture change together, not one before the other nor one without the other.*

All crises bring opportunity as well as danger. Sociocultural metamorphosis does not come easily, but history has proven that radical changes can be set in motion when we integrate personal awareness, courage, and engaged action with interpersonal collaboration and collective action. Remembering cases of this emancipatory process in the United States, we can appreciate the abolition of overt slavery, women's suffrage, and the civil rights movement. Each was a truly consciousness-altering, culture-altering response (although immense work still remains).

## The Wisdom of Symptoms: Wounds to Our Narcissism Can Be Liberating

It is difficult to let go of sedimented stories because they have helped us navigate a life that is often painful and challenging. Our separatist sense of self and species is strangely reassuring even while being pathological and pathogenic. It can feel threatening to realize that sociocultural reality is constructed rather than objectively real because comforting "realities" are instantly called into question. However, if we can learn to bear the anxiety, this awareness can be liberating and empowering. Building on a clue offered by Freud, let us reconsider three transformative events that radically deconstructed, and then creatively reconstructed, our story of reality. Freud's theory of the dynamic unconscious disrupted conventional notions that (over)valorized rational thought, individual autonomy, and personal agency and control. It did so in such a profound way that Freud (1955) considered his discovery to be one of three historical wounds to humanity's excessively elevated self-esteem. The others were Darwin and Wallace's discovery that we humans are animals, and Copernicus' discovery that earth is not the center of the universe. Each of these startling revelations subverted a *normative yet grandiose fantasy of separation, superiority, privilege, and power.* In the light of ecopsychology, we can see that each transformative movement decentered humans from a supposedly separate, elite, and masterful position that had been taken for granted, and resituated us as creatively responsive participants in a deep and wild relational field: a cosmic field, an ecological field, and a psychic field.

These paradigm shifts did wound humankind's narcissism, breaking through a collective hubris about our position in the world. Yet the ramifications of the "wounds" were liberating, and still are. In this respect we need to *realize who is being wounded* or, at best, *humbled.* That is: (1) the conventional "cultural self" that—based upon religious and philosophical conditioning—had imagined our home planet held a supreme "God-given" place in the center of the universe; (2) the collective "species-self"—similarly socially constructed—that presumed it was discontinuous with, elevated above, and entitled to dominate all other species; and (3) the supposedly independent, sovereign, rational, ego-self that had thought itself to be the center and master of the psyche. When we remain fearfully attached to such stories, clinging to them for security, identity, and fulfillment, we do tend to feel humiliated and terrified when they are disrupted. However, *the healthy cousin of humiliation is humility*. Each of these revolutionary realizations places a real constraint on human autonomy and power. *And this is immensely frustrating if our point of view comes only from an ego-centered identification*. But the humbling implications of these discoveries actually relieve us of an impossible burden, that of striving to fulfill a fantasy of unilateral mastery and control. We are thereby freed to engage collaboratively with the depth dimensions of our psyche and with all our relations in this shared earth community. When we actually stand on the earthy ground and open our sensuous body-self—looking, listening, smelling, feeling—it is obvious that we are not a detached self (or species) mastering an objective world but rather a self-in-inseparable-relationship with an animate, intelligent, expressive world.

## A (Short) Story of the Isolated "I," and Ecopsychological Alternatives

The next chapter is critical exploration of the (apparently) separate ego as our *exclusive* identity. As a prelude, I would like to share a (short) story of "I." My reference is to the actual word "I," and to lived experiences associated with it. It is curious that the personal pronoun used to designate myself—"I"—is a single-letter word that stands alone in sentences, isolated and capitalized. This is unlike any other word in English. In Old English the word was spelled *ic*, in Middle English, *ic*, *ik*, or *ich*. For reasons that are not clear, the final consonant began being dropped in the twelfth century, with the word becoming "i." It was not until the fifteenth century that the capitalized "I" appeared in some areas of England, and not until much later did it become common. Perhaps all of this is simple coincidence. Yet the practice of writing "I" came to prominence in the modern era, mirroring that era's belief—delusion—that each person is merely an isolated self. While humans are inherently relational beings, the visual appearance of the word "I" suggests the exact opposite. *Nonetheless, no "I" can ever really stand alone.*

Guided or misguided by culturally constructed narratives, human societies can live in conviviality or antagonism with the rest of nature.

An "I-centered" adversarial approach rules right now, but things may be turning. Throughout history subcultural movements have created viable alternatives to mainstream culture, and these innovations have become integrated into the larger society. Countercultural initiatives in the United States, a country responsible for immense ecological destruction, actually created the world's first national park (Yellowstone); the Clean Air Act (1963), Clean Water Act (1972), and Endangered Species Act (1973); Earth Day (1970); and ecopsychology (1990s–present). The great work continues.

As we come to the end of this theory-heavy chapter, to vivify things we might simply step outside, open our body-mind-heart, and welcome the solicitations of our neighborhood companions—those meeting us by way of two legs or four, or by wing, leaf, or breeze. *After all, such direct experiential encounters are really where good stories come from; and where the best stories send us again and again, ever responsively and (at best) responsibly.*

Chapter Five

# The Supposedly Separate Ego

## Delusion, Paranoia, and Greed in Conventional (Co)Existence

[The] ego is not master in its own house.

—Sigmund Freud (1955, p. 143)

It is a delusion that the self is so separate and fragile that we must delineate and defend its boundaries, that it is so small and so needy that we must endlessly acquire and endlessly consume, and that it is so aloof that as individuals, corporations, nation-states, or species, we can be immune to what we do to other beings.

—Joanna Macy (1991, p. 187)

[In this experience of the sacred] I had given myself to the moment. . . . I was not caught in anything, any insecurities, or fears, or expectations. That was all gone. . . . I had this image of being . . . something inside of a rock case. And boom! Just everything fell off and there I was, exposed to it all!

—Sarah, massage therapist and research participant

## Overture

"Who am I?" Our lived answer to this classic existential question has great bearing on our relations with the rest of nature. By way of cultural

133

convention and normal personal development, it seems obvious that I am an independent, autonomous, skin-bounded self. But this belief comprises the fundamental mistaken identity of humankind, one that brings suffering to us and all our relations. Indeed, the *supposedly separate* ego is an intrinsically confused, fear-filled, and avaricious structure, but ultimately an illusory one. Fortunately, there are life-enhancing alternatives that include but transcend the apparently independent ego.

## Growing Beyond Stories of Separation in Individual Development

Thomas Merton (1968b) observed that Christianity and Buddhism agree that something is fundamentally awry in our usual sense of self and way of relating with others. Both traditions

> are aware that man is somehow not in his right relation to the world and to things in it, or rather, to be more exact, they see that man bears in himself a mysterious tendency to *falsify* that relation, to spend a great deal of energy in justifying the false view he takes of his world and his place in it. . . . It is a disposition to treat the ego as an absolute and central reality and to refer all things to it as objects of desire or of repulsion. (p. 82)

The concern is that the self-sense or identity we adopt exerts a powerful influence on how we see and respond to the world. In this regard, I would like to offer an interpretation for mutual exploration, one that I hope will be both disquieting and generative. Stated strongly, here is the idea: *our conventional sense of self is an intrinsically delusional, paranoid, and greedy structure, yet ultimately an illusory one.* I am referring to our (supposedly) separate, sovereign, self-sufficient, skin-bounded, ego-centered self; and to the ways of being that follow from our efforts to defend or aggrandize such a self. Thankfully, there is a deeper life beyond the ego. And contact with nature provides an opportunity to awaken to these depths.

Understanding the origin and functioning of the apparently autonomous self can help us surpass its tyrannizing grip on us, and our fear-filled grip on it. As a point of orientation, note that traditional theories of developmental psychology hold that the ultimate goal of individual growth is the cultivation of a strong, stable independent ego.

Transpersonal psychologists agree that this is important but go further to disclose deeper possibilities (Wilber, 1977, 1980, 2000b; Washburn, 1995; Loy, 2018b; Ferrer, 2002; Engler, 2003). Development is usually thought to unfold from a prepersonal phase in infancy and childhood, wherein our self-boundaries are permeable and our immature self-sense is mostly drawn from internalizing the views and values of others, to a personal phase in adolescence and adulthood wherein we establish firm self/other boundaries and cultivate a distinctive personal sense of identity, agency, and values. Mature versions of the latter are usually deemed to be the deepest possibilities of human development. Transpersonal research extends the developmental path, demonstrating that we have the potential to grow into an even more mature transpersonal phase wherein our self-boundaries open and our sense of self transcends the skin-encapsulated ego.

At the outset here let us ponder a statement that highlights the chapter's theoretical themes. It comes from a great mystic, but the name may surprise you. In a letter of consolation to a man whose daughter had just died, Albert Einstein (1950) wrote:

> A human being is a part of the whole, called by us "Universe," a part limited in time and space. He experiences himself, his thoughts and feelings as something separated from the rest—a kind of optical delusion of his consciousness. This delusion is a kind of prison for us, restricting us to our personal desires and to affection for a few persons nearest to us. Our task must be to free ourselves from this prison by widening our circle of compassion to embrace all living creatures and the whole of nature in its beauty.

The natural world and conscious care for it can help liberate us from this egoic prison, thereby freeing us for loving relations with others, both human and more-than-human.

## The Intersubjective Construction of a (Supposedly) Separate Sovereign Ego

As we discussed in chapter 4, modern culture constructed an unprecedented worldview based upon the story of humankind's elevation above the rest of nature. Given this shadow side of modernity, the conditions were set for a *concordant re-storying of our sense of self on the individual level.* Culture and self are mutually co-constituting, after all. In the Euro-American world, peoples' taken-for-granted sense of self came to be construed as a (supposedly) separate structure of identity, self-coherence, continuity, and agency—an independent sovereign self that can master and control the external world. A variety of forces influenced the establishment of this new notion of self. Changes in economics, politics, religion, and science were especially notable. This included the increasing value given to individual freedom, independence, and autonomy in opposition to authoritarian oppression by the church and state. Across time the feeling of being an isolated self-interested entity became fortified by (and reciprocally fortifying of) the burgeoning ethos of capitalism and consumerism. Further, there is another formative force we have not yet discussed, one imbued with these collective influences yet distinct from them: namely, our early *intersubjective* relationships and the way they become internalized and incorporated as *intrapsychic self-structure* in the course of personal psychological development.

Constructs carry diverse meanings across various traditions of psychology, philosophy, and spirituality. Therefore, when critiquing our misguided identification as an exclusively separate self or ego, it is important to clarify that I am *not* referring to the skillful use of "ego strengths" as traditionally conceived: self-coherence, self-esteem, self-continuity, self boundaries and self/other differentiation, individual agency, will, relative security, critical reason, memory, anticipation, imagination, the ability to reflect on experience, the ability to bear intense feelings without repressing them or acting impulsively, and so forth. Relatedly, this book's invitation to transcend our felt-sense of being merely a skin-bounded egoic self is not directed (without careful qualifications) to people suffering severe forms of psychopathology such as schizophrenia, nor to anyone else who cannot rely on a stable personal sense of self nor the ego strengths just noted. For our purposes, "ego" refers to the most common sense of self in modern (and now postmodern) Euro-American culture, together with the ways of living that emerge from this identity. I will use the terms ego and separate self interchangeably. It is useful to distinguish *self-representational* qualities of the ego and *functional* ones: that is, respectively, my favored *ideas* about myself and the *ways of being and interrelating* that follow accordingly. The representational aspect of the ego refers to my conventional, habitual, affectively felt sense of self, self-concept, self-image, personal identification, and prepackaged life narrative. *Herein, the primary characteristic of the ego is the basic felt-sense of existing as a separate self.* I come to feel that I am really and necessarily separate from others, from the natural world, and often from my own body and non-egoic aspects of myself. I take myself to be a definite, reified, independent, autonomous, abiding, sovereign, skin-bounded subject who is (or should be) self-sufficiently in control of my life and thereby able to manipulate the world around me. The *functional* aspect of the ego is my way of being, perceiving, and interacting when I am (consciously or unconsciously) defending, fortifying, aggrandizing, or willfully imposing this objectified self-representation. As we shall see, *my egoic self is characterized by a dissociation intrinsic to its very structure, a presumed split between me in here and others out there.* This leaves me subtly but chronically afraid, and thus driven to excessive defensiveness, self-aggrandizement, and efforts at control.

Psychoanalytic research in developmental psychology has given us a subtle understanding of something most people know without appreciating its real significance. That is, our sense of self does not exist fully formed in infancy but is built over time through our inter-responsive contact with others. Indeed, *our personal self is constructed through our interpersonal relationships,* especially by way of repeated interactions with our parents or other caregivers. This insight was not available prior to the findings of twentieth-century psychology. All through life, but especially when we are very young, existence can be confusing, frightening, and dangerous. Attentive nurturing from our caregivers is absolutely essential for our physical survival and psychological health. To a significant degree, in these vital interactions, *we become like our closest relations.* We internalize, identify with, and enact their qualities; the ways they describe, prescribe, proscribe, and define us; and the ways they love, support, encourage, celebrate, punish, neglect, abuse, abandon, blame, shame, or otherwise induce us to be. This process happens mostly outside of our conscious awareness. A child's newly developing self is immensely malleable vis-à-vis the intersubjective field. The first ways we experience things have a profound effect, not just for the moment but across our lifetime. Each time our mother or father responds to us they are lending meaningful coherence to our experience, thus providing formative messages about who we are and who we are supposed to be. Our felt-and-imagined sense of self and world are thus built through this relational involvement. At the same time, our parents' personalities and parenting styles are primarily influenced by their own identification with the values of the culture in which they are members.

The intersubjective construction of identity takes on a special poignancy when we consider that, compared to all other animals, *human infants have the longest period of absolute dependency upon their caregivers.* With horses, for comparison, a foal can stand and begin walking within an hour of its birth. And it can gallop the very next day! Such rapid physical development is a life-saving resource when faced with hungry predators in the wild. Yet humans only begin crawling at 6 to 10 months and walking at 9 to 16 months. It is funny to imagine a newborn baby standing right up and running around! After a 9-month gestation period, human infants come into the world relatively *premature* in their neurological, cognitive, and motor development. The brain and cranium of fetuses grow so rapidly that if they were to stay in the womb much longer their heads would not fit through the pelvic opening of most mothers. Natural selection apparently tends toward an early birth in order to reduce maternal and infant mortality. Psychologically speaking, this condition is profoundly influential because it leaves us almost totally helpless for an extended developmental phase. During this time our very survival is completely contingent upon the care of others.

From the baby's perspective, they are vulnerable in a strange new world. Hopefully it is a loving and supportive one, yet it will inevitably be painful, confusing, and scary at times. Infants are immersed in an ever-changing unfolding of events: interpersonal yearnings, instinctual urges, bodily feelings, sensations, relational interchanges, physical tasks, and so forth. Some are pleasurable, some are painful or frightening, and all are new to them. Babies do not have the abilities to handle these ordinary challenges alone. Parental responses are essential in helping them gather their experiential flux into relatively coherent and meaningful patterns. Every encounter shapes the infant's understanding of who they are and what this world is like. Susceptible to the various pangs of daily existence—hunger, heat, cold, injury, illness, external threats, relational rupture—the baby is completely reliant on the loving attention of others, not just for physiological nourishment and protection but for psychological needs too: loving connection; warm, intimate touch; security; support; responsive interaction. Such involvement provides crucial assistance in bearing the anxieties of everyday life, and in relishing the joys as well. *These are life and death matters.* Without caring relationships the infant would die.

The French psychoanalyst Jacques Lacan (1977) described how the child's ability to recognize themselves in a mirror, at around 18 months, exerts a major formative effect on their developing sense of ego and their ability to mitigate anxiety. An actual mirror provides the child with a reliably coherent, stable, supposedly separate self-image to hold on to and be oriented by. Even more importantly, caregivers' responses serve as a kind of mirror, reflecting the child back to themselves in relatively consistent ways. This happens nonverbally via others' affective tone, gaze, and behavior. And it happens when others define the child with objectifying messages. *The most formative message is that you are separate from me.* (A more familiar example is the way children are shaped with gendered stereotypes.) A child takes these reflections in, mostly unawares, and thereby forms feelings, concepts, and images regarding their self. Unable to survive on their own in an often scary world, and yearning for connection with their beloved parents, the child readily shifts their emerging identity in accordance with the parents' directives (be they overt or covert). In this process, *the child's felt, imagined, and conceptualized sense of self becomes consolidated as a kind of defensive strategy to master fear and anxiety.* Notice that the messages of others not only direct us in navigating immediate challenges. Further, via a process of internalization, *others' responses—especially their objectified and objectifying characterizations of us—become a relatively stable part of who we take ourselves to be and how we see the world.* In this way, *interpersonal relations metamorphose into intrapsychic self-structure.* Over time, this self-sense is then expressed and defended in further relations with others. We should be aware that parental responses are not simply an unbiased mirror image of their child's self-presentation but are actively formative forces conditioned by the parents' own personality, history, culture, desires, and state of consciousness. In the modern world, parents are predominantly (dis)oriented by stories of separation, independence, self-sufficiency, and autonomy. And this separatist ethos is passed on in the developmental construction of their children's identity and ways of being.

## As Our Sense of Self Contracts, Sources of Perceived Threat Expand

Typically the conventional self/other, self/world split is never questioned. My self appears to be inside my body (or, more narrowly, inside my brain); and other people, the human-built world, and the rest of nature appear to be out there, separate from me, definitely not-me. This belief is understandable since my personal body-mind is the locus of my distinct individuality.[1] However, ecological science, contemplative spirituality, and transpersonal psychology offer a radically alternative story. Seen from any of these perspectives, *there is no such thing as a separate self.* Not only is every self a self-in-relation-with-others, but every person is an expression of a transpersonal reality that is infinitely deeper than any isolated individual. For example, as Thomas Berry says, "The human is more a mode of being of the planet rather than a separate being on the planet."[2] This is mysterious, but it should not be mystifying. The psychologically significant point is this: *my self is not merely mine alone, not in any fully autonomous, self-contained, self-sufficient way.* What I call my "self" consists of my felt-sense of identity, coherence, continuity, and agency. Yet when "I" think or feel or relate with others, something beyond my individuality is always acting through my skin-bounded self. This is why the world's spiritual traditions teach that my real self is not limited to my (supposedly separate) body-mind. Uncannily, *my true self is not myself.* Not as I conventionally imagine it, at least. Such realizations do not deny our relative agency but place it in a usefully humbling context. We could claim that culture comprises the transpersonal dimension to which I am alluding. This is true as far as it goes, but it does not go far enough. Nature precedes, exceeds, permeates, and includes culture. Joining with Berry, we could say—or better, *realize experientially*—that the whole, dynamic, animate, intelligent, inter-responsive field of nature is an especially significant version of my transpersonal self. When my ego is decentered, when it relinquishes its presumed preeminence and finds its place in a more embracing context, then my (co)existence begins to flow from a deeper, relationally responsive dimension of my being.

In releasing my habitual identity as a small separate self, I am given an intimately felt sense of my connection with others, and of a deeper self and life coming forth through me. *I may realize that there is an infinite, seamless, dynamic, inter-responsive life that transcends but includes my individual self, and know I am that.* All the great wide earth—all the whole vast cosmos in fact—is seamlessly gathered in and springs forth *as my very self.* Such an affirmation points to the least common sense of self, yet the one with the greatest potential for liberation, compassion, love, and justice. Wise ones across the ages have long celebrated this great transpersonal reality. For example, Dōgen implored his students to realize that "the whole universe throughout the ten directions is in itself the Self; this Self is the whole universe throughout the ten directions"

(Abe, 1992, p. 126). And as Jane Goodall (1999) once put it: "Your soul, the Universe" (p. 33).

Who I actually am surely must include the life-giving activity of the larger animate earth, but I often act as if it does not. When I establish a dualistic self-boundary that deems the natural world "not me," I am dissociating a deeper dimension of my being. In making this basic self/other severance, I construct a narrow notion of self. Yet, out of fear, I often contract far more than this. Having imbibed modernity's ideals (such as Descartes' mind/body separation) by way of my cultural and familial milieu, rather than identifying with my whole body-mind I begin to identify only with my conscious mind or rational ego. My animal body gives rise to natural impulses and feelings that are outside my conscious will and control: pleasure, pain, fear, sex, aggression, intense emotion, ecstasy, and so forth. And my tender body leaves me vulnerable to injury, illness, and death. *Better, it seems, to take my thinking mind as my real self, an egoic self that strives to master and control that unruly and mortal body.* Carrying this dissociative process even further, I often become troubled by aspects of my ego that I do not like, qualities that feel dangerous, unacceptable, shameful, or unlovable. So I banish these to unconsciousness where they live on dynamically as a threatening shadow self. Through such repression I am left to identify exclusively with my favored, conscious, socially esteemed self-concept, my persona (as Jung would say). This is the most contracted self-sense of all, yet tragically the most common. For most of us most of the time, this extremely constricted self-representation becomes the lens through which we see and interact with the world.

The conventional sense of being merely a separate ego (or, smaller still, a persona) is created, largely unconsciously, by internalizing stories from caregivers—stories that typically insist that we draw strict boundaries that detach self from others. A story told or boundary line drawn may seem a flimsy foundation for one's sense of self, and it is true that separatist stories are not based on any substantial reality. But we should not underestimate their power. Make no mistake, *the self-boundaries we adopt come to be taken for granted, simply the way (we imagine) things really are and have to be, even though they are mostly arbitrary constructions* based upon cultural, interpersonal, and intrapsychic processes. In truth, I can never be disconnected from aspects that are split off. Each is an inherent dimension of my very being, yet I commonly cut off and lose touch with each. But nothing dissociated can ever really be banished.

*Thus, I tend to feel threatened by my body, shadow, other people, and the rest of nature, because each expresses an alter-agency that operates beyond my willful expectations, preferences, and power.*

All these various dissociations create a *low-grade pathology of normality*. (Remember that the present chapter is focusing on *normal* ego development.) It is telling that *all forms of clinical psychopathology involve a partial person relating partially to a partial world*. Someone who is depressed typically lives merely as a guilty, unworthy, devitalized person in a depleted relationship with a critical, dark, devitalized world. Likewise, we are seeing how ego-oriented life involves a partial self relating partially to a partial world. For example, when we exist merely as an egoic self we typically see nature as exploitable material, an impediment to our wishes, or a danger to defend against. This problem is compounded by our efforts to guard ourselves against life's inevitable wounds, especially ruptures in close relationships. For protection, we often make our self-boundaries excessively solid, rigid, and fixed. Rather than flexibly differentiating ourselves from others by crafting distinct yet still permeable ego boundaries that facilitate connection, we often enclose ourselves with *impermeable ego barriers that detach us from intimate contact*. As we make this isolating move time and again, defensive reactions unwittingly become sedimented into habitual ways of being. We temporarily gain safety by cutting ourselves off, but we abdicate a reciprocally enlivening interchange with others. Beyer (2014) offers a humorously revealing analogy, comparing our supposedly separate ego to the shell of a barnacle.

> The "common land barnacle" belongs to the class "Homo Sapiens Pseudo Crustacean." Human beings are the only known species of land barnacle. . . . We, like the marine barnacle, attempt to separate ourselves from danger by building our own type of impermeable walls—psychological walls—and escaping to the inside. Like marine barnacles, throughout our development we attempt to protect our vulnerable selves from harm by vacating our way too organic bodies and fleeing into our cerebrally enhanced and fortified heads. And in time, we, too, attempt to attach to something—our now constricted and impermeable egoic identity—and we commit ourselves to it, passionately, and we hold on as if our survival depended on it. (p. 128)

I hope Beyer's satirical tale made you laugh. But I am guessing that, like me, you also felt somewhat anxious in recognizing yourself in his characterization. Bolstering this presumably detached, masterful ego is often the primary but (mis)guiding motivation of our existence. However, the anthropologist Clifford Geertz (1983) makes a striking observation: "The Western conception of the person as a bounded, unique, more or less integrated motivational and cognitive universe, a dynamic center of awareness, emotion, judgment, and action organized into a distinctive whole and set contrastively both against other such wholes and against a social and natural background is, however incorrigible it may seem to us, a rather peculiar idea within the context of the world's culture" (p. 59).

## The Ego Is a Delusional, Paranoid, and Greedy Structure

From the Buddha's interpretation of ego-centered craving to Freud's view of unconscious motivation, wise teachers have long demonstrated that *people often do not really know who they are or what they authentically desire*. Taking oneself to be a separate sovereign subject is the key case in point. *Suffering is intrinsic to egoic existence* because I (as ego) am out of touch with deeper, transpersonal dimensions of my being (including the rest of nature); because any fixed self-representation is misleading; because the ego is nothing substantial or real in the first place; because egoic desires are intrinsically insatiable; and because life or nature itself is wildly beyond the ego's drive for mastery and control. Since I can never really be isolated and self-sufficient, I am rightly plagued by a sense that something vital is missing (see Loy, 2008, 2018a, 2018b; Wilber, 1977, 1980, 2000b). A feeling of unsatisfactoriness lingers in the back of my awareness, as if there is something not quite good enough about me, the world, and life itself. Loy (2008) states it with succinct power: "separate self = *dukkha*" (p. 105). "Suffering" is the usual translation of this Sanskrit term. And there is indeed a form of *dukkha* associated with conditions that are intrinsically painful: the death of loved ones, illness, injury, interpersonal wounding, and so on. However, *dukkha* primarily connotes a pervasive feeling of dis-ease and discontent that inevitably haunts ego-centered existence. As Loy has brilliantly shown, *in misunderstanding the source of* dukkha, *I believe I need to acquire something more or better in order to fill my lack and thus be secure and happy.* So I defensively turn to anything that gives me a consoling sense of safety and control: fame, money, power, possessions, food, drugs, screens, exploitation of other people or the natural world, and so forth. *The fantasy is that if only I had these things, then I could really be secure and fulfilled.* When I actually get them to some degree, the painful sense of lack may go away temporarily. But this is brief at best. Such false solutions are necessarily unsatisfying because they never address *the real source of suffering: our fundamental misidentification as a separate self.* Worse yet, *my real needs remain unrecognized and unaddressed, especially my holy yearning for conscious loving union with other people, nature, and the great unnamable mystery (G-d, the Dao, life).*

> Since our usual sense of self is a construct, it does not corre-spond to anything substantial, which is why it is inherently anxious and insecure: because there's nothing that could be secured. The self usually experiences this ungroundedness as a *lack*: the sense that there is something wrong with me, a basic discomfort often experienced on some level as *I'm not good enough.* Unfortunately, we often misunderstand our dis-ease and try to secure ourselves by identifying with things "outside" us that (we think) can provide the grounding we crave: money, material possessions, reputation, power, physical attractiveness, and so forth. [Including, especially, clinging to favored ideas of our self.] Since none of them can actually ground or secure one's sense of self, no matter how much money (and so on) we may accumulate, it never seems to be enough. (Loy, 2018a, pp. 7–8)

The *ego's craving is insatiable* since fear, insecurity, and lack are built into its structure as the exclusive locus of identity. The compulsive search for (substitute) satisfactions to fill our lack is simply another project of the ego, striving as always to bolster itself and its illusion of control.

We can see how the sociocultural forces addressed in the previous chapter are interwoven with the conventional operations of our (appar-ently) separate self. The ego's basic defensive strategy is avoidance, but its most overt tactic is the other side of avoidance: namely, grasping for things in order to banish unpleasant feelings. This ranges from holding tightly to our familiar self-sense to craving material objects or power. Contemporary culture fans the flames of this inevitably doomed approach. Throughout most of history, economic practices were situated within, and designed to serve, the local human community and natural world. But now the situation is reversed. Supported by the dominant political and legal systems, the economic system is given primacy and everything else is situated within it. This is egocentrism on a massive scale. Capitalism worships (presumed) "progress" via heedless economic expansion and the technological exploitation of nature. For many individuals, consumerism serves as a new secular religion, the predominant source of value, meaning, and motivation. Big box stores have become our temples and retail websites our sacred texts. Marketing executives act as priests who promote compulsive rituals of consumption as the means of our salvation. *The felt-lack intrinsic to our ego is preyed upon by this exploitive process, with the manipulative lure of endless products that promise to fill our lack.* The ego's insatiable desires are amplified by corporate-consumerist culture, and in turn amplify that same toxic culture. Whether by individual acquisitiveness or massive extraction of natural "resources," excessive consumption is ravaging the natural world while still leaving us unhappy. Further, to the ever insecure ego, the world is comprised of people for me to defend against or to use to satisfy my self-interested cravings. When I feel separate, afraid, and focused on getting things to overcome my apparent lack, then I presume others are doing the same. This escalates my drive to defend or aggrandize my self-concerned self. Such suffering cannot be healed by egoic means because the ego is the source of the suffering. Clinging to the ego as our only identity is the primal trauma, the core wound itself.

This whole analysis leads us to a disturbing insight: *the normal ego is an intrinsically delusional, paranoid, and greedy psychic structure (but ultimately an illusory one).* Delusional because who I am is infinitely deeper than my small contracted self-sense; paranoid because all that is other than ego appears as a threat to me; greedy because I am chronically driven to fill a lack that can never be filled by egoic acquisitions; illusory because the ego is merely a provisional mode of being and self-representation, with no substantial reality. However, when we realize that our true self extends infinitely beyond our skin-bounded ego, surrendering the fantasy that the ego-self is exclusively who we are, then egoic capacities can serve skillfully in our life. All the traditional "ego strengths" continue operating well when the ego is appropriately situated within more encompassing dimensions of our being. In fact, *one of the ego's most exquisite capacities is that it can freely release its tight grip on us and consent to its own transcendence.* As is often emphasized, *the ego can never really be a master, but it can mature into an able servant.*

## Clinging to the Ego as a Defense against Death

The felt-story of being a solid, separate, autonomous, abiding ego is intertwined with *the intrinsic tenuousness of our very going-on-being.* After all, my egoic sense of self first emerged in infancy, when I was absolutely vulnerable and dependent. In those early days I surely had a bodily-affective sense that I would perish without the support provided by people close to me. At that time I grasped on to self-defining images and concepts reflected by others because they lent a fear-abating coherence to my nascent self, a consoling sense of being secure, real, and enduring. And they provided a sense of mastery in an often painful, baffling, and even life-threatening world. These formative experiences live on mostly unconsciously throughout our life, so it is no wonder that I hold on so fiercely when my favored self-concept is threatened.

It is significant that our earliest experiences of self-formation are imbued with the dreadful threat of death or nonbeing. The ego identity constructed in this process becomes the prototype that colors our subsequent self-sense and later relational encounters. Later in life it can feel like our very survival depends upon defending the egoic self that originally emerged to help us manage our primal dread. In the fringes of awareness, we are plagued with the fear of death, of losing love and loved ones, of not being real or whole or worthy. Theorists such as Martin Heidegger (1996), Norman O. Brown (1959), Ernest Becker (1973), and David Loy (2018b) have offered profound studies of a key existential fact: *when not faced and clarified consciously, the fear of death leads to a fear of life.* Our natural fear of death can lead to an excessive withdrawal from being fully alive and responsively engaged. Conversely, when we make peace with the fact that we and our loved ones will die at some unknown time, we can open more intimately into the life we are being given here and now. However, our understandable concern about death is disproportionately amplified when we identify only with our supposedly separate self. When basing my identity, security, and fulfillment on this narrow self-sense and its wishes, *all that is other than ego appears to be dangerous.* And to be clear: all that is other means all the rest of the whole world! That is to say, non-egoic dimensions of my individual self (body, animal instincts, affects, repressed shadow qualities, transrational creativity, wisdom, compassion, and intuition); other people, who threaten to impose their own ego upon me; the natural world; and life itself. While each of these has ways of its own that often contest my self-centered wishes, each can be life-enhancing when welcomed openly. At times we do need to defend ourselves because people or other natural forces are in fact hurting us. But natural vigilance for survival can easily morph into surplus vigilance and excessive self-aggrandizement. This is a bitter bargain, because in fortifying our reassuring self-concept we often hold ourselves back from living fully, from daring to venture into encounters or projects that are uncertain in outcome and beyond our control: that is to say, into almost all the truly meaningful endeavors of our life!

*Aversion* and *clinging* are the basic ways we defend our preestablished sense of self. Aversion takes two well-known forms, fight or flight. These originally arose to preserve our physical survival, yet they usually appear in more subtle, psychologically relevant ways. Fighting includes aggression, domination, control, exploitation, violence, and so forth. Fleeing includes avoidance; denial; repression; dissociation; self-numbing by alcohol, drugs, screens, consumerism; and so on. Clinging comes in variations of greed, narcissism, self-entitlement, acquisitiveness, possessiveness, overconsumption, addiction, and so on. This includes, especially, a rigid attachment to our preferred self-concept and ego-centered desires. (Clinging is often called "attachment" in the spiritual literature, but this is completely different from healthy "attachment" to others à la the relational theorists.) I have shown how identifying exclusively as a separate self is the fundamental confusion of humankind. To be con-fused is to be fused with something, in this case a fear-driven fixed fusion with an objectified image of our self. Clinging and aversion are motivated by *an anxious craving that is intrinsic to the supposedly separate self's existence.* Although our egoic identity first arose as a defense against anxiety, *the overall mood of the ego is one of anxiety, dis-ease, unsatisfactoriness, resentment, and even paranoia.*

Uncannily, to even refer to "the ego"—much less to ground our identity in it—is misleading because the ego is never a substantial entity but only a relatively stable, recurring pattern of self-representation, believing, feeling, perceiving, and interacting. Despite our apparently incorrigible clinging, the ego-self is ultimately illusory, merely a *provisional conceptual construction* with no real existence or ultimate ground. As my Zen teacher once remarked, with serious capriciousness: "I rarely speak of 'the ego' because I don't like to talk about anyone in their absence" (Bruce Harris, personal communication, 2015). Similarly, as Harris Rōshi's dharma brother David Loy demonstrated, the *ego's intrinsic absence* leaves us feeling anxious, lacking, unreal, and craving for something to alleviate this painful sense. I am thus haunted by "the quite valid suspicion that 'I' [as ego] am not real" (Loy, 2018b, p. 1). I try to bolster my ego to ward off dangers, *especially the loss of love or my inevitable but unpredictable death.* Yet it is not only some future threat that I defend against. As Loy shows, I also grasp tightly to my egoic self-sense in order to banish *the present and accurate feeling that my conventional self is not fully real, whole, abiding, and secure.* (Indeed, it is not!) However, there is a vexing irony in this. *I remain fiercely attached to reified self-images and self-concepts because they serve (temporarily) to ease anxiety about who I am and how to be. But the way I typically imagine and live my egoic self—as separate and masterfully self-sufficient—leaves me feeling incomplete and afraid of all that is other than this small, objectified self-sense.*

## The Ego Is an Object of Awareness, Not the Subject Who Is Aware

By cultural convention, we normally locate our subjectivity in our ego. However, in its representational form, *the ego is not a subject who is aware but an object of awareness*—a reified concept that is constructed interpersonally, socioculturally, and linguistically. To be objectified is the very nature of the ego, especially in imagining that one is a separate self. But who I truly am can never be objectified. I might rightly say I am a husband, father, teacher, psychotherapist, tennis player, Zen practitioner, nature lover, and on and on. Yet each characteristic leaves out so much. The "on and on" continues endlessly. To explore this I invite you to sit with a trusted friend and have them ask: "Who are you?" After you answer, the friend will pause briefly and ask: "Who are you?" And you respond anew. The friend kindly poses this existential question, again and again. If you stay with it for 10 minutes (or more), if you are willing to bear anxiousness, silence, and not knowing, I trust you will be intrigued. Most basically, you will realize that no finite concept can ever really name you. But this is not meant to deter inquiry. Wise ones across the ages have encouraged careful searching so as to "know thyself." Self-descriptions can be useful, provisionally, when I hold them lightly. They work well when serving my larger life, but they tyrannize me when I let them totally define me or guide my life. Even the most exquisite idea I have of myself is not who I am most deeply.

*Any reified self-representation inevitably is way too much and way too little:* too much in that the particular quality is too static, fixed, exclusionary, totalizing; too little in that my real self goes infinitely deeper. Nothing I can say about myself, no quality I identify with, is even close to being sufficient. (The same is true for anything I say about another person or the natural world.) This is the case whether I say, "I am good and deeply loved" or "I am bad and unlovable." It is even the case if I say, "Nature goes infinitely deep, and that is who I truly am." Sandor Ferenczi, grandfather of relational psychoanalysis, once declared that "character-traits . . . are secret psychoses" (Becker, 1973, p. 27). It does seem rather crazy that I would imagine that any personality characteristic could really define me, and that *I would stake my happiness and security on upholding this delimited self-definition.* Yet, implicitly, I do this much of the time. Identifying with fixed characteristics gives me a sense of safety, solidity, and control in a challenging, impermanent, uncontrollable world. However, I often become so rigidly fused and attached to these objectified self-concepts that I defend them as if my very existence depended on it. This can feel like a life and death matter. Our primal fears originate in infantile helplessness, but ordinary life can be scary at any age. To ease our anxiety—about death or loss of love in the future, about not being real and secure right now—we tend to cling to preestablished notions of self and world and reject experiences that contradict these reassuring preferences. But this impedes our capacity to respond flexibly and fittingly in the present moment. *Most of the ever-new appeals that life sends us differ significantly from our most wise and compassionate presumptions, much less those oriented by craving for self-confirmation, mastery, and control.*

*I can never find or know or grasp my self objectively, because my true self is not an object (although my familiar ego is). I can only really know my deepest self by consciously being that self.* Spontaneous mystical experience, contemplative practice, and intimacy with nature can give us an intuition of this non-graspable, non-objectifiable, yet vividly present self.

## The Reciprocity of Identity and Ethics: Self Creates Love, Love Creates Self

We can now address a key point, namely, that *identity and ethics are intertwined.* Who we take ourselves to be guides how we treat (or mistreat) others. As we view our self, so shall we act and interact. Our sense of self is given tangible expression in our loving actions (or their absence).

Reciprocally, being loving (or not) recurrently recreates our sense of self. Many authorities have claimed that the world's spiritual traditions share a common transpersonal understanding. Jorge Ferrer (2002, 2008) offers an important perspective on this issue. Citing a classic metaphor, he agrees that the various religions, in their deepest expression, are different rivers leading to the same ocean (p. 138). But to avoid oversimplification, and to avoid reifying an infinitely mysterious dynamic reality, Ferrer (2008) distinguishes the crucial quality of this one ocean. "The ocean shared by most traditions does not correspond to a single spiritual referent or to 'things as they really are,' but, perhaps more humbly, to *the overcoming of narrow self-centeredness* and thus a liberation from corresponding limiting perspectives" (p. 138). This metamorphosis is central for ecopsychology.

In a revealing developmental model that builds upon the work of Lawrence Kohlberg, Carol Gilligan, and others, Ken Wilber (2000a, pp. 116–117, 197, 208, 209) emphasizes the interconnection between our sense of self and our ethical engagement.[3] Figure 5.1, my adaptation and elaboration of Wilber's (2000a) clear view, depicts increasingly expansive spheres of consciousness, identity, and love. As one's self-sense and consciousness evolve they become more inclusive, thus sponsoring decreasing ego-centeredness, narcissism, and anthropocentrism; increasing awareness, wisdom, compassion, love, justice, and identification with and service to others; and deepening freedom, agency, and empowerment in relation with others. Our spheres of care expand together with our spheres of identity. "What is it that you call *yourself*? With what do you identify this self of yours? For that *identity* expands from egocentric to ethnocentric to worldcentric to pneumocentric [spirit-centered]—you actually feel that you are *one with* each of those expanding worlds" (Wilber, 2000a, p. 116). And your care for others will extend accordingly. Thus, at the egocentric level: I am exclusively a contracted, supposedly separate ego. From this self-sense, I only take care of what is good for me. Ethnocentric: I am my individual body-mind plus people like me—my group, tribe, race, class, country, religion, sexual orientation, species, and so on. So I only take care of what is good for "us," the exclusive group with whom I identify. Others who appear different from us are excluded from my care. Development often gets arrested here, but there are deeper possibilities. Worldcentric: I am my individual body-mind, plus all people, plus all this great wide earth. (This marks the emergence of a genuinely transpersonal identity.) From this self-sense, I take care of what is good for *all of us*, including the beings and presences of the natural world. Spirit-centric, theocentric, pneumocentric, omnicentric: as my true, deep, transpersonal

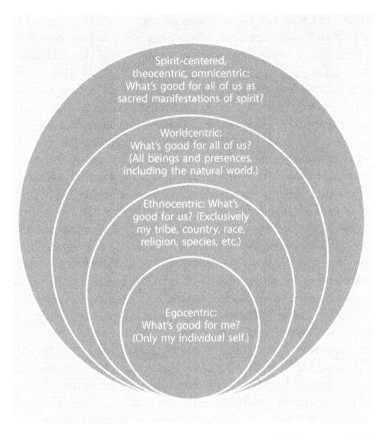

Figure 5.1 Developmental Transformations of One's Self-Sense and Ethical Orientation. Adapted from Ken Wilber, 2000a.

self, I am my individual body-mind plus the great wide earth plus the whole cosmos (manifest and unmanifest)—all of reality, being, G-d, the Dao, the one great life—in its complete dynamic holy functioning. From this supreme self-sense, I care for each and all as perfect expressions of the sacred or divine.

## Reorienting Our Self via Lessons from Harry Harlow and Jane Goodall

The present chapter has been rather complex theoretically. *Yet our egoic dissociation from others and nature is not primarily a theoretical matter. It is an acutely (co)existential one.* It makes an enormous difference whether I feel myself to be a separate self or a relationally involved one. To show how this is so, I will pose a strange juxtaposition: *Harry Harlow is to Jane Goodall as* _____ *is to* _____? As you probably know, Goodall is a world-esteemed primatologist and ecological activist best known for her field studies of wild chimpanzees in Tanzania. Harlow too was a scientist of great renown. Through his laboratory experiments with monkeys he lent empirical evidence to the burgeoning relational and attachment theories. And he served as president of the American Psychological Association, the world's most influential psychological organization. I will not try to present a comprehensive study of either one's life or work, neither of whom I ever met. But I will consider some of Harlow's personal characteristics because they illustrate the kind of ego-centered self-sense that contributes gravely to our ecopsychological distress. (His research also demonstrates the field of psychology's historical, and sometimes continuing, alienation from the rest of nature.) Goodall's life and work point to a radically different, ecologically attuned alternative.

Like John Bowlby, Harlow believed that behaviorist explanations for mother-infant attachment were overly simplistic. Surely more was going on than positive reinforcement, tension reduction, and the satisfaction of physiological needs. Harlow knew that intimate, physically affectionate, loving relationships are crucial for our well-being. However, in the 1950s, experimental research psychologists did not talk about love. When Harlow was speaking of love at a conference, a fellow scientist "corrected" him with this criticism: "You must mean *proximity*, don't you?" To his credit, Harlow challenged him with a strong retort: "It may be that proximity is all you know of love; I thank God I have not been so deprived" (Slater, 2004, p. 133). To demonstrate the importance of loving relations and warm bodily touch in the development of the mother-infant bond, and to document the long-term pathological effects of relational rupture, Harlow conducted a series of famous (now infamous) experiments on maternal deprivation and infant isolation. He did so by studying rhesus macaques, a species of monkey widely distributed through Asia. In the wild these intelligent, aware, emotionally connected animals live in structured social groups of 20 to 200 members. Mothers and infants are known to create powerful, mutually affectionate relationships. In his most recognized series of studies, Harlow removed the infants from their mothers and raised them in isolation. Each baby was placed alone in a cage with two types of so-called surrogate "mothers."[4] These were inanimate models that only vaguely resembled a real monkey. Rather crudely built by today's standards, one surrogate was made mostly of wire. The other was shaped the same but covered with a soft terrycloth towel. Harlow did various experiments with somewhat different foci, but his main findings can be summarized as follows (Harlow, 1986; Harlow & Mears, 1979; Harlow & Suomi, 1970, 1986; Harlow et al., 1971). Even when a baby monkey was "fed" only by the wire "mother" (with a milk bottle secured to the model), they would quickly move away from the food provider and cling to and snuggle with the soft cloth "mother." The monkeys overwhelmingly preferred the physical touch and "contact comfort" available there. The babies would also use the cloth mother as a secure base from which they ventured out to explore the surroundings, and to which they returned for comfort when feeling threatened.

In a different study, Harlow created four types of what he called "evil" or "monster" mothers (Harlow & Mears, 1979). He also referred to this type of surrogate as an "iron maiden" (p. 220), named after an actual torture device: "We next concocted a mother who shook until the baby's teeth chattered, and finally one far removed from the concept of contact comfort, a surrogate covered like a porcupine with brass spikes" (p. 220). Even after being assaulted by such a mother figure, the infant macaques would return and cling to "her," so powerful was the soothing support provided by close physical contact. Each of Harlow's studies was more disturbed and disturbing than the previous one. Here is a particularly chilling instance. In an effort to experimentally induce psychopathology in monkeys, Harlow and his associates removed infants from their real mothers—ignoring screams and wails and mothers banging their own heads against the cages—and reared the babies in total social isolation for up to 12 months. (Remember, this is with beings who are known to have deep social connections in the wild.) Some of these monkeys died, often by starving themselves. But Harlow persisted in studying what kind of mothers the surviving monkeys would turn out to be. However, due to the severe trauma of total isolation, they would not mate. To acquire the offspring required in his study, Harlow coldly reported that "we resorted to an apparatus affectionately termed the rape rack" in order to forcibly impregnate them (Harlow et al., 1971, p. 545). (Note that Harlow's unabashed comments were published in esteemed scientific journals.) "Most of the monkey motherless mothers ignored their infants . . . but other motherless mothers abused their babies by crushing the infant's face to the floor, chewing off the infant's feet and fingers, and in one case by putting the infant's head in her mouth and crushing it like an eggshell" (p. 545). Frankly, I am repulsed by Harlow's work. Yet the horrific violence enacted by Harlow and his associates are *symptoms of the collective insanity of a culture gone terribly awry*. The animal rights movement in the United States gained momentum by publicizing and resisting his abuse of the monkeys (Singer, 1990, pp. 31–36). Jane Goodall singled out Harlow's work in her critique of animal experimentation. Thanks to her advocacy and that of others, the National Institutes of Health in the United States stopped funding research on chimpanzees in 2015.

We will address these major ethical breaches later. For a moment, however, imagine that we knew nothing about Harlow's traumatic procedures and were only aware of his research results. Given the interrelational focus of the present book, we would readily agree with his primary findings: loving, affectionate contact with a caregiver is crucially important for psychological health. Conversely, depriving babies of relational contact and comforting touch leads to long-term psychopathology. Now an obvious question might be: who would deny the importance of affectionate relationships and benefits of love? Few would argue otherwise. However, far too many people and institutions certainly do *act* otherwise. In Harlow's day, many psychologists and pediatricians contended that the mother-infant bond was motivated exclusively by physical hunger, and that parents should force babies to break their emotional attachments and become independent as soon as possible. The legacy of John Watson's detached behavioral approach to child development was still strong in the field of psychology. Consider Watson's (1928) advice to parents: "Never hug and kiss them, never let them sit in your lap. If you must, kiss them once on the forehead when they say good night. Shake hands with them in the morning. . . . Try it out. In a week's time you will find how easy it is to be perfectly objective with your child and at the same time kindly" (pp. 81–82). Harlow rightly thought this was nonsense. Nonetheless, a critical turn is certainly called for. Harlow's abuse of the monkeys was extreme, but let us not deceive ourselves: these days the earth finds itself *in extremis* even in the ordinary course of events. We must acknowledge the basic fact that many people in Harlow's era believed that scientific evidence was required to "prove" that a loving parent-infant relationship is crucial for children's well-being. Otherwise, his research would not have been done in the first place. *The perceived need for such research demonstrates the severe extent to which our culture had lost touch with the inherently relational nature of human beings*. Like other animal researchers, Harlow's basic rationale for studying monkeys was that they are so much like human beings (Harlow et al., 1986). Rhesus macaques are intelligent, aware, socially and emotionally involved animals who share 94 percent of our genes. Therefore, the widely accepted argument goes, research results can be generalized to humans. But this discloses a terrible irony. *We torture infant monkeys because they resemble us so much. Then, seeing them suffer and die at our own hands, we convince ourselves such methods are justified because they are "only animals" or mere "lower forms of life."*

A 2010 study found that rhesus macaques can recognize themselves in a mirror (Rajala et al., 2010). This ability has long been seen as evidence of self-awareness and intelligence. And I recently came across the touching story of a monkey in India who risked their own life to save an injured companion ("Monkey to the Rescue," 2014). One monkey had been severely shocked by high-tension wires and had fallen to the ground unconscious. A fellow monkey quickly came to the rescue—shaking, tapping, biting, and placing their friend in water to revive them. Setting one's self-interests aside in the loving service of another is often considered the preeminent ethical act, a capacity mistakenly thought to be exclusively human. Harlow was well aware of the macaques' exquisite capabilities, but as far as I know he never expressed regret for how he (mis)treated them. After having many years to reconsider his work—its contributions but also the serious ethical concerns raised by other researchers, animal advocates, and by the anguished macaques themselves—Harlow made this chilling remark: "The only thing I care about is whether the monkeys will turn out a property I can publish. I don't have any love for them. Never have. I don't really like animals. I despise cats. I hate dogs. How could you like monkeys?" (Blum, 1994, p. 92).

In a profoundly alternative voice, Jane Goodall often speaks of the great love she has felt for animals throughout her life. Indeed, she entitled one of her books *The Chimpanzees I Love* (Goodall, 2001). And she compassionately interweaves the plight of people and other animals:

> I have seen that appeal for help in the eyes of so many suffering creatures. An orphan chimp tied up for sale in an African market; an adult male looking out from his five-by-five-foot sterile cell in a medical research lab. . . . I've seen it in the eyes of street children, and those who have seen their families killed in the "ethnic cleansing" in Burundi. All around

us, all around the world, suffering individuals look toward us with a plea in their eyes, asking us for help. . . . If we dare to look into those eyes, then we shall feel their suffering in our hearts. . . . Together we can bring change to the world, gradually replacing fear and hatred with compassion and love. Love for all living beings. (Goodall & Beckoff, 2002, p. 171)

I said that Harlow never showed concern for the monkeys. However, many people were concerned about him, particularly his heavy drinking, chain-smoking, and severe recurring depression. Harlow's biographer described him as a "man who lives at the lab, dawn to dusk, fueled by smoke, cigarettes, alcohol, and obsession" (Blum, 2002, p. 140). Students and colleagues said it was not uncommon to find him drunk and in need of assistance (Slater, 2004, p. 148). It does not take a psychologist to see that something serious was troubling him. I imagine his distress was complex, but abusing the monkeys must have been both a symptom and source of his suffering.

## Harlow Is an Exemplar, Not an Exception: The Trauma Is Being Repeated Today

To avoid simplistic idealization or devaluation, I trust that Harlow was not always so low, nor Goodall so good. There is something touching in the fact that Harlow, in his own perverted way, was trying to speak up for love in a scientific community where that treasured word was sadly taboo. He appears in our ecopsychological story as a kind of rhetorical foil. However, this is only because his work is a tragic exemplar of a more pervasive pathology in our relations with the natural world. Lest we imagine that Harlow's views and actions are aberrant ones of bygone days, I have two disconcerting stories to share. (1) The chair of psychiatry at the University of Wisconsin–Madison—the very place Harlow worked—recently submitted an institutional review board (IRB) proposal to conduct experiments with rhesus monkeys similar to Harlow's (Kalin, 2015; Wahlberg, 2015). This included separating infant monkeys from their mothers and exposing them to stressful events in order to experimentally induce anxiety and depression. Kalin (2015) explained that "rhesus monkeys have been selected because [of] their similarities to humans in social behavior, emotion, hormonal responses and brain structure" (p. 6).

Then, with truly perverse logic, he argued that researchers are justified to methodically traumatize baby monkeys because it is unethical to do the same thing to human infants (p. 5). The review board initially approved Kalin's study. But after widespread public and academic protest, the study was redesigned to eliminate the maternal deprivation. (2) At the very moment I am writing this (June 2018), the US government is actively separating babies and other children from their parents when they try to immigrate to the country. At least 2,300 children are now incarcerated in detention centers away from their parents. Many are actually being held in cages. Government officials have made the unconscionable argument that *because* parent-child bonds are so important, we should separate children from their parents to deter others from immigrating.

Ecopsychological transformation depends upon our capacity to deconstruct the story of separation and its fear-filled enactment. With this in mind, we can see that the assaults that took place in Harlow's lab stem from a triple dissociation: one sociocultural, one interpersonal, one intrapsychic—with all three being mutually reinforcing. Conversely, Goodall's compassionately engaged work stems from a triad of relational supports: a subculture concerned for the welfare of other animals; a network of interpersonal allies, including her mother and Louis Leakey; and her transpersonal self-sense, wisdom, courage, embodied compassion, and love. Despite screams of protest from moms and babies, Harlow severed key relational connections in order to confirm inevitably pathological results. After witnessing the agonizing consequences of his actions, he continued to do so for nearly two decades. I see this as a tragic interpersonal dissociation, with Harlow separating himself emotionally from the monkeys' obvious suffering and from many people who were pleading with him to stop his sadistic experiments. *While claiming to study love, he repeatedly tortured the monkeys, even allowing abused mothers to kill their helpless babies.* Eerily, here was a researcher celebrating warm attachment while demonstrating cold detachment from the beings who were victimized by his experiments. Harlow was enacting a dissociative value central to modernity, that of mastering and controlling the supposedly expendable, inferior natural world. Finally, there must have been a dissociation within Harlow himself. To repeatedly abuse the monkeys, he must have created an intrapsychic split between his thinking and feeling self, and between his power-and-fame-seeking self and his ethical self.

The strongest evidence of Harlow's threefold dissociation is the very existence of his long-term program of research. But here is a situated example. Harlow and Bowlby drew theoretical support from one another and also developed a personal relationship. During a tour of Harlow's lab, Bowlby looked at all the monkeys isolated in individual cages and shook his head upon seeing them "sucking themselves, rocking back and forth, cuddling their own bodies" (Blum, 2002, p. 214). According to Harlow's own report, Bowlby said to him: "You already have more psychopathological monkeys in the laboratory than have ever been seen on the face of the earth" (Harlow & Suomi, 1970, p. 8). Bowlby located the craziness in the tormented monkeys because it was most acutely obvious there. But the primary source of the insanity is the shared cultural story that we humans are separate from, superior to, and entitled to exploit other animals. This is a mad fantasy that Harlow must have internalized, and it surely interacted with his own personal psychology. "In later years, Harry would laugh [not cry] about Bowlby's ability to see what he himself had been blind to" (Blum, 2002, p. 214). After all those hours in a lab that reeked of feces, urine, and terror, a place that was filled with animals screaming, banging their heads on cages, and mutilating themselves, Harlow seemed surprised by Bowlby's remark about the psychopathology in the lab. (In a revealing slip, I first wrote "psychopathy" here.) Where was Harlow's conscience and felt-understanding of the monkeys' suffering? Rationalized away or banished to unconsciousness, apparently. The "blindness" Blum noted earlier is certainly a version of dissociation. Like today's denial of the climate emergency, Harlow would not see what was right before his eyes.

All this is in vast contrast with Jane Goodall's intimacy with the natural world. When Goodall was only 18 months old, she gathered earthworms from the family garden and took them to bed with her. Upon discovering this her mother gently said, "Jane . . . if you keep them here they'll die. They need the earth" (Goodall, 1999, p. 5). Little Jane understood and carried the worms back to their natural home. As a child Goodall loved to sit up in her favorite tree, which she named "Beech." She would place her cheek on its trunk and feel "the lifeblood of Beech, coursing below the rough bark" (Goodall, 1999, p. 20). In this tender contact, her self-boundaries became permeable and the illusion of separateness dissolved. She knew that she was "a part of the life of the tree" (p. 20). She also developed a close rapport with a furry companion, Rusty, the family dog. Rusty and other pets "had taught me well. They had made it abundantly clear that animals had personalities, could reason and solve problems, had minds, had emotions" (p. 74).

Dissociation is a fascinating psychological phenomenon because it means that *part of us is aware of something and, simultaneously, another part is unconscious of it.* I imagine Harlow's dissociative moves were facilitated by various means. Surely one of these was his heavy drinking, numbing himself to the reality of the suffering all around him. Another was the cultural and professional support he received. But in my view an even more important source of dissociation was also operative in Harlow's life. This involved a driving obsession to bolster his ego with personal achievement and fame, thereby screening out care for the monkeys and apparently for other people in his life. Harlow took this to extremes, but it involved a normal structural dissociation built into almost everyone's personality, a confused sense that our egoic self-image is really who we are.

Harlow adopted a position of domination and exploitation in relation not only with the laboratory macaques but also with people, especially women. Another psychologist recounted how Harlow "was so insulting to women. . . . [He] was a sexist" (Blum, 1994, p. 93). Harlow frequently referred to female monkeys as "the bitches" (p. 93). And in his own words: "Both of my wives . . . knew a man was more important than anything else" (Slater, 2004, p. 144). These misogynistic remarks lend further support to chapter 4's connection between the oppression of women and that of the natural world. The structure of oppression is the same: separation-elevation-superiority-devaluation-domination. *In every case, the scourge begins with separation.* Harlow's sexism is also consistent with our analysis of the ego and its efforts to avoid a felt-sense of lack. His detached alienation from the monkeys and women was obviously coupled with a sense of entitlement, self-interest, and self-aggrandizement. Along with his arrogant posturing and contempt for others, fame and power were major preoccupations throughout his life. In his high school yearbook, Harlow did not name a career he wished for in the future but instead stated that he wanted to "be famous" (Blum, 2002, p. 13). It seems that Harlow's professional life was dominated by an anxious drive to actualize his earlier fantasy for fame, as if that would give him the reassuring security he craved. At the height of his acclaim, Harlow was awarded the National Medal of Science. To receive this prestigious award he attended a ceremony at the White House hosted by Lyndon Johnson. But on the eve of being honored by the president of the United States, Harlow uttered a sad self-obsessed lament: "Now I have nothing left to strive for" (Slater, 2004, p. 152). *No honor, accomplishment, or fame could fill his anguishing sense of lack, because those things do not even come close* to touching the malady intrinsic to ego-centered existence: the felt-sense that we are really separate from others, and the associated notion that our egoic self-concept defines us, affirms our worth, and secures our existence.

Jane Goodall has taken up her international acclaim quite differently. In interviews spanning decades, she rarely focuses on herself but gives credit to others who supported her: her mother and grandmother; Louis Leakey; her family dog and a special tree at her childhood home; the youth of today who are devoted to earth's well-being; G-d; and, of course, the beloved chimpanzees of Gombe. Far from feeling she has nothing to strive for, Goodall—now in her 80s—travels over 300 days each year in support of ecological awareness, justice, and conservation. I do not really know why Goodall has lived so differently than Harlow. But I trust that it is at least partly grounded in her early and ongoing intimacy with other people and the natural world; and that it involves two sensibilities that evidently pervade her life: a compassionate understanding that we humans are indivisible from and ethically responsible toward the rest of nature, and a transpersonal (trans-egoic) sense of self that guides her (co)existence. "One thing the chimpanzees have helped to do is to open science's closed mind to understanding that we are part of and not separate from this amazing animal kingdom" (Goodall, in "How Dr. Jane," 2017). A brief story will illustrate the transpersonal point. In her late teenage years, apparently, Goodall (1999) was touched emotionally by a duck that flew close by. In response, she penned a poem that ended with this celebration: "The lovely dunes; the setting sun; / The duck—and I; / One Spirit, moving timelessly / Beneath the sky" (p. 30). Similarly, decades later, Goodall (1999) commented on her early fieldwork in Tanzania:

> Together the chimpanzees and the baboons and monkeys, the birds and insects, the teeming life of the vibrant forest, the stirrings of the never still waters of the great Lake, and the uncountable stars and planets of the solar system formed one whole. All one, all part of the great mystery. And I was part of it too. . . . More and more often I found myself thinking, "This is where I belong. This is what I came into this world to do." (p. 81)

Notice how Goodall's conscious embodiment of a transpersonal sense of self—"All one, all part of the great mystery. And I was part of it too"—spontaneously gave rise to deep ethical devotion: "This is what I came into this world to do." *When we know vividly that we are inherently connected with others, then compassion, love, and service spring forth naturally.*

## There Is a Life beyond the Ego

After considering the views of various esteemed authorities, I would like us to listen to two other women you have never heard of, but who are equally wise. Their testimony comes from an empirical, qualitative, phenomenological-hermeneutical research study that I conducted on "experiencing the sacred in everyday life" (Adams, 1996). Significantly, all of the volunteer research participants underwent a transformative movement from a habitually contracted, defended, egoic stance to one of open intimate communion with the natural world, another person, and/or the depths of their self. "Joan" was a 39-year-old nurse. Taking us right to a key point, she says: *"To me the 'sacred' is the interruption of what I routinely consider 'my self.'"* Here Joan is describing a profound shift that occurred during a "really painful" and "angry" conversation with her beloved boyfriend. As she reports, "The first part is knowing that it hurts and you're feeling pain together. But not deciding to move away from the pain, either by attacking and trying to hurt the other person or avoiding it by running away." Joan did not resort to the aversive reactions to pain that characterize the habitual ego, neither avoidance nor attack. "And it occurred to me that having the openness of heart—the willingness to go *through* it rather than just avoid or get around it in some way—is a miracle." As the intimate conversation unfolded, she began to experience "more permeability, in and out . . . a little bit of a dissolving of . . . what the usual, clear delineation is. That there's Francis and here's me. . . . And in a moment like this you can see how usually impermeable you really are." Such impermeability is simply the defensive functioning of our conventional egoic self-boundaries, blocking intimacy and obscuring understanding and care. Usually, as she remarks, "You don't ever really see the other person. I felt like I could really see him . . . without a whole lot of fear or defensiveness." Letting go of her guardedness, a radical metamorphosis occurred: "It was as if suddenly he just emerged as real from this fog of my own self-absorption. . . . He was alive." In the most vivid moments of contact, having surrendered the common absorption in her ego-self, Joan felt like she was a permeable "membrane" through which "love," "life," and "energy" were flowing, back and forth. It was "almost like a screen . . . air flow or fluid flow or whatever is not stopped by it, on either side. But rather some of which goes out comes back in and some of which comes in goes back out. There's not so much of a delineation between what's in and what's out. . . . That really is it. That's the sacred. . . . That is an emergence, a thing, me, through which life is flowing. . . . That's when you're really alive."

It is worth emphasizing the fact that life is flowing through us all the time. If not, we would cease to exist. What made Joan's experience distinctive is that she became lucidly conscious of participating in this intimate and holy process. (This is one of humankind's greatest capacities.) As she suggested, we cannot really make contact with another person when we hold ourselves separate and "impermeable," when captivated by "fear or defensiveness," when lost in the "fog" of our own "self-absorption." And yet—*given some mysterious mix of support, courage, and grace*—when we let go and open our heart, the sacred is suddenly revealed.

Such sensitive transpersonal contact can also transpire between people and the animate earth. "Sarah," a 33-year-old massage therapist, was blessed with an experience of the sacred while watching the sun set over a bay. Although the content is different, the structure of her experience is almost exactly the same as Joan's encounter with her boyfriend. "Early one evening," said Sarah, "I was sitting on the table watching the sky change colors while the sun set. . . . I guess it was like a meditation because . . . I allowed myself to be open to whatever was going to happen." As the sun was dropping below the horizon, glowing light started filling the sky: "red, orange, yellow, green, blue into violet." Soon, she said, "I felt as if the energy from my body was flowing out and I was getting energy back in from the light change. . . . I felt as though my energy was saturating the darkness and the energy was coming back from the darkness. . . . I felt as though I was blending with all things that are natural. Even though I still felt discrete . . . my whole being had come together with the simplicity and continuum of life. . . . I was boundaryless and expansive. . . . I wasn't separate. I didn't tread on it. I was part of it." At the "apex" of the experience, "I thought, 'Oh, I'm blending! . . . I don't end. There's no beginning and end to me. It's all continuous.' I was continuous. . . . It felt as though I had no real edge. I was just a continuum of everything else. . . . I am part of what is beyond my skin and it's a part of me and whatever else is in the room or in the universe is all just a part of me and I'm a part of it."

I was touched profoundly by the beauty of Joan and Sarah's stories, by the gratitude they both felt, and by their conviction that such precious experiences are always accessible but usually obscured by our fear-filled, ego-centered identity. Indeed, as Sarah passionately declared: "People have so much shit that they have to go through in order to see something. . . . [But in experiencing the sacred] all inhibitions were gone. I had given myself to the moment. . . . I was not caught in anything, any insecurities, or fears, or expectations. That was all gone. . . . I had this image of being . . . something inside of a rock case. And boom! Just everything fell off and there I was, exposed to it all!"

*"Shit." A "rock case." The "fog of my own self-absorption." These intense images are not depicting some extreme form of self-contraction and self-protection like often occurs in temporary reactions to acute trauma. Rather, they express—still quoting—the ordinary "insecurities, or fears, or expectations," "defensiveness," "impermeability," and feeling of being "separate" that comprise our conventional ego.*

All the work of this chapter brings us to a disquieting realization: *we presume our normal, supposedly separate, ego-centered identity and ways of being are life-enhancing, but they are actually life-diminishing*—for ourselves and for all our relations. Such exclusionary self-interest draws a tightly contracted circle around us, leaving merely an isolated, impoverished self in an impoverished world. We are chronically frustrated because happiness and fulfillment depend on the world cooperating with our ego and granting its wishes. But such an ego project is doomed to fail because the world often does not comply! Not only are we still unhappy, but we have missed the opportunity to bring care and life to others. In this way, settling for an egoic identification is doubly problematic. But we need not settle. An exclusively ego-centered self-sense is certainly not an absolute given of our existence but the most fundamental form of what Blake (1988) called "mind-forg'd manacles" (p. 27). "It is a delusion that the self is so separate and fragile that we must delineate and defend its boundaries, that it is so small and so needy that we must endlessly acquire and endlessly consume, and that it is so aloof that as individuals, corporations, nation-states, or species, we can be immune to what we do to other beings" (Macy, 1991, p. 187). As long as this coexistential fact is left undiscovered, we will feel unconsciously compelled to keep forging egoic manacles. But when we intuit that such self-contraction is imprisoning us and afflicting others, we also intuit a heartfelt path of liberation, love, and justice.

*There is a life beyond ego.*

Chapter Six

# No Longer I

## Christian Mysticism, Self-Surrender, and Transpersonal Realization

G-d is one; and you shall love G-d with all your heart and with all your soul and with all your mind and with all your strength. . . . You shall love your neighbor as yourself.

—Jesus Christ (Mark 12:28–31)

In this breakthrough, I know that I and God are one.

—Meister Eckhart (1980, p. 218)

It is no longer I who live, but it is Christ who lives in me.

—Saint Paul (Galatians 2:20)

## Overture

Letting go of our tight grip on the supposedly separate ego as our exclusive identification, we discover a transpersonal life that is infinitely deep, open, free, and dynamically inter-responsive. Living from our depths, love and wisdom flow more freely and fully to all our relations, human and more-than-human. This chapter explores the Christian mystical version of this archetypal human process and demonstrates its relevance for ecopsychology.

## Transpersonal Realization in Mystical Christianity

Wise ones across the ages have affirmed that there is an infinitely deep life and self beyond our ego. This is a heartening reminder, a precious invitation and opportunity, and a profound ethical imperative and responsibility. I state this ardently because we will remain driven by subtle feelings of paranoia and greed as long as we presume ourselves to be a sovereign ego separate from all others. Clinging defensively to a contracted sense of self, we deprive ourselves of the psychospiritual nourishment offered by others, the natural world, and our own trans-egoic depths. And we deprive all our relations of the care we could otherwise offer.

Clearly, we need to find ways of transforming this normal yet afflictive state of affairs. But what does this healing step consist of? What does it mean to awaken from our fantasy of separation? What does it mean to transcend our conventional ego, to realize our true self or essential nature, to live more deeply, intimately, lovingly? These subtle questions have long been addressed by the world's spiritual and philosophical traditions, especially in their mystical, contemplative versions. More recently the field of transpersonal psychology has taken up this timeless inquiry. Most basically, transpersonal psychology explores modes of consciousness and ways of being-with-others that flow from sources beyond the ego. As Stanley Krippner puts it, "Transpersonal psychology is commonly defined as one that examines states of consciousness and stages of human development that go beyond the bounds of the self as normally defined, as well as the aspirations and paths of practice directed at transcending the conventional 'I'" (Friedman & Hartelius, 2013, p. xvii). Unfortunately, prior to the emergence of transpersonal studies, these profound dimensions of human existence were incomprehensible to the major schools of psychology. If not simply ignored, they were often deemed pathological (as will be evident later in Freud's views).

This chapter will draw out the transpersonal (eco)psychology that is implicit in the mystical tradition of Christianity.[1] Throughout its history, transpersonal psychology has been most influenced by Asian spirituality, with Buddhism being especially prominent. Thanks to people like Thomas Merton, Howard Thurman, Martin Luther King Jr., Thomas Keating, David Steindl-Rast, Matthew Fox, Cynthia Bourgeault, James Finley, Richard Rohr, and Pope Francis, the contemplative wisdom of Christian mysticism has been introduced into our larger society. But Christian perspectives have been significantly underrepresented in transpersonal psychology. This chapter is a small contribution toward addressing this gap.

Given our critical discussion in chapter 4, it may seem odd to welcome Christianity as an ally for ecopsychology. This is a tradition whose sacred text begins with a "God" who authorizes humans to subdue and have dominion over all other living beings; a "God" who demonizes the rest of nature by making a snake into a manipulative villain who arranges humans' (supposed) fall from grace; a "God" who retaliates punitively against the snake, and against Adam and Eve for eating a piece of fruit (Genesis 1:28, 3:1–22). Speaking humorously about these serious problems, the Zen scholar D. T. Suzuki remarked: "God against Man. Man against God. Man against nature. Nature against Man. Nature against God. God against nature—very funny religion!" (Campbell, 1988, p. 56). I share these concerns. Yet the authentic Christian mystical tradition tells a very different story, thereby offering real resources for ecopsychology.

The most famous example of a transpersonal realization, at least in the Western world, actually comes from Christianity. I am referring to Jesus Christ's awakening to his nondual union with and supreme identity *as* G-d. In his renowned testimony, "My Father [G-d] and I are one" (John 10:30). Of course, kindred teachings are found across the various spiritual traditions. Here is a classic Hindu version: "An invisible and subtle essence is the Spirit of the whole universe. That is Reality. That is Truth. THOU ART THAT [YOU ARE THAT!]" (Mascaró, 1965, p. 118; *Chandogya Upanishad*, 6:12–14). These cherished teachings point to the heart of contemplative spirituality: I consciously realize that I am inherently one with the ultimate mystery that we call G-d (or Brahman, the Dao, being, life), that I am a distinctive expression of that very mystery. Compassion and love spring forth naturally from this realization.

The great Christian mystics—starting with Christ—emphasize that such transformative discoveries are not limited to the historical Jesus. Thus does Christ pray: "May they *all* be one. As you, Father, are in me and I am in you" (John 17:20–23). While Jesus was unique in many ways, the capacity to consciously realize one's divine, transpersonal nature is not one of those. Rather, the Christian mystics insist that wakeful union with G-d is everyone's birthright and developmental possibility. A little story makes this point with an amusing twist. William Blake (1946) was once asked about "the imputed Divinity of Jesus Christ. He answered: 'He is the only God'—but then he added—'And so am I and so are you'" (p. 680). One of the most esteemed of all mystics was Meister Eckart, a fourteenth-century German theologian/philosopher. Like Christ, Eckhart (1980) speaks of breaking through all narrow, ego-centered notions of who we are, proclaiming that "in this breakthrough, I know that I and God are one" (p. 218).

Similarly, Marguerite Porete (1993)—a medieval mystic whose writings likely influenced Eckhart—takes up Christ's spiritual summons in a most radical way. Offering an extraordinary contemplative dialogue between "Love" and "the Soul" (or we could say the transpersonal self), Porete passionately celebrates our deep spiritual identity with G-d: "I am God, says Love, for Love is God and God is love, and this Soul is God by the condition of Love" (p. 104). She continues, "Such a Soul . . . is so enflamed in the furnace of the fire of Love that she has become properly fire, which is why she feels no fire [separate from her true self]. For she is fire in herself through the power of Love who transforms her into the fire of Love" (p. 107). With appreciation, let me paraphrase Porete's contemplative testimony. G-d, love, and fire are different names for the one great unnamable dynamic mystery. Correspondingly, the soul is graced with a crucial transpersonal discovery: G-d-love-fire, this is what I am. Love—that is to say, G-d—transforms me into love. More precisely, love allows me to become aware that I am always already love. And my loving responses to others (and indistinguishably to G-d) follow freely.

Eerily, Porete wrote the preceding passage when the Inquisition was executing supposed heretics at the stake. Women with mystical sensibilities were special targets. Staying true to her realization even after being accused of heresy and knowing her likely fate, Porete was burned alive in Paris in 1310. Eyewitnesses reported that she remained completely peaceful during the horrific event, bringing tears to those watching (Sells, 1994). Porete spoke of becoming fire itself, love itself. As evidenced by her composure, I would say she also became peace itself: "the peace of God, that surpasses all understanding" (Saint Paul, Philippians 4:7). This is fiercely tragic evidence for the transformative power of a contemplative existence (although, had she screamed and cried, her deep transformation would not have been diminished).

This is a life open to each of us, as our ever-present nature and our engaged responsibility. As Saint Paul avows, the discovery of such a transpersonal way of being is a (co)existential opportunity for every single person: "We have the mind of Christ" (1 Corinthians 2:16); "Let the same mind be in you that was in Christ Jesus" (Philippians 2:5). Let us awaken in us the same consciousness, self-sense, and way of relating with others that Christ realized. Thomas Merton (1953) offers a more recent version in this poetic prayer: "Thou in me and I in Thee and Thou in them and they in me: dispossession within dispossession, dispassion within dispassion, emptiness within emptiness, freedom within freedom. I am alone. Thou art alone. The Father and I are One" (pp. 361–362). To let go and allow our ego-self to be dispossessed, to become aware of our transpersonal union with G-d (or life, if you prefer), and to relate wisely and compassionately by way of this realization: this is the great mystical invitation, a call that is sent to everyone continuously (whether or not we couch it in religious language).

One of the most eloquent contemporary authorities on mystical Christianity is James Finley, a clinical psychologist, spiritual director, and former novice monk under Merton at the Abbey of Gethsemani. In his exquisite book *Christian Meditation*, Finley (2004) tells us: "In this mystical realization of oneness with God we are liberated from our tendencies to derive our security and identity from anything less than God. [Especially from our supposedly separate self and the objects of its cravings.] In specifically Christian terms, we enter the mind of Christ, who realized oneness with God to be the reality of himself and everyone and everything around him" (p. 17). The contemplatives urge us to discover that such nondual oneness is the actual ever-presencing fact of everyone's existence. Thus the great sixteenth-century Spanish mystic Saint John of the Cross attests, "Union between God and creatures always exists" (1991, p. 163). Similarly, Zen master Dōgen (2012) affirms that there really is "nothing lacking" (p. 7) in our self and life: "Know that fundamentally you do not lack unsurpassed enlightenment, and you are replete with it continuously. But you may not realize It" (p. 10). Indeed, for most people most of the time, the reality of this dynamic oneness operates unconsciously. Yet conscious awareness makes a tremendous difference in terms of our well-being and ethical engagement. Intrinsically, everything and everyone is an expression of a single seamless mystery. Therefore, each of us is always already one with the one great life (G-d, in Christian terms). This is a completely evident ontological fact that does not require religious language or affiliation. What is required, the mystics say, is *ongoing experiential verification, clarification, and relational actualization* of this core existential truth. Saint Catherine of Genoa (1989), an Italian mystic who lived from 1447 to 1510, states it quite powerfully: "My *self* is God. . . . My being is God, not by participation only but by a true transformation and annihilation of my proper being" (p. 46).

I am sure Saint Catherine knew that it sounds strange, even heretical, to claim that "my self is G-d." But to be clear, it is *not* that

I—exclusively, as an isolated ego—am G-d. That belief would comprise a psychotic delusion of grandeur, or self-satisfied narcissism in a spiritual guise. Rather, my finite self is a unique incarnation, expression, or mode of the infinite, all-inclusive, all-pervading reality of G-d. *I am never detached from or other than this one great dynamic nondual reality.* G-d precedes, exceeds, and thoroughly permeates me. Finley (2004) stresses this key point: "We are given to realize that although we are not God, neither are we other than God" (p. 51). Similarly, Christ depicts our nondual union by way of a metaphor borrowed from the natural world. (Please appreciate that when Christ says "I" he means G-d, because he is speaking from his deepest transpersonal identity, not from his small ego-centered self.) Thus he proclaims, "I [G-d] am the vine, you are the branches" (John 15:5). In contemplating this image, notice that each particular branch is an *inseparable manifestation of the whole vine.* As it grows in its own distinctive way, every branch is a unique form that the vine is taking. Likewise, every encounter, person, and nonhuman natural phenomenon is one form that G-d is taking, a radiant theophany, a unique form of that which is ultimately formless. In the same way, everyone and everything is a unique form nature is taking.

The Christian mystical tradition insists that we all yearn to consciously realize our absolute union with G-d. Speaking intimately with G-d at the beginning of his early fifth-century *Confessions*, Saint Augustine (1997) says, "Our heart is unquiet [restless, without peace] until it rests in you" (p. 3). The great sixteenth-century Spanish Carmelite mystic Saint Teresa of Ávila (2007) agrees: "The soul will not be content with anything less than God" (p. 225). As we saw in chapter 5, when living from an ego-centered stance we are haunted by an anguishing sense of lack. This is a perpetual feeling that we and life itself are not good enough, that something is missing, that happiness depends on acquiring things that might fill the apparent dearth in our being. Yet, as Saint Teresa says, "Whoever has God lacks nothing: God alone is enough" (Vogt, 1996, p. 33). When we are aware that this great dynamic life completely embraces us, permeates us, in fact *is* us—is our true (transpersonal) self—then there can be nothing lacking. Otherwise, we are haunted by a feeling of deficiency. "For God made our hearts in such a way that only God will do. Or we might say infinite love made our hearts in such a way that only infinite union with infinite love will do" (Finley, 2004, p. 28). But misunderstanding the source of our nagging sense of insufficiency, we are compelled to self-aggrandizement by means of money, power, control, and so on. The fact that Finley interchanges G-d and love is immensely significant, and consonant with my invitation to play with substituting various names when exploring the lived reality of the mysterious word "G-d." The mystics perennially avow that "G-d is love" (1 John 4:8) and that conscious oneness with G-d naturally springs forth as love. "What a man takes in by contemplation, he pours out in love," says Eckhart (Aitken, 1984, p. 113).

We cannot actually *become* united with G-d or *achieve* oneness with G-d, because this notion presumes a real gap that needs to be overcome. But all such dualistic separation from G-d is illusory—we are always already one with G-d—just as our discontinuity from nature is illusory. Life simply asks that we open ourselves and consciously experience the "fullness of the divine mystery giving itself, whole and complete, in and as each thing that is, just as it is" (Finley, 2004, p. 161). Contemplative practice creates favorable conditions for discovering this *experientially*, time and again. Thus, "we meditate that we might realize that the present moment, in its deepest actuality, *is* the perfect manifestation of the mystery we seek. . . . The present moment, just as it is, manifests the mystery we call God" (Finley, p. 160).

Such teachings may appear astonishing. However, it is undeniable that we (and everyone and everything) are expressions of the holistic reality of the cosmos or nature itself—the reality the mystics call G-d. Consider the way a contemporary physicist puts it: "You are the universe pressing into an awareness of itself. . . . You *are* that star [i.e., the big bang or great flaring forth], brought into a form of life that enables life to reflect on itself. . . . We are the creative, scintillating, searing, healing flame of the awesome and enchanting universe" (Swimme, 1984, pp. 132, 59, 171).[2] Unconscious union in the great mystery is the condition of everyone and everything. But intimately felt awareness of this is something else. That we are graced with the capacity for awakening to this is quite profound. That we rarely actualize it is a grievous thing.

The mystics insist that humans cannot overcome a (supposed) separation from G-d because, being a particular form of G-d's infinite presencing, we are never separate from G-d in the first place. Likewise, humans cannot overcome a (supposed) separation from nature because we *are* a particular expression of nature. Each of us individually, and our species as a whole, *is* nature appearing in human form. What needs to be surpassed—what must be released to heal our eco-catastrophe—is the constructed, affectively charged *sense* of separation. Merton (1961) warns of the dangers of living from "the assumption that my false self, the self that exists only in my own egocentric desires, is the fundamental reality of life to which everything else in the universe is ordered" (p. 35). The Buddha and Christ also addressed this concern, so it seems people have long struggled with such a contracted self-sense. But modernity consolidated the skin-bounded, sovereign, self-possessed ego as our exclusive, taken-for-granted identity. Stuck there, we are doomed to discontent, left anxious and frustrated we cannot manipulate the world to match our wishes.

## Oneness, Union, Nonduality

The spiritual language of "oneness," "union," and "nonduality" calls for clarification. First, notice that ordinary living is actually nondual (nonseparate). In drinking coffee or tea, nothing in my experience resembles this: "I am over here and that cup is over there. So I as a separate subject need to grab that separate object and take drink." Rather, in a seamless spontaneous flow, the cup beckons my hand and I lift it to my lips and enjoy the rich taste. When, instantaneously, I see a glowing autumn leaf I am not conscious of my self looking at something beautiful. Rather, what is given in direct awareness is something like: "Ahhh!!"—just pure beauty, wonder, joy. Like one Zen teacher exclaimed, "When I heard the temple bell ring, suddenly there was no bell and no I, just sound" (Haku'un Yasutani Rōshi, in Kapleau, 1980, pp. 113–114).

Approaching nonduality in another way, consider that Moses and Jesus Christ both proclaim that "G-d is one" (Deuteronomy 6:4; Mark 12:29). This classic affirmation has often been taken up in crude, childish, oppressive, tribalistic ways, as in: "There is only one real God, and (of course) my God is better than your God!" However, the mystics offer an immensely clearer and more loving view: *there can only be one all-inclusive reality or being or life: the wholeness of all that is, the totality of the cosmos—manifest and unmanifest—in its integral dynamic functioning.* Christian contemplatives refer to this all-encompassing, all-pervading reality as "G-d." Thus, nothing can be other than, excluded from, or outside of G-d. There is only one: "One without a second," as the Hindu *Upanishads* say of Brahman (Easwaran, 1987, p. 183; *Chandogya Upanishad* 6.2.2). In fact, "the one" is another classic name for the great infinite mystery. And "the many"—all the various particular participants in the shared earth community—are different expressions of "the one." The contemplative critique of *dualism* is more precisely a critique of *separatism.* In mystical language, oneness and nonduality mean *not two separate, independently existing things*: self versus others, self versus G-d, humans versus nature, mind versus body, and so on. In nondual experience there is no sense of a subject-object severance or dissociation. Yet nondual union does not sweep away difference, multiplicity, and interrelationship. "The one" and "the many" are identical in their depths, simply different faces of G-d. All of earth's singular participants are seamlessly involved with each other in the all-inclusive, ultimate mystery. Their inter-responsive relationship with each other is how the one grand life shows itself and freshly recreates itself.

Mystical oneness has another, complementary meaning: sameness that includes difference. Think of how our body is made up of different constituents: hands and eyes, heart and lungs, blood and bone, and so on. Every single one has its own distinctive function, while all the constituents work together in an integrated way. Now, the very same life, energy, spirit, or love that comprises and courses through our heart is also comprising and coursing through our hands and eyes. Likewise, the same life-energy-spirit-love is animating every person, nonhuman animal, plant, stone, cloud, mountain, house. Swimme (1984) offers a scientific (and mystical) description of this dynamic, many-formed, cosmic oneness: "Everything that exists in the universe came from a common origin. . . . This universe is a single multiform energetic unfolding of matter, mind, intelligence, and life" (p. 28). Likewise, in a classic nondual metaphor, G-d is a vast ocean and each individual (human or otherwise) is a particular wave. Each wave can be distinguished from every other wave and from the rest of the ocean; and each wave is always a *particular embodiment of the one unified ocean.* Individual waves and the whole ocean itself are all equally water, all equally saturated with the divine.

## Letting the Names of G-d Work in the Service of Nature

I hope it is beginning to be clear how contemplative spirituality is relevant for ecopsychology. From a Christian perspective, mystics invite us to go beyond merely learning *about* spiritual matters secondhand and from a distance; beyond hearsay or intellectualization only; beyond relying only on texts, teachers, and preachers; beyond clinging to our sedimented sense of self, world, nature, and G-d; and beyond waiting for fulfillment, awakening, and liberation to occur later, after we die, in some imagined otherworldly heaven. Accordingly, they invite us into a direct experiential discovery of G-d's presencing and love in and as our very self and life. We embody this as engaged loving care for our fellow companions—human and more-than-human—who are equally the very presencing of G-d. The basic analogy between Christian mysticism and transpersonal ecopsychology comes from this realization.

Surpassing our felt-sense of separation from the rest of nature (or seeing it was illusory all along), and thereby responding in the service of others: this is the core aspiration of ecopsychology. Essentially, this is the core aspiration of contemplative life as well. In liberating ourselves from the felt-sense of separation from G-d and our neighbors, we become more understanding and loving with all our relations. And our other-than-human companions must be included as neighbors. Transpersonal ecopsychology encourages us to discover our inherently indivisible union (and in fact, identity) with something that goes infinitely deep, namely, the animate, sapient earth (and all-inclusive cosmos). So too do Christian contemplatives encourage us to discover our indivisible union (and identity) with something that goes infinitely deep, namely, G-d. Some Christian mystics explicitly affirm our analogous union with the infinite depths of nature. Thus, in one ecstatic writing after another, John Muir (2013) celebrates his "unconditional surrender to Nature" (p. 90).

The mystics—and indeed, life itself—call upon us to embrace our union with G-d, and to live and love accordingly. But what does oneness with G-d actually mean? This is impossible to say, because whatever the word G-d intimates is ultimately unsayable, inconceivable, ungraspable. "If you comprehend it, it is not God," as Saint Augustine cautions.[3] Nonetheless, it can be helpful to say the unsayable in order to initiate further experiential inquiry and discovery. As I discussed in the introduction, G-d is a classic name for _____. Well, as you see, any term, characteristic, quality, concept, image, or description I could place in the blank is inadequate. *That is, it is inadequate if I am trying to name a particular referent.* However, rather than presuming the word "G-d" represents something objective or definitive, what if we *allow the ancient sacred word to act on us generatively, thereby sponsoring a fresh new experience?* For example, we could say that G-d is a time-honored name for the true nature of the very presencing that is transpiring right here and now, say the sound of rain falling; and, identically, for the dynamic depths of life, for the one great mysterious reality, all-inclusive and all-pervasive.

Yet when we dare to invoke any name for the ultimately unnamable, to suggest any quality of the unqualifiable, it is important to remember the spiritual traditions' warning against idolatry. No reified attribution or identification will ever do. That's why contemplative teachers humbly attest that the absolute mystery is *not this, not that: neti, neti* (as in the Sanskrit saying). Sometimes the Christian mystics make the startling proclamation that G-d is "nothing"—no thing, no definite, objectifiable, separable thing. In this spirit, Meister Eckhart (2009) confronts us with a challenge: "If God is neither goodness nor being nor truth nor one, what then is He? He is pure nothing: he is neither this nor that. If you think of anything He might be, he is not that" (p. 287). Still, as we will see in our discussion of love, the apophatic avowal of nothingness (no-thing-ness) is far from nihilistic. Thus, from Advaita Vedanta, the nondual school of Hinduism, Nisargadatta Maharaj offers one of the most beautiful formulations that has ever come my way: "When I look inside and see that I am nothing, that's wisdom. When I look outside and see that I am everything, that is love. Between these two my life turns" (Loy, 2015, p. 54).

Since no single meaning is sufficient (for G-d or nature or our deepest self), nor even all qualities in total, the mystics often work provisionally with several meanings, contemplating and articulating them in a dynamic, mutually complementary and supplementary way. We just heard Eckhart proclaim that G-d is pure nothing. Yet he also says, "God is life" (1980, p. 89) and "God is like nothing so much as being" (p. 84). Life, love, being, presence, reality, awareness, spirit, the infinite, the cosmos, the way, nature: all these are potentially felicitous metaphors for G-d. Turned the other way, G-d is a potentially felicitous metaphor for each of these.

We can carry our meditations further by pondering a famous image that has been embraced by sages across history: *G-d or nature or the cosmos is a sphere whose center is everywhere and whose circumference is nowhere.* This metaphor can be traced back to ancient Greek authors such as Hermes Trismegistus (ca. second century CE) and Empedocles (fifth century). Later it was esteemed by diverse writers including Giordano Bruno, Blaise Pascal, Voltaire, Arthur Schopenhauer, Ralph Waldo Emerson, and others (Small, 1983). Keeping alive a potentially generative slippage among classic names for the one great mystery, consider three versions of the recurring formulation. "We can securely declare that the universe is all center, or that the universe's center is everywhere and the circumference is nowhere" (Bruno, in Small, 1983, p. 96). "[Nature] is an infinite sphere whose center is everywhere and circumference nowhere" (Pascal, in Small, 1983, p. 96). And Emerson speaks of the "nature of God as a circle whose center is everywhere, and its circumference nowhere" (Small, 1983, p. 93). We can connect these affirmations with a revealing proclamation from Christ: "It is I who am the All. . . . Split a piece of wood, and I am there. Lift up the stone, and you will find me there" (Gospel of Thomas 77, in Robinson, 1977, p. 126). Imagining G-d as a boundless omnicentered sphere can foster an intuition of G-d as the dynamic totality of reality. Coupled with Christ's remark, we can realize this infinite reality is centered in and coming forth as every single participant and relational encounter: a piece of wood, a stone, a hornet's sting, a hug, reading these very words.

All of these suggestions can sponsor a lived sense that G-d is everywhere and nowhere—*nowhere exclusive, limited, objective, or fixed*. Thus did Saint Augustine (1997) pray: "O God, most high, most deep, and yet nearer than all else, most hidden yet intimately present . . . you are everywhere, whole and entire in every place, but confined to none" (p. 100). In fact, the mystics insist that nothing at all could possibly be excluded from G-d. Stated affirmatively, *everything* is necessarily and inextricably included. (How could anything be excluded from an infinite sphere?) Raindrops and fireflies and global warming and you and me, for example, must be involved in the sacred depths of life. In just the same way, since "G-d is one"—nondual, one without a separate second—nothing at all could possibly be other than, outside of, or dissociated from G-d (even if things appear otherwise). "Whatever is one, from that all that is other has been removed" (Eckhart, 2009, p. 287). Thus, when splitting a piece of firewood, lifting a river stone, planting a spinach seed, listening to the wind, talking with you, being myself: I discover G-d right there. In this realization, every particular presence shows itself as the living center of G-d. Correspondingly, every particular one—as the dynamically centered body of G-d—radiates out inter-responsively, infinitely, with no circumference. Thus we can realize our union with G-d in any moment of conscious contact. Herein, our existence is theo-centered or eco-centered, depending on how we want to describe it. From a transpersonal perspective, these are equivalent and interchangeable. In contrast to any reified dogma, the center is not preestablished, fixed, or static but always emerging freshly in every relational encounter. A life guided by such awareness is radically different than one (mis)guided by our supposedly sovereign, self-interested ego.

## Nature as the Embodiment of G-d

"In the beginning was the Word [*Logos*] . . . the Word was God. . . . The Word became flesh" (John 1:1, 14). This famous Gospel passage is conventionally read as a reference to the incarnation of Christ: G-d—as the formless transcendent "Word" (*Logos*)—becomes immanently embodied in and *as* a particular human being, the historical Jesus. This interpretation certainly holds true from a mystical perspective. Yet the mystics go further and add a radical supplement. Seen through contemplative consciousness, *the whole world and every single participant in it is the body of G-d.*[4] Thus Eckhart (1980) attests, "God is equally in all things and in all places. . . . The one who knows God best is the one who recognizes him equally everywhere" (p. 139). This realization is open for everyone, yet it requires that we see in ways that are far deeper than our egoic consciousness. The challenge, as Blake (1988) says, is that conventionally "man has closed himself up, till he sees all things thro' narrow chinks of his cavern" (p. 39). But there is a marvelous alternative: "If the doors of perception were cleansed every thing would appear to man as it is: infinite" (p. 39). And Blake was clear about the spiritual significance of this transformative shift in consciousness: "He who sees the Infinite in all things sees God" (p. 3). By way of deep, intimate perception, *everything*—the squirrel outside our window, the distant coral reef, the single mother and her hungry children—everything is revealed to be infinite, indeed, to be the infinite incarnated. And "the infinite" is a classic metaphor for G-d, the precious sacred one we are called to love, to love in the multifarious forms of each and all our neighbors. Thus the feminist theologian Sallie McFague (1993) poses a core question:

> What if we dared to think of our planet and indeed the entire universe as the body of God? . . . We might begin to see (for the first time, perhaps) the marvels at our feet and at our fingertips: the intricate splendor of an Alpine forget-me-not or a child's hand. . . . We might realize what

this tradition has told us, although often shied away from embracing unreservedly: we live and move and have our being *in* God. We might see ourselves and everything else as the living body of God. (pp. 19, 132)

Likewise, Hafiz sings, "there is just one flesh to wound [or care for], and it is His—the Christ's, our Beloved's" (Ladinsky, 2002, p. 159). Rather than a collection of physical objects to be exploited by a separate self, what if we really did see the earth as the sacred body of G-d? What if, through a reliable, consistent mode of (transpersonal) consciousness, this was the reliable, consistent way the natural world spontaneously appeared to us? What if, perceiving from the depths of our self, the depths of life were opened to us, and our responses followed accordingly? *When we see G-d in nature, in the face of our fellow humans, and in our own deep heart, then what? The mystics give one preeminent answer: We respond with love, quite naturally and spontaneously.* Thus, when the planet is dangerously overheated, when a person is attacked because of the color of their skin or their sexual orientation, when a mountain range is annihilated for coal and profit, we know the tangible body of G-d is being assaulted. When an endangered species is saved or a hungry person fed or a meadow preserved instead of bulldozed for commercial development, the tangible body of G-d is nurtured. "Truly I tell you," says Christ, "just as you did it to one of the least of these who are members of my family, you did it to me" (Mathew 25:40). To G-d. Along with all oppressed peoples today, our neighbors in the natural world must be included among the "least."

As we are seeing, there is significant overlap between a family of time-honored sacred words, especially G-d and nature. I am not proposing a simple equation of G-d and nature, even when we agree that the nature we are speaking of is not merely the physical or biological world. (Adopting a nondual mystical perspective, there is no such thing as mere materiality or biology. From so-called gross forms like boulders to subtle forms like thrush-songs and dreams and air, everything is saturated with spirit, is G-d made manifest.) Without claiming they are identical, I would like us to keep open the ambiguity and the potential for interchange and provisional substitution between words such as G-d, nature, buddha-nature, the Dao, the way, being, presence, reality, love, and life. This invitation comes from my desire to see what new understandings and creative, compassionate actions can be released by the interplay between such words. As a key case in point, seeing the natural world as the body of G-d calls forth a profoundly different response than seeing it as a stockpile of resources.

## No Longer I:
## Ego-Death, Self-Surrender, Self-Realization

Anxious about death in the future and not feeling real and secure in the present, the ego strives to master and control the world. But an ego-centered way of being is not our only option. Suffering points the way beyond suffering—if, that is, we can stay aware and sustain contact rather than resorting to defensive fortification and self-aggrandizement. The challenge is getting out of our own way. Merton often emphasized that there is no actual barrier to realizing our union with G-d. Rather, "The obstacle is in our 'self,' that is to say in the tenacious need to maintain our separate, external, egotistic will. It is when we refer all things to this outward and false self that we alienate ourselves from reality and from God" (Merton, 1961, p. 21). This mistaken identity generates paranoia and greed, and the natural world is turned into an alien threat or a corporate supermarket. Alternately, by releasing our grip on the separate self, the separate self's grip on us is released. Although we can let go in any moment, this is far from easy because we are fiercely attached to our sedimented self-identification—to reified concepts and images of who we are—and the ways of being that follow. Fortunately, the Christian mystics are experienced guides along this transpersonal path. They invite us into a radical metanoia, a profound turning of our consciousness and self-sense wherein we release into our transpersonal heart-mind. We are not who we ordinarily think we are, so the contemplatives teach. Who we really are is infinitely deeper than *any* self-defining notion, much less a contracted, ego-centered one. But realizing this involves surrendering or "dying to" or transcending our conventional identification with our "false" separate self and thereby opening to our true self, true nature, divine nature—the one nature that is always infinitely open, complete, lacking nothing, freely functioning.

Well before his death on the cross, Jesus had already surrendered his small, contracted identity and realized his supreme identity to be no other than the great way of G-d. Thus he avowed: "My teaching is not my own. It comes from the one who sent me. . . . Whoever speaks on their own does so to gain personal glory" (John 7:16–18). Christ knew that there is really no such thing as speaking or acting totally on one's own, as a completely independent self. I imagine that he felt his every word and action flowing from an infinite source, from G-d and G-d's will, yet inflected responsively and responsibly through his uniquely irreplaceable self. Similarly, after sharing a last supper with his disciples Jesus went with them to a cherished place in nature, the garden of Gethsemane at the foot of the Mount of Olives. Aware that grave danger was imminent, he knelt down to pray: "O Father, if you are willing, remove this cup from me . . . . . . yet, not my will but yours be done" (Luke 22:42). I added the extended ellipsis to distinguish the initiation of this transformative event from its culmination; and to highlight a key moment, Jesus' pregnant contemplative pause in between. Fear and doubt understandably arose when he sensed that he would die very soon. Jesus was human, after all. The wishes of *Jesus as an individual ego* are indicated by the phrase "my will." From this stance, he asked G-d to spare him the impending ordeal. But in the midst of this anguish, by way of a meditative opening of consciousness, he surrendered his own willfulness to the transpersonal will of G-d.

It is not that Jesus released his ego-centered wishes and was thereby freed forever. Transpersonal transformation rarely if ever happens that way, even for Christ. Instead, life asks us to let go again and again, in circumstance after circumstance. Soon after the aforementioned events, Jesus was arrested and condemned to be crucified. In agony on the cross, near death, Jesus' separate self-sense surged up again. He cried out, "My God, my God, why have you forsaken me?" (Matthew 27:46). But then, surrendering his resistance (once again) and confiding himself into a mystery infinitely beyond his control, he openly avowed: "Father, into your hands I commend my spirit" (Luke 23:46). Jesus' supposedly self-sufficient ego is released, his last breath is released, and he dies. Yet we know that the Christian story continues beyond this moment. When read psychologically, Christ's death and resurrection can be understood as an archetypal portrayal of the process of ego-transcendence. In other words, this crucial experience is not limited to Christ but is available for us all. Releasing into open awareness, we each may "die" to our exclusive identification as a merely ego-directed, skin-bounded self and be reborn as a transpersonal self. Christ emphasized this to his disciples, declaring that "whoever loses their life for my sake will find it" (Matthew 10:39). The word rendered as "life" is the Greek *psyche*, one's soul or self. Likewise, Saint Paul describes this death-and-rebirth metamorphosis: "It is no longer I who live, but it is Christ who lives in me" (Galatians 2:20).

In releasing our egoic self-representation and identity we release into a reality that goes infinitely deeper: G-d, in Christian terms. Herein, we discover a freer, more loving way of being. This timeless story—*experience*—is beautiful. But it is not immediately clear what it means to surrender one's own ego-centered self and to follow G-d's will instead. It is clear what it does not mean, however. (1) *We need not actually do away with our ego*—it was never a substantial reality in the first place—*but we do need to help it find its humble place within the infinite depths of our transpersonal self*. (2) "Ego strengths" (such as reason, memory, critical discernment, and personal agency) continue functioning as called for by our circumstances, but now they operate from a different ground: the groundless ground of G-d, life, or nature as it is appearing in and as our current experience and its relational summons. (3) Authentic psychospiritual release has nothing to do with masochistic submission to any authoritarian figure or organization. Since the mystics avow that "G-d is love," the experience of ego-transcendence is one of *surrendering to love*. Or to life. Or to nature. Or, quite tangibly, to the relational call of the presencing moment—to the fresh scent of a pine tree, or to the stench of an oil "spill." Indeed, to *free ourselves from* narcissistic attachment to our self-preoccupied ego and its fantasy of controlling the world *is to free ourselves for* wise, just, compassionate, and loving contact with others.

I hope this commentary is bringing the experience of self-surrender down to earth. These are not primarily theoretical points but nitty-gritty matters involving real suffering and health. Christ stated it with great urgency: "If you bring forth what is within you, what you bring forth will save you. If you do not bring forth what is within you, what you do not bring forth will destroy you" (Gospel of Thomas 70, in Pagels, 1998). Likewise, Goethe celebrated what he called our "holy longing" to let go of our self-preoccupied existence and awaken into union with the depths of life. Yet in doing so he offered a vivid warning: "So long as you haven't experienced this: to die and so to grow, you are only a troubled guest on the dark earth" (Bly, 1980, p. 70). Because the ego is ever haunted by the dread of death, the mystics offer a startling resolution: Go ahead and die! Christ may be the most renowned exemplar of this great metamorphosis, yet—because it is an archetypal human process—the same counsel is given across spiritual traditions. " 'Die before you die,' said the Prophet Muhammad" (quoted by Rabia of Basra [Sufi saint, ca. 717–801], in Ladinsky, 2002, p. 7).[5] And my Zen teacher states it acutely: "Die now! Be thoroughly dead, so that you may reemerge and live freely" (Bruce Harris, personal communication, May 2, 2020). This experience involves realizing that who we are goes infinitely deeper than our favored self-image. And with this discovery we consent to let go of our insistence that life conform to our will and wishes.

Elaborating on the Zen ethos of consenting to one's death and being reborn anew, Harris shares a revealing insight: "This is actually how reality is functioning all the time. The whole of existence is simultaneously dying and emerging freshly, right now. And you are that!" Each experience presents itself to us instantaneously. In no time that experience is gone and a fresh one arises. Such impermanent yet ever fresh presencing is occurring every moment. Consider an actual encounter with the natural world, say with a snake slithering next to my house. One sheer seeing-feeling flash: "Ah, what's that?!" Instantly that dies with the next new flash: "Wow, a big snake!" In this moment, as in all encounters, I can release myself into life's intrinsic death-and-rebirth process. Or I can resist and try to impose my egoic presumptions and preferences. By definition, I am seeing a "garter snake." But this quick conceptual categorization is crudely insufficient, hardly doing justice to this particular being and this particular relational event. If I do not let that static characterization perish and give birth to a new moment of seeing-feeling, then I will miss the actual relational contact (which really means missing out on my very life). Alternately, in some mysterious but completely ordinary way, when I do not stay stuck to my initial (but now dead) notion, when I let die what has already died anyway, when I confide myself into whatever is transpiring here and now, something new arises. "Oh my, the snake is eating a frog! Maybe he'll also catch some of those mice that keep coming into our house."

We also find the same ceaseless, dynamic, death-and-rebirth process when we turn to search for our self. In the encounter with the snake, where was my self? Who or what was I? Was I an egoic subject observing and analyzing things from a distance? No, not at all. That common contracted self-sense was totally gone, already released before I did anything. Was I my startled body? Not exactly. Was I my thoughts ("Garter snake!") or excited feelings ("Wow!")? Not exactly. To be honest, I can't really say who I was. But, to get close, I might venture that *I was the presencing and dying away of each single instant of the encounter*, full and complete for the time being. "You are that!" as Harris Rōshi proclaims. Really, even saying "I" is extra.

## Freud's Critique of Religion and a Transpersonal Critique of Freud

This discussion of ego-transcendence may be raising some concerns, and rightly so. "No longer I." "Not my will but yours." "Die!" The mystics claim that these experiences involve a psychospiritual transformation that is crucial for living well. But how can this be, since it seems to require that we give up ego capacities that are essential for human health, in particular our agency and personal power? Especially with forces of fascism resurging these days, why would we want to surrender our will to something beyond our self? Is this a form of childish dependency? Abdication of our real abilities and responsibilities? Passive submission to authoritarian powers? Even masochism?

Sigmund Freud raised similar concerns in his psychoanalytic critique of religion. I find it helpful to explore Freud's ideas because—up to a point—they exemplify truly liberating insights that arose in the modern era. However, I will also show how he grossly misunderstood the nature of mature transpersonal spiritual experience. Remedying this mistake is important for ecopsychology. When critiquing a theory—or when disagreeing with a friend—*our first move should be an effort to appreciate how what they are saying makes sense.* So we can begin by asking, "How was Freud right?" When Freud looked at the conventional versions of religion that were popular in his day—and are still prevalent—he saw people abdicating capacities that are crucial for mature healthy existence: reason, (relatively) autonomous self-direction, the ability to handle the inevitable pain in human existence, and the courage to be fully engaged in this one earthly life. These, he argued, are given up in favor of consolation from an illusory, anthropomorphic, fatherlike God who supposedly directs our lives from afar; who rewards and punishes us depending upon our behavior; and who promises a heavenly afterlife that is more real, happier, and everlasting. In 1927 Freud published a critical work entitled *The Future of an Illusion*, with religion being the so-called illusion. Freud saw religion as an irrational and self-constricting defense in the face of life's inevitable challenges, "born of the need to make human helplessness bearable, and constructed with the material of recollections of the helplessness of one's own childhood and that of the childhood of the human race" (2012, p. 83). Religious beliefs and practices reminded Freud of the avoidant neurotic fantasies he had seen in his analytic patients, and of the prerational magical thinking of children. The fact that Freud proclaimed himself a "completely godless Jew" (Meng & Freud, 1963, p. 63) added a personal intensity to his critique. He frequently spoke of religion with great derision. "Religious consolations can be likened to a narcotic" (Freud, 2012, p. 108), to "illusions" (p. 94), to "delusions" (p. 94), to a "childhood neurosis" (p. 111). Stated concisely, Freud deemed *all* religion to be pathological, immature, or regressive.

The only psychologically healthy alternative, according to Freud, consists of the hard work of psychological development and cultural transformation. (In my view he is right as far as he goes. But he does not go nearly far enough because he has no awareness of our authentic potential for transpersonal development.) "Is it not true that infantilism must be surmounted? . . . People cannot remain children forever; they must ultimately go out, into 'hostile life.' One may call this 'education to reality.' . . . One must depend on one's own strength" (Freud, 2012, p. 108). Herein he gives preeminent allegiance to what he calls "our God *Lógos*" (p. 111). In this case, *Lógos* means rational thinking. And Freud insists that "there is no higher court than the court of reason" (p. 91). Yet transpersonal/trans-egoic realizations—like being identified with the whole of nature while remaining my distinctive self—are *transrational* (but not irrational).

Magical, childlike views of G-d are common today. Even worse are rigidly hateful ones such as those justifying violence in the name of G-d. That's why Freud's insights remain directly relevant. However, he simply did not understand the transpersonal modes of consciousness and ways of being that are characteristic of the spiritual mystics. In his view, the most mature version of adult development is the emergence of a strong, relatively autonomous ego with firm self/other boundaries, an ego that uses reason to channel the id's primitive instinctual urges, negotiate the critical demands of the superego, and respond to the challenges of daily reality. While Freud is correct that infantilism must be surmounted, the contemplative traditions teach that eventually our exclusive identification with our ego has to be surmounted as well. Jack Engler (2003), a psychoanalytic psychotherapist and Buddhist teacher, puts the issue succinctly: "You have to be somebody before you can be nobody" (p.

35). He rightly emphasizes "the importance of being 'somebody'—that is, facing crucial developmental or life tasks head on instead of attempting to avoid them in the name of spirituality or enlightenment" (p. 36).[6] Consistent with our analysis in the previous chapter, Engler also celebrates "the importance of being 'nobody'—recognizing that the integration or enhancement of the self is at best a resting place, not the goal, that the experience of being or having a self is a case of mistaken identity, a misrepresentation born of anxiety and conflict about who I am" (p. 36). Transpersonal psychology, mystical experience, everyday contemplative life—and Freud's own observations on love—provide abundant evidence that we are endowed with deeper, trans-egoic potentials. It sounds odd, but the development of "ego strengths" helps us surpass our egoic insecurities, enabling us to surrender the excessive drive to aggrandize or defend our self-constricting ego, thereby opening to our transpersonal depths. Meditation practice actually cultivates such ego capacities while supporting growth beyond all separatist notions of our self. It is not these abilities that are transcended, but our small, fear-and-greed-driven, egoic self-representation.

Following the publication of *The Future of an Illusion*, Freud received a letter from Romain Rolland, a renowned French playwright, novelist, essayist, biographer, peace activist, art historian, musician, and Nobel Laureate in literature. Over the previous four years, through letters and occasional face-to-face meetings, the two men had developed a personal friendship filled with mutual respect. Rolland thanked Freud for his incisive analysis and said that he agreed with Freud's critique when applied to the most widespread versions of religion. Like Rolland, the mystics would concur with much of what Freud proposed even though he was speaking from the position of a modern atheist. The mystics certainly do not imagine G-d as a heavenly Santa Claus figure or omniscient behavioral psychologist who is watching to see if we are good or bad and dispensing positive reinforcement or punishment. Nietzsche (1974) famously proclaimed that "God is dead. . . . And we have killed him" (p. 181). Spiritual contemplatives agree in the following specific way: childish views of G-d need to die—to be outgrown and released—so as to enhance human empowerment and freedom. But the mystics go on to attest that the authentic mystery of G-d goes infinitely deeper.

Rolland encouraged Freud to recognize a mature form of spiritual experience not based upon childish fantasies, nor upon uncritical obedience to doctrine or church authority. He argued that this less common form was based upon direct experience, and was completely compatible with critical reason. He thus urged Freud to undertake a fresh "analysis of *spontaneous religious sentiment* or, more exactly, of religious feeling"—"totally independent of all dogma, all credo, all Church organization, all Sacred Books, all hope in personal survival, etc., the simple and direct fact of *the feeling of the 'eternal'* . . . simply without perceptible limits, and like oceanic" (Doré & Prévost, 1990, p. 86). Rolland considered this "'oceanic' sentiment" to be "the true subterranean source of religious energy" (p. 87). In contemplative literature spanning various traditions, the oceanic experience has long been a metaphor for relaxing one's self boundaries, surrendering one's egoic identification, and realizing one's identity with the divine depths of life. Each individual is a raindrop, a stream, or a wave who awakens in and *as* the infinite ocean, and who naturally responds in its loving service. In Hindu parlance, this is the conscious union of Atman and Brahman: "As the rivers flowing east and west / Merge in the sea and become one with it, / Forgetting they were ever separate rivers, / So do all creatures lose their separateness / When they merge at last into pure Being" (*Chandogya Upanishad* 6.10.1–2, in Easwaran, 1987, pp. 184–185). In Islam, this is the realized union of the self and Allah. (The word Islam means surrender.) As Rumi (1992) says: "Let the drop of water that is you / become a hundred mighty seas. / But do not think that the drop alone / becomes the Ocean— / the Ocean, too, becomes the drop!" (p. 149). In Christian mysticism, this is the conscious union of the self (or soul) and G-d. "The spiritual marriage . . . is like rain falling from the sky into a river or pool. There is nothing but water. It's impossible to divide the sky-water from the land-water. When a little stream enters the sea, who could separate its waters back again?" (Teresa of Ávila, 2003, p. 270). Such realizations are open for everyone, and the natural world is an auspicious context for their unfolding. In my study of the sacred in everyday life, Sarah's dualistic self-boundaries fell away upon being enamored by a lovely sunset: "I had become elastic or I was dissolving. I was a sugar cube in water. I was becoming a part of everything else."

Notice that the "oceanic feeling" derives from lived experiences in an actual ocean. Strangely, in all the commentaries I have read, I have never seen anyone discuss the natural world. But tangible contact with the ocean must have been the original, *experiential source* of this spiritual metaphor of union. Even now we can imagine—or recall—the sensation of our body being buoyed by the salty water as we are rocked gently by the waves on a sweet summer day. We can conjure up the sense of being held by the warm ocean and releasing into those pleasurable sensations. We can feel the usually firm boundaries between our self and the water relaxing and becoming permeable. We can enjoy the liberation that comes when the anxious tension of holding our self together as a separate ego disappears. And we can intuit an awakening into something immensely deep: the vast ocean—truly, an even deeper reality appearing as the ocean—revealed to be our transpersonal body or true self.

## Through and Beyond Freud's (Mis)Interpretation of Mystical Spirituality

Freud (2010) addressed Rolland's questions in his next cultural critique, *Civilization and Its Discontents*. He reports that a friend had written a letter asking him to study "the true source of religious sentiments . . . a feeling as of something limitless, unbounded—as it were, 'oceanic'" (p. 24); a "feeling of an indissoluble bond, of being one with the external world as a whole" (p. 25). Freud acknowledges that "I cannot discover this 'oceanic' feeling in myself" (p. 24). But he goes on to say that it "sounds so strange and fits in so badly with the fabric of our psychology that one is justified in attempting to discover a psycho-analytic—that is, a genetic [i.e., developmental]—explanation of such a feeling" (p. 26). Having no experiential access to the oceanic feeling, he claims he is justified in fitting it into psychoanalytic theory. This approach reminds me of Procrustes, a figure from Greek mythology who tortured visitors by making them fit precisely into his guest bed—cutting off their legs if they were too tall, pounding and stretching them with a blacksmith's hammer if they were too short! I believe Freud misunderstood the oceanic feeling partly because of the limits of his theory and method of inquiry, aggressively wielding psychoanalysis like a Procrustean bed; partly because transpersonal experience was foreign to his lived experience; and partly because he was so understandably troubled by life-diminishing effects of immature, defensive forms of religion that he could not bring himself to consider the possibility of mature, life-enhancing ones.

Reacting to Rolland, Freud proceeds forcefully with his psychoanalytic take on the oceanic experience. Discussing the self's permeable boundaries in this experience, Freud (2010) says, "Pathology has made us acquainted with a great number of states in which the boundary lines between the ego and the external world become uncertain or in which they are actually drawn incorrectly" (pp. 26–27). I know what Freud means. Once I met with a young man for a psychological assessment. After I introduced myself as Will Adams, the man called me "Bill" several times. I noted to myself that *his* name was Bill, but I also recognized the similarity between our names. A bit later I sneezed and he instantly responded, "Thank you." That surprised me because ordinarily he would say something like, "Bless you," to which *I* would reply, "Thank you." After an old radiator made the room quite hot, I took off my sweater. As I did so the man relaxed back into his chair and said, "Ah, that feels so much better." His self-boundaries were so extremely permeable that he could not discern the difference between his experience and mine, an experience that is rather common in schizophrenia. Apparently he felt a kind of "union" between the two of us. However, this was not a wakeful, transpersonal union, or even an ordinary empathic one, but a confused prepersonal fusion.

In reflecting on how the boundaries between self and world dissolve in the oceanic experience, Freud was also reminded of the fact that in our earliest experiences—in the womb, at the breast, throughout infancy and toddlerhood—the lived boundaries between self and others are very permeable. These experiences are characteristic of a prepersonal phase of development prior to the establishment of demarcated self-boundaries and a uniquely personal self-sense and worldview (Wilber 1977, 1980, 2000b; Washburn, 1995). As Freud (2010) tells us, "An infant at the breast does not as yet distinguish his ego from the external world" (p. 27). Imagine a baby who falls while learning to walk, but who suffers no injury in the process. For a moment she may not know how she feels or how to respond. If her well-intentioned parents overreact by lifting her up and wailing, "Oh no! Are you hurt my sweet one?," the baby will almost certainly begin wailing too. But if her parents lift her up and calmly say, "Oh, my sweet one, you had a little fall. It's OK. Let's walk some more," she will almost certainly become calm and ready to walk again. The boundaries between self and others are naturally porous at this stage, so it is difficult for her to distinguish between her direct experience and others' reactions. Across time it will be important for her to differentiate herself from others. In childhood and especially in adolescence this involves the construction of relatively firm ego boundaries but, quite crucially, not rigid ones that detach her from others.

With these clinical, developmental, and sociocultural issues in mind, Freud (2010) viewed religion with great scorn: "The whole thing is so patently infantile, so foreign to reality, that to anyone with a friendly attitude to humanity it is painful to think that the great majority of mortals will never be able to rise above this view of life" (p. 39). However, right in the midst of such harsh judgments, Freud makes a particularly significant observation. He begins by saying, "Normally, there is nothing of which we are more certain than the feeling of our self, of our own ego. This ego appears to us as something autonomous and unitary, marked off distinctly from everything else" (p. 26). But he then goes on to acknowledge—hesitantly and conflictedly—that our sense of being a separate autonomous ego is an illusion. He says that psychoanalytic work has revealed "that such an appearance is deceptive, and that on the contrary the ego is continued inwards, without any sharp delimitation, into an unconscious mental entity which we designate as the id" (p. 26). This is one way of reaffirming a key insight of psychoanalysis, that the conscious rational self we take for granted is actually not (all of) who we are. The self-reflective ego rests upon the depths of the unconscious. This includes the primordial id as well as aspects of the ego that function outside of awareness. As Freud rightly suggests, the psyche is unfathomably deep. But as an heir of Descartes' dualistic views, he insists on a necessary separation between self and world. The psychic depths celebrated by Freud go only one way, intrapsychically, into one's so-called interior. "But towards the outside . . . the ego seems to maintain clear and sharp lines of demarcation" (Freud, 2010, p. 26).

However, transpersonal (eco)psychology and contemplative spirituality demonstrate that boundaries between our self and the "outside" world are permeable in mature spiritual experience. Similarly, these traditions disclose psychic depths that extend "outwardly" into and throughout the world, including others and the whole shared earth community. As the Greek sage Heraclitus avowed, "You could never discover the boundaries of the psyche, even by traveling along every path, so deep is its *logos*" (see Haxton, 2001, p. 45).[7] Freud would not go nearly that far. Yet he does single out one major phenomenon that contradicts his theory. As much as he would like to hold on to the belief that self/other separation is an ontological necessity (except in infantile, regressive, or pathological cases), he admits that this strict claim breaks down in the face of lived experience. It does so due to the nature of a profound human phenomenon: *love*. "At the height of being in love the boundary between the ego and object threatens to melt away. Against all the evidence of his senses, a man who is in love declares that 'I' and 'you' are one" (Freud, 2010, p. 26). In moments of loving contact—be it intimate conversation, open perception, sexual intimacy, or otherwise—conventional boundaries become porous or fall away.

In interpreting—actually, *misinterpreting*—the oceanic feeling, Freud makes a peculiar move when he comes upon the profound reality of transpersonal versions of love. A hallmark of mystical experience is the realization of our inseparability from and deep identity with others, the world (including the natural world), and G-d or life itself. When Freud approaches this archetypal phenomenon by way of the oceanic experience, he is first reminded of infantile immaturity and psychopathology. *But he is also reminded of the loving union of two adults.* Elsewhere Freud (1964) wisely proclaimed that being loving is an essential quality of psychological health: "A strong egoism [i.e., genuine ego strength] is a protection against falling ill, but in the last resort we must begin to love in order not to fall ill, and we are bound to fall ill if . . . we are unable to love" (p. 85). And he emphasized that being well depends on actualizing our capacity "to love and to work" (Freud, in Erikson, 1980, p. 102). Therefore, one would hope that he would pause and think further about the analogy that he himself recognized: the deep affinity between intimate loving encounters and the oceanic feeling. But no. Following his appreciative remarks about love and open boundaries, Freud quickly dismissed such cherished experiences with no further comment and returned to a discussion of pathology in the very next sentence. Wilber (1983, 2000b) shows how such views are based upon a "pre/trans fallacy." That is, mature, healthy, transrational, transpersonal experiences are often reductively interpreted as immature, pathological, prerational, prepersonal, experiences.[8] Due to Freud's stature, his (mis)understanding ended up (mis)guiding psychology's assessment of transpersonal, mystical, and spiritual experiences for decades.

## From Supposed Separation to Union and Love

The fact that Freud initially caught the connection between transpersonal experience and love is significant, even though he immediately dismissed the insight. Indeed, the affinity between love and mystical experience is one of the core themes of the present book. It is impossible to say what G-d is. But one of the best contemplative offerings—not to represent

G-d but to evoke fresh experience—is the affirmation that "G-d is love" (1 John 4:8). Christ was once asked to name the most important commandment of all. This is a moment when one of history's most esteemed sages articulated his sense of what it is to live well, and he essentially said: Our life really comes down to love. "*G-d is one; and you shall love G-d with all your heart and with all your soul and with all your mind and with all your strength*. This is the first and greatest commandment. And there is a second one that is like it: *You shall love your neighbor as yourself*" (Jesus Christ, Mark 12:28–31). We have acknowledged that it is difficult to understand what it means to be one with G-d, or to let go of self-centered willfulness and follow G-d's will. Yet if we sense that G-d is love, then oneness with G-d must involve love. So too in following G-d's will. In her great mystical text *The Interior Castle*, Saint Teresa of Ávila (2003) elaborates on Christ's imperative. "On the spiritual path, the Beloved asks only two things of us: that we love him and that we love each other. . . . The most reliable sign that we are following both of these teachings is that we are loving each other. Although we might have some clear indications that we are loving God, we can't be sure that we really are, but it is obvious whether or not we are loving each other" (p. 140). What does it mean to love G-d? Teresa brings it right down to earth: loving our neighbor is loving G-d. Christ's two teachings are really different versions of a single ethical summons. *And it is far easier to love our neighbor when we are not totally identified with a small, supposedly separate, fear-driven self*. In the renowned Gospel passage we just considered, notice that the other whom we love is not really other, not really separate from us. Christ does not say that we should love our neighbor like we would love our presumably independent individual self. Rather, we love each neighbor *as* our self, as our true or transpersonal self. Identically, following the Christian mystics, this means loving G-d in the form of every relational partner we encounter, be they human or other than human. Thus does Mother Teresa of Calcutta (1997) describe the contemplative life: "We . . . are called to be contemplatives in the heart of the world by: Seeking the face of God in everything, everyone, all the time. . . . Seeing and adoring the presence of Jesus, especially in the lowly appearance of bread, and in the distressing disguise of the poor" (p. 33). "I see God in every human being. When I wash the leper's wounds I feel I am nursing the Lord himself" (Mother Teresa, in Kelly-Gangi, 2006, p. 19).[9]

It is relatively easy to love those who are close and familiar to us:

192 | A Wild and Sacred Call

family, friends, members of our tribe, and so forth. But Christ's ethical appeal is far more radical: to compassionately welcome "strangers" (Matthew 25:35) and to "love your enemies" (Matthew 5:43–48). In the spirit of this teaching, our neighbors comprise an all-embracing group—and the natural world must be included. Indeed, throughout history, the beings and presences of nature have been our cherished neighbors. Even with today's ecological desecration, the natural world can be seen as G-d in a distressing disguise. Thankfully, nature's splendor still remains as well.

Based upon experiential contemplative inquiry, the Christian mystics point out that there cannot be anything severed from, other than, outside of, or lacking in G-d. (What could be separate from or lacking in "the All?") They avow that G-d precedes, exceeds, and thoroughly permeates my individual being, so of course I am always connected with G-d. And they affirm that whatever the unfathomable mystery of G-d is, that is my supreme identity. This is true whether I realize it or not. But when I do realize it, a liberating reality is disclosed: my true self is intrinsically whole, complete, divine, lacking nothing. Correspondingly, I realize that I am participating in a sacred field of interrelationships. Thus, every participant in the field and the whole dynamic fellowship are likewise never other than G-d, indeed are the very presencing of G-d in and as everyday life. When things become clear in this deeply heartfelt way, the ego's anxious insecurity dissolves. Compassion and love spring forth in its place. Importantly, there is an ecopsychological analogy to what I have just articulated. Waking up to the reality of nature, I see that it always precedes, exceeds, and permeates me. As a vivid existential fact, I realize that I am (a particular incarnation of) nature. Herein, nature is my supreme identity. I know I am distinctively different from but surely not separate from the whole dynamic, inter-responsive, ecological field; different but not separate from the beings and presences who share this one earth with me and who, in their own wildly wondrous ways, are not other than the sacred presencing of life. Whether we couch it in spiritual language or not, this means that *an awakened consciousness is an ecological consciousness*. Whether invoking G-d or not, when we let go of our tightly contracted self, we can sense that we are rooted in a deep source of life and energy that we did not manufacture and that is naturally flowing through us. Opening in this way, we are free to live and love accordingly.

## "Who Am I?" Turns into "How Can I Be of Service?"

Just to be clear, so-called ego-transcendence does not mean getting out of this messy, challenging, impermanent, vulnerable, embodied life and into some supposedly better, heavenly realm rumored to exist *somewhere else*, say an imagined life after death. Granted, there are exclusively ascetic, ascendent, or transcendent spiritual schools that devalue our incarnate life and earthy world. But this is not at all what authentic nondual spirituality involves, nor what we are exploring in this book. Far more radically, surrendering our ego involves being carried beyond all self-centered contraction and into intimate involvement in this very life—embracing life in all its beauty and pain, yet with greater awareness, freedom, and love. After all, Christ insisted, "The kingdom of heaven is within you"; "The kingdom of heaven is among you" (Luke 17:21).[10] The "Kingdom of the Father is spread out upon the earth, but people do not see it" (Gospel of Thomas 113, in Pagels, 2003, p. 241). Why don't people see the sacred, precious, heavenly quality of this earthy life? Because we are usually looking through the lens of the apparently separate self. *The egoic mode of consciousness bends the divine rays of the world such that things appear merely as threats to our existence or as objective resources to exploit.* To realize heaven, then, we must transform our consciousness. "Ascending to heaven" does not mean moving to an "other world" somewhere else, but growing into a deeper (nondual) way of being, one that allows us to discover another world inside this earthly one, and thus to live with unreserved openness, intimacy, and compassion. Fortunately we do not have to go to some other place, because there is really nowhere else to go. And we do not have to wait until later, because the only time we can actually live and love is now.

"The Spiritual Canticle," by Saint John of the Cross, provides a beautiful example. This is a love poem to his beloved, G-d. Indistinguishably, it is a love poem to the natural world. "My Beloved, the mountains, / and lonely wooded valleys, / strange islands, / and resounding rivers, / the whistling of love-stirring breezes" (John of the Cross, 1991, p. 473). "These mountains *are* what my Beloved is to me. . . . These valleys *are* what my Beloved is to me" (p. 527, emphasis added). Mountains, woods, valleys, islands, rivers, breezes: via contemplative consciousness, Saint John knows these are G-d becoming flesh, G-d stirring his love. Welcomed by Saint John's mystical heart, the mountains are mountains, of course—but not merely objective, material, biophysical mountains.

(Really, there is no such thing as a merely biophysical object, so deep does everything go.) Standing in Saint John's place, we could say: (1) I see mountains (just a physical landscape over there, apparently separate from me); (2) No longer I, no longer mountains, no longer any subject-object severance, there is only G-d; (3) *I really see the mountains, appearing freshly and clearly as a form of my beloved G-d.* This corresponds to the Zen depiction of realization from chapter 1: first I see mountains; then the mountains and I disappear; eventually there are mountains anew, mountains as the very presencing of buddha, my own deepest self.

In our busy, fast, modern-turning-postmodern world, it may not be easy to hear the call to love G-d. But surely we can hear the earth calling for our care. This is true whether the summons is coming from climate emergency, mass extinction, and nature-deficit disorder; or from the beauty and wisdom of nature. Since, with the mystics, we are affirming that nature is the very presencing of G-d (or of transpersonal life, if you prefer); and since the natural world is severely wounded and asking for our care; then, from a contemplative perspective, we may hear nature's call as an appeal from G-d to love G-d. We may also feel grateful that nature (or life or love or G-d) has brought us into being—in fact, *is now* bringing or loving us into being—and thereby hear nature summoning us to respond with loving service. Felt and known deeply, these two perspectives are interchangeable. It all comes down to conscious love. "My sole occupation is love" (John of the Cross, 2007, p. 10). Explicating this expression, John remarks: "This refers to the soul's surrender of itself to the Beloved in this union of love, wherein it devotes itself with all its faculties . . . to His service" (p. 218).

This selfless sensibility is not just the domain of ancient saints. Upon watching myrtle warblers hunting insects one day, Merton felt a "sense of total kinship with them as if they and I were of the same nature, and as if that nature were nothing but love" (Deignan, 2003, p. 110). He could have equally used the word G-d for that "same nature," because his writings repeatedly avow that "G-d is love." This takes us to a vital contemplative point. No one can know G-d objectively, because G-d is not an object. Rather, the mystics know and love G-d experientially, nondually, by realizing that G-d is the source of their being and that their very being is a distinctive presencing of G-d; and by seeing clearly that this is the case for absolutely every other being and presence as well, each of whom is calling to be loved. "God's being is my life. If my life is God's being, then God's essence must be my essence, and God's self-identity my self-identity, neither more nor less" (Eckhart, 2009, p. 330). *The mystics know G-d by lucidly being a uniquely tangible manifestation of G-d; and they love G-d by loving other uniquely tangible manifestations of G-d*: a myrtle warbler, a widow who is lonely, a living forest threatened with clear-cutting. A compassionate, conversational, call-and-response life flows from this realization. Indeed, a core ethical imperative comes naturally with nondual awakening: to love all our relations, both human and more-than-human, to love them *from* our deepest self and to love them *as* our deepest (transpersonal) self, *as* G-d in earthly form. "Two as duality [separation] does not produce love; two as one naturally gives willing, fervent love" (Eckhart, 1980, p. 198). When being contacted by particular others who are calling upon us for care, and to whom we are responding with a smile (for the warbler) or time and attention (for the widow) or ecological activism (for the forest), we can appreciate that these others are not really other than or separate from G-d, not really other than or separate from our own deepest self.

It is not enough to "love" the earth abstractly, as in: "Let's save the planet!" The mystics say the same about our love for G-d. As Blake (1988) insists, "He who would see the Divinity must see him in . . . friendship & love" (p. 251). "He who would do good to another, must do it in Minute Particulars" (p. 205). From a nondual perspective, whether we are putting out seeds for chickadees, or removing invasive plants from our local woods, or working to resist the toxic effects of corporate pollution: *oneness with G-d, loving G-d, loving our neighbor, loving the natural world—these are identical and indistinguishable*. When the world is seen through an awakened consciousness, no authority or sacred text—or ecopsychology book!—has to tell us to be loving. Rather, our depths are touched by the other's depths, and we spontaneously respond with heartfelt care. "Our / union is like this / You feel cold so I reach for a blanket to cover / our shivering feet" (Hafiz, in Ladinsky, 2002, p. 154).

## Who Is the One Who Loves?

The ethical promise of Christian contemplative life centers on loving G-d, which takes place by loving our neighbors. Stories of mystics' loving service abound in the literature. Intriguingly though, in all humility and truth, these teachers acknowledge that they are not simply being loving as independent individual agents. As Christ puts it, "The words I say to you I do not speak on my own [egoic] authority. Rather, it is the Father, living in me, who is doing his work" (John 14:10). Regarding their selfless service, contemplatives often say things like, "It's not me doing this." Instead, they avow that love is happening through them, flowing from an infinitely deep, mysterious, transpersonal source: G-d's love. Love freely without reserve, the mystics say, but do not presume that the one who is loving is your conventional self. Your real identity goes infinitely deeper, and those mysterious depths—imbued with your unique gifts—are the source of your loving actions. Correlatively, the mystics encourage us to let go of our attachment to the fruits of our action, to let go of the fantasy that our ego can really master and control the world.

"It is I who am the All. . . . Split a piece of wood, and I am there" (Gospel of Thomas 77, in Robinson, 1977, p. 126). When working with this affirmation earlier, we celebrated the marvelous realization that G-d—this inter-responsive life in all its dynamic depth and wholeness—is omnipresent and all-permeating. I would like to draw out another implication of the same passage. The text presents readers with an implicit challenge: *Who is speaking when Christ says "I"?* This question might sound strange but it provides a crucial perspective for understanding mystical texts. It is easy to assume that the one talking is Jesus of Nazareth. This is accurate, but it is not the whole story. Christ actually tells us that he is speaking not only as a finite historical person, but *as* "the All." In other words, G-d. This is the very heart of Christian spirituality: Jesus' true, real, deep, transpersonal self *is* G-d. This helps us appreciate an often-quoted proclamation that sounds offensive if Jesus were speaking only as a single individual or from an exclusively Christian stance. In the culminating conversation with his disciples, Christ proclaims, "I am the way and the truth and the life" (John 14:6). Please recall that "way," "truth," and "life" are classic synonyms for "G-d." Read with a mystical sensibility, we understand that Jesus is not claiming some elitist authority for himself or for (what became) the Christian religion. Rather, he is affirming his (and our) supreme, divine, transpersonal identity. "Who are you?" someone might ask Christ (or us). And he (we) could respond: "The great way, the great truth, the great life—this is who or what I am! And this is who you are as well!" Here the phrase "the way" is being used like the phrase "the Dao" in Asian spirituality. When translators venture an English version of this revered Chinese word, they render it as "the way." For many people, the most tangible, accessible manifestation of the Dao is the larger natural world, the great way of this mysterious life, the transpersonal life we are ever comprised of, participating in, and ceaselessly transforming by way of our responsiveness. Right after making the proclamation we just cited, Christ places it in a key context: "I am in the Father and the Father is in me" (John 14:11). Not only is G-d my deepest being and supreme identity, but I (as a unique body-mind) am in G-d and G-d permeates my unique body-mind-self. Theologians call this realization not pantheistic—G-d is (immanent in) all things—but panentheistic: G-d is in all things (immanently) and all things are in G-d (as transcendent and all-encompassing).

## Nature Has No Ego!

Although Freud mounted a fierce critique of religion, he did urge people to accept the fact the ego is not the center of the psyche. Given our primitive instinctual drives and all the things we have repressed, the forceful influence of the unconscious deserves great respect. In a famous declaration, Freud (1955) insisted that "the ego is not master in its own house" (p. 143). The contemplative traditions heartily agree. However, they would say that the ego rests not only on unconscious dimensions of our personal psyche, but on even deeper, more encompassing, transpersonal dimensions of our being: life, nature, G-d, the Dao (by various names).

From this view, the most exquisite gift of the ego is its capacity to consciously surrender its presumed sovereignty, consenting to be a responsive servant rather than a willful, domineering master. Herein, we open to compassionate inter-responsive participation in a deep dynamic life that transcends our ego-centered self. Angelus Silesius, a seventeenth-century German mystic-poet, puts it wryly: "God, whose love and joy are present everywhere, can't come to visit you unless you aren't there" (Mitchell, 1989, p. 87). Because there is never any real separation in the first place, we as ego have a paradoxical role to play: not resisting the solicitation of life's depths that come from beyond our will, in the call of each situated encounter. Saint Paul shared some details about this great metanoia: "Be of the same mind [as Christ], having the same love, being in full accord and of one mind. Do nothing from selfish ambition or vain conceit. Rather, in humility, value others above yourself, not looking to your own interests but each of you to the interests of the others. . . . [Though Christ] was in the form of God . . . he emptied himself, taking the form of a servant" (Philippians

2:1–8). The reference is to Jesus' physical death on the cross, but also to a self-emptying (*kenosis*) process we can all give ourselves to: letting go of egoism in a psychospiritual "death," confiding oneself into the one great mystery. This is naturally followed by rebirth as a transpersonal self, one devoted to serving G-d via serving all our companions in this shared earth community.

"The only true joy on earth is to escape from the prison of our own false self, and enter by love into union with the Life Who dwells and sings within the essence of every creature and in the core of our own souls" (Merton, 1961, p. 25). Upon surrendering our self-absorption, "true joy" springs forth from a mysterious source—G-d, life's depths, the present encounter—and begins moving freely through us and onward compassionately to all our relations. Mystics often speak of feeling nourished by a boundless, ever-flowing fountain of life, energy, and love: "a fountain that was not made by the hands of men" (to invoke a wonderful Grateful Dead song) (Hunter & Garcia, 1970). As John Muir avows, "Rocks and waters, etc., are all words of God and so are men. We all flow from one fountain Soul. All are expressions of one Love" (Badè, 1924, p. 332). Renowned as a gifted naturalist, environmental activist, and writer, Muir was also a deep-seeing Christian nature mystic—two aspects of a unified sensibility.

Today we are being summoned to do all we can to foster the well-being of the earth, and thereby to foster human health as well. Yet, as transpersonal ecopsychology and the contemplative traditions teach, we cannot do it alone, by dint of our individual egoic agency and power. But when we get out of our own way, when we release our exclusive identification with our self-contracted ego, the depths of life begin to flow through us more freely, moving in wise and healing ways. Our unique and irreplaceable inflection of these depths must be included in all that we offer to this glorious and suffering earth, but the real source of our every gift is the great mystery or life or nature itself—G-d, in the language of the mystics. Like Macy (1991) says: "As we work to heal the Earth, the Earth heals us. . . . As we care enough to take risks, we loosen the grip of ego and begin to come home to our true nature. For, in the co-arising nature of things, the world itself, if we are bold to love it, acts through us" (p. xii). While transpersonal experiences can occur in any moment, serendipitously, several existential contexts are especially auspicious: *love, death, sexuality, beauty, embodied engagement, art, music, pain and suffering, spirituality, and nature.* All these have a way of drawing us out of our usual self-preoccupation and opening us for intimate contact with whatever is being sent our way. (Formal meditation can also avail us to nondual realizations, and help us integrate such fleeting experiences into more stable modes of being.) A work of art may take our breath away, indeed take our separate self-sense away. In a kind of time-out-of-time, there is not a separate objective painting over there with me as a separate subject looking at it from over here. Rather, there is only a single seamless seeing. Inspired by the Christian mystics, T. S. Eliot (1962) celebrates "music heard so deeply / That it is not heard at all, but you are the music" (p. 136). Athletes can open into a state of flow wherein they feel intimately interconnected with the whole field of play: no gap between the player, their teammates, the opposing players, the ball, and so forth. Sometimes physical or emotional pain can exceed our capacity to manage it and we surrender our efforts at mastery, releasing ourselves not just into acceptance but into a different kind of well-being that is infinitely deeper than any pain. Sitting on the deathbed of a cherished companion, holding hands, breathing together, and gazing silently into one another's eyes, time and eternity can intersect in a moment of true transpersonal communion. In intimate conversation or lovemaking, the conventional dualistic boundary between my beloved and me may dissolve, and we are graced with a sense of lively nondual presencing: no lover, no loved one, only love. Staying in contact with what we discovered in that blessed event, our heart knows that whatever befalls our beloved befalls us. The other's pain is my pain, the other's joy as well.

In much the same way, the natural world calls us out of our small, contracted self, induces us to let go of our habitual defenses, and opens us to the transpersonal depths of life. Floating in an ocean, standing on a mountain peak, holding our child's hand—in any such instance we may suddenly lose our self. That is to say, lose the chronically anxious, self-preoccupied sense of being merely a finite, skin-encapsulated ego needing to defend or bolster itself. What emerges in its place feels radically more real or alive: a freshly vivified mountain, ocean, or child-parent encounter; and a freshly open, liberated, relationally attuned self. Our sense of separateness can also dissolve in response to the earth's suffering. A student once told me about driving behind a truck that was carrying logs from trees recently cut near her mountainside home. With great distress, she said: "When I saw the sap dripping from those pines, I felt my skin being slashed and my blood dripping." Including yet going beyond her skin-bounded body, she knew the beloved forest to be her deeper, extended, transpersonal body (self). And thus she did bleed. When the natural world suffers, so do we. When it flourishes, so do we.

There are many reasons why encounters with nature often open us to depths that surpass our ego. Until recently we have always lived in intimate rapport with nonhuman folk, and our hearts yearn for this contact. The natural world is beautiful and mysterious, and these qualities spontaneously invite us beyond our self-absorption. Further, along with loving encounters with our human companions, the natural world is often the most accessible circumstance for the disclosure of a key psychospiritual reality: that we are expressions of and responsive participants in an infinitely deep, inclusive, wild, and sacred mystery. For many of us today it is far from obvious that we are participating in the infinite life of G-d. But with only a little attention, it is completely obvious that we are participating in the deep, dynamic life of the animate earth. From the perspective of Christian mysticism, to be aware of this is to consciously welcome G-d's love, love that is ceaselessly bringing us and everything into being, now and now and now. Without any contradiction, we can also appreciate that nature is always giving rise to our very existence, loving us into being breath by living breath, encounter by living encounter. Known vividly, this is the ultimate grace, namely, *that we actually are at all!* Instantaneously, this evokes gratitude and the inspiration to live with love for all our relations.

But even though we find joy on the other side of egoic self-preoccupation, the transformative process can be frightening from the side of the ego. It is quite telling that the Christian archetype of ego-transcendence is Christ's death-and-rebirth, because at the threshold of letting go it can feel like we are physically dying. But when "ego-death" gets conflated with biological death, an authentic psychospiritual breakthrough can appear to be a terrifying breakdown. Our habitual self-sense is certainly not relinquished easily. Recall that our egoic identification emerged in infancy as a defense against the inevitable anxieties of simply being in the world, ultimately as a defense against death. Thus we remain fiercely attached to this contracted self-sense, grasping it as if our life were at stake. *Significantly, we cling most tightly to our egoic identity (or defensive false self) when we are feeling threatened by someone else who is holding tightly to their own intrinsically insecure ego. In contrast, the natural world does not function in an ego-centered way, but in a dynamic, participatory, inter-responsively flowing way.* (We could call this way eco-centered. We could also say that *nature is centered everywhere and nowhere*: centered anew in every relational encounter, which means centered nowhere exclusively, nowhere fixed.) We need to be mindful of dangers in the natural world, but not in the same way that we are wary of the risks involved in encountering other humans. *People tend to hurt us when they are identified only with their supposedly separate ego, especially when this reified self-sense feels threatened.* Driven by fear and greed they try to protect or aggrandize their ego, often exploiting others in the process. *But nature does not have an ego that it is trying to defend, bolster, or impose.*[11]

The forces of the natural world can definitely hurt or kill us. But nature has no personal, narcissistic, malicious intention to assault us for our personal qualities. This is in notable contrast with a dangerous possibility that often haunts our relations with other people. Hurricanes can take our life, but they are not trying to do so. Wild animals may attack us on rare occasions, but only because they are frightened, injured, sick, starving, or protecting their young. When we tune into our direct experience in the natural world we can sense that nature has no egoic will to force upon us. Therefore, nature fosters the dissolution of our *excessive defensiveness or "surplus vigilance,"* to borrow a felicitous phrase from Jeff Beyer (personal communication, June 29, 2019). Releasing the tense effort of fortifying our egoic identity, we can be sensitively vulnerable, opening fully into the present encounter. It can be liberating to let this chronically defensive stance die away. *Surrendering our egoic ways and surrendering into intimate contact can be as natural as opening our hand, relaxing our tight grip on something no longer needed. So simple and direct. And truly the practice of a lifetime.*

## "What Do I Want?" Turns into "What Does Life Want from Me?"

Transpersonal ecopsychology affirms that I am the tangible display of a mysterious sacred reality—one that is infinitely deeper than my supposedly independent self, one that I am called to love and serve. In Christian language, this reality is called G-d, in whom "we live and move and have our being" (Saint Paul, Acts 17:28, paraphrasing Epimenides, an ancient Greek poet-philosopher). A key component of this experiential discovery is the corresponding insight that everyone and everything else are also expressions of the same transpersonal reality. With this realization, the human ego and the human species are displaced from their self-presumed centrality. For Freud, the conscious ego is decentered due to its prepersonal rooting in the primitive, instinctual id and its merely relative autonomy in relation to the dynamic, repressed unconscious. For the Christian mystics, the ego is decentered in the conscious realization of our inherent union with—and supreme identity *as*—the great transpersonal mystery, G-d. For transpersonal ecopsychology, the ego is decentered in favor of the omni-centered or eco-centered or centerless reality of every presencing encounter.

From the perspective of the utilitarian ego the world is comprised of separate people and objects, and the question that drives me is: "How can I use (and discard) these to fulfill my own self-possessed desires?" When my consciousness turns and a transpersonal perspective emerges, the world—as the body or the play of G-d—is a nondual field of sacred presences and relationships, each one summoning my understanding and care. This awareness gives rise to very different kinds of questions. The primary question comes not from me (as a separate self) but from the whole animate world, from life itself or from G-d. That is, life asks something of me via a "minute particular" right there before me: a honeybee trapped in my house who is yearning to escape; a neighbor spraying Roundup (which might kill the bee after I take it outside); a national energy policy that is unwise, unkind, and irresponsible. It is my responsibility to understand the request and craft a fitting response. Herein, the ego-centered question is inverted. *It is no longer "How can I use the world?," but "How can the world or life use me?"* "What is life asking of me?" "How can my life serve the greater life?" Christian mystics would wonder: "What is G-d asking of me?" "Beyond my egoic will, what is the will of G-d?" *These are ethical questions centered in the present moment's relational contact.* And each encounter is centered in a vast inter-responsive field of beings and presences. Thus it is the same thing to speak of an ecocentered, theocentered, or omnicentered existence, none of which have a fixed center. Practically speaking, it is not enough to know that we coexist interdependently with each other; or to know that our deepest being is an infinite, unitive, transpersonal field, say, the field of nature or the being of G-d. Our real summons is to offer our daily (co)existence for each other, in compassionate service. When Saint John of the Cross (2007) celebrates what he calls "mystical wisdom," he immediately presents another sacred name as a synonym:

"love" (p. 3). *Mystical union grows to fruition in simple acts of love. When it comes down to it, in our everyday relationships, knowing and being and loving must be actualized as one.*

## Deep Calls to Deep:
## Life's Sacred Depths Ceaselessly Appeal to Our Sacred Depths

Saint Augustine once remarked that "God is more intimate with me than I am with myself."[12] Likewise, nature is more intimate with me than I (as a conventional ego) am with myself. Human beings are natural beings, cultural beings, and spiritual beings—inseparably so and, potentially, consciously so. This means that when humans are relating with the natural world, this is one form in which nature is relating with itself. Equally, when experienced through contemplative eyes—through mystical ears, skin, nose, tongue, heart-mind—this involves the sacred depths of life responding to the sacred depths of life; or, to put it boldly, G-d responding to G-d. Stretching the metaphor of "self"—true self, as contemplatives say—this is nature attuned to itself. Such intimacy is transpiring all the time. (It cannot really be otherwise.) We usually are not aware of it, but we can be. And loving care follows naturally. This is what we mean by the transformation of consciousness, culture, and sense of self.

Holding these ideas in mind and heart, I would like to comment on something that has been implicit throughout our study. Saint Teresa of Ávila (2003) claims that "God calls to us in countless little ways all the time" (p. 57). This includes the various ways nature addresses us in our day-to-day life. In my view, our eco(psycho)logical crisis is due to the fact that we typically hear these relational appeals from a relatively superficial and merely utilitarian stance, by way of our self-centered ego. In contrast, life calls upon us to appreciate the natural world's sacramental quality and our responsibility toward it. *But to perceive these depths we must perceive from our depths.* Described the other way around, *when we confide ourselves into earth's wild and sacred call, we thereby allow the infinite depths of nature to reach, touch, and move our own infinite, wild, and sacred depths.* Psalm 42:7 conveys this beautifully: *"Deep calls to deep in the voice of your waterfalls."* In this passage, the word "your" refers to G-d, and so does each invocation of "deep." The initial deep is G-d in the form of the waterfall. The second deep is our own depths (sacred, divine, transpersonal). These are the depths in us that G-d—*as the waterfall*—is calling upon. "Every purely natural object is a conductor of divinity, and we have but to expose ourselves in a clean condition to any of these conductors, to be fed and nourished by them" (Muir, in Wolfe, 1938, p. 118). Much like Blake's cleansed "doors of perception," Muir's phrase points to the quality of consciousness we bring into our relationships. When looking through eyes emptied of merely self-serving motivation, we see clearly that our companion's being goes divinely deep, be they human or otherwise. And we naturally respond with compassion and care. Correlatively, when knowing and loving any other in their infinite depths, *the self we are loving from*—our true self—goes infinitely deep, far beyond our conventional ego. Such a *deep-to-deep or heart-to-heart relationship* is radically different from an ego-to-ego or ego-to-object one.

Contemplative consciousness discloses a sacred world that functions interdependently, conversationally, by way of ceaseless calls-and-responses. G-d calls us to love our neighbor, so the mystics say. Simultaneously and indistinguishably, loving our neighbor is loving G-d. And our neighbors include "Brother Sun," "Sister Moon," "Brother Wind," "Sister Water," "Brother Fire," "Sister Bodily Death," "Sister Mother Earth," as Saint Francis of Assisi sings (Armstrong & Brady, 1982, pp. 38–39). A glowing maple tree, a river polluted by commercial toxins, ivory-billed woodpeckers on the verge of extinction, this one glorious, irreplaceable, overheated planet: seen via mystical eyes, these natural sisters and brothers are G-d appearing in the flesh. Whether these divine depths present as beauty or suffering, we are summoned to reply with understanding and love. *How we treat nature is how we treat G-d; how we treat every child and their children to come; and how we treat our self, as none of these precious and sacred ones are ever really separate.* We are now being given the opportunity—indeed the responsibility—of turning today's ecological breakdown into a psychospiritual breakthrough. May we cleanse our doors of perception; allow the infinitely deep, wild, sacred nature of our companions to touch our corresponding depths; and thereby free our understanding and compassion to flow forth for all our relations without exclusion, those familiar and nearby, those unfamiliar and far away, those who look like us and those who don't. Each is the one calling for our love.

Chapter Seven

# Nature's Conversational Consciousness

## Awareness as an Ecological Field of Relations

Looking out the window, I said to a store clerk, "Wow! That's an intense thunderstorm. I didn't think it was supposed to rain this afternoon." She replied, wisely, "Mother nature really has a mind of her own."

—Personal conversation

I came to realize clearly that Mind is no other than mountains and rivers and the great wide earth, the sun and the moon and the stars.

—Eihei Dōgen (Kapleau, 1980, p. 215)

You forget that the eco-mental system called Lake Erie is a part of your wider eco-mental system—and that if Lake Erie is driven insane, its insanity is incorporated in the larger system of your thought and experience.

—Gregory Bateson (1972, p. 484)

## Overture

The whole interdependent earth community, including our home bioregion, is structured and functions by way of a transpersonal, conversational, ecological consciousness. Awakening in this participatory conversation, we may realize that nature's dynamic inter-responsive field is simultaneously our deep self and that for which we are called to responsibility and loving care.

## Today's Dominant Construction of Awareness, Consciousness, Psyche, and Mind

Over the last several centuries the dominant tradition in Euro-American culture has constructed an idiosyncratic view of nature, self, and awareness. While enhancing the material conditions of life for many humans, the shadow side of this modernist perspective is proving to be immensely destructive. The conventional view posits that awareness, consciousness, mind, and psyche exist exclusively in human beings, or, contracting even further, only in our brains. With a hierarchical ranking that devalues all who are not human, this narcissistic story of separation, elevation, domination, and exploitation has become terribly captivating. The pioneering anthropologist and systems theorist Gregory Bateson (1972) puts it forcefully: "As you arrogate all mind to yourself, you will see the world around you as mindless and therefore not entitled to moral or ethical consideration. The environment will seem to be yours to exploit. . . . The whole of our thinking about what we are and what other people are [and what nature is] has got to be restructured" (p. 462) An intriguing intimation is embedded in this passage, namely, that there is *a kind of "mind" in and as the larger natural world*. The present chapter embraces Bateson's suggestion in order to reconstruct our understanding of consciousness, self, and relationship. Beyond arrogating mind only to ourselves, how might we live and interrelate?

To begin, let us consider how the discipline of psychology usually constructs a family of important phenomena: awareness, consciousness, psyche, mind, and intelligence. To develop a sense of the field's conventional construal of these concepts, I will provide definitions from a landmark text: the APA *Dictionary of Psychology*, published by the American Psychological Association (VandenBos, 2007). The following verbatim review is rather dry. But patient reflection will support our case that the definitions are constituents of a larger, socially constructed story that carries benefits and perils for various parties.

awareness *n*. a consciousness of internal or external events or experiences. There has been a continuing controversy over whether nonhuman animals have self-awareness. (p. 96)

consciousness *n*. 1. the phenomena that humans report experiencing, including mental contents ranging from sensory and somatic perception to mental images, reportable ideas, inner speech, intentions to act, recalled memories, semantics, dreams, hallucinations, emotional feelings, "fringe" feelings (e.g., a sense of knowing), and aspects of cognitive and motor control. (p. 218)

mind *n*. 1. most broadly, all the intellectual and psychological phenomena of an organism, encompassing motivation, affective, behavioral, perceptual, and cognitive systems . . . 2. the substantive content of such mental and psychic processes. 3. consciousness or awareness, particularly as specific to an individual. 4. a set of EMERGENT PROPERTIES automatically derived from a brain that has achieved sufficient biological sophistication. In this sense, the mind is considered more the province of humans and of human consciousness than of organisms in general. 5. human consciousness regarded as an immaterial entity distinct from the brain . . . 6. the brain itself and its activities: in this view, the mind is essentially both the anatomical organ and what it does. (pp. 580–581)

psyche *n*. in psychology, the mind in its totality, as distinguished from the physical organism. The term also refers to the soul or to the very essence of life. (p. 747)

intelligence *n*. the ability to derive information, learn from experience, adapt to the environment, understand, and correctly utilize thought and reason. (p. 488)

Take special note of four characteristics in these definitions: (1) the focus is on supposedly separate individuals; (2) human beings are elevated to a privileged status, with nonhuman nature correspondingly diminished; (3)

all terms are designated as nouns (implying a static, thinglike quality); and (4) the meaning of all these terms has long been contested.

## The Shared Earth Community's
## Conversational Awareness

This chapter will explore how alternative constructions of these phenomena—*emerging via lived experience*—can enhance the well-being of humans and the rest of nature together. As a prelude, I would like to set up a small thought experiment. First, think of a chipmunk. Second, is a chipmunk a conscious being? You might imagine a small, brown, squirrel-like rodent with darker brown and white stripes and a somewhat bushy tail. For anyone who has watched a chipmunk it might be obvious that this little animal has its own kind of consciousness: sensing, feeling, perceiving, experiencing pain and pleasure and desire, interacting with others, and so forth. If you live with a dog or cat, you do not need to be convinced that nonhuman animals are aware, intelligent, empathic, and loving. But countless scientific studies and other reports have provided compelling evidence. Jane Goodall showed that tool use, once believed to be unique to humans, is common among chimpanzees. We now know this is true for elephants, dolphins, ravens, and crows. Many different animals have demonstrated self-awareness by way of the mirror self-recognition test, first developed by psychologist Gordon Gallup in his work with chimps (Gallup, 1970; Pachniewska, 2015): gorillas, chimpanzees, bonobos, orangutans, elephants, dolphins, orca whales, birds, and even ants. In such research, paint is placed on an animal where they cannot see or feel it. But by using a mirror they are able to notice and strive to remove the mark, thus indicating awareness of their own distinctive self. The use of symbolic language was another characteristic presumed to elevate humans above other animals. But birds have different calls for connection, mating, danger, and indicating the location of potential predators. Similarly, research has shown that prairie dogs have extraordinary linguistic abilities (Slobodchikoff, 2012, 2019). Using a language comprised of differentiated squeaks, chirps, and yips, sometimes combined with gestures, prairie dogs can specify the particular species, location, size, shape, color, and pace of another animal approaching. Further, we frequently hear eyewitness accounts of dogs, dolphins, and many others acting compassionately to assist others. I read recently about a mother orca whale whose calf had died soon after birth. In a moving expression of grief, she carried her dead baby with her for 17 days (Dwyer, 2018). Suffice it to say, there is abundant evidence that every animal is gifted with their own kind of consciousness, intelligence, and compassion.

Taking a further step, the present chapter will focus on a different kind of consciousness: namely, a participatory, conversational awareness that exists in, through, and *as* the inter-responsive community of nature. Ecological awareness is another good name for this, but I am not talking about someone being *aware of* the local ecology (as important as that is). Rather, I am invoking a transindividual awareness that is structured and functions ecologically—that is to say, by way of interdependent, inter-responsive participants who are dynamically involved with each other in a holistic sentient-sapient field. Because this transpersonal notion is unusual, I could quickly launch into elaborate theoretical support. Instead, preferring to ground our inquiry in experiential evidence, I will begin with a revelatory encounter in a mountain meadow.

One spring morning I was sauntering happily through the glorious wilds of West Virginia. Eventually the wooded valley trail allowed access to an open meadow nestled between a river and the surrounding mountains. I soon found a comfortable place at the boundary of the woods to settle in attentively. To my delight the meadow was animated with the dance of hundreds of monarch butterflies and about a dozen ruby-throated hummingbirds. They were all weaving among one another as they fed on purple-pink milkweed blossoms. A pleasant breeze was blowing. Through my binoculars I watched indigo buntings, black-throated green warblers, magnolia warblers, Carolina chickadees, blue jays, and red-bellied woodpeckers, all singing and otherwise involved in their new-day activities. After about a half hour I noticed a chipmunk across the meadow who was eating an acorn. After a while he ambled on but then stood up abruptly, turning his head sharply and scanning vigilantly. I realized that most of the birds had stopped singing and dropped out of sight. They had also disappeared when I first arrived, but once I was still and quiet for a time they had returned to their nonthreatened baseline (inter)activity: singing, feeding, courting, playing, and doing plenty more that I had no clue about. All this had suddenly ceased. However, just before things turned silent again, I had heard a few birds—mostly chickadees and jays—not singing but sounding out urgent alarms. I caught these calls only vaguely, in the periphery of my awareness. But listening to the agitated cries growing louder as the meadow grew quieter otherwise, I sensed a heightened energy all around. Something important was happening but I did not know what. Glancing back I saw the chipmunk darting away. Then a blurry flash in the corner of my eye morphed into a red-tailed hawk: swooping down rapidly, catching the chipmunk, and dashing away to eat. Breathtaking! A visceral shudder of empathy coursed through me, as if the bird's sharp talons were piercing my own flesh. In one instant the little chipmunk was enjoying breakfast, in the next he had become breakfast for the hawk. Upon catching my breath it dawned on me that prior to hearing the alarm cries of the jays and chickadees I had half-heard the squawking of crows and the high-pitched retort of a hawk. Those back-and-forth voices had come from the distance, far back down the river and far back in my awareness. This was almost certainly the same red-tail. The jays and chickadees had fully heard the crows harassing the hawk, and perhaps they had seen the big raptor land on a branch above the meadow. They were signaling warnings of its dangerous presence. The songbirds heeded these conversational cues and dropped out of sight. The chipmunk also heard the messages of growing threat but, alas, just a little too late.

Chipmunk-interacting-with-acorn-with-meadow-with-chickadees-with-hawk-and-on-and-on . . . I became keenly aware that this was a coherently inter-responsive network of beings and presences. A complete list of participants in this conversation would never end. For example, a breeze from the river, an opening in the tree canopy, and previous meals in the meadow had guided the hawk toward this particular site. The breeze was intimating a thunderstorm brewing in the next county, which drenched me later that day. Earlier, a half mile back down the trail, I had watched some turkey vultures rising in a circular pattern above the sun-bathed river. The red-tail probably enjoyed the same thermal lift and then glided along until he perched high over meadow and caught sight of that tasty chipmunk. Appreciating this complex conversational dance is important, as I sensed that this was not just a linear sequence of cause and effect relationships. It was not simply that the hawk's screeches made the jays cry, which made the chipmunk anxious, but something far subtler and more complex. A deeper kind of order, intelligence, and awareness was being disclosed. Each situated participant and responsive interchange was resonating across time and space, being gathered together, and carrying forward a wild, free, and ultimately infinite field of being. In the hawk seizing the chipmunk, past occurrences and distant places were concentrated right here and now: think of the oak that bore the chipmunk's acorn and the sociocultural practices that legally preserved that place as a designated wilderness area. Future occurrences were gathered as well: think of the other creatures relaxing a little as the hawk flew away with a soon-to-be-full belly. This is not a one-dimensional line of separate stimulus and response, but a boundless multidimensional sphere of mutually resounding interrelationships. Even this extended description can only hint at the dynamic depth of what was occurring. Truly, an infinite fellowship of interdependently coexisting beings and presences revealed itself to me—and taught me something new about the nature of consciousness and (inter)subjectivity.

Was that chipmunk a conscious being? Of course! But that question is simply too limited, focusing as it does on a single individual in isolation. Going further, I sensed a unitive interrelational mystery that included that single chipmunk but inseparably transcended him. I felt palpably immersed in a coherent, nondual, conversational community, one that was pervasively aware, expressive, and intelligently responsive. It was astonishing. Yet I realized that *something like this is transpiring everywhere and all the time.* Then the intuition came clearly and vividly: *this* is a special kind of awareness, consciousness, mind, psyche.

We have already explored our capacity for real dialogue with the natural world, and this is part of what I experienced. But dwelling at the meadow's edge, the conversation I found myself in involved countless participants speaking with each other in a diverse yet coherent multilogue. To be sure, each individual was bringing forth its own distinctive consciousness and subjectivity, yet each was freshly arising into existence via meaningful conversational exchanges with countless others in an integrated intersubjective field. Every participant's being and that of all its relational companions were responsively interpermeating every other, in an intimate, ever-changing, communicative communion. Each encounter was a unique living center in a vast omnicentered, omnidirectional, freely circulating field of awareness and communication. It was evident that *such consciousness could not exist only inside single members, but was flowing conversationally between them, among them, through them, and beyond.* This inter-responsive world was thoroughly orderly yet infinitely open, wild, and free—extravagantly exceeding any totalizing grasp, understanding, prediction, or control.

Like each of the other participants, I remained a distinctive beneficiary of and contributor to this multifarious conversation. At the same time I realized, "Ah, *this* is what life is. *This* is who or what I am." My very being, self, and life *are* that which is transpiring *in and as* this situated encounter, *in and as* the whole, intertwining, inter-responsive, communal consciousness. And not only my being, but that of all others too. This conversational awareness is their being as well. Such nondual participatory consciousness is always occurring, regardless of whether we are aware of it. But being attuned to nature's ecological awareness changes things—liberating us from the confines of a mistaken identity and freeing us for intimate understanding, compassion, and service. Such is the precious teaching the chipmunk and all his relations gave me.

## Ecological Consciousness in Context: Indigenous Wisdom, Etymology, and Meditation

It still seems a little strange to speak of this kind of conversational aware-ness, as I have been powerfully conditioned by modern Euro-American culture. But in many indigenous cultures it would be strange to suggest that reality is otherwise. Therefore, I would like to situate the phenome-non in three different contexts: (1) indigenous people's sensitivity to the intelligent earth; (2) the revealing way that words resonate meaningfully across time and culture (etymology); and (3) contemplative teachings from Buddhism and Christianity.

David Abram (1996) emphasizes that "humans, in an indigenous and oral context, experience their own consciousness as simply one form of awareness among many others" (p. 9). For folks living in daily intimacy with the natural world, being attuned to nature's conversational awareness is integral to their sense of self and reality, their place in the community and cosmos, and their shared health and well-being. As Richard Nelson's (1983) ethnographic research shows, for the Native American Koyukon people of Alaska, "all that exists in nature is imbued with awareness and power. . . . All actions toward nature are mediated by consideration of its consciousness and sensitivity" (p. 31). "Traditional Koyukon people live in a world that watches, in a forest of eyes. A person moving through nature . . . is never truly alone. The surroundings are aware, sensate, personified. They feel. They can be offended. And they must, at every moment, be treated with proper respect" (p. 14). Nelson is not only implying that a particular being may become aware of us walking through the woods, like a blue jay who squawks as we approach. But further, in the Koyukon experience, "the surroundings" as a whole are "aware." This sensibility contravenes any thought that the natural world is merely a utilitarian resource for human exploitation. When I experience the local eco-community as "aware, sensate, personified," as responsive to me (and others) in a kind of conversation, then I spontaneously take care to live with more sensitivity, understanding, and love. I know I am involved in a real dialogue with a wise world that precedes and exceeds me yet includes me and is shaped by my responsible participation with it. This humbly decenters me from any presumption of being an independent, supposedly superior, sovereign self. And it recenters me as an inseparably responsive participant in a deep and sacred world, a precious communal world that sustains me and my loved ones while simultaneously calling for and depending upon my care.

To situate this ecological, conversational awareness in a complementary context, consider the etymology of this chapter's key words/ phenomena. In contrast to psychology's conventional construction, the history of these words attests to the lived experience of an inter-responsive, participatory phenomenon. The word "consciousness" comes from the Latin *con-* (or *com-*), together or with + *scire*, to know. Intriguingly, the *OED*'s first definition of consciousness is "joint or mutual knowledge" (1971, p. 522). Herein, consciousness is "knowing-with," knowing together or being mutually aware. *Consciousness is not just consciousness of an other, but consciousness with an other.* Similarly, the word "mind" is rooted in the Old English *gemynd*, where *-mynd* connotes understanding, thinking, remembering, and intending. The prefix *ge-* signifies *together or with*. Thus mind (as *gemynd*) originally had cooperative conversational connotations. In this sense we can construe mind as understandings that transpire through and as our participation with others. The word "awareness" comes from the Old English *gewaer*: *-waer* means aware, watchful, or wary; and *ge-* is the same prefix as in *gemynd*. Again, an implicit mutuality is disclosed: to be aware is to be aware together, inter-responsively, communally. The word "intelligence" is rooted in the Latin *intellegere* (to see into, perceive, understand), which comes from *inter-*, between, within, plus *-legere*, to bring together, gather, pick out, choose, catch with the eye, read. Through intelligence—between oneself and others—things are brought together, read together, understood together. The English "psyche" comes from the Latin *psyche* and Greek *psykhe*, breath, life, soul, spirit; and the older Greek *psychein*, to breathe or to blow (like air). The ancient word conveys a sense of the vital breath that animates all beings. This breathing psyche or psychic breath blows and flows freely throughout the sentient-sapient earth, like—or *as*—the dynamic flow of nature's participatory awareness. Today psyche is often used synonymously with mind, soul, spirit, awareness, and consciousness. Thus we come full circle with this family of words/ phenomena: consciousness-awareness-mind-intelligence-psyche.

A third context for appreciating nature's conversational awareness is provided by transpersonal discoveries from the contemplative/mystical branches of the world's spiritual traditions. In support of ecopsychological sensitivities, I find it helpful to contemplate a revelatory image bequeathed to us by Hua-yen ("Flower Garland") Buddhism (Cook, 1977). This school of Mahayana Buddhism emerged in China in the second century and later became a major influence on Zen. Perhaps you are already familiar with the "Jewel Net of Indra." If so, I encourage you to consider it afresh in light of our relations with the natural world. Imagine a boundless net comprised of interconnected jewels, each one precious, shimmering, and multifaceted. The net flows throughout and comprises all of space and time. Every single jewel in the net is absolutely unique and irreplaceable, differing from every other by the type of stone; its coloring, size, and shape; the way it has been cut, polished, damaged, restored. Further, each jewel coexists inseparably with all the others, in dynamic, reciprocally responsive affinity. Every jewel is simultaneously reflecting and being reflected by every other jewel. Let us view every "reflection" as a meaningful, expressive response in a particular present-moment encounter. Each jewel and each encounter is a dynamic interrelational center that momentarily gathers all the other reflections-encounters-communications that are transpiring throughout the whole net. In this confluence, all the temporarily assembled reflections are transformed instantaneously and passed on responsively in further conversation, rippling out infinitely through the whole net. Each jewel is not merely reflecting all the others in precise duplication, as if in a mirror, but each one is creatively shining forth in its own idiomatic manner in response to the idiomatic appeal of the present encounter. All the jewels together create a mutually vitalizing alliance, an infinitely open, indivisible, freely functioning inter-responsiveness to all, with all, as all, and for all. Each jewel shares its irreplaceable gifts yet always via responsive interplay with others and always via the supportive background functioning of the entire integral net. *Each unique jewel is itself a function of the whole communal net. Indeed, each is the whole net coming forth in and as one unique member.* Simultaneously, *the whole communal net is freshly*

*coming into being by way of each singular jewel's irreplaceable responsiveness.*
Like the third Chinese Zen ancestor Sengcan avows, "Each thing reveals
the One, the One manifests as all things" (Seng-ts'an, 2001, n.p.). Let
us appreciate that in each participatory moment the whole net lovingly
re-creates and nurtures each jewel anew, while each jewel re-creates and
(at best) lovingly nurtures the whole net anew.

Indra's Net portrays an infinite omnicentered call-and-response
interplay, with nothing solid or fixed to stand upon or cling to—including,
especially, an apparently static separate jewel (or separate self). I trust
you understand that each jewel depicts a unique person, being, presence,
or event—like the chipmunk, hawk, their interaction, and on and on.
And like you and me as well. (I trust that you truly are a jewel, shining
forth in your own unique way with all your fellow jewels in this one
precious life!) The whole net depicts the wide open conversational field
of life—nature or the Dao or G-d—in its total dynamic functioning.
Notice that this is a life of *mutual identity*, *mutual causality*, and *mutual
love*. The astonishing yet commonplace reality of Indra's Net is most
accessible as the ecological community of our home bioregion. Every animal, plant, elemental presence, and relational encounter is a jewel, each
one comprised of the whole transpersonal net—ecosystem—as it gathers
itself centrally and comes forth freshly. Since all of us are members of an
ecosystem, this means that *you and I are the functioning of the whole net
right here and now*. This also means that the whole net is created anew
by our response to the relational appeals of our companions.

Indra's Jeweled Net beautifully discloses the "interdependent
co-arising" of all phenomena that we discussed in chapter 3. It is no
accident that interdependent co-arising is sometimes referred to as "buddha-mind," "natural mind," "buddha-nature." We could simply call it an
ordinary ecological community or the functioning of everyday life. For
the time being, I am calling it nature's conversational awareness. Such
is the life I discovered in that mountain meadow, so too the life that is
transpiring precisely where you are. When Dōgen (2012) and other Zen
teachers proclaim that "*the mind itself is buddha*" (p. 43), this is the kind
of awakened mind they mean (and not our conventional individualistic
cognitive mind). "Nothing . . . is outside of mind-nature. All things
and all phenomena are just one mind; nothing is excluded or unrelated"
(Dōgen, 2012, p. 15). "When we try to pick out anything by itself, we
find it hitched to everything else in the universe" (p. 110), as John
Muir (1988) famously remarked. Of course, Muir's trans-egoic insight

came from intimate contact with the natural world. Since Indra's Net functions like an ecosystem, I wonder if the *experiential source* for this Buddhist image was careful attunement to interrelationships in the local natural world? After all, "all of us are apprenticed to the same teacher that religious institutions originally worked with: reality" (Snyder, 1990, p. 152). For "reality," we could say nature, or life's communal, conversational, ecological field.

Once a young child and a wise elder were out walking together. Pausing beside a stream, the child asked, "Why does the stream flow?" And the mentor responded, "Earth tells water how to move." Later they stepped onto a bridge that spanned the stream far below. The child wondered, "Why is the canyon so deep?" And the elder replied, "Water tells the earth how to move" (Seung, 2012, p. 276). It's obvious that these two people were having a wonderful conversation. Yet so were the water and canyon! Similarly, consider the recent discoveries about the so-called "wood wide web" (see Macfarlane, 2016; Simard, 2016). Researchers are realizing that meaningful "underground conversations" (Macfarlane, 2016) are always taking place between trees and fungi and soil. The fungi send out tiny tubes (hyphae) that join with the tree roots and soil, thereby comprising vast mycorrhizal networks (*myco* = fungus, *rhizo* = root). In this mutually beneficial, collaborative relationship, the fungi draw nutrients (like carbon-rich sugar) from the trees while passing on nutrients (like nitrogen and phosphorus) to the trees that they have absorbed from the soil. This network allows individual trees to be connected with each other across great distances. One "mother" tree can be intertwined with hundreds of other trees. By way of such connections, trees share resources and support one another. A tree who is about to die can bestow valuable nutrients to its companions. Mature trees can do the same for youngsters who need a boost. And when one tree is being attacked, say by aphids, it can send out chemical messages that alert companion trees to increase their defenses.

Neuroscience also points to the holistic, inter-responsive nature of our existence. Thus, using an image reminiscent of an ecosystem or Indra's Net, Sabastian Seung (2012) explains that "a connectome is the totality of connections between the neurons in a nervous system" (p. xiii), including the electrochemical communications between them. Then he states his key point: "*You are your connectome*" (p. xv). This is fascinating. Unfortunately, by restricting the interrelational connections to networks within our brain, this view is extremely reductionistic. If we believe that who we are is only what is happening inside our brain, we leave ourselves lonely indeed, sadly cut off from the rest of life. But what if the real connectome is the whole (local and global) conversational eco-community, and *that is who we are?*!

Beyond all egocentrism and anthropocentrism, nature—Indra's Net, or our very (co)existence—functions dynamically in an all-embracing and ecocentered way. Here I am emphasizing the mutually interdependent connotations of *eco-* as in ecology's understanding of ecosystems, but more primarily as in the lively interbeing that characterizes all natural communities. Ecologists teach that the holistic, communal web of life supports and is affected by particular situated encounters between individual participants—for example, in the relationship between trees and fungi and the soil, bees and flowers and pollen, bears and salmon and rivers, a mining company and a mountain and money, activists for ecological justice and that same mountain. Along with implying a coherent community of inter-responsive participants, the Greek root *eco-* also means a home or dwelling place. Bringing both meanings into play, when living in an ecocentered way we come home (time and again) precisely where we are, centering our distinctive awareness, self, and being in the living relational encounter, yet always within a larger fellowship of being. Like every jewel in Indra's Net, "We are in the center of the world always, moment by moment" (Suzuki, 1970, p. 31).

## Gary Snyder and Gregory Bateson on Nature's Participatory Awareness

If we listen only with a conventional ear, then it sounds odd to hear about nature's conversational "awareness," "consciousness," "mind," "psyche," "intelligence." But so many of our conventions are failing miserably today. What I encountered in the mountain meadow was not a typical version of consciousness, but not totally different either. The ways we speak exert a powerful influence on the ways we think, perceive, interact with others, and co-create our shared realities. Modernity preferred mechanical metaphors over organic ones. Following Descartes, Newton, and others, the ruling discourse banished mind and G-d from nature, claiming the natural world worked like a clock.[1] Today it is popular to banish psyche (and nature) from psychology and deem the mind to be a computer. But ecopsychological attunement gives rise to something very different, something inherently animate, sentient, sapient, and inter-responsive.

I recently discovered that what I am calling nature's conversational consciousness was a major focus for two wise authorities, Gary Snyder and Gregory Bateson. As Snyder (2008b) avows, "Ultimately we speak on behalf of the elegance, the orderliness, and the freedom of the mind, which is to say, of the natural world." Here he nominates "mind" as an alternative name for "the natural world," or "the natural world" as another name for "mind." Joining Snyder, I hope that the present book will contribute to new ways of languaging and co-creating our relationship with our companions in the community of nature. Notice that "companions" evokes care far more readily than "lower" or "subhuman" forms of life, even when the same beings are involved. We relate differently with "humus" versus "dirt," even when it is the same physical stuff. We might reconsider unbounded industrial-technological expansion when its misleading equation with "progress" is exposed. Likewise, when we move beyond the presumption that consciousness is limited to isolated individuals, and only human ones at that, we foster better ways of carrying on together. Bateson (1972) agrees: "I now localize something which I am calling 'Mind' immanent in the larger biological system—the ecosystem" (p. 460). "The individual mind is immanent but not only in the body. It is also immanent in the pathways and messages outside the body; and there is a larger Mind of which the individual mind is only a sub-system. This larger Mind is comparable to God and is perhaps what some people mean by 'God,' but it is still immanent in the total interconnected social system and planetary ecology" (Bateson, p. 461). This larger mind may appear perplexing initially, but Snyder (1990) offers a common example: "The world is watching: one cannot walk through a meadow or forest without a ripple of report spreading out from one's passage. The thrush darts back, the jay squalls, a beetle scuttles under the grasses, and the signal is passed along. Every creature knows when a hawk is cruising or a human strolling. The information passed through the system is intelligence" (p. 19). In their own ways, Snyder and Bateson are invoking a kind of participatory consciousness that manifests in three interdependent forms: (1) in each singular participant; (2) in each interrelational encounter; and (3) in a more all-encompassing, all-permeating manner, in and as the dynamic functioning of the whole inter-responsive community. We usually think of consciousness in the first way. Regarding the second, remember the awareness streaming through our two focal actors: hawk-responding-to-chipmunk-responding-to-hawk. Likewise, Bateson

(1972) asks us to contemplate what actually happens as a tree is being chopped:[2] "Each stroke of the axe is modified or corrected, according to the shape of the cut face of the tree left by the previous stroke. This self-corrective (*i.e.*, mental) process is brought about by a total system, tree-eyes-brain-muscles-axe-stroke-tree; and it is this total system that has the characteristics of immanent mind" (p. 317). Seeing that mind is immanent in the seamless chopper-chopped-chopping interchange, we are led to a further realization. Every encounter is a localized expression of an infinitely deeper, vaster mind—a mind that *is* the whole participatory ecological community or great wide earth, brilliantly alive, awake, and communicative. An inter-responsive awareness transcends each relational event, while being immanently embodied in and as every particular one. Each event of relational contact is a dynamic center, gathering messages from endless others and radiating messages to endless others.

I cited Bateson's evocative remark that some might use the word "G-d" when speaking of this great inter-responsive mind. Let us also note that Buddhist teachers often speak of "buddha-mind," "natural mind," or "big mind" when invoking this transpersonal awareness. Suzuki Rōshi (1970) emphasizes that Zen meditation "is just an aid to help you realize 'big mind,' or the mind that is everything" (p. 33). He urges us to release our small, ego-centered mind and "enjoy all aspects of life as an unfolding of big mind" (p. 36). And Dōgen celebrates a great transformative discovery: "I came to realize clearly that Mind is no other than mountains and rivers and the great wide earth, the sun and the moon and the stars" (Kapleau, 1980, p. 215). In the mountain meadow I was clearly involved in a special form of awareness that manifested as a participatory fellowship of being: no separate self or chipmunk; no isolated individual or presence; no mind located exclusively within an independent, self-sufficient being; but rather a *conversational consciousness* co-created via the inter-responsivity of all the various participants. Even so, our egoic identity still has a powerful hold on us. As most of us would, a typical tree-chopper "says 'I cut down the tree' and he even believes that there is a delimited agent, the 'self,' which performed a delimited 'purposive' action upon a delimited object" (Bateson, 1972 p. 318). But Bateson, Buddhism, and phenomenology show that this individualistic and dualistic belief is a conceptual abstraction, a reified idea far removed from what transpires spontaneously in our direct experience. "The 'self' is a false reification of an improperly delimited part of this much larger field of interlocking processes" (Bateson, p. 331).

## Singing Loons and the Spirit of a Place

The ecological consciousness we are exploring is our very being, readily accessible when we attend carefully. But we need allies to help us appreciate it. We cannot do it alone, especially because the fantasy of solo sovereignty is our core malady. As our wise ally Abram (1996) says:

> Each place its own mind, its own psyche. Oak, madrone, Douglas fir, red-tailed hawk, serpentine in the sandstone, a certain scale to the topography, drenching rains in the winter, fog off-shore in the summer, salmon surging in the streams—all these together make up a particular state of mind, a place-specific intelligence shared by all the humans that dwell therein, but also by the coyotes yapping in those valleys, by the bobcats and the ferns and the spiders, by all beings who live and make their way in that zone. Each place its own psyche. (p. 262)

Like Abram implies, through our sensitive attunement we discover that mind is "all these together." *This mind or consciousness is the conversational interchange* transpiring among the participants in a local ecosphere, far beyond the ego's best conceptualization, much less its control. While it is unconventional to speak of a natural community's consciousness, this does call up a common notion: the "spirit" or "soul" of a place. People use such phrases to invoke the felt-ambiance of a particular habitat, intuiting a kind of subtle, meaningful energy that circulates like breath ("spirit") through a distinctive locale. Yet we rarely articulate just what we mean. In my view, people are giving voice to their lived sense of an enveloping conversational awareness, one comprised of the distinctive relationships among the various participants that recur in a relatively consistent pattern in a particular place.

After returning home from Algonquin Provincial Park in the wilds of Ontario, Canada, a friend asked me to tell him about the "spirit of that place." Pausing to sense my way into the question, the sound of loons soon filled my body and heart. I told my friend that the spirit of Algonquin has to do with the marvelously haunting songs of these birds. Immediately I knew that what I said was true, yet crucial ingredients had been left out. Trying to convey things more fully, I shared a story of an early morning when I was enchanted by the ethereal singing of a pair of common loons. These are striking black and white birds with glowing red eyes and a vertically striped "necklace"—so-called "common" but far less so now, alas.[3] Floating on the still water, the loons were conversing with each other and occasionally diving for fish. I told my friend about how I stood and smiled silently on the bank of the lake with mist rising as the sun was just appearing. I described how the loons' echoing tremolos and wails made me tremble with wonder, joy, and gratitude. I shared how their singing resounded with me and beyond me—beyond in space, throughout the whole lake and into the dense coniferous forest where, out of view, I sensed other wild neighbors carrying on with their lives as they do day by day; and beyond in time, into the night before, when we were graced with a black-domed, star-strewn sky and the primal howling of wolves in the distant hills. I tried to put into words how the loon's singing was interwoven with my reverent attunement; how I felt our contact resounding seamlessly throughout the whole place; and how the whole place was gathered vividly in one singular loon-note, and then another, and another. I tried to express how the birdsong-with-my-present-awareness—they were one indivisible fact—were already joined with the scents of pine and animal musk; with faint sounds emanating from a bay hidden around the bend, rustling and sloshing sounds intimating—could it be?!—a moose munching water lilies (like we were blessed to see the day before); and with countless other participants within my sensorial field and beyond. By depicting this inter-responsive community in some detail, the spirit of that exquisite place—that interdependent network of awareness—came alive for my friend. Yet I was still only hinting at the unique depth and subtlety of Algonquin's conversational consciousness.

## Participatory Awareness Encompasses Us, Permeates Us, Is Us

Although the wild lands of West Virginia and Algonquin are truly glorious, a version of what I experienced in those places is happening everywhere and always. However, due to the momentum of our ego-centered stance, nature's conversational awareness is not apparent to our conventional sensibility. I understand that it may sound outlandish to speak of earth's consciousness, or to say that the natural world is aware of us and responds intelligently. It is, quite literally, out-land-ish. That is, when we step out of our human enclosures and into the open lands around us, and when we devote our attention to what is transpiring between the beings and presences there, including us, then a participatory conversational awareness is revealed. Thus, let me appeal to an experience most of us have shared in one situation or another, a common version of what I intuited in the mountain meadow. Remember a time when you were walking in the woods or a park. Upon hearing some birds calling or animals scurrying about, you headed over to see what was happening. But when you got closer things suddenly became quiet and still. "Those birds were right here, but now I can't see even one of them!" A tangible sense of concealment pervades the whole area, bestowing an uncanny ambiance. We could choose to focus on just a single participant, say the vireo who stopped singing or the squirrel who ran away. Yet things actually change collectively and coherently in such circumstances. The silent stillness is conveying a communal awareness, one constituted and communicated via the shared attentiveness and inter-responsivity among all the animals involved. *This* is nature's conversational consciousness, and it is far more ordinary than the phrase first suggests.

Although such a transpersonal field of awareness is thoroughly embodied in our daily communion with the local ecosphere, it usually functions without us noticing. But we can consciously discover it and let ourselves be guided accordingly. "By acknowledging such links between the inner, psychological world and the perceptual terrain that surrounds us, we begin to turn inside-out, loosening the psyche from its confinement within a strictly human sphere, freeing sentience to return to the sensible world that contains us. Intelligence is no longer ours alone but is a property of the earth; we are in it, of it, immersed in its depths" (Abram, 1996, p. 262). This deep conversational consciousness does not exist simply inside you or me or a chipmunk, say, inside our personal bodies or convoluted brain. Rather, "we are in it, of it." This awareness in which we are always immersed *is* the meaningful inter-responsivity among all the animals, plants, and elemental presences. This is astonishing, completely ordinary, truly transformative, as the philosopher and Zen priest Jason Wirth (2017) suggests: "To realize that the earth has the same deep structure of your own mind is to realize that the Mind has the same deep structure as the Great Earth" (p. 8). Awakening to earth's conversational awareness as our deeper identity, we can no longer delimit psyche to presumably separate individuals who are secondarily related to presumably separate others. Instead, we see that consciousness, awareness, mind, and psyche are always arising anew—in, through, and as the inter-responsive participation of the shared earth community, centered, as it always is, in each presencing encounter. Once again, Snyder (1990) puts it beautifully: "The world is our consciousness, and it surrounds us" (p. 16). Herein, the human ego is radically decentered. Its supposed sovereignty is dissolved but its functional role welcomed within the deeper conversational psyche. An ethical call to responsibility is given with this transpersonal appreciation, because our involvement in the ecological field freshly recreates that field. "The Earth awakens through the human mind" (Swimme, 1984, p. 34). More primarily, since the earth should come first, the human mind (and heart) awaken through the mind of the earth! Yet our capacities do give us a special role: "The human provides the space [or, a space] in which the universe feels its stupendous beauty. . . . The universe shivers with wonder in the depths of the human" (p. 32). *When you smile at a sunset, or challenge a corporation's polluting practices, you are the earth cherishing itself!*

## Merleau-Ponty and the Earthiness of Mind

I take special note when different traditions concur on unconventional views, so let me briefly include one more ally: phenomenological philosophy. In a work cut short by his untimely death, Merleau-Ponty (1968) was articulating a nondual yet inter-responsive ontology that is deeply consonant with our present inquiry. He had grown concerned that it is misleading to locate consciousness only in an individual subject, a subject (supposedly) constituting a meaningful world that is structurally separate from it. This notion is not faithful to the nondual nature of actual experience. Expanding our understanding of consciousness, Merleau-Ponty stressed an uncanny characteristic of ordinary perception: "What begins as a thing ends as consciousness of the thing, what begins as a 'state of consciousness' ends as a thing" (p. 215). He went on to describe a (co)existentially primary, interrelational phenomenon that he variously named "flesh," "the intertwining," and "the chiasm." Studying perception, he was intrigued by the chiasmic, crisscrossing, inter-responsive interchange between our lived body and other beings and presences: "There is a reciprocal insertion and intertwining of one in the other" (p. 138). Involved—inter-volved!—with one another via a mutually participatory chiasm, our flesh and the flesh of the world are discovered as a single seamless participatory flesh. "Grasp this chiasm. . . . That is the mind"

(p. 199)—*mind as nondual chiasmic inter-responsiveness*! Continuing, he emphasized how "'subjectivity' and the 'object' are one sole whole, that the subjective 'lived experiences' . . . are part of the *Weltlichkeit* of the 'mind'" (p. 185). The German *Weltlichkeit* is usually translated as "worldliness" or "worldhood," yet it also means "earthliness." Either way is revealing: *the worldliness of the mind, the earthliness of the mind!*

## Nature's Conversational Awareness Springs Forth as a Situated Ethical Call

Our ethical responsibilities toward the natural world are inherently intertwined with the psychology of consciousness and self. Consider the following Native American perspective, as reported by Nelson (1983): "The country knows. If you do wrong things to it, the whole country knows. It feels what's happening to it. I guess everything is connected together somehow" (p. 241). Here we can recall the grieving orca mother who swam around carrying her dead baby for two and half weeks. One whale expert wondered whether the mourning mother was also communicating with humans about the anthropocentric defilement of the ocean: "It's a message. These are pretty amazing animals. They know they're being watched, they know what's going on and they know that there's not enough food. And maybe they know that we have something to do with it" (Dwyer, 2018). To indigenous people, who have long lived in intimate rapport with the rest of nature, there is an obvious connection between nature's conversational awareness and humankind's ethical calling. "In the Koyukon world . . . human existence depends upon a morally based relationship with the overarching powers of nature. Humanity acts at the behest of the environment. The Koyukon must move *with* the forces of their surroundings, not attempting to control, master, or fundamentally alter them" (Nelson, 1983, p. 241).

The world of nature is conventionally constructed as a passive, insentient object. But as we are realizing, the natural community ceaselessly addresses us, invites us, engages us in a dialogue, poses obscure questions for us, makes requests of us. The particular appeal is different depending on context: say, simply to marvel at the majestic flight of an egret; put on a coat when it is cold outside; reduce our consumption, reuse stuff we might throw away, and recycle what we can; turn away from fossil fuels and turn toward solar and wind; or join with activist allies to resist the ecological destruction afflicting our local community. But the basic request is this: to *let go of* our delusion of separation and our drive for domination; and to *let go into* conscious, caring consonance with the conversational forces of the natural community. Shall we act according to our small, self-centered wishes? Or shall we respond according to the behest of a natural ecological intelligence that is infinitely deep and timeless and ever fresh and new?

These ethical questions allow us to pick up a thread from the ecopsychological alliance we developed with the Christian mystical tradition. The mystics claim that our core responsibility is to follow what they call "the will of G-d." "Not my will but yours" (Luke 22:42), as Christ avows. But what can this time-honored yet enigmatic notion mean, experientially? I would wager that we cannot know "the will of G-d" in any definitive way. *Yet we can attend to what life is asking us in the present encounter, and thereby respond fittingly.* And "life" is a classic name for G-d. We have introduced the phenomenon of nature's conversational consciousness and linked this with Bateson's (1972) suggestion that "this larger Mind is comparable to God" (p. 461). We have also described it as the inter-responsive functioning of Indra's Net. Recall that the reflective communication among all the jewels—the multifarious voices that comprise nature's vast participatory awareness—are gathered in each situated relational encounter. In a truly unfathomable way, every experience is comprised of a centripetal confluence of life's infinite relational influences, centered in the present moment's contact. In this way, the whole of life itself is transmitting a message that is unique in each eco-centered circumstance. Our responsibility is to respond harmoniously. Thus, in an effort to make a classic spiritual value phenomenologically accessible and ecologically grounded, I would like to offer a proposal: we could think of "the will of G-d" as the relational-ethical summons we are given in each distinctive encounter. Rather than imposing our ego-centered will and agenda, we listen from our depths to our partner's appeal and craft a complementary response.

## Crises Awaken Us to Nature as an "Eco-Mental System"

It has taken an ecological and economic collapse (generated by an underlying psychological-cultural-spiritual crisis) and a worldwide pandemic to disrupt the tightly held notion that humans are discontinuous from and able to control the rest of nature. The rippling effects of global warming and the coronavirus plague make our interdependence evident.

> When you narrow down your epistemology and act on the premise "What interests me is me, or my organization, or my species," you chop off consideration of other loops of the loop structure. You decide to get rid of the by-products of human life and that Lake Erie will be a good place to put them. You forget that the eco-mental system called Lake Erie is a part of *your* wider eco-mental system—and that if Lake Erie is driven insane, its insanity is incorporated in the larger system of your thought and experience. (Bateson, 1972, p. 484)

Bateson realized that Lake Erie is a genuinely eco-mental system. *As a participatory whole, the lake could be driven insane because it is a special kind of mind or psyche.* When industries wantonly dumped phosphorus, heavy metals, and other pollutants into the great lake and its tributaries, native plants and fish were killed en masse, algae grew rampant, and the water emitted a putrid smell.[4] These were—and to a significant extent still are—symptoms of the desecration of the aquatic eco-community, of Lake Erie being traumatized into madness. Beachgoers, swimmers, and fish-loving anglers were driven away by the stench, the ugliness, and the fear of being poisoned. Some were contaminated physiologically with toxins leading to cancer, hormonal disruption, and other illnesses. Most or all suffered psychospiritually with grief, anger, sadness, or anxiety upon losing the beaches, waters, fish, birds, and beauty of that special place. In all these ways, Lake Erie's insanity was incorporated into their—our—very being. But let us be clear, the lake was driven insane by humankind's insanity: confused dissociation from the rest of nature; arrogation of consciousness exclusively to human beings; fear-and-greed-driven efforts to dominate and control the natural world; care only for our tribe.

After this grim story, some good news is more than welcome. Following decades of activist work, the New Zealand Parliament granted legal standing to the Whanganui River in 2017 (Te Awa Tupua, 2017; Warne, 2019).[5] The great river is sacred to the indigenous Māori people, especially the Whanganui tribes who drew their name from it. The Whanganui have such an intimate relationship with the river that they know all 239 of its rapids. The eels, fish, mussels, crayfish, and shrimp who live there have been sustainably nourishing the people for seven centuries. To the Whanganui, the river and its encompassing ecosystem are not only physical presences to be utilized for practical purposes, but are imbued with spiritual power and significance. They experience the river as a living being, like a mother, father, sister, or brother. And they identify with the animate ecosphere as a deeper (transpersonal) dimension of their very being. In truth, the river as a discrete entity is not only what the Māori cherish, nor what was granted legal status. Rather, it is Te Awa Tupua: "Te Awa Tupua is an indivisible and living whole from the mountains to the sea, incorporating the Whanganui River and all of its physical and metaphysical elements" (Te Awa Tupua, 2017, p. 14). Human beings are naturally included in this dynamic, inter-responsive, spiritual network. In the "Te Awa Tupua (Whanganui River Claims Settlement) Act," the New Zealand government made this formal declaration: "Te Awa Tupua is a legal person and has all the rights, powers, duties, and liabilities of a legal person" (p. 15). The act, negotiated and written in collaboration with Whanganui Māori, deemed the river a "legal person," the closest approximation to how the Māori experience the river.

For the Whanganui, the river has always had a voice, culturally and spiritually. But now it has a voice by formal statute. This legal achievement is remarkable, yet only by Euro-American standards. The reality it affirms has long been completely evident to the Whanganui Māori. The Māori "see the living world as an extended relationship network, in which humans are neither superior nor inferior to any other life form" (Warne, 2019). The Whanganui people know that Te Awa Tupua is who they most deeply are. As they avow, "*I am the River and the River is me.*" This is a key line from an ancient proverb, and I cite it from the recent Parliamentary act (Te Awa Tupua, 2017, p. 15, italics added). The saying is a "life-defining [and self-defining] reality" for most Whanganui (Warne, 2019). The very next line in the same legal document is equally crucial: the Māori "have an inalienable connection with, and responsibility to, Te Awa Tupua and its health and well-being" (Te Awa Tupua, 2017, p. 15). Here we see a vivid affirmation of the inseparability of cosmology, identity, and ethics.

Tragically, beginning in the mid-nineteenth century, White colonists from Europe and Australia arrived with a very different cosmology, one oriented by an ethos of separation-elevation-superiority-devaluation-domination. Not only was their worldview radically different, but they used advanced weapons and other technology to enforce their Euro-centered stance. The Māori were stripped of their rights, and the river desecrated and degraded. Its rapids were dynamited to make them easier for tourists to navigate, land was appropriated for colonists' livestock, headwaters were diverted for hydroelectricity, raw sewage was released into the river, and habitat for fish and other animals was destroyed. Gerrard Albert, a Whanganui leader and chief negotiator of the landmark legal statute, lamented, "When you are dealing with a sick river, you feel sick yourself, because that river is you and you are that river" (video in Warne, 2019). When the natural world is assaulted, we ourselves are wounded. Grievously, we become incomplete. We lose something at the heart of being human. Yet when the natural world flourishes, we are more whole and healthy. As Albert put it, "The river completes me."

## Bringing This All Back Home

In chapter 2 we considered Aldo Leopold's (1949) moving encounter with a mother wolf who was dying from bullets from his gun. In good hermeneutic fashion, let us revisit a crucial moment in this story in order to carry our explorations further. "We reached the old wolf in time to watch a fierce green fire dying in her eyes. . . . There was something new to me in those eyes—something known only to her and to the mountain. . . . I thought that . . . no wolves would mean hunters' paradise. But after seeing the green fire die, I sensed that neither the wolf nor the mountain agreed with such a view" (pp. 129–130). Leopold emerged from this encounter with a radically ecocentered self-sense and ethos, including a version of the participatory awareness we are exploring. The renowned ecologist urged us "to think like a mountain" (p. 132). Yet what kind of "knowing" is possible for a mountain? How can a mountain agree or disagree? As far as I can tell, Leopold never explained it fully. But I want to suggest that the mountain's thinking—its knowing, its awareness—*is* the ongoing inter-responsive conversation among all the plants, animals, and elemental presences that dwell together therein. Chipmunk-responding-with-acorn-hawk-meadow-and-innumerably-more: *that* was a mountain thinking! What if we really found a way to release our habitual take on things and open humbly to thinking like a mountain? Or like any healthy eco-community? Or a whole human being? This means thinking-feeling-loving in consonance with all our companions.

Gary Snyder (1990) can help us bring the fruits of the present inquiry back into our home territory. Celebrating an *experientially based etiquette that arises via intimate contact with the natural world*, he guides our attention to the fact that "human beings, in their ignorance, are apt to give offense. There's a world behind the world we see that is the same world, but more open, more transparent, without blocks. Like inside a big mind, the animals and humans can all talk, and those that pass through here get power to heal and help. They learn how to behave and not give offense. To touch this world no matter how brief is a help in life" (p. 164). To say it again: "There is another world, and it is inside this one" (Tarrant, 1998, p. 4). The "big mind" or the "world behind the world" is other than the world we construct from our ego-centered and human-centered stance, but not other than the deeper nondual one we are always already participating in. With its power to heal and help, this open mind-world of interspecies rapport is the very world we all share, the very consciousness we all share. Unaware of this, we generate great suffering for ourselves and the rest of nature. Thus Snyder (1990) implores us to realize that "we are always in both worlds, because there really aren't two" (p. 165).

It is our responsibility to consciously embrace this and act accordingly. This truly is a matter of life and death. Each of us is able to kill and to love. These are immense powers. They are especially profound because whenever we bring them forth, we do so in relationship with our fellow humans and with kindred animals, plants, and elemental presences. This means that our very being and responsiveness radiate interdependently throughout the world, for ill and for good. It is not just that we have the capacity to kill and love. More crucially—since we often kill unconsciously and even try to love unconsciously—we also have the ability, and indeed the response-ability, to bring awareness to bear on these truly sacred powers.

What is awareness? Consciousness? Mind? Psyche? Regarding the mysterious referent of these familiar words, we might better ask: What is actually transpiring right here and now? Might there be a deep, participatory, conversational consciousness in and as the natural world, one that includes but transcends the individual consciousness we are familiar with? How is it functioning? How might we participate more wisely and compassionately? If such awareness may be said to have or *be* a self, our true self as the mystics say, might awareness itself be the everyday inter-responsiveness among all of nature's participants, centered in every encounter and locale and extending infinitely? Sparked by this inquiry, how then might we all carry on together? More personally, for each of us: How may I, irreplaceably, listen more deeply and offer my unique contribution to this wild, sacred, participatory conversation? These are endlessly open questions. Ultimately, we can only answer with our day-to-day (co)existence. But we can always begin by attending to our relationship with the natural world close to home, let ourselves be guided by whatever is happening right there, and thereby discern our next move.

Walking along the sidewalk in front of my family's house, I feel the morning sun caressing my face, together with a summer breeze wafting up from the Allegheny River a mile down the hill. A butterfly drifts past, drawn by bright red lilies and sweet lavender bee balm in our garden. The flowers are growing well, far enough from the drip line of a grand old oak tree and close enough to the house that most have been bypassed by our hungry four-legged neighbors, those glorious white-tailed deer. The bee balm is alive with honeybees. I've been glad to see a few more coming for their "balm" this year and freely distributing pollen in turn. I also notice bumble bees and a couple of incredible hummingbird moths interacting with the flowers. This little natural community is flourishing and I am smiling joyfully. Is the sun making me smile? Or the breeze? The butterfly? The flowers—their color, form, scent? The bees or amazing moths? It feels like "my" joy is not mine exactly, not something I possess as an individual, but an event that involves all these participants and more. I could say the joy is that of life itself. I, the others, and every encounter are unique nodes in a vast dynamically involved and aware fellowship. I was already happy because a few minutes ago, looking out our kitchen window, my wife and children were delighted by a ruby-throated hummingbird hovering at our feeder. I went outside to look more closely, and thereupon saw the butterfly. I smile even more as another hummer arrives, this one a male, his neck glistening red with sunshine. Our dear cat Rumi once caught such a glorious bird, but he died a year ago from cat food tainted with toxic ingredients. It is so strange that this sad loss now makes our yard safer for these little winged ones. The second hummingbird approaches and initiates a competitive dance with the butterfly and bees and moths, and then an erotic dance with the flowers and their energizing nectar. Physiologically, the nectar is actually *becoming* the bird as I watch. This common event is wondrous. But even more awesome is the realization that, psychospiritually, the tiny bird's being is actually becoming part of my very being—my grateful smile and feeling of wonder. And my being is becoming part of the bird's being. My wife and I planted the bee balm not only for our pleasure but for the pleasure and health of various winged companions in the neighborhood. The nourishing flower nectar was created interrelationally through a confluence of the animate flesh of the flower, the sun's energizing rays, yesterday's rain, the rich humus of our garden bed, and carbon-dioxide-rich breath released by my family and deer and squirrels. I could continue forever with these endless participants, all co-creating this eco-community by way of their very inter-responsiveness: sun—rain—humus—our cat and his grievous absence—bee balm—hummingbirds—breeze—my family and me. Ah, yes, my family: my sweet-curious little girl and baby boy would love all this, and my beloved wife too. I have to go find them so they can join this ordinary and thoroughly marvelous interchange.

Conversational awareness, shall we say? Participatory, ecological awareness? Consciousness not just in but *as* a dynamic, interdependent, eco(psycho)logical field? A sentient-sapient fellowship of being? The infinitely open, alive, inter-responsive wisdom of nature? The deep mind of the shared earth community? What a wild and sacred life, *this*!

Chapter Eight

# Bashō's Contemplative Therapy for Narcissus

## From Ego-Centered Alienation to Eco-Centered Intimacy

I am in love with myself. . . . What I want, I am. But being all
that I long for—That is my destitution.

—Narcissus (Hughes, 1997, p. 76)

To study the Way is to study the self. To study the self is to forget
the self. To forget the self is to be enlightened by all things of the
universe.

—Eihei Dōgen (in Kim, 2004, p. 104)

Buddhist awakening occurs when I realize that I am not other than
the world: I am what the world is doing, right here, right now.

—David Loy (2002, p. 214)

## Overture

Contemplative practices such as meditation—and an overall contemplative
sensibility in everyday life—can serve as a countercultural "therapy," one
that helps us surrender our narcissistic ways and open into compassionate
contact with all our relations in this glorious and wounded world. The
Zen poetry of Bashō may guide us along this great way.

233

## Narcissus' Self-Absorbed Estrangement
## from Intimate Contact

Imagine that you are preparing for an important event, say an intensely vulnerable conversation or a risk-filled wilderness adventure. Whom would you choose as a mentor, Narcissus or Bashō? This juxtaposition may appear whimsical, but the issue I am raising is very serious. The mythical youth and the great Zen poet both underwent profoundly formative experiences at an old pond, yet in radically divergent ways. Returning freshly to their tales, we can see that the differences between them hinge on their sense of self(-in-relation) and their corresponding capacity to be moved (or not) by the depths of others.

The classic account of Narcissus' (mis)adventures is given by Ovid in the *Metamorphoses* (ca. 2–8 CE). The story is quite familiar but I will retell it to initiate an alternative, ecopsychological interpretation. Narcissus was a youth of spellbinding beauty, and countless admirers sought his affection. However, he avoided all genuine relationships: "His pride was icy; his heart, cold" (Ovid, 1994, p. 53). He scorned everyone's approach, never letting them "touch his haughty heart" (Ovid, 1986, p. 61). Once, when Narcissus was out hunting, the wood nymph Echo saw him and was immediately infatuated. Suffering from an earlier curse, she could speak only by reiterating the words of others. Nonetheless, she managed to choreograph what could have been a mutually enlivening encounter. Yet when she reached out he shouted, "Keep away! I'd sooner die than have you touch me" (Ovid, 1994, p. 54). Echo could only cry, "Touch me, touch me" (Ovid, 1994, p. 54), as she retreated heartbroken into the woods. As we will see, Narcissus' remark about dying was eerily prescient, albeit unwittingly. Perhaps his unconscious was speaking, expressing a fatal dissociation he felt but could not acknowledge.

After rejecting Echo's affections, Narcissus ran away "all unaware" (Ovid, 1994, p. 55). He came upon "a pond, a small but perfect body of water way off in a distant part of the wood. . . . Its surface was burnished silver, and grass and waving reeds framed it and kept the winds from touching its pristine surface" (Ovid, 1994, p. 55). In the midst of this beautiful natural place, he gazed into the water, saw his own reflection on the surface, and was enamored. "Not recognizing himself He wanted only himself" (Ovid in Hughes, 1997, p. 74). Over and over he reached to embrace this self-image, and each time it disappeared. Eventually he discovered his "delusion," as Ovid called it (Hughes, 1997, p. 74). Yet he felt compelled to persist: "I am in love with myself" (1997, p. 76). "What I want, I am. But being all that I long for—That is my destitution" (1997, p. 76), as he rightly proclaimed. Unwilling to let go of this craving for no other than himself, Narcissus could only weep and then die. "So, by love wasted," he dissolved away (Ovid, 1986, p. 65). But even the shock of death did not awaken him from his self-absorbed dream, for upon reaching the underworld Narcissus "ran straight to the banks of the Styx / And gazed down" (Ovid in Hughes, 1997, p. 78). Sadly, he was still looking only for his superficial, ego-centered self. Alas, being so narrowly self-engrossed is what he might have better wept over.

Because Narcissus cut himself off from Echo and all others, this tale has often been cogently applied to disturbances in human relationship. Yet isn't it interesting that our familiar interpretations of the story lack any mention of Narcissus' estrangement from the rest of the natural world? Not only does Narcissus detach himself from other people, but in a glorious natural setting he sees merely himself and absolutely nothing of nature. Gazing into a mountain pool, he only allows the natural world to be a superficial surface mirroring his own superficial, supposedly self-sufficient desires, reflecting them back untransformed. He does not even see the pond right there with him, merely feet away but infinitely distant psychologically. He thus forecloses any contribution from the real depth, otherness, and intelligence of the community of nature. Anyone who could be welcomed as a genuine other is immediately reduced to the selfsame, to a servile extension of his own self: a self that is constructed and lived in a terribly constricted way—a self-possessed, desensitized self. This truly is "destitution," as Narcissus concedes. The words narcissus and narcissistic, like the word narcotic, come from the Greek root narke, meaning "numb." *Defensively numbing himself time and again, Narcissus remains insensitive to the meaningful solicitations coming from a life that infinitely transcends his egoic self. And this is precisely what killed him, his refusal to open his heart to real others, be they other humans or other participants in the larger ecology.* Tragically, what he avoided is the very thing that could have saved him, an authentic relationship with a real other. It is said that Narcissus' dead body was never found, but in its place bloomed a lovely flower with white petals and a yellow center. We now call this a "narcissus." Might we take this as poetic justice, a testimony to our inherent intimacy with the rest of nature, and to the dangers of our grandiose delusion of separation, sovereignty, and self-sufficiency?

## This Chapter Is Not about Narcissus, but Us: The Pathology of Normal Narcissism

Much like Narcissus, we can all get stuck in bolstering, imposing, or defending our egoic self-image. The mythic youth is a more extreme example of inclinations we all share. Beyond the realm of clinical psychopathology, I am concerned that our overall relations with nature are becoming increasingly narcissistic. I remember happily walking in the woods one late May morning. Soft spring sunlight was bathing the trees and path. Earthy scents were drifting on the breeze. A pair of wood thrushes were singing notes that would have inspired master flutists. My baby daughter was all attentive while nestled sweetly in a carrier on my back. In the distance I spotted a huge tree with smooth gray bark, an American Beech whose presence I had enjoyed before. But I was wrenched out of my delight by an inscription freshly carved into its flesh: JFL. Wanting to understand (and not just be sad and angry), I imagined JFL as an adolescent striving to find their way in a confused and confusing culture. It seems likely that JFL felt an anxious need to secure their identity and worthiness: "See this monument to me!" But from such a perspective, the old beech tree is not seen as a real being with whom we may relate, but merely as an ego-affirming mirror that functions (briefly) to appease our insecurity.

However, the ego's craving for aggrandizement is intrinsically insatiable. When living by way of the egoic self's low-grade paranoia, we are chronically driven by fear and greed. Not realizing the source of our pain, we exploit tree after tree—or something or someone else in far worse ways. Further along the trail I was pained but not surprised to find "JFL" carved into three more trees. One monument to our ego is never enough. Even if we slice into a hundred or a thousand more trees, we will still feel insufficient. Likewise, blasting away entire mountain ranges for coal and drilling for oil in yet another wilderness area will never be enough. As Gandhi acutely observed, "For greed, all of nature is insufficient" (Snyder, 2007, p. 35). This is because we are attempting to resolve our anxiousness in ways that never come close to touching the primary source of our distress: namely, the ego's delusion of separation and autonomy, and its effort to control the wild, uncontrollable presencing of life. Far from expressing an idiosyncratic conflict, JFL's actions illustrate a shared (co)existential challenge. Youth have carved their names into trees for generations. But much more insidiously, powerful economic, political, and legal forces are cutting up our world in accordance with their craving and will. Supported by an anthropocentric, economically elitist culture that is (dis)oriented by a grave dissociation from nature, those holding power and privilege have chosen to carve national heroes into the face of the earth at Mount Rushmore and Confederate heroes into Georgia's Stone Mountain. Both were sacred sites for Native Americans and, in a different way, for the more-than-human beings who lived there. Although the damage is magnified in such racist and ecologically ruinous cases, the psychology is similar to carving our name into a tree.

## Bashō and the Contemplative Way

Another famous literary figure, the Japanese poet Matsuo Bashō (1644–1694), may offer a therapeutic alternative to these confused and destructive ways. I have selected Bashō to be exemplary for several reasons. First, his poems are simply beautiful and they often involve the natural world. Further, his life and work are imbued with the spirit of Zen, a tradition renowned for seeing the natural world as an embodiment of buddha-nature, our own true nature. Zen practitioners appreciate nature as an infinitely deep, precious, sacred presence with which they are identified and from which they can never be severed. Bashō's haiku and travel journals are exquisite expressions of this convivial human-earth relationship. "Follow nature, return to nature, be nature" (Bashō, 1998, p. 177): this was Bashō's way in art and in his larger life.

At age 42—already a revered poet, and having long practiced meditation as a lay Zen monk—Bashō was graced with a profound encounter at a pond, one that was radically different than that of Narcissus. Commentators consider this to be his preeminent awakening or enlightenment experience. The initiatory event is conveyed in the world's most famous haiku: "The old pond, a frog jumps in, Kerplunk!" (Bashō, in Gach, 1998, p. 197).[1] "The sound of water" (p. 28) is Robert Aitken Rōshi's (1978) more traditional translation of the last line. As the story goes, Bashō is talking with friends and students in a garden beside a pond. In a moment of silence . . . kerplunk! sounds forth. With lucid clarity and astonishment, Bashō looks up and exclaims "frog-jump-in water-sound" (as rendered literally from the Japanese) (Henderson, 1958, p. 20). Soon thereafter he composes the renowned haiku.

Let us trust that Bashō's encounter was truly a transformative spiritual awakening. According to Buddhist psychology, awakening involves a vivid discovery of our essential nature, or true self. Like so many Zen practitioners, Bashō's realization transpired by way of intimate contact with the natural world. The great precedent was the enlightenment experience of the historical Buddha. Readied by years of meditation and existential inquiry, and sensing that he was ripe for a fresh realization, Siddhartha Gautama sat down for an extended period of meditation under a fig tree. (This would later be called the bodhi tree, the tree of awakening.) As his meditation deepened through the dark night he was attacked by Mara, a powerful "demon" who did everything he could to block his awakening. Speaking psychologically, we can understand Mara as the shadow dimension of Siddhartha's psyche, a personification of his—our—existential conflicts: confusion over being a separate self (when Mara tempted him with power and fame); fear and avoidance (when Mara's monsters threatened him); greed and clinging (when Mara's beautiful daughters lured him with sex); and shame (as described a bit later). Although nature has no ego, we imagine that we really do. And we feel anxiously driven to protect and bolster this conventional but illusory self-sense. We can recognize Siddhartha's challenge as an archetypal one. The Christian version—a near precise analogy that also occurred in nature—is when Jesus faced the devil's temptations in the wilderness.

Staying true to his contemplative practice, Siddhartha handled Mara's torments without giving in or turning away. Near the end of this intense psychospiritual conflict, Mara resorted to one of the fiercest attacks of all: he tried to shame Siddhartha. Shame involves the felt-belief that we are basically unworthy and unlovable, that there is a real flaw at the core of who we are. This may well be a universal human vulnerability, and Mara definitely took advantage of it. As legend has it, he taunted Siddhartha by asking who could bear witness to his capacity for enlightenment. It was as if Mara sneered, "Who do you think you are to believe that you can wake up?" In response to this hateful assault, Siddhartha touched the earth with his hand, grounding his identity in something infinitely deeper than his personal self. Immediately, the whole sentient-sapient earth responded to bear witness for him. Mara fled and Siddhartha kept meditating. At dawn he opened his eyes, saw Venus—the "morning star"—shining in the eastern sky, and was graced with a profound realization, one that actually answered the question of who he is but not in the way Mara expected. It is said that the new

Buddha exclaimed: "I and all beings and the whole wide earth are awake together!" Each one of us really is unconditioned wakefulness itself, pure aliveness, graceful love, lucid presencing. We are all radiating as brilliantly as that "star!"

Like Siddhartha with the morning star, "Bashō changed with that *plop*" (Aitken, 1978, p. 28) of the frog into the pond. *And so may we all be changed.* Bashō's true self is no other than our own, and countless "*plops (!)*" call to us every single day. Bashō's heart-mind had long been cultivated by meditation, poetry writing, and attentive contact with the world of nature. In the core moment his awareness must have been wide open (like the old pond), intimately attuned to whatever the world was sending his way. Suddenly, the whole of life came together for him in the kerplunking! *Just that!*

Across his literary work, we find Bashō welcoming various manifestations of nature as genuine companions in conversation. "Every form of [supposedly] insentient existence—plants, stones, or utensils—has its individual feelings similar to those of men" (Bashō, in Hass, 1994, p. 237). Whether it be the frog splashing for Bashō, or, for us, a fox peeking around a boulder, bees missing from our gardens, the climate overheating, or a meteor streaking across the night sky: the larger field of nature is addressing us, entreating us to engage in a real relationship and to respond with understanding and care. We can welcome our partner's expression even if we don't understand what it means at first. The wild-free mystery of nature's real alterity precludes any presumptuous (pseudo)comprehension. "What fish feel, birds feel, I don't know" (Bashō, in Hass, 1994, p. 49). But if—like Narcissus or the creators of the Mount Rushmore monument—we are content to see only our projected egoic face in the face of the earth, we will look superficially and find only what we already believe or wish: namely, our own image and agenda. *Yet nature is infinitely more subtle, deep, wild, and free than our ego can ever fathom, much less command.* Like an insecure emperor, the ego-self craves mastery and domination. But efforts to dominate end up being mutually impoverishing, as global warming and mass extinction teach. The larger-than-human fellowship of being invites, beckons, or sometimes shocks us *out* of our small self and *into* a truly sacred, mysterious, yet thoroughly ordinary way of being. To "transcend our ego" is to become a more conscious and humble participant in a marvelously expressive world. Accordingly, an awesome responsibility is bestowed: rather than imposing our egoic wishes, we "learn how to listen as things speak for themselves" (Bashō, 1998, p. xviii).

Bashō is affirming an inherent link between the experience of awakening—or, more stably, wakeful experiencing—and our capacity to meet others intimately. The twentieth-century Zen master Yasutani Haku'un Rōshi agrees: "From morning to night, vividly, immediately, the original face of universality moves briskly in detailed particulars. Whenever, wherever, it is the full presentation" (in Aitken, 1978, p. 67). A complete presentation of buddha-nature—our deepest nature—transpires in and as every situated experience. This is true whether we appreciate it or not, but our responses flow far better when we do. From this perspective, awakening involves indivisible intimacy with a unique companion: the morning star, a crying friend, a beautiful but polluted river. Releasing our ego-centered stance and opening to an eco-centered one, *our being is centered on the present encounter as it is coming forth right here and now.* Our response—our very life, for the time being—emerges from whatever is revealed in the meeting between the other's expressive appeal and our openly attuned awareness. Our being comes to fruition in being-*for*-others, in the conscious loving actualization of the present moment's ethical summons. I should add that our responsibility is to attend to the well-being of the *singular other* right here before us and, inseparably, to *all other others* (some nearby, some far away) and to our own self. When a fracking executive argues for a permit at a town council meeting, and I ask, "If you lived in this neighborhood, would you really be willing to poison your children?" I am speaking to that individual to be sure, but also in responsible service to everyone who lives in that community.

## Awakening as Intimacy

Following Buddhist psychology, if the event at the pond is Bashō's enlightenment experience then he must be awakening to life's "oneness," "nonduality," and "buddha-nature." Yet what *lived experience* is being addressed by these abstract-sounding concepts? Recall Bashō's (1966) contemplative advice to his students: "Go to the pine if you want to learn about the pine. . . . And in doing so, you must leave your subjective preoccupation with yourself" (p. 33). Dōgen makes the same point: "To study the Way is to study the self. To study the self is to forget the self. To forget the self is to be enlightened by all things of the universe" (Dōgen, in Kim, 2004, p. 104). Likewise, Meister Eckhart (1980)—

Dōgen's brother in spirit—insists that "the soul wanting to perceive God must forget itself and lose itself" (p. 140). And as my teacher's teacher once put it, "Zen practice is a matter of forgetting the self in the act of uniting with something" (Yamada Kōun Rōshi, in Aitken, 1996, p. 81). At best, when a pine tree, a polluted river, a work of art, or a person calls upon us, we spontaneously surrender into responsive involvement with their unique presencing. In such intimate, aware contact, the ego-self falls away. As Aitken (1996) says, "To unite with something is to find it altogether vivid—like the thrush, say, singing in the guava grove. There is just that song, a point of no dimension—of cosmic dimension. The 'sole self' is forgotten" (p. 81). In Bashō's initiatory realization, there is such complete intimacy that suddenly there are not even two partic-ipants to unite. It is not that Bashō (over here) awakens *to* a *kerplunk* (over there). Rather, he disappears into the *kerplunking*. There is only that vivid *sounding*. *Plop!* That's it! No self there. No other, either. No thing to objectify, no self to subjectify. *Just this!*

Zen challenges us to realize that "the other is no other than myself" (Aitken, 1984, p. 169)—my true transpersonal self, of course, not my egoic self. The "fundamental delusion of humanity is to suppose that I am in here and you are out there" (Yasutani Rōshi, in Aitken, 1984, p. 169). And in my favorite description (or *experiential invitation*), David Loy (2002) attests that "Buddhist awakening occurs when I realize that I am not other than the world: I am what the world is doing, right here, right now" (p. 214). In an auspicious moment, Bashō *becomes* the kerplunking—and that kerplunking is all-inclusive and all-pervasive. A monk once asked about the essential nature of Zen, and the great Chinese master Zhàozhōu (Japanese: Jōshū) replied: "The oak tree there in the garden" (Yamada, 2004, p. 177). In the language of Zen, the oak tree is one gesture of my nondual "true self," "original self," "true face." Realizing this, the whole of existence springs forth as that very oak tree. Identically, I am one gesture of the true face of the Dao, the buddha way, nature, this one great life.

# Meditative Transformations of
# Our Conventional Self-Sense and Way of Being

What can help us awaken from the compulsive spell of supposed separation, and from the self-centered anxiety, narcissism, greed, and defensiveness that come with it? "Harden not your heart," we are counseled in the Psalms (95:8). Bashō would surely agree. But how can we heed this advice when life is so harsh so often? It is not enough to know cognitively that this is a good idea, as if mere information is sufficient; nor to be told by authorities that nature is holy or that our rigid ego boundaries need to be dissolved, as if we need more preaching of morality. Rather, we must come to know the world's sacred nature (and our own sacred depths) by way of direct embodied experience. Sometimes we are spontaneously drawn into these depths, like Bashō with the *plop!* Such experiences cannot be created by force of will. They transpire gracefully, *contingent on mystery*. And yet formal contemplative practice can sensitize us for, and help us relax and release into, these initiatory moments. Bashō encouraged the young poets to surrender into the pine. Yet I trust that he also said, "Practice zazen!" While there is no calculative prescription for transformation, and while no egoic agency can willfully accomplish this, contemplative practice can help dissolve the tyrannizing grip of our fear-filled, contracted self-sense. Most deeply, this occurs by *seeing clearly that there was never a real separate self in the first place*. While honoring the "therapeutic" power of contemplative practice, I should emphasize that meditation is not about progressively achieving some idealized enlightenment at some point out in the future. Rather, in meditating, our resistance to life in the present is released, allowing us to be more consciously involved with what is transpiring right here and right now. This is pertinent off the meditation cushion as well. It is not even the case that I (as a separate self) am autonomously doing an activity called meditation. Rather, letting go of goal-seeking desires and opening with uncontrived naturalness to life in the present moment, a mysterious, transpersonal process takes over. In a graceful influx of energy, awareness, and love, it is as if life begins meditating me. Truly, this life and meditation and I are all the same.

Meditation practice, and a larger contemplative existence, go against the grain of our dominant culture. Silence, stillness, and present moment awareness are fiercely obscured by today's fast-paced lifestyles, superficial enticements from the media, and fantasies that our wishes be easily fulfilled. Powerful sociocultural forces are inducing us into exclusively self-centered, human-centered values. As a countercultural response, contemplative practice can bolster our resistance to these oppressive influences. There are countless transformative methods, "hundreds of ways to kneel and kiss the ground" as Rumi (1995, p. 36) says. Perhaps one's path is meditation, contemplative prayer, art, yoga, intimate relations with other humans, intimacy with nature, some integration of these or other ways. What all these approaches have in common is that they interrupt our habitual, narcissistic, all-too-certain, fear-filled, possessive, and controlling attitudes. Far from trying to conjure special experiences in an isolated sitting period, meditation cultivates our capacity to live and love more freely. This means that *meditation is ultimately an ethical practice.* One of meditation's exquisite benefits is that it readies us to welcome—many times each day—the serendipitous revelation of life's mysterious presencing. The everyday world truly is our zendō (meditation hall). Herein we allow the depths of others to touch our depths, and we respond accordingly. And we realize that these two depths are one, complementary "sides" of the unified flowering of life.

## What Difference Does All This Make?

Bashō loved pilgrimages—"every day is a journey, and the journey itself is home" (Bashō, 1998, p. 4)—and he engaged in countless treks until the day he died. His most famous travel journal is entitled *Narrow Road to the Interior.* For Bashō, the "interior" is the mountain heartland of Northern Japan. And it is also the depths of his very being. These are indivisible forms of a single sacred reality. During one of his journeys, Bashō rejoiced over a marvelous event. It is so simple we might miss it: "We stretched on a rock to rest and noticed the opening buds of a three-foot cherry tree. . . . It's all here, in these tiny blossoms!" (Bashō, 1998, p. 24). There is abundance and completeness in a single cherry blossom, with absolutely nothing lacking: *just this one fact, this sheer event*—the blossom unfolding just as it is, the whole world unfolding just as it is, we unfolding just as we are. Via this awareness, wherever we find ourselves, we know: wonder of wonders, it *is* all here. *This* is it! This is the way things are. *This* is (my) life, *this* is who I am. And this is what I am here *for.* Of course, nature is not always sweet cherry blossoms. From mosquitoes and sharks to hurricanes and earthquakes, the world can be dangerously harsh. During one trek Bashō (2004) encountered: "fleas, lice, / a horse peeing / by my pillow" (p. 94). Surely he was uncomfortable, yet the poem conveys no sense of resentment. This too is nature; this too is my life. In our interdependent world, everything is included inherently.

However, Buddhist psychology never prescribes passive submission to pain, much less to malevolence, abuse, oppression, or injustice. In contrast, authentic practice fosters our agency and empowerment as distinctive individuals. In vigorous support of these strengths, we are encouraged to be aware of our egoic confusion, fear, and greed—three classic "poisons"—and to transcend the unconscious enactment of this limited way of being. Transcending the ego means *moving out of* our constricted, defended, narcissistic stance and *moving into* intimate, appreciative, loving engagement in our day-to-day relations. Here we are carefully attuned to our partners' particular presencing: lavender's luscious scent, oil pipelines leaking crude(ly). When intimately attentive, human hubris drops away and compassion is summoned forth spontaneously. Hearing this call, our ethical responsibility is self-evident. No extrinsic moral authority needs to tell us how to act. No instrumental moral calculations need to be made. We simply do not desecrate trees with our initials or annihilate mountain ranges. Most likely we prefer not to harm a fly, as the saying goes, and instead work for the well-being of others. And if it is a deer fly biting our child's flesh we might vigorously brush it away, while feeling for the plight of this fierce little companion in the shared earth community.

## Walking Wakefully, Falling Down, Humbly Getting Up Again and Again

If there is one thing that all the world's contemplative traditions agree upon, it is that the quintessential human path involves (repeatedly and radically) letting go of our self-centered identity and desires and letting go into the loving service of others. Bashō awakened via a vivid *ker-plunk!* What really matters, though, is not what happened in that event but how he personalized his realization in the nitty-gritty challenges of daily life. Even before disappearing into that now famous sound, Bashō was a sensitive and compassionate soul. Consider his poignant response to a family whose life was turned upside down by the trauma of their child's death: *"a withered, leaning, out-of-joint world— | bamboo | upside down under snow"* (Hirshfield, 2015, p. 65). This achingly beautiful haiku was composed relatively early in Bashō's career. His mature writings suggest that his contemplative journey further deepened the tenderness we feel here. Before we consider another poem, note that kenshō and satori are Zen terms for awakening. But Bashō was fiercely suspicious of the so-called "stink" or "sickness of Zen." With such cutting phrases Zen masters challenge any elitist or self-satisfied attachment, even to the deepest of experiences. Here Bashō warns of such spiritual hubris: *"how admirable— / a man who sees lightning / and not satori"* (Hirshfield, p. 63). This perspective is an antidote to misguided fantasies that easily emerge on the contemplative path. A common yet misguiding notion is the belief that spiritual life has to do with some special realm removed from our ordinary world, as if experiencing lightning is one thing and satori something completely different. In contrast, Bashō celebrates the one indivisible fact, precisely as it appears here and now. Flash! Or, kerplunk! Or, "Hello friend, would you like a cup of coffee?" That is it.

Another (pseudo)spiritual notion is the belief that awakening will resolve our conflicts and struggles once and for all. But Zen masters repeatedly send their students—and themselves—back to the endless practice of personalizing their realizations and carrying them further in everyday life. Life is messy, painful, and challenging. It is often said, and aptly so, that contemplative practice reveals our true nature to be infinite, whole, and complete. And, inseparably, each of us is also finite, limited, and fallible. At times we all get lost, confused, and afraid. We are all vulnerable to hurting others with self-absorbed reactions. Zen practice or no, there is no immunity to making mistakes time and again, before *and* after any awakening. Bashō was well aware of this from his own personal experience. For example, trekking with a friend, he came upon a little two-year-old boy who had been abandoned by the side of a river. Bashō (1998) felt the toddler's "sobs stirring our pity" (p. 40) and was aware that the boy could easily die. But his next comment shocks our contemporary sensibilities: "I left him what food I could" (p. 40). Then, it seems, he just walked away with his traveling companion.

Yet Bashō carried the child's suffering with him, along with guilt over his own lapse. Soon after the incident he wrote in his journal, "How can this happen?" (Bashō, 1998, p. 40). Apparently reproaching himself for not doing more for the vulnerable boy, while also critiquing the out-of-joint society of his day, he composed a haunting haiku: *"the cries of monkeys / are hard for a person to bear— / what of this child, given to autumn winds?"* (Hirshfield, 2015, p. 78). We all have lapses, many minor ones to be sure, but grave ones also. We are awake at times and asleep at times. In walking with others in this shared life, we inevitably fall down again and again. None of us is immune. In our relations with the natural world as with other people, we can recover, humbly do what we can to repair the rupture, and carry on again and again.

## There Is Still Time: Embracing
## Our Bittersweet Condition

A frog splashed into a pond. In one way, that is all that happened in the crucial moment. Surely Bashō had heard such things hundreds of times before. Still, in a meeting of his depths and the world's depths, a common occurrence was received as truly revelatory. Time upon time others call for us to welcome their solicitations, call *upon* us to shift our consciousness and way of responding: the twinkle in our child's eye, the scent of cedar in the woods, the cry of an immigrant child isolated from her parents, the cry of a forest scarred by a corporation's assault. Walking with Harry Harlow one night, a graduate student was struck by the glow of a golden moon. In an act that Bashō would heartily commend, the student paused appreciatively and called his mentor's attention to the beautiful sight. Unfortunately, Harlow sarcastically dismissed the student's wonder-filled attunement, sharply remarking that the moon had "been there a long time. I've seen it before" (Blum, 2002, p. 3). Cut off from both nature and his student, Harlow plowed ahead with his own self-preoccupied agenda. But he is far from alone in this. We all have a tendency to get caught up in the momentum of our ego-centered existence.

On occasion, the spontaneous events of daily life can instantly dissolve our bedeviling sense of egoic detachment, liberating us to be touched by an other's sheer presencing. At times we need only breathe, blink, or smile, and there we are, in intimate contact. This happens before we *do* anything, even before we *can* do anything. Prior to our conscious intention, will, or consent, life comes to us unbidden, with grace or fierceness or both. No distance. No separation. Just the face of a homeless man in winter, the face of the mine-ravaged mountain—each traumatized and beckoning. The face of a radiant red rose, the face of the glowing Milky Way arching across the dark night's domed sky—each beautiful and beckoning. Our heart opens freely, or is discovered to be inherently open when we get out of our own way, and we do our best to answer the appeal. Maybe we give the homeless fellow our lunch, or the hat off our head. Maybe we gather allies and sue the mining corporation for an end to mountain range annihilation. Maybe we smile before the rose or gasp in awe before the star-strewn sky.

Bashō's poetry brings alive the vivid singularity of unique participants in the community of nature. At the same time, he shows how each irreplaceable individual comes forth as inherently one with all its relations. Thus, simultaneously, *nature is utterly other (than our ego) and nature is our deeper transpersonal self.* Both are implicit in Bashō's radical motto: "Follow nature, return to nature, be nature" (1998, p. 177). In these days defiled by anthropocentric destruction, we would do well to follow the calls coming from the more-than-human world. But what about *being* nature? As awareness grows, we can realize that *we are nature* in far deeper ways than just biologically. We realize that we are an inseparable expression of the larger animate and intelligent earth. And we know the whole dynamic field of nature to be our transpersonal self. Ultimately, *we cannot really return to nature because we can never leave in the first place. We always already are nature* (although we often forget and act otherwise).

Perhaps the enticement of an ego-centered approach is an intrinsic condition of being human, because it appears as a concern across eras, cultures, and religions. But egoic attachment is magnified by the culturally constructed anxieties and confusions peculiar to modern and postmodern techno-corporate-capitalist society. In either case, Bashō's contemplative therapy for Narcissus is really a therapy for all of us, whether we practice formal meditation or not. At last, or once again, we may hear the appeals these others are making to us and go on to respond in our own uniquely caring way. Surely we know that one else can answer the summon for us. *What immense responsibility, yet what joy as well, since our very life is the rejoinder we offer.*

How then might we live? This is an existential question we each must answer through our replies to the calls of daily life. But we can draw inspiration from another Zen poem. This one comes not from Bashō but from Dongshan (Tōzan, Japanese). In a wonderful inversion of Narcissus' self-entrancement, Dongshan was enlightened upon seeing his reflection in a river! Awakening involves consciously realizing one's true self and living accordingly. In Dongshan's encounter, we can be assured that the self he discovered went far beyond any ego-centered, skin-bounded one. In a verse he composed later, he reminds us that these opportunities are always available: "The song of the cuckoo / calls me home."[2] Really hearing such singing may awaken me from my self-obsessed trance—if

I consent to it, confide myself into it. I can always come home to and quintessentially *for* my fellows. Identically, this means coming home to my deepest self as well. Here I am surrendered into life's wide-open heart ground, into my own true heart and yours, into intimacy with all my relations, and into loving service. The beings and presences of nature spring forth each time I release into open attunement, and we all are refreshed together.

Let us tenderly remember how easy it is for us and for others to become lost in narcissistic spells, time and time again. And let us not forget how anguishing it is to be cut off from others, from our very self, from this very life—as yet unable or unwilling to hear the bird's song, the distress of our coworker, the laugh of a child, the voice of the beckoning earth. "Ah, not to be cut off" cries Rilke, "not through the slightest partition shut out from the law of the stars" (Mitchell, 1995, p. 191). Bashō was well aware of this great challenge. After years of meditative practice, he composed this bittersweet haiku: *"even in Kyoto, / hearing a cuckoo, / I long for Kyoto"* (Hirshfield, 2015, p. 54). Whether in Kyoto or our own home, often we are not really here, not attuned to the gifts that life is freely bestowing or the appeals it is making to us. How bitter it is to feel exiled from the infinite depths that are always already presencing. But susceptibility to such lapses seems intrinsic to our finite and fallible condition. And yet—still, still, still!—upon hearing the cuckoo or a neighbor's voice, the illusion of separation can dissolve. Sensing their depths from our depths, we respond anew. How sweet!

The song of the cuckoo calls us home, from ego-centered alienation to eco-centered intimacy, conversation, conviviality, and responsibility. So also does global warming, rich humus nourishing our garden, cancer growing in a loved one, the economic/political systems sponsoring insatiable consumption, the smell of a summer thunderstorm, the military mindset eager to wage war on those deemed "other," and the old oak tree in the garden—in truth, all our human and more-than-human sisters and brothers in this participatory earth fellowship. We are called home by each of these. With intimate communion—aware that home is present in every encounter, that every place is the center, and that every other is uniquely other while simultaneously being one face of our deepest self—may we embrace this awesome sacred summons and bring forth our irreplaceable gifts in reply.

Chapter Nine

# Nature-Healing-Body-Healing-Nature-Healing-Body

## From Desensitization to Embodied Attunement

Only human beings have come to a point where they no longer
know why they exist. . . . They have forgotten the secret knowledge
of their bodies.

—John Fire Lame Deer (Lame Deer & Erdoes, 1972, p. 147)

My body is a sort of open circuit that completes itself only in things,
in others, in the encompassing earth.

—David Abram (1996, p. 62)

Listen, are you breathing just a little, and calling it a life?

—Mary Oliver (2005, p. 142)

## Overture

Today's dominant culture afflicts us with a twin dissociation. We are
estranged from the natural world and from vividly felt experiential
contact with our embodied wisdom. In a countercultural therapeutic
move, conscious involvement with nature can help heal our desensitized
body(self). Correspondingly, our sensitized body(self) can help heal the
desecrated and exploited natural world. Herein, we may realize that the

shared earth community is our deeper, transpersonal body(self), just as our body(self) is the earth taking form as our unique body(self).

## Our Sensuous, Wise, and Compassionate Body

To initiate this chapter's inquiry, let me take the liberty of posing a question. Please notice the first thing that comes to mind. *Did you see the weather today?* . . . This is a common query, since the weather is such a powerful force in our daily lives. Most people think first about a weather *report*, about information gleaned from their phone, computer, radio, or television. No one is immune to the pervasive (and largely eco-alienating) influences of our technologically enthralled society. Nonetheless, this association—conditioned, disembodied, distant-from-experience—is troubling because the actual weather can only be found in our bodily felt contact with the elemental presences of nature. "You don't need a weatherman to know which way the wind blows" as Bob Dylan (1965) once challenged us to realize.

The real weather is a wild, freely functioning field of embodied powers all interacting with each other: airy forces interplaying with watery, fiery, and earthy ones (and now with economic/political forces in their complicity with climate disruption). Further, the weather involves not only atmospheric elements in themselves, but such elemental forces *in relation with* our sensuous and intelligent body. The weather consists of the cool breeze caressing our cheeks and caressing the willow's leaves; the fall sunshine warming our skin and a kestrel's feathers; clouds, threatening or inviting; lightning bolting and thunder cracking; rain drizzling or pouring upon everyone; fresh snow with bears hibernating, children sledding, cars skidding; pulling the blanket up at night or removing a vest in the afternoon; summer heat in our flesh, and in the kindred flesh of cougars, and in the contrasting yet still kindred flesh of giant redwoods. We all "see" and are touched by the weather every day. Yet our proclivity to construe the weather as something bestowed by a screen is a minor symptom of a major alienation: the estrangement of us human animals from aware contact with the rest of nature.

"Listen, are you breathing just a little, and calling it a life?" (Oliver, 2005, p. 142). We tend to be alienated not only from the surrounding natural world, but from our naturally attuned embodiment. Our bodily felt responses to the solicitations of others are the way nature sponsors our understanding and care, but cultural conditioning can suppress (or support!) such crucial relational capacities. As we immerse ourselves in phones, zoom screens, office cubicles, or experience-distant concepts, it is as if we have left our body behind, forgotten it, devalued it, or desensitized it. At other times we numb our bodies—psychologically and/or chemically—in efforts to flee emotional wounds. Or we try to subdue or repress our animal body due to fantasies that it is intrinsically violent or excessively sexual. Even when we do focus on our body, we often treat it merely as a burden (when injured, ill, or fatigued) or a machine (that needs a technical tune up at the gym).

In speaking of the ways we often construe our body, I just wrote that we often forget and desensitize "*it*." Even while trying to honor our bodily intelligence, I unintentionally got caught in the dominant culture's devaluation of embodiment. The sentient-sapient body I want to celebrate is not an "it," not an object. (Neither are an eagle, a river, or a mountain, although "it" is a designation we often give them too.) Rather, *my body is me*. I do not mean my merely physical body (because no living body is ever just physical), but my intelligent body-self. Tellingly, however, when we hear someone say "myself," the inherently embodied and relational qualities of "self" are often lost in translation. Even the word "*embodied*" is misleading because it suggests that some subjective mind exists separately from an objective, physical body; and that this presumably disembodied mind must somehow place itself "in" the body. Nonetheless, we surely need to bring more consciousness into our bodily experience and more of our bodily experience into consciousness. *Gravely, we have lost touch with touch, and thereby end up out of touch with the animate earth.* Joining with Mary Oliver, we all need to breathe more fully so as to connect more deeply with our self and others.

In contrast to the dualistic, separatist, desensitized stance previously noted, when I speak of embodiment I mean our (potentially) lively, sensuous, sensitized, wise, resonant, creative, caring body that is always in relation with others. This includes but transcends our strictly biological body. Such a wakefully attuned body is the experiential nexus of real understanding, compassion, and love. We could call this our body-self, body-mind, heart-mind, or heart, or simply our "self." The present chapter will show how attunement to our bodily felt contact with others facilitates care for the rest of nature, and how conscious contact with nature enhances our embodied vitality, awareness, and holistic health. By interrupting the viciously reinforcing circle of disembodiment and desecration of nature, this move can sponsor a reciprocally enlivening, interrelational circuit of transformation: *nature-healing-body-healing-nature-healing-body*.

## Remembering the Secret Knowledge of Our Body (It's an Open Secret)

John Fire Lame Deer, a Lakota Sioux holy man, expressed grave concerns about the body-and-nature-estranged ways of modern Euro-American culture: "Only human beings have come to a point where they no longer know why they exist. . . . They have forgotten the secret knowledge of their bodies, their senses, or their dreams" (Lame Deer & Erdoes, 1972, p. 147).

We are certainly the heirs of Descartes and his fellow champions of dualism (separatism). Their ghosts continue to haunt us for good and ill. The good has to do with modernity's important accomplishments: critical reason, science, health care, democracy, and so forth. Among the "ills" are the dissociative denial of our intelligent carnal inherence in the animate world. Having diminished our somatic sensitivity in relation with others and with our own self, we become confused about why we exist, about what we are here for in the shared earth community. Captivated by disembodied fantasies of human preeminence and materialistic progress (for a privileged few), bulldozers run rampant over rainforests, we blind ourselves to fossil fuel addiction and global warming, and corporations carry on unconscionably with business as usual.

As a psychocultural therapeutic, ecopsychology aspires to foster holistic, nondual healing possibilities for embodied being, knowing, and loving. Remember that *health* and *healing*—and *holy* as well—all derive from an ancient word meaning whole. When we live as if dissociated from our body, our self is split. The small part with which we identify—our egoic mind, or more narrowly our persona—is far from whole. And when we live as if dissociated from nature, our self is split in another way. We become less whole, and we go on to destroy countless species, habitats, and relational possibilities. In doing so, we make the world less diverse, less whole. Estranged from the wisdom and compassion of our body(self), we live merely as a partial self relating partially to a mere part of the world. Such a fixed, fortified partiality is a definitive sign of psychopathology. In today's crazy-making world the incidence of clinical disorders is terribly high, with approximately 20 percent of adults experiencing mental illness within a one-year period ("Mental Health," 2019).

But far more pervasive is the subclinical malady of being out of touch with our sensuously intelligent body. This is yet another version of the *normative pathology* afflicting our world. Desensitized knowing with our heads but without our hearts is a symptom of our larger alienation from nature. Our incarnate self is one form of nature, after all. Our bodies do have "secret" knowledge that we have forgotten, as Lame Deer said. But in the healing venture that is at hand, be assured: this is a secret open to all.

## Embodied Awareness and Intimate Relations

One summer I was participating in a body-oriented Gestalt therapy conference at the renowned Esalen Institute. I was there to learn from others, to share my ecopsychology work, and to enjoy the extraordinary beauty of the place. Located in California's Big Sur bioregion, where rocky cliffs meet the vast Pacific Ocean on the west, and giant redwoods grace the hills on the east, Esalen is truly an awe-inspiring place. During an early morning walk I noticed an Allen's hummingbird hovering over a bush and relishing the nectar of some small pink blossoms. Smiling with delight, I felt tingling currents of excitement coursing through me as I watched the little bird and plant dancing with each other. Approaching slowly, I sensed a lively erotic charge all around the blooming bush. This subtly felt energetic awareness was flowing initially between the hummer and the flowers yet soon began reverberating outward to touch me (and to be touched by me, as the bird clearly felt my presence). The experience was joyful. Yet, because I am blessed with ruby-throated hummingbirds around my home on the other side of the country, up to this point things seemed fairly familiar. But I was in for a great surprise, something I had never seen in nearly 20 years of avid birding. The contact between the bird, the bush, and me grew more intense, and I sensed a dynamic intimacy taking form in two "places." A warm vibratory energy was coursing through my individual body(self). Inseparably, there was a flowing energetic-relational intercourse between me and all the others in the natural field. I was primarily aware of the humming-bird-with-flowers-with-me. Simultaneously, I also felt intimations of all-of-us-together-participating-with-the-encompassing-air-and-waves-and-sea-and-trees-and-mountain-and-sky-and-on-and-on-endlessly. (Another example of nature's conversational consciousness.) As the experience continued to transpire, the participatory partnership opened even further in an extraordinarily lucid way. I realized the leaves and flower petals were moving in exquisite inter-responsivity with the hummingbird's flapping wings. I could actually see the viscous air being pushed down from the rapidly beating wings to the small green leaves below, the leaves bending down pliantly in response and then springing back up in turn, sending a tangibly thick cushion of air up to the hummer's tiny wings, thereby supporting the bird's flight and facilitating the nourishing and pollinating interaction between the little bird and plant. With this intimate contact, warm tears of joy flowed from my eyes.

I had been privileged to encounter hundreds of hummingbirds in my life, but I had never before been graced with such an experience. Such interactions between birds, insects, and flowers are surely common. And yet—right then, right there—I was blessed to see and feel it directly. Upon returning home I watched our ruby-throated neighbors feed on bee balm in front of our house, and indeed, the petals and leaves and wing beats were moving in unison! I also made sure our feeders were filled with nectar or seeds, in support of our avian allies' preparations for fall migration. Did Esalen's marvelous natural field vivify my bodily attunement, such that I met the hummingbird-and-petals as if for the first time? Did my lively embodiment, having been refined via the conference, open me anew to nature and thereby sponsor greater care? Both conditions are true and mutually generative: *conscious contact with our nonhuman companions enhances our embodied awareness and well-being. In a complementary way, embodied attunement fosters empathic awareness of the rest of nature and devotion to its well-being.* This gives us the opportunity to cultivate a spiraling, inter-responsive way of being together: *nature heals our body, which further heals nature, which further heals our body(self), and on and on.* In this call-and-response conversation, notice that *nature comes first.* But even this is a bit misleading, since we humans are a mode of nature's being. When we benefit from earth's healing overtures, this is a version of nature healing nature. When we offer our ministrations for earth's well-being, this is a different version of nature healing nature.

## The Lure of Disembodiment and the Reciprocal Dissociation from Nature

Driven by the fantasy of splitting body from mind, and self and species from the rest of nature, Euro-American culture has long valorized the (supposedly) disembodied intellect. Our cognitive abilities are great gifts. But in overemphasizing them we often dampen our intelligent sensuous attunement with the world, thereby fabricating a desensitized, anesthetized, and thus relationally impoverished existence. Although the body "is open in a circuit with the world" (Merleau-Ponty, 2003, p. 217), we often short-circuit life's naturally meaningful, inter-responsive currents. To illustrate this dire point, instead of living as if we were elevated above our body and the rest of nature, what if we decided to intentionally enact this spurious severance? Presuming to be detached and self-sufficient, we might refuse physical nourishment from the waters of the earth and the bodies of plants or animals. But it is obvious how such folly would turn out. This thought experiment instantly subverts our separatist fantasies.

I find it helpful to remember that there are powerful forces inducing us to adopt dissociative ways of being. Life itself can be immensely challenging. The pain it sends our way can be too much to bear at times. Three major circumstances lure us to disavow our embodied sensitivity: (1) trauma, especially the experience of being intentionally hurt by another person, particularly by one who was supposed to care for us; (2) today's socially constructed, separatist paradigm: mind/body, self/others, self/world, humans/nature; and (3) the basic (co)existential conditions of being human, especially our vulnerable body-self and our awareness that death is inevitable for us and our beloved ones. The most acute source of defensive disembodiment is interpersonal trauma. At some point each of us will be wounded in a relationship. Such pain ranges from ordinary misunderstandings to empathic failures to mean-spirited attacks to shaming to active violence, abuse, neglect, or abandonment. Psychotherapists know that one way of coping with trauma is to identify with only part of our self and disidentify with or dissociate other parts (or other ways of being)—say, our thinking mind over our vulnerable body. And when trauma is followed by ongoing lack of understanding from others, our originally creative, life-saving defenses congeal into habits that congeal into constrictive personality structure, worldviews, and ways of being. Defenses get enacted automatically, when they are no longer called for, thereby impoverishing ourselves and others in the process.

Estrangement from our sentient bodies is supported by the (mis)guiding sociocultural forces that became preeminent in the modern era: especially the notion of a mind-centered self divorced from body, others, world, and nature. These presumed disconnections are the "shadow" of modernity's emancipatory accomplishments. *Body and nature are the primary victims of this splitting and denigration*—indeed, two forms of the same dissociation. *This still prominent cultural construction of reality functions as a mostly unconscious ground that compellingly structures our experience.* However, in today's techno-corporate-consumerist society we should not critique "anthropocentric" practices in general, but the practices of relatively anonymous, noncentralized systems of economic/political/ legal power. These systems are led by *a small number of privileged people who tend to make life-changing decisions in relatively distant, disembodied, detached ways.* It is far easier to order a military attack from the White House or Kremlin, where leaders are detached from a viscerally felt bodily experience of the real people who will kill and be killed. And it is far easier to order the annihilation of a rural mountain range when sitting in the city boardroom of a coal company.

Along with trauma and sociocultural conditioning, we can also be pushed away from bodily attunement by circumstances intrinsic in all of human existence. Ordinary life can be painful and dangerous indeed. Sickness, injury, aging, and death are unavoidable. Nature's powerful forces can be terrifying and deadly. We know we will die, inescapably but unpredictably. And we know we will lose the people we love most, whether they die before us or we before them. Our tender animal bodies remind us of our mortality each time something goes wrong. We are ever vulnerable to the "the heartache and the thousand natural shocks That flesh is heir to" as Hamlet lamented in agonizing whether "to be or not to be" (Shakespeare, *Hamlet*, act 3, scene 1). We do not have to find ourselves stricken with cancer, accidentally swimming with sharks, or lying on the ground with a broken neck after tumbling from a bike to appreciate that simply being here is dangerous, tenuous, and impermanent. Our fleshy, feeling self is inherently exposed to violation. We can try to deny this, but the truth keeps resurfacing. For each of us there comes a time when we see the lifeless body of a dead animal, say a dear dog or cat who passed away in our home or a raccoon crushed on the road. And there comes a time when we witness the body of a beloved person fade away. After all, the people most intimate with us are mortal animals too. In seeing these deaths we foresee our own. Our lively animal body is destined to perish. Ultimately, there is no denying that our end-time will come. Even though we are ever vulnerable in the face of nature's forces, we often pretend that we are not really an incarnate animal but somehow elevated above the natural order. These defensive strategies are doomed to fail, but they are understandable.

The cultural anthropologist Ernest Becker raised serious concerns about the common disavowal of our tender bodily condition. And he traced this to our avoidance of a thoroughly natural phenomenon: death. It is unclear if other animals are aware that they will die at some unknown future time. But it is very clear that we human animals are burdened (and gifted too) with a poignant awareness that death looms on the horizon. Becker (1973) showed how the "denial of death" drives much of our daily existence, but mostly outside of our awareness. In a brilliant existentialist formulation, he pointed out that *"consciousness of death* is the primary repression, not sexuality" (p. 96). If death were always at the forefront of our awareness, the sustained intensity of this reality would be unbearable. And yet, when we shrink back from our incarnate animal mortality we are shrinking back from engagement with the one existence we are given. *Fear of death quickly morphs into a fear of being fully alive.* A haunting, low-intensity dread often hovers in the background—not only a dread that something bad will happen in the future, but a dread of letting go into intimate, bodily felt contact with the wild, glorious, fierce, and ultimately unmasterable reality of the present encounter. *Ironically, we preemptively deaden ourselves to avoid dying.* Life is hard. *Simply by being here we will be wounded, inevitably so.* Each of us is managing as well as we can under the circumstances. But captivated by a largely unconscious presumption that our past injuries will be repeated—that this new encounter will overwhelm or even kill us—our fears and defenses grow out of proportion to the present risk. In dissociating our embodied attunement and wisdom, we settle for a partially lived life.

## Daring to Bring Our Bodies Alive with Others

Our animal susceptibility and mortality are unavoidable givens of human (co)existence. What is not given—what we have much say in—is how we take up and respond to these existential facts. We can try to extricate ourselves from the inextricable—using drugs, screens, overconsumption, hyperactivity, money-grabbing, power-grabbing, and emotional detachment to diminish our bodily felt sense of life's intensity. But there is another way. A vital, bodily felt awareness of death holds surprisingly life-enhancing possibilities. "We experience the sensuous world only by rendering ourselves vulnerable to the world" (Abram, 2010, p. 58). Bearing the consciousness of our finite temporal existence can be inspiring, returning us to this precarious life with a renewed sense of its preciousness and of our sacred responsibility. This sensibility is conveyed by Merton in his journal. I imagine he was walking among the rolling hills of his monastery when he penned this sensuous appreciation of nature's marvelously impermanent presencing: "A sweet summer afternoon. Cool breezes and a clear sky. This day will not come again. . . . Blue hills. Day lilies nod in the wind. . . . This day will not come again" (Merton, 1968a, p. 45). No moment, no encounter, no life ever comes again. The moments I miss, the relational interchanges that pass by as I sleepwalk, numb, or detach myself—*these are my very life.*

Merton's testimony reminds me of a poem by Kobayashi Issa (1763–1828), Japanese poet and lay Buddhist priest. Issa's existence was marked by death after death. He lost his mother when he was three. He was raised by a loving grandmother, but she died when he was 14. Issa's first child died soon after birth, and two others perished when they were quite young. His wife died not long afterward. Yet Issa found a way to stay fully alive when death repeatedly arrived. He wrote this poem after his daughter died: "Dew evaporates— / And all this world is dew: / So dear, so fresh, so fleeting."[1] I am poignantly aware that all finite things will pass away. This is a bitter truth when resisted from an ego-centered stance. Yet when I make peace with this fiercely felt fact, I find that those dear to me shine more brightly and my loving appreciation flows more freely in the present (and only) time we are being given. I am thinking here of beloved human companions but also of more-than-human ones—the pileated woodpecker drilling for grubs in a decaying oak tree, all the endangered beings in this era of mass extinction.

It is true that I live by eating others, be they plants or animals. And so too will I be eaten. This is intrinsic to the great venture of (co)existing. The challenge is to consent consciously and responsibly to this sacramental fact, while graciously participating in another dimension of the same great venture: it is through nurturing others and being nurtured by them that I live. To honor impermanence and the certainty of eventual death is a profound opportunity, an intense but open invitation ceaselessly presented to each of us. The invitation sends shudders through me as I make felt-contact with the truth that, all too soon, I and those whom I love will no longer be. Yet shuddering is my animal body's natural way of allowing the currents of life to keep flowing through me. When I clamp down on my shuddering, I clamp down on my life.

*Interpersonal trauma, misguided cultural conditioning, and (co)existential vulnerability: with this trio of afflicting forces in the mix, it is no wonder that we try to remove ourselves from our bodies and take up residence elsewhere. But elsewhere is not a real option. There is nowhere else to be than in and as our vulnerable, mortal, sentient, sapient bodies.* While defenses do help us bear otherwise unbearable situations, it is not sustainable to keep distancing ourselves from our lived bodies. We cannot not be in contact with people and with the rest of nature. Our only option has to do with the relative depth, subtlety, and flexibility of awareness and responsiveness we bring into our embodied connections with others. In this wounded and wounding world, painful encounters will inevitably occur when we open up our somatic sensitivity. Yet being more deeply sensitized bestows creative resources with which to respond to life's challenges. Thankfully, our pleasure and joy and loving-kindness are enhanced as well.

## Body(self) as a Dynamic Site of Ethical Contact

Between my sensuous body and the phenomenal world "there is not a frontier, but a contact surface" (Merleau-Ponty, 1968, p. 271). My incarnate body-self is the primary locus of my engagement with the world, the sentient-sapient nexus that gives rise to my understanding and (inter)actions. My eyes and nose allow the beauty of a rhododendron blossom or the ugliness of a clear-cut forest (and the timber company's unconscionable bottom line) to touch and move me. I do not have to conceptually imagine the pain of the oriole who crashed into my glass door and died. I know it directly, via my lived body. The boundaries of our sensitive, inter-responsive body are "more like membranes than barriers, they define a surface of metamorphosis and exchange" (Abram, 1996, p. 46). By cultural convention, I think of myself as a skin-bounded self. *However, my body-boundary does not really separate me from the rest of the world. Rather, being open, aware, permeable, receptive, and expressive, my embodiment joins me in conversational intercourse with all my relations, with fellow participants who may be loving or dangerous or in need of my care.* Indeed, "The body is precisely my insertion in the common, or intersubjective, field of experience" (Abram, 1996, p. 44). Even as my personal body differentiates me from you and from the blooming cherry tree and from the great blue heron flying across the lake, it functions simultaneously as a porous medium of interchange between me and all others: between your hand and mine, between your heart and mine, between the sweet cherry blossoms and my relishing nose, between the heron's graceful glide and my awe-filled eyes. And as we are seeing with transpersonal ecopsychology, the permeable corporeal boundary where I and my companions meet is one that opens into infinite depths—the depths of self, others, world, and life, all ultimately the same depths.

Merleau-Ponty calls our attention to the obvious fact that our sensorial body is inherently *inter*corporeal. Time and again we find our body(self) meeting another body(self)—the body of a person, chair, skunk scent, beach sand. Pondering the implications of an ever-recurring condition of life, Merleau-Ponty (2003) names the (co)existential fact of "my body standing in front of the upright things, in a circuit with the world, an *Einfühlung* [empathy] with the world, with the things, with the animals, with other bodies" (p. 209). In being upright on two legs, we humans open upon a wildly diverse world and move through it with our tender hearts exposed to all the blessings and threats that others send our way. Thus, an interrelational and ultimately ethical orientation is built into the very structure of our embodied (co)existence. Our lived body is the nodal source of empathic, caring engagement, with our senses being gates through which others nourish us and we go on to nourish them in turn. Serving as our openness to the world, our body naturally yearns for and welcomes (as well as defends against) contact with different beings and things. When we inquire about the location of our felt experience-in-relation-with-others, is it inside our body? Not exactly. Outside our body? Not exactly. Looking/feeling into our direct experience, we can find no real separation of self and other. "The concern is to grasp humanity first as another manner of being a body . . . not as an other substance [as Descartes would have it], but as *interbeing*" (Merleau-Ponty, 2003, p. 208).[2] Inherently, our very being, the being of our body (self), is interbeing with other bodies (selves).

Our body's capacity for sensory awareness is what allows us to meet the rest of the world. But that is just the beginning of the story, not the end, because what matters is not merely any kind of somatic contact. As the source of compassion, a vivid consciousness of our embodied responsiveness is what makes all the difference in our lives and the lives of others. In contrast, our lack of bodily attunement skews our perceptions and actions toward preestablished beliefs and self-centered wishes. With a committee meeting on my mind I drive on without heeding the icy conditions, foreclosing awareness of the wary caution my body might otherwise convey. With profits in mind and embodied empathy out of mind, corporate and political policy decisions authorize continued reliance on fossil fuels while dismissing the rise in respiratory illnesses (exacerbated by polluted air) and disastrous storms and fires (due to global warming).

## The Natural World (Mis)Construed through the Lens of Disembodiment

A sycamore may be seen as a home (by an oriole), as a challenging climb (by a child), as smooth flesh to caress (by a nature lover), or as lumber (by a businessman). These are very different trees even if they are the same material presence. Clearly, the meanings of lived experience are not given objectively by way of physiological stimuli. Rather, the functioning of our consciousness (imbued with history and culture) participates in *organizing, constructing, or constituting experiential meaning.* This psycho-cultural lens bends the overtures the world sends us, and does so in a relatively stable, preestablished way. Oriented—actually, disoriented—by a mostly disembodied self that is imbued with the separatist fantasies of modernity, how then do we constitute nature? What does the natural world look like and how do we tend to relate with it? To begin with, I feel relatively desensitized and detached from the felt immediacy of my direct experience. Distanced from conscious sensuous involvement with others, I lose access to much of my somatic vitality, intelligence, empathy, and relational repertoire. My perceptions, motivations, and interactions are organized via a constricted part of my being. And I thereby perceive merely a constricted profile of the natural world. Disavowing my bodily felt engagement with others and with the depths of my own being, I imagine myself to be a cerebrally centered, autonomous, self-sufficient individual who is intrinsically detached from others and the rest of the natural world. My identity, security, agency, and relational responses emerge from this abstract notion of who I am and what I want. Rather than welcoming the natural world as a genuine conversational companion who is intelligent and communicating with me, nature tends to appear woefully reduced: as irrelevant, as a feared threat, as an impediment to my self-centered wishes, or merely an objectified resource to exploit.

## Embracing or Disavowing Our Lively Body:
## A Continuum of Sensitivity

A variety of formal methods are helpful in reawakening our bodily sensitivity and wisdom. Consistent direct contact with nature may be the most auspicious path of all. Others include body-oriented psychotherapy, yoga, Qigong, conscious sex, and socially/ecologically engaged service. Some actual examples of recovering the richness of our embodied awareness may be helpful here. We might begin with a simple body-awareness exercise. I often do this for myself, and sometimes with students, psychotherapy patients, and ecopsychology workshop participants. If you are willing, begin by looking up from this book and becoming aware of your ordinary experience. Simply notice how your body feels, and how the things around you appear . . . Now please stand up. Welcome in some deep breaths and breathe out vigorously. To amplify the experience, briskly pat your body with your open hands. Actively tap your arms, legs, torso, shoulders, and back. (Yes, give yourself a pat on the back! You deserve it.) Gently tap your head and face as well. Notice the sensations in your body and how the things around you appear now. And compare this with your experience before you started. I do not know what happened for you, but I often hear things like, "Those flowers are glowing." "At first I was focused more internally, but now I feel myself being out there in the room." "The whole room is brighter." "Everything is vibrating—me, all of you, that chair, everything." "It's strange, but that ink pen looks beautiful to me." "We're all smiling now!"

Similar experiences often arise in my practice of psychotherapy, work that is deeply informed by ecopsychology. A man in his 40s sought my assistance at a turning point in his life. Paul, as I will call him, was a kind, intelligent, articulate man who was yearning for a real change. He was long burdened with shame; pulled back from the world and focused inwardly with self-criticism and self-loathing; devitalized but unaware of his slow, heavy comportment and bodily anesthetization. He was essentially unavailable for his wife and indeed for his very life. To say that he was depressed only hints at his suffering. We had been working with each other for almost a year (interrelationally, bodily, and verbally), focusing by way of conversation and experiential exploration on his present concerns and life history, his disconnection from his wife, his desensitized body, sadness, shame, and so on. Then one day in session, as Paul was starting to feel angry at his work supervisor, I noticed that he was sitting up a little more fully. I shared this with him so we could get interested together. This was in contrast to his habitually heavy comportment—downward-and-inward slouching, with drooping head and shoulders and caving-in chest. I described how, in the present moment, his head and torso appeared to be stretching upward and slightly forward. He allowed this into his awareness and surprisingly found himself enjoying a small surge of energy, even a little sense of power. Then we tuned into the fact that he was breathing more deeply than usual. I wondered with him if he could discover the *bodily* processes that supported this upward-for-ward-energized experience. When he could not at first, I shared that I was "trying on" in my own experience a version of his movement, and that I was aware of my sit-bones sinking into the chair and helping me rise up. He engaged his experience anew, and noticed that he did indeed sense a movement upward from his bottom-in-contact-with-the chair. Then he added that he felt his feet firmly on the ground. I encouraged him to stay with that contact and stay aware. Eventually, with excitement and fear, he exclaimed, "I'm really here. I feel more real." His chest was a little more open and exposed, his face had more color, his eyes were brighter. I smiled and replied that I too felt him coming across as really here, really present with himself and with me as well.

At first this encounter may not seem related to nature. However, our embodied existence—part of our human nature—is a manifestation of the larger natural world (while being deeply enculturated at the same time). Several months later Paul looked around my office and remarked that he was enjoying all the plants growing there. He asked if I had renovated the space. Long before my first session with him, my office had been filled with plants and other natural presences such as feathers and smooth sea-stones. But now, with a more lively body(self), he was moved by the lively plants. In later sessions, *in ways he could not even imagine before*, he began playing with the beautiful stones, caressing them with pleasure and savoring the feeling of his body being correspondingly touched by them. One day Paul pointed across the room and said, "That poor plant needs some water!" And he was right! Further, such sensitive changes were not limited to my therapy office. He bought some house-plants to enliven his home, and—not unrelatedly—he and his wife found ways to create a more vital, intimate existence together.

For a contrasting example, consider the case of René Descartes. As we have discussed, Descartes' thinking exemplifies the values of the modern era, including a dissociation from embodied life. Seeking for a truth of which he could be certain, Descartes arrived at the peculiar idea that mind and body (and so too mind and world) are completely separate. He claimed that "the concept of body includes nothing at all which belongs to the mind, and the concept of mind includes nothing at all which belongs to the body" (Descartes, 1984, p. 158). With this strange turn of thought, he contrived a logic that led him to identify solely with his (presumably) rational mind, and to deem the body and the natural world as insentient, material objects. "I do not recognize any difference between the machines made by craftsmen and the various bodies that nature alone composes" (Descartes, in Capra, 1983, p. 61). Ironically, while valorizing reason, this is a very irrational thought! These dualistic and mechanistic notions became pivotal in Descartes' philosophy, even though they are removed from the evidence of direct experience. More significantly, they became incorporated into the dominant cultural views and scientific/technological program of the modern era. This includes a sense of being entitled to exploit the supposedly mechanical, merely material natural world. Over time these views also began shaping people's taken for granted sense of self.

Two events were especially significant in leading Descartes to cling to such experience-distant ideas. He presents the first in support of his most famous philosophical proclamation:

And noticing that this truth—*I think, therefore I am*—was so firm and so assured that . . . I judged that I could accept it without scruple as the first principle of the philosophy I was seeking. . . . Then, examining with attention what I was, and seeing that I could pretend that I had no body and that there was no world nor any place where I was, I could not pretend, on that account that I did not exist at all. . . . I knew that I was a substance the whole essence or nature of which is simply to think, and which, in order to exist, has no need of any place nor depends on any material thing. (Descartes, 1998, pp. 18–19)

A merely thinking, disembodied "I," what an eerie first principle to be guided by! A few years later Descartes (1984) argued further for a mechanistic mind/body split: "Were I perchance to look out my window and observe men crossing the square, I would ordinarily say that I see men themselves. . . . But what do I see aside from hats and clothes, which could conceal automata [i.e., mechanical robots]?" (p. 68).

Both experiences were formative for Descartes, and by extension for the newly emerging modern worldview. But if we heard these without knowing that they were philosophical thought experiments, they would sound either psychotic or sociopathic. How bizarre to imagine that I could exist without depending on "any material thing." Stop eating. Stop drinking. Abdicate the nourishment the earth is always providing. Really, Monsieur Descartes? And, truly, upon seeing another person, the thought that they are a machine would not even occur to us. To claim such a thing would be frighteningly out of touch with shared reality, indeed psychotically delusional. Alternatively, lacking a conscience grounded in embodied empathic connection, a sociopath might dehumanize another person in order to better manipulate them, stripping the other of their feelings and their ability to suffer. It is terribly disturbing that someone could look at another person and see a robot, yes? But it follows rather consistently if we float along detached from our relationally attuned body. When captivated by such a disembodied fantasy, how could we feel empathy for the real others we encounter? It is said that Descartes wept openly when his five-year-old daughter died. If only this experience would have informed his philosophy!

## The Pernicious Confluence of Disembodiment, Deanimation, and Capitalism

Descartes' take on things is quite chilling. And lest we think that his views are merely the idiosyncratic musings of an eccentric individual a long time ago, let us consider an egregious analogue in our contemporary society. From the 1970s to the present, coal corporations have used an extreme strip-mining method across the Appalachian region in the eastern United States. The procedure is known as "mountaintop removal," but this deceptive euphemism hides the devastation wreaked by this ruthlessly violent practice (see "Mountaintop Removal 101," 2019; Reece, 2006).[3] Far more severe than the "top" of a single mountain being "removed," entire mountain ranges are being demolished from their peaks down. So let us call it what it actually is: *mountain range annihilation*. At numerous sites in West Virginia, Kentucky, Tennessee, and Virginia, miners who formerly tunneled underground have been laid off and replaced by colossal machinery and powerful explosives. Armed with these massive weapons, coal companies are destroying entire mountain ranges and their surrounding watersheds, obliterating everything except the seams of coal. Once the valuable mineral is collected, remnants of formerly flourishing natural communities (now mere debris) are deposited as "waste" in the valleys, filling streams and killing wildlife in vital wetland ecosystems.

These beautiful lands were—and those that survive still are—the most ancient mountains on earth, home to unimaginably diverse natural communities. But now, rather than looking up at a glorious green mountain one must look down into a vast lifeless rubble-pit resembling a crater on the moon. Families who lived in these lands for generations are being paid or coerced to move away. Others are driven away by the air and water pollution generated by the carnage. Human homes and neighborhoods, black bears and white-tailed deer, broad-winged hawks and indigo buntings, monarch butterflies and honeybees, maples and hemlocks, ferns and trillium, rich humus and rippling springs: after these are destroyed or displaced, the ancient, ecologically rich ridges become mere commodities. The living mountains-cum-fossil-fuel meet our short-term energy demands while amplifying global warming; polluting the air and water; generating acid rain poison; bringing asthma, cancer, depression, anxiety, and substance abuse to people who live nearby; and filling the pockets of corporate executives.

Having heard the anguished concerns of citizens living near these mines, a journalist from the *Pittsburgh Post-Gazette* sought the industry's perspective by interviewing the president of the West Virginia Coal Association. Mr. Bill Raney acknowledged (apparently in total seriousness) that mountaintop removal mining may create, in his words, "a reduction in elevation" (Jones, 2006, p. A-14). Nonetheless, he argued that this is a good thing because it creates flat pieces of real estate in a mountainous state. As he put it, "Level land is such a rare commodity that it's a shame not to coordinate future development" with mountaintop removal (p. A-14). Now, imagine standing before a thriving mountain eco-community and seeing only coal and flat land to exploit. Such a detached, insensitive perspective would be outright psychotic if it were not sponsored by a culture that fosters our dissociation from the natural world and from our bodies. Or if not mad, then sociopathic? Or just business as usual? Or all three in some nefarious mix? It has been said that John Denver's popular lyric, "Almost heaven, West Virginia . . . ," must now be sung as a lament: "Almost level, West Virginia . . ." Yet mountain range annihilation continues to be largely supported by our economic, political, and legal systems.

## The Field of Nature as Our Transpersonal Body

My wife and I lived for eight years in the glorious mountains of West Virginia, and during that time it was our great fortune to become acquainted with Mr. Larry Gibson. What brought us together was our shared devotion to preserving (what was left of) Appalachia from the ravages of mountain range annihilation. Mr. Gibson's home was Kayford Mountain, a wonderful place his ancestors first settled in the 1700s. On three different occasions I visited him at his humble cabin, located as it was on a beautiful piece of land surrounded by a cluster of huge strip-mine craters. Incredibly, this was all the living territory that remained after the mountain had been razed by the coal company. Where a 50-square-mile mountain range once rose magnificently to the sky, I was shocked to see a gigantic barren pit. In his initial encounter with this abominable mining method, Mr. Gibson was assaulted by extreme noise while his whole house was shaking. Of this incident he remarked, "Didn't know what it was. Didn't know it was legal to blow up a mountain. I mean, who does that?" (A Hero, 2012).

I have deep respect for Mr. Gibson and his incredulity. I mean, who does that indeed?! But the answer is clear: disembodied corporate executives entranced by a narrow view of profit. If only the *corp-* (body) of a mining corporation was a living, feeling, interrelational body! After working as a janitor for many years, Mr. Gibson devoted the last three decades of his life to fighting for his cherished homeland and its inhabitants, and in fact for all the mountains in this spectacular ecoregion. His adversaries were wealthy corporations with allies in high political and judicial positions. For over 50 years the coal companies have been buying up vast swaths of territory. In economically impoverished Appalachian communities, the money has been hard to resist. Nonetheless, Mr. Gibson forever refused to sell the place he so dearly loved. As he put it, they "say this land is worth 650 million dollars to the industry. . . . I know there's not enough money that's been printed or made that can buy this place. Some things money shouldn't be able to buy" (A Hero, 2012). He told me that many people had tried to intimidate and even kill him for his conscientious resistance. His house had been hit with bullets and set on fire. I was chilled to see bullet holes left in his home after these violent attacks. And he had been run off the road by thugs allegedly associated with the coal industry.

Mr. Gibson adored the wild, beautiful, besieged lands of West Virginia. His love is evident in this wry recollection of a conversation with his wife:

She says, "Do you cheat on me?"

I said, "Sure I do."

"Do I know her?"

"Sure you do."

"Is she pretty?"

"Most beautiful woman you ever seen."

"What's her name?" she says.

I said, "Kayford Mountain. Prettiest lady I ever met." (A Hero, 2012)[4]

One afternoon Mr. Gibson and I were standing on the edge of (what remained of) Kayford Mountain, looking down at the ongoing desolation of an active mine site. Pointing up and across the way, he said, "That ridge is where we played and picked apples when we were kids. Over there is where my uncle Dirk had his farm" (personal communication, April 2002). Sadly, he was pointing into empty space because the beloved ridges he saw in his mind's eye had been totally annihilated. Laid to waste, all that was left was mutilated ground, hundreds of feet below.

For nearly 30 years Mr. Gibson kept meeting with local and national politicians, industry representatives, environmental activists, and ordinary citizens. He risked his life for the life of the mountains, and for the lives of others' children and grandchildren. "Hell, I cried myself to sleep many a night thinking 'What could I have done better that day, and then what can I do different tomorrow to make a difference?'" (A Hero, 2012). In this video interview, Mr. Gibson gestures to the massive destruction taking place beside his home. He removes his glasses, rubs tears from his eyes, and shakes his head in dismay: "I just can't get used to it." Then his justifiably righteous anger rises to the occasion: "Truth is, my heroes are the people who don't get used to it. The one that gets used to it is the one who won't do anything about it."

Larry Gibson was a short man of great psychospiritual stature: vigorously embodied, passionately and compassionately rooted in the wild and sacred land. Visiting him one afternoon at his mountain home, he became teary as we talked about the relentless attack occurring all around. Touching his hand to his heart, he lamented: "When they destroy these mountains they are ripping out my heart. I feel my life's blood draining away" (personal communication, October 2005). Mr. Gibson was expressing grief and outrage at the violence being wreaked upon his beloved Kayford Mountain. But that is not all. *His words and gesture conveyed a vivid sense that he was inseparable from the local animate earth, that he tangibly felt this living (and now dying) mountain to be his deep heart or body(self).* We could call it his transpersonal heart, transpersonal body. The glorious natural community was his heart—metaphorically, yes, but also in tangible experience. When his home territory was pillaged—marvelous ridges, bounding deer, flowing fish-filled streams, all vanquished—his expansive heart was torn out. When the natural world is destroyed, we lose an essential dimension of our very being. As Abram (1996) remarks, "My body is a sort of open circuit that completes itself only in things, in others, in the encompassing earth" (p. 62). Like Larry Gibson knew, we actually become incomplete when our companions in the natural world are destroyed. Something at the very heart of our being is lost.

As Kayford Mountain was broken to bits, Mr. Gibson's heart was broken time and again. It is no accident that the word courage comes from the French *coeur: heart*. And Larry certainly fought on and on with heartfelt courage. But eventually the coal company's atrocious actions took the ultimate toll. Sadly, Larry Gibson died of a heart attack at his Kayford Mountain home in 2012. The mountain truly was his deep heart, indivisible from his psychophysical heart. Both hearts—which are really one heart—were being attacked by mountain range annihilation. Tragically, what killed him was a broken heart. His premature death remains a grievous loss, even as his inspiration lives on in the work of countless activists and in the words of this book.

The natural world is other than my small, individual, skin-bounded body. But it surely is not other than my transpersonal body (self, heart). As Merleau-Ponty (1968) says, in the relationship between our lived body

and the rest of the world, "there is a reciprocal insertion and intertwining of one in the other" (p. 138). This conversational interchange is
happening all the time, prereflectively, as it is the very way perception
functions. But I can participate more consciously in its call-and-response
unfolding. With deepening our awareness I see that "the things [of the
world] are the prolongation of my body and my body is the prolongation
of the world" (Merleau-Ponty, 1968, p. 255). Like Mr. Gibson, or like
Dōgen (2012), who implored us to "know that the entire earth is your
own true body" (p. 879), I can realize that my distinctive body(self) is
*an articulation of* and creative *participant in* something infinitely deep, a
subtle dynamic mystery that is ultimately inconceivable and ungraspable
but that takes tangible form as me and you. I can also feel that the life
coursing through a stream, a leaf, and a bear is the same life that courses
through me. And I can know, truly, that *I am the one great transpersonal
life* in which all things "live and move and have their being" (Saint
Paul, Acts 17:28).[5]

This is a version of the core mystical realization shared perennially
by the world's nondual spiritual traditions. I realize that the transpersonal
field of nature is my true body or true self. Identically, I know this deep
body to be the very body of G-d, the Dao, spirit, life (by whatever name).
This is the body of that which is most holy, precious, beloved, the body
that draws me out of my contracted ego and into caring communion
with all my relations. And not only is this sacred life appearing as my
body(self), it is appearing as *everyone's body*. Recall the tearful lament of
my research participant Nora: "I never thought I would live to see this
happen to the life systems of the planet, to the body that is the great
body, that is the mother body. That is for me the sacrament of God. I
do not know what is going on in the rest of the universe. I don't know
how many of these little blue gems there are. But for me, it is an attack
on God." When we realize the body of mother earth *is* the body of
G-d, the buddha-body, the body of life itself; when we realize that this
great sentient-sapient body is our true body and the body of all those
we love; and when we know this deep in our flesh and bones and heart,
we simultaneously treat the earth with the utmost care.

Like versions of other religions, there are versions of Christianity
that denigrate the body. This is ironic because at its core Christianity
is a spirituality that venerates the divine depths of embodiment by
appreciating Christ as an incarnation of G-d. Since Christ emphasizes
that the same is true for each of us, how could Christians ever think

the body deserves denigration? Indeed, across spiritual traditions, mature contemplative realization resolves and dissolves all dualistic oppositions: spirit-flesh, mind-body, self-others, self-world, us-them, heaven-earth, nirvana-samsara, humans-nature. Speaking from Advaita Vedanta, Ramana Maharshi proclaims: "The world is illusory; / Brahman alone is real; / Brahman is the world" (Wilber, 1999, p. 202).

## Embodied Awareness Sponsors Care
## for the Bodies of Others

As we traverse life's great way in connection with others, we are recurrently challenged to negotiate basic questions of selfhood and responsibility. "Who am I?" "And given that my tender body is ever vulnerably exposed, how shall I interact with others?" Ultimately, both questions arise as ethical-relational concerns because I cannot answer either one with a final, comprehensive, definitive fact—certainly not one I have prepared ahead of time—but only with a tangible response. *Yet when I become sensitively attuned to my individual body, I simultaneously become sensitively attuned to the bodies of others—be they singular individuals (like my friend with terminal cancer or the insect-ridden old pine tree next to my house) or a larger community (like the Gulf Coast crudely smothered with oil).*

Thankfully, in relationship with the rest of nature (as with other people), it is not only embodied pain that draws me to them but eros—eros as an infinitely deep and pervasive life force encompassing but not limited to our sexual energies. Think of Larry Gibson's love for Kayford Mountain. Remember my patient enjoying his sensuous contact with the stones in my office. Even better, recall your own direct encounters with the glories of nature. And consider this fortunate and hopeful fact: we respond instantaneously to the lively spirit and beauty of others, including beauty that goes further than skin deep. Painful experiences can teach us a great deal. Yet our pleasurable encounters are equally or even more crucial. Indeed, enjoyable contact with others may be the original source of our compassionate response to suffering. Surely we have all felt an unbidden bodily response to the glowing splendor of autumn leaves, or some other marvelous gesture of nature: unbidden by our personal will and calculative intellect, that is, but bidden by sheer presencing of these radiant color-shifting companions. In an exquisitely erotic interplay of call-and-response, fiery red and yellow leaves bid for the attention of our body-heart-mind. Our body(self) is predisposed to being moved by that beautiful bidding, leading us to respond with care. And that encounter lays down traces that sponsor further attunement and compassion in the future. This is the loving resonance of eros, living on as part of our very being, a vital source that is always ready to spring forth in our engagement with life.

In this book we are celebrating wondrous encounters with nature, and grieving many disastrous losses. Let me offer a contemplative exercise that draws from both of these aspects, thereby demonstrating that *our embodiment is situated at the center of the ethical dimension of existence.* Let us say you are with a close friend and their trustworthy, affectionate, smart, and beautiful dog.[6] You have played with this furry companion on several occasions, and you feel great fondness for her. Imagine her happily cavorting with you and your friend in an open field—running to connect with you, running away, chasing a squirrel, coming back again and again. As if you are actually there, take a few moments and notice your embodied sensations, feelings, thoughts, desires, and interactions. I presume that you feel some version of affection, pleasure, fun, and care. Focusing again on your felt-sense, picture the dog playing in the distance. She turns and bounds toward you like before. But this time she steps into an unseen hole and crashes to the ground with a sharp wail. What is your response? Shock? Pain? Fear? Empathic resonance with her? Perhaps you even felt your body's compassionate inclination to dash over and help? We have all undergone experiences like these contrasting ones. They are basic (co)existential situations, wherein we are called to respond as best we can. As in this instance, notice how *beauty, intelligence, and suffering all spontaneously summon forth our love.* Whether in glory or pain or some mix of these, the earth surely needs our wise and loving care.

In today's precarious relationship between us human-folk and the rest of nature's folk, our bodies surely sense an urgent cry from the world's nonhuman beings and presences. "You can hold yourself back from the suffering of the world: this is something you are free to do . . . but perhaps precisely this holding back is the only suffering you might be able to avoid" (Franz Kafka, in Macy, 1991, p. 21). Their health surely depends on our reply, yet so too does ours. When we are sensitively attuned, the natural world shows itself to be an intelligent, communicative field inhabited by kindred companions, human and otherwise, each one glori-ous and suffering at times, each one summoning our conscious attention and ultimately our love. When hearkened with an openly embodied and grateful heart, we can turn this appeal into a devoted inter-responsive practice: nature-healing-body-healing-nature-healing-body.

Chapter Ten

# Living Means Being Addressed
## Embracing Earth's Wild, Sacred, Ethical Call

Deep calls to deep in the voice of your waterfalls.

—Psalm 42:7

Living means being addressed . . .

—Martin Buber (1965, p. 10)

I am he who finds the resources to respond to the call.

—Emmanuel Levinas (1985, p. 89)

## Overture

Coming to us unbidden, beyond our freedom and prior to our consent, the wild and sacred earth addresses us, summons us, asks something of us encounter by encounter. Global warming, the coronavirus pandemic, racist oppression, mass extinction, a summer thunderstorm: we often do not know precisely what we are being asked, nor quite how to respond. But our embodied heart knows that we are being called upon, undeniably and irreplaceably. In this tender time of eco(psycho)logical peril, it is crucial that we muster the resources to answer the call.

## Relational Responsibility
## Is the Very Structure of Subjectivity

Let us build upon the previous chapter's exploration of the life-enhancing potential of our embodied involvement with others. At the outset, consider Martin Buber's (1965) powerful description of our (co) existential condition and responsibility: "Living means being addressed" (p. 10). While typing the previous sentence I heard my dog crying to go outside and join my wife in the garden, so I paused to open the door for her. That is a tiny example of what this chapter is about. Today's urgent ethical imperatives are far more profound than this, of course. But life keeps making appeals and imploring me to respond. In every encounter, "a word demanding an answer has happened to me" (Buber, p. 10). Emmanuel Levinas (1985) agrees and stresses the crucial point: "I am he who finds the resources to respond to the call" (p. 89).

Guided by existential phenomenology and Judaism, Levinas developed an inspiring philosophy of the face-to-face relationship. Although his writings are focused almost completely on human interactions, I find them directly relevant for our relationship with the animate earth. Levinas' work centers on disclosing the "primacy of the ethical, that is, of the relationship of man to man" (1969, p. 79). He is concerned with the responsive and ultimately responsible relationship between self and other, the same and the other, I and the face of the other. (When "the other" is invoked, please think of both humans and nonhumans.) "The way in which the other presents himself, exceeding *the idea of the other in me*, we here name face" (Levinas, 1969, pp. 50). In other words, who my relational partner is, and what their expression means, transcends any conceptual representation that can be constituted by my ego. The other's depths (or heights) are infinite, as Levinas avows. Thus each encounter resists being incorporated into my same old way of thinking and being. In their radical alterity, every other calls me to be open in conversation with a mystery beyond myself, thereby summoning my responsibility. To find a fitting response is my core ethical calling. And love is the essential quality of such contact: "That which I call responsibility is a love, because love is the only attitude where there is encounter with the unique" (Levinas, in Bernasconi & Wood, 1988, p. 174).

Exploring the phenomenology of the face-to-face encounter, Levinas articulated a radically embodied and relational notion of (inter)subjectivity. As he shows, to be a self or a subject is to be subjected to the ethical summons of the other, to be called to respond in my own unique and irreplaceable way to the unique and irreplaceable singularity of my conversational partner. This means responding to the other's depths from my very depths. Here subjectivity is not primarily active, assertive, agentic individuality. Rather, it is receptive, responsive, responsible involvement. "I speak of responsibility as the essential, primary and fundamental structure of subjectivity. . . . Ethics, here, does not supplement a preceding existential base; the very node of the subjective is knotted in ethics understood as responsibility" (Levinas, 1985, p. 95). That is, I do not first exist independently, from a "preceding existential base" of autonomous ego-centered individuality, and then go on to reply to the other's appeal. That mistaken notion is consistent with the modern Euro-American construal of what it means to be a self. In contrast, Levinas (1969) repeatedly presents "subjectivity as welcoming the Other, as hospitality" (p. 27), especially hospitality in the face of the other's need and suffering. *The ethical call that occurs in my contact with others actually constitutes my subjectivity. My unique being is drawn forth in and as my response to their unique being.*

## What a Little Rabbit Taught Me: The Other Beseeches Me Prior to My Freedom and Consent

Early one summer morning I was watching several cottontail rabbits grazing and frolicking in the dewy grass outside my house. I felt a bit frustrated because this little clan had recently been nibbling away at the vegetables in our garden, cleverly sneaking through the fence in ways we could not discern. Nonetheless, I felt a real fondness for them. I was especially delighted by the young bunnies who were playing a zig-zagging game of chase, dashing around, hopping, and tumbling over each other. Suddenly, a wailing shriek filled my body and my consciousness and the whole interrelational field. Coming out of the blue, this anguished plea made me gasp. An intense yet tender pain arose in my chest. Immediately aware that someone was hurting, my body turned to assist I knew not whom. These initial responses flowed spontaneously and prereflectively. Some animal was in agony, terrified, and crying for help. The sound seemed to come from our fenced garden, behind where the bunnies were playing. Instantly I was rushing over, wondering what was happening and what I could do. Upon arriving I saw a baby rabbit tangled in chicken wire that my wife and I had laid out to deter the critters from devouring our tasty strawberries. One of her legs was trapped and she was jerking to get free. A powerful heartrending (heart-opening) response arose in my chest: painful, quivering, sorrowful, caring. She froze as I leaned down closer. I tried to move the wire, but this did not help. A fearful fantasy of getting bitten and contracting rabies came to mind momentarily. But I took a deep breath, grasped the trembling rabbit in my trembling hands, and found a way to release her. Her little body shook vigorously before rushing frantically around the garden. Eventually I guided her out the open gate, whereupon she darted away into the brush. Disquieted but relieved, I was left wondering how she would fare after that trauma. To be clear, I never felt that this rabbit was crying out specifically to me. But I did know *I was being called to respond, irreplaceably so*. I had no doubt that she was crying not only in pain and fear, but *for help*.

In earlier chapters we emphasized the *constitutive, constructive, meaning-bestowing capacity of consciousness*. As important as it is, I would like us to place this agentic meaning-making capacity in the background for now and look carefully at what transpired between me and the rabbit. When the shriek pierced my heart in that first fierce moment, I was touched to the core and drawn toward the pained animal *before I had any choice in the matter*. In that initial shocking instant I was immensely more constitut*ed* than constitut*ing*. My very being was *constituted as summoned* by her traumatic plea, implored to assist the unknown one asking for care. Prior to any explicit thought or willful action, I was seized by the call. Simultaneously, my intelligent body-heart turned to help even before I knew I was turning, *before I as an active agent chose to generate any movement at all*. It was not "I" as a separate self opting to act compassionately. Rather, compassion was flowing forth on its own. I was suffering (*pathos*) with (*com-*) a not-yet-known but vividly beckoning being. Indivisibly intimate with the sounding cry, my ethical responsibility and response-ability were activated before I as a reflective subject could cognize or articulate it.

Primarily, before the rabbit's plight was formed into thinkable language, my sentient flesh felt the little animal urgently appealing for my care. Venturing to translate her cries into English, I dare say that I felt-heard her saying, "I'm hurt and scared! Please, please help!" Secondarily, I might have broken away from the primordial contact that insisted upon my ethical responsibility. But first, foremost, and undeniably, I sensed a kindred being addressing me, asking something of me—just me, because no one could replace me in that moment. As this encounter demonstrates, a radical responsibility is inherently placed upon us in our bodily felt contact with others. In the initial moment of being contacted, we are given a "responsibility that rests on no free commitment . . . without any choice" (Levinas, 1981, p.116). This does not "arise in decisions taken by a subject 'contemplating freely'" (p. 112). Rather, "responsibility for the other . . . signifies . . . the exposure of me to the other, prior to every decision. There is a claim laid on the same by the other in the core of myself" (p. 141). Through the basic (co)existential fact that I am an embodied relational being, the very condition of "incarnation . . . exposes [me] naked to the other" (p. 109). I am always already tenderly susceptible to their appeals, and I know this through my intelligent-compassionate somatic sensibility. As with the baby rabbit, my very life is structured by an open, vulnerable "exposure without reserve to the other" (p. 168)—directly given in my carnal involvement with everyone who comes my way.

Levinas (1981) emphasizes that bodily felt, face-to-face encounters bestow upon us "an extremely urgent assignation—an obligation" (pp. 100–101). My exposed body turned toward the wailing cry in one moment, my eyes filled with tears in another: both responses sprang forth instantaneously. Before even realizing that it was a rabbit, a cry from her depths spontaneously solicited a response from my depths. Before any free consent or refusal is even possible, I am always already exposed to the other's "extremely urgent" assignment. *Ultimately, I am assigned to be compassionate, loving, to kindly provide a helping hand as best I can for the time being.* My experience with the rabbit points to something that is transpiring ceaselessly, an existential given of human life-with-others, one we often live unconsciously yet are implored to bring to fruition consciously: each of us is always already involved with human and nonhuman, wild precious ones who are *contacting us before we make, sustain, and nurture our contact with them.* A primordial ethical imperative is intrinsic to this conversational engagement.

## I Am the One Who Finds Resources to Respond

Drawing upon this example, we discover a *nondual, bodily felt responsivity and responsibility at the heart of being-with-others.* As we have discussed, the dominant ethos of Western culture gives preeminence to the (supposedly) separate, sovereign, assertive, agentic, individual, ego-centered self. "The ego" or "the same" are two names Levinas uses for this conventional self-representation and mode of being. And he consistently subverts the overvalorization of this (presumably) autonomous ego. His philosophy— like everyday life!—begins not with the self but with the other. The other is one who infinitely transcends any idea I have about them, the one who bears the holy, the one to whom I am infinitely responsible.

In a beautiful paradox, Levinas points out that the other comes to me from a position of transcendent height and from a position of poverty, presenting simultaneously as more than and less than me, as one who is both master and destitute. "There is a commandment in the appearance of the face, as if a master spoke to me. However, at the same time, the face of the Other is destitute; it is the poor for whom I can do all and to whom I owe all" (Levinas, 1985, p. 89). The other is ever *"the first one on the scene"* (Levinas, 1981, p. 86). *This means the other always comes first, and the self comes in (and as) our response.* Applying this to ecopsychology, nature ever precedes and exceeds me, even when I act as if my ego comes first. Levinas insists that in every instance, but especially when my partner is suffering (as the natural world surely is), the other is always already elevated above me, ethically speaking. The other approaches me "from a dimension of height, a dimension of transcendence whereby he can present himself as a stranger without opposing me as obstacle or enemy" (Levinas, 1969, p. 215). Therefore, my responsibility is not simply equal to or reciprocal with my companion. Rather, "the Other counts more than myself" (1969, p. 247). Significantly, the Dalai Lama (2000) concurs: "With genuine compassion you view others as more important than yourself" (p. 104). This can be as simple as saying, "Please, you go first" when arriving at a doorway. Or it can be as subtle as saying the same thing to the natural world: "Please animals and plants, please mountains and meadows, please air and water, please, you go first." This could take the form of: "No! We do not need an expansion of fracking"; or, "Yes! Let us be bold and turn to solar, wind, and geothermal energy." "No! We do not need to elevate our species over the rest of the earth." "Yes! Let us embrace our grounded place as humble dialogue partners in the shared earth conversation."

Levinas (1969) provides a powerful image of this asymmetrical relationship. In the ethical dimension, he says, there is always a distinctive "curvature of intersubjective space" (p. 291). Therein, "the Other is placed higher than me. . . . Man as Other comes to us from the outside, a separated—or holy—face. . . . This 'curvature of space' is, perhaps, the presence of God" (p. 291). I would say *differentiated instead of separated*, outside our ego but not outside our deeper transpersonal being. Still, Levinas' remark is reminiscent of teachings we have heard from Christian mystics and Zen teachers. That is to say, *every* finite other is an incarnation of infinite depths—holy, sacred, or divine depths: "transcendence embodied, embodied transcendence" (as my Zen teacher says). We know the "infinite" is a classic name of G-d, and it is an existential quality of the other who arrives to call upon us. "The dimension of the divine opens forth from the human face. . . . It is here that the Transcendent, infinitely other, solicits us and appeals to us" (Levinas, 1969, p. 78). Thus, the infinite depths of the divine are the real source of the truly sacred summons we receive. Whether appearing in the form of a person or a river or a forest, these depths deserve our infinite care.

In realizing that our relational partners—including the natural world—come from a dimension of depth (or height, depending which metaphor you prefer), all ego-centered and human-centered elitism is subverted. So too are our masterful attitudes. I might be surprised by a bright red wildflower or the cool wet grass under my bare feet. I might be disturbed by the disastrous realities of global warming, the COVID-19 pandemic, White supremacy, or the mass extinction of species. Either way, before I even know it cognitively, the other touches me; interrupts the momentum of my self-centered way of being; and implores me to muster a kind reply. My plans, expectations, and wishes are called into question. My fixed sense of self is also disrupted. Given the emotional attachment I feel toward my familiar egoic identity, the latter can be immensely stressful to handle. Indeed, *the other's overture can be felt as a narcissistic wound, a threat to what I (mis)take to be my very core*. The other "strips the ego of its pride and the dominating imperialism characteristic of it" (Levinas, 1981, p. 110). In response I can fortify my defenses and try to impose my will. Or I can open to the address of my relational partner and discover something new, letting them teach me what they and the precise circumstances call for.

## I Am Constituted before Constituting:
### *Constituted as the One Who Is Called*

When the beings and presences of the natural world arrive in all their unique freedom, expressivity, beauty, intelligence, and suffering, we must acknowledge that we are in the midst of a real wildness that far surpasses our capacity for prediction and control. After all, "wildness is not just the 'preservation of the world' [as Thoreau says], it *is* the world" (Snyder, 1990, p. 6). But even though nature is far beyond our comprehension and mastery, it is not beyond our ability to be responsive, loving, and just. Surpassing the death-denying temptation to dissociate our vulnerable mortal bodies, both Levinas and Merleau-Ponty emphasize our corporeal sensitivity to the appeals of others. As Merleau-Ponty (1962) says, "My body is the pivot of the world" (p. 82). And, I will add, the world is the pivot of my body(self). In this case "the world" means fellow beings and presences—human loved ones, strangers, falcons, redwoods, oceans. These others actually turn on my response to them. I might be tempted to shut down defensively or selfishly, and I do react like this too often. *But first and foremost I find my body already turning intimately with their overtures*, summoned, say, by their beauty or by their suffering.

Going further, Levinas (1981) avows that "the body is . . . that by which the self is susceptibility itself" (p. 195). But susceptible to what? Susceptible to being touched by others, to having my preestablished plans and self-sense interrupted, to being moved to respond responsibly to the calls my fellows inevitably present. Herein, "there is deliverance into itself of an ego awakened from its imperialist dream" (p. 164). As we have shown, in its habitually presumed stance as a separate self, the ego is a paranoid and greedy structure. And ultimately a confused, illusory one. Intrinsically insecure in its presumed sovereignty, and thus motivated primarily by fear (which often manifests as avarice or violence), the ego's dream-fantasy is to be a grand emperor. Fixed in this position, the imperialistic ego—*each of us when lost in this conventional mode*—tries to master and control those wishfully subjected to its rule: namely, nonegoic (prepersonal and transpersonal) dimensions of our own being, other people, the rest of nature, even life itself. *To control others, nature, and life itself—what madness!* Yet we are often driven to live like this, while rarely being aware of the false self-sense that drives us.

In contrast, encounters like the one that transpired with the rabbit disclose the healing, transformative potential of our somatically felt, interrelational life. I am especially struck by the primary ethical summons generated in our initial prereflective yet meaningful felt-contact with others. We can compare this distinctive moment with a different one, namely the way we reflectively construct an understanding of a situated event or of my larger life circumstances. The latter notion has long been a key principle of psychotherapy. It is important indeed to realize that my consciousness contributes to the constitution of experiential meaning. This can be tremendously empowering, helping me actively tap into my creative agency and power; liberating me from being a passive victim of oppressive institutions, people, and self-limiting constraints; and initiating alternative understandings. However, an ethos focused exclusively on my meaning-bestowing power can easily be wielded for narcissistic purposes, desensitizing me to the genuine appeals of others. Here is the danger: wittingly or unwittingly, I tend to keep seeing others only within the constitutive horizon of my conventional, self-serving, and defensive perspective; I tend to reduce them to my expectations and wishes, usually without noticing that I am doing so; and I likely miss, distort, or efface their unique singularity and summons (which are way beyond anything I can conceive or control). The opportunity for dialogue with a real other is reduced to a monologue with my selfsame presumptions and wishes. Treating nature as an objective material resource for my gratification is a key case in point.

It can be liberating to know that our well-being is not just dependent on what happens to us, but on what we make of it. However, isn't there something heartening about those moments of encounter wherein our consciousness is not actively constituting but constituted? More precisely, when our embodied awareness is originally constituted by the call of another embodied self, as mine was by the rabbit's shriek? I am *not* referring to the phase of an encounter wherein someone explicitly characterizes me by way of particular attributes: as in, "Will is a husband, father, professor, psychotherapist, assistant soccer coach, tennis player, contemplative, nature lover, and so on." And then I reflect upon and respond to their construal. Instead, I am intrigued by something far more immediate, by that initial instant of contact wherein, almost subliminally but with subtle somatic awareness I feel not defined by this or that notion but, simply and profoundly, *constituted as summoned, as called to respond as best I can.* Someone is asking something of me, as yet I know not what, but I know acutely that I am in fact being beckoned. *For the time being, their existence (and mine) turns on my response. Traces of my response will live on in them, in me, and in all the others we each go on to meet. This responsibility is so awesome that it makes me tremble.*

## I Cannot Not Be Summoned: My Body Knows This (Co)Existential Fact

Levinas claims that our vulnerable, corporeal exposure to the other's call is unavoidable. And he insists that we cannot recuse ourselves from the radical ethical responsibility that comes in the encounter. What are we to make of these assertions? Surely we know that people do act with heartless irresponsibility at times, traumatizing each other and the natural world in truly grave ways. For example, not long ago I was driving across Pennsylvania to attend a conference and present an ecopsychology workshop. As my car was climbing a small hill on the interstate highway, I saw a tractor-trailer truck up ahead and shifted into the other lane to pass. Then, in my rearview mirror, I noticed a distant car approaching at an extremely fast pace. It quickly arrived right behind me, racing up to only a couple of feet away. With both of us halfway around the big truck and moving at 70 miles per hour, I felt anxious but also annoyed at the aggressive intrusion. I presumed I would simply get around the truck and the other guy would zoom on past. I felt some relief when I glanced in the mirror and saw the man slowing down and dropping back. But then he sped up rapidly and rammed into the back of my car! Shocked, frightened, and then angry, I steadied my car and steered on past the truck. I looked sharply at the other driver as he went by, trying to express something like "What was that crazy exploit?! You're going to kill somebody!" I wanted him to see my fierce glare of concern, so I was glad (and somewhat scared) when I saw his head pivot ever so slightly toward me. But just before making eye contact he actively turned away from my gaze and speedily drove away.

People could have easily died in this event. Once safe, however, I felt uncannily fascinated. I said to myself, with dark dismay, this is precisely the misguided madness I am going to address in my conference workshop! The driver must have had his own motives that made sense to him. But his careless way of (non)relating with me was an extreme version of a common mode of being with others: detached, self-enclosed, self-concerned; dissociated from responsible contact with the real alterity of others; and dreadfully driven to gratify one's own narcissistic wishes. How then can Levinas claim that our ethical responsibility is unavoidable? As I drove on toward my destination I felt haunted by something I could not quite name. Then it occurred to me: right after the collision the man turned toward me before turning away. It did not feel like he consciously chose to confront me, say in an angry or arrogant way. No, it wasn't like that. Rather, I had an intuition that his body-self had acted involuntarily in response to crashing into me. Some *corporeal sense of responsibility* must have been thrust upon him, unwittingly, even though he quickly shirked it. My sense was that the lived ethical call was momentarily compelling, otherwise his body(self) would not have moved toward me. Such moments testify to a core ethical sensitivity, one that is *inherently given* in our embodied intersubjective contact with others. "The will is free to assume this responsibility in whatever sense it likes; it is not free to refuse this responsibility itself" (Levinas, 1969, pp. 218–219). By dint of my bodily sensitivity, I am always vulnerably exposed to others' entreaties. After each irrevocable summons, I might evade my responsibility (like the driver who hit me). But this defensive move actually affirms that I was already affected by the responsibility-conjuring call.

Similarly, Merleau-Ponty (1962, 1968, 2003) explores how our shared existence is structured by embodied, call-and-response encounters. The "world exists in the interrogative mode" (Merleau-Ponty, 1968, p. 103). The world is ever asking something of me. In an inter-responsive circuit comprised of open inter-corporeal contact, life presents me not just with a question but a plea, an appeal for responsible action that I receive via my exposed bodily attunement. And when these appeals come to me the responsibility is uniquely mine, even when I am blessed with allies who are offering support. "My responsibility is untransferable, no one could replace me" (Levinas, 1985, p. 100). I am beckoned by a rabbit's wail, by a student's earnest inquiry, by a whale breaching, by my dear child's illness, by wildfires raging again this year, by shape-shifting clouds floating across the sky. Take one of these instances (or recall one that occurred in your life) and notice: in the initial instant of contact we cannot even try to block the world's overture, because it has already occurred; nor can we block our initial felt-sense of this call, because we have already been touched. And even when we are not experiencing an acute summons, countless others are always already there in the background, implicitly calling for our care. *We might say yes or no to the summons, but we cannot not be summoned. However, what we do with the other's appeal makes all the difference.*

## Embracing the Other's Overture: Contemplative and Phenomenological Resources

Levinas' writing style actually makes us feel the acute intensity of the other's claim upon us—feel it viscerally, deep in our body and heart. Thus he asserts, "The more I divest myself, under the traumatic effect of persecution, of my freedom as a . . . willful, imperialist subject, the more I discover myself to be responsible" (1981, p. 112). Trauma and persecution refer to the way an other's sudden relational plea disrupts my contracted, self-enclosed identity and narcissistic concerns. Especially when moving in an ego-centered manner, I feel the other's overture as a raw bodily affective shock, sometimes subtle but sometimes quite intense. Either way, the felt-sense is a message to awaken, to realize I am being asked something, to find a fitting reply, thus giving myself fully into the encounter. At times the shock is pleasurable, like when my eye is caught by a dragonfly's multihued luminescence. At times the other's address is unsettling and painful. Such disturbances frequently occur in mundane events, say, when my preconceived plans are interrupted by a fallen tree on the road, a request from a neighbor, or a bus that is late. Sometimes they are far more anguishing, like when I let the reality of our climate catastrophe touch me; when a coal executive is troubled by a true nightmare regarding the unsustainable future of fossil fuels; or when I find dead fish floating in a river poisoned by industrial chemicals. Such events arrive unforeseen and unforeseeable, beyond my desires, plans, or expectations. Attached to my preestablished projects and identity, and averse to their interruption, I often try to reimpose my wishes by way of attack or avoidance.

Wise ones across various disciplines have emphasized the crucial importance of hospitably receiving my partner's overtures in these striking moments when we are contacted unawares. Levinas (1969) remarked that his main philosophical task was to "present subjectivity as welcoming the Other, as hospitality" (p. 27). Speaking of his renowned approach, Jacques Derrida asserted that "to prepare oneself for this coming (*venue*) of the other is what can be called deconstruction" (Caputo, 1997, p. 114). And the hermeneutic phenomenologist Hans Georg-Gadamer (2011) affirmed that "every experience worthy of the name thwarts an expectation. . . . The experienced man knows that all foresight is limited and all plans uncertain" (pp. 350–351). These are the challenges and joys of meeting others who arrive from a place outside our expectations; and, crucially, outside the supposedly masterful ego's circumscribed capacity for prediction and control. That "place" is life itself, in its ordinary and often bewildering—be-*wilding*—display. Joining with these thinkers, note that nonhuman beings and presences are even more radically "other" and uncontrollable than members of our own species.

Since I usually move through life gripped by and griping on to an ego-centered mode, *how may I ready myself to welcome the presencing of nature as a real other in all its wild-free mystery?* How can I offer attentive hospitality and generous service? What capacities might help me heed the other's summons, bear it, sustain the contact, and thereby sponsor a life-enhancing reply? How might I transmute the call—first *given to me* absolutely by the other—into something *to give myself to,* to freely confide in, to surrender my (small) self-centered identity, fear, greed, and willfulness, and thereby respond wisely and kindly? If it were merely a matter of cognitive insight or objective ethical principles, we might readily affirm the value of letting go of our self-centered agenda. We might open the door for a stranger. We might give someone the coat off our back. We might—if only!—put the health of the natural world over corporate mega-profits. However, to do this reliably in the heat of the moment is one of life's great challenges. Especially when things are difficult we like to hold on to our long-established and often self-concerned ways and identity. The problem lies in the fact that every singular other has their own ways, ways that often contradict our own preferences and plans. "The relation with the Other as a relation with his transcendence . . . introduces into me what was not in me" (Levinas, 1969, p. 203). My partner's transcendence is infinitely beyond any pretensions of egoic mastery. Just by carrying on with their life, others recurrently breach our comforting horizons. This is certainly true of the larger natural world. Such experiences can be surprisingly painful because they disrupt our (wished-for) capacity to master the present encounter and control the outcome. Our familiar self-sense is often shaken in these moments. We can easily default into fearfully avoidant or greedy reactions. From this stance we feel compelled to forcefully impose our will upon the rest of nature. But we impoverish ourselves and the natural world in the process, as our eco(psycho)logical crisis demonstrates.

## Contemplative Resilience and Hospitality

We hear another horror story about global warming and deem it something far distant that has nothing to do with us. A stand of old fir trees next to our house seems like a nuisance, and we decide to cut them down to enlarge our driveway. In actual practice, how can we transcend the forceful momentum of our ego-centered ways? Beyond avoidance or attack, how can we release into and respond in consonance with the constituting call of the other—the summons we feel when, say, we are enchanted by the sweet song of a wren or disturbed by our childhood woods being made into a shopping mall? *How, in fact, may we transform the other's appeal into our own authentic desire*, bringing forth real compassion, love, understanding, and justice? Here we are addressing a crucial (co)existential assignment, the wild and sacred call of our very life. Responding well hinges on *our capacity to consciously embrace and creatively transmute our instantaneous, pre-volitional, bodily-turnings-to-the-other*. Meditation and other contemplative practices can support us. Another path is psychotherapy. Experiential ecopsychology (like in workshops) can be truly transformative. Intimate relationships—with other people and with the natural world—are especially important. Most crucially, we are asked to body forth the fruits of these practices in everyday encounters, like helping my child and myself keep breathing when a tantrum is brewing, or acting in concert with others when the local water supply is being polluted. *Ultimately, it is all one embodied relational practice: life itself.*

I have suggested that a meditative sensibility can help us along this great way. Earlier I invoked a famous psalm: "Be still and know that I am G-d" (Psalm 46:10). The contemplative message is that real knowing depends upon stopping and being still. Whether we aspire to know "G-d" or one other person or a single expression of nature—all of which are infinitely deep—something must stop in order for us to see clearly and deeply. But what is it that must stop? The poet John Keats provides a wonderful pointer. He invites us to cultivate a *"Negative Capability,"* that is, to be "capable of being in uncertainties, Mysteries, doubts, without any irritable reaching after fact & reason" (Keats, 1959, p. 261). Poets, phenomenologists, and contemplatives all warn that our preconceived ideas can rule us unwittingly. We are all attached to our favorite ideas, of course, especially the fantasy of our separate self but also the illusion of separate others with fixed characteristics. Regarding these concerns, the Buddhist sage Nāgārjuna makes a radical point. Really being awake, he says, involves "the coming to rest of all ways of taking things, the repose of named things" (Nāgārjuna, in Loy, 1996, p. 92). By "taking things" he means reifying them, that is, mis-taking an infinitely deep dynamic reality—our self, another person, a cougar, a desert—to be an isolated objective entity with a predefined and fixed essence. Reification sets in when words and concepts lose their evocative, generative function; and when, instead, they entrance us into believing that we and the world are separate, static, solid, definable things. Without interrupting this process—epistemologically and ethically—we unconsciously subsume the other in our selfsame presumptions, thereby ignoring their real alterity. When Nāgārjuna speaks of *taking* things, the connotations of grasping, acquisition, and possession are spot on. "I've got your number. I know what you are like." It feels terrible when someone treats us in such a reductive way. In contrast, recall your experience of a thunder-and-lightning storm, a baby looking into your eyes, or another instance where you felt touched by the real presence of your relational companion. Don't they convey some sense of mystery, power, and beauty—so much so that it transcends your comprehension? The other can never be who or what the ego thinks or wishes they are. This is true of other people and of the natural world, as the wild mystery of each goes endlessly deep. Wolf, willow, sparrow, stream, stranger, lover: *every other is unfathomably mysterious, simply by being their unique self.* Each one, in their actuality, goes far beyond our most sensitive suppositions, much less our automatic, self-absorbed ones.

Others frequently challenge not only our preconceived ideas about them, but our own emotionally felt sense of safety, self-esteem, and identity. Thus *we often strive to manipulate mystery into certainty, into something we can master and control for our own ends.* But in freeing ourselves from such imperialistic designs, we can allow the other to show themselves and teach us something in accordance with this particular circumstance. A core opportunity and responsibility are bestowed upon us in each encounter: "To let be—that is, to let beings be as the beings which they are" (Heidegger, 1977a, p. 127).[1] Letting our partner "be as they are" is not to attribute some preestablished, fixed essence to them, but to carefully—lovingly—foster the relational conditions for them to be most fully and uniquely themselves in this particular encounter (and hopefully beyond). Every time an other's summons stops us in our tracks, we are given a chance to embrace the pause and stay in conscious contact with our companion. Herein, we allow our response to emerge from a source far more vital, wise, and compassionate than our habitual ego. That source is the dynamic intertwining of our partner's depths and our own.

The capacities of consciousness that are cultivated in meditation can serve us well in such circumstances. I am thinking of the fundamental meditative attitude: being present, open, and aware, welcoming all that arises in experience without aversion or attachment, without pushing anything away or clinging to anything.[2] Rumi (1995) celebrates this hospitable, all-embracing, openhearted, courageous, contemplative awareness: "This being human is a guest house. / Every morning a new arrival. / A joy, a depression, a meanness, / ["a bird dipped in a rainbow," another species driven extinct, another f'ing fracking well![3]] / some momentary awareness comes / as an unexpected visitor. / Welcome and entertain them all! . . . / Be grateful for whoever comes, / Because each has been sent / As a guide from beyond" (p. 109). A crucial ingredient in formal meditation—and, by extension, in daily living—is our ability to be a good host for whichever visitor comes to call: thoughts, feelings, sensations, images, urges, realizations, pains, joys. We keep consenting to and confiding in the presencing moment, allowing experience to unfold just as it is (rather than as we wish it to be), allowing the depths of this encounter to guide our corresponding reply. And since we will inevitably avoid or grasp at times, a contemplative sensibility helps us recover, returning again and again to a conscious capaciousness of heart.

Bringing this sensibility into everyday encounters, we find ourselves involved in a kind of spiraling movement *from conversation to meditation to revelation to further conversation*. That is, I open my heart in dialogue with my companion, letting them come forth just as they are. Such contemplative awareness may foster a direct revelation wherein I see my partner freshly and vividly, thereby allowing them to teach me. "The other is . . . the first teaching, the condition for all teaching" (Levinas, 1969, p. 203). *The primary thing the other teaches me is the very fact that they are asking for a caring reply.* Growing from this realization, I can let myself be mentored about what they and the larger circumstances are asking. Welcoming such guidance and letting it resound in my depths, I am more likely to find a consonant response. New understandings may then be disclosed, held lightly, and tested as the conversation continues.

The following is a cautionary tale of a missed opportunity for such open, meditative engagement. Once I was walking along a rocky trail when I came upon a family whose preteen children were excitedly taunting a snake with sticks—pretending to "charm" the animal like in a cartoon. When I looked closely I saw that it was a small timber rattlesnake. Its tail was raised, its rattle vibrating rather loudly—clear warning signs for the two-legged intruders. I cautioned them emphatically to step back and let the rattlesnake be. The parents just scoffed and said, "There aren't any poisonous snakes around here." But that snake actually was quite venomous. The kids probably would not have died if they had been bitten, although that is uncertain. What is certain is that wild rattlesnakes are not playmates, characters in a Disney movie, or evil unfeeling creatures to be tormented. Eventually I walked on, hoping the children would be alright while shaking my head in dismay at our epidemic estrangement, arrogance, and captivation by a domineering, ego-centered agenda. Later I imagined how things could have gone differently. What if the parents had simply stopped; heeded the rattler's obvious warning; reminded the children that nature can be wondrous and dangerous at the same time, and always deserving of attentive respect; guided them to listen to the embodied fear that arose naturally upon first seeing the snake; reassured them that the snake would only strike out if they approached aggressively; helped them see that they would be very unhappy if a giant stranger burst into their home and threatened them with a stick (!); and supported them into a conscious, kind, relational etiquette. Ah, what if, what if?

In the midst of this discussion, perhaps you have wondered: How does the proffered sensibility—both contemplative and Levinasian—apply when confronted by a bully, an abusive spouse, or a political/economic system that supports the plundering of the natural world? The type of unseeing aggression depicted in the rattlesnake story is far more pernicious when enacted on a massive scale, as in the ravaging of the Amazon rainforest and the exacerbation of global warming. Holding in my care (as best I can) every singular being and the all-inclusive community, I may well be called to bring out a strongly assertive defense or counterchallenge. Consciously channeled anger and aggression may be the most loving, understanding, and just response to others' unloving, confused, unjust, hurtful actions. A forceful "No!" to violence can be a compassionate "Yes!" for myself and others—even for the violent one who might (at best) reconsider their ways.

## The Fine Risk of Welcoming the Holy:
### Scared but Not Scared Away

A key theme of this study is the ethical sensibility evoked by the sacred or holy dimension of nature. Rudolph Otto's (1978) classic text *The Idea of the Holy* can help us carry these explorations further. According to Otto, two major qualities are transmitted when we encounter the holy (*Das*

*Heilige*), what he calls *fascinans* and *tremendum*. That is, the holy or the sacred is a mystery that is immensely *fascinating and dreadful*, profoundly *attractive and repulsive*. Trying to express the inexpressible, Otto coined the term "numinous" to evoke these uncanny, awe-inspiring qualities. *Depending on the depth of our consciousness, absolutely anything can disclose the sacred—not as a mere isolated object, of course, but in its infinite, precious radiance.* "What is Buddha?" a student asks in all earnestness. "Three pounds of flax!" declares his Zen teacher, challenging him to really see (Yamada, 2004, p. 89). Or an even more provocative master proclaims, "a dried shit-stick!" (p. 102). (A tool used instead of toilet paper in ancient times!) Authentic, non-exclusionary wholeness is truly liberating. Still, sacred presences tend to come to us in two consummate forms: another human and another being or presence of the natural world. I could add a third time-honored form—G-d, the Dao, being, life—but I would just be repeating myself because, from a transpersonal perspective, humans and the rest of nature are no other than tangible forms of the one great formless mystery. In any case, the natural world is widely appreciated as a privileged site of the holy.

The bivalent attractive-and-repulsive quality of the sacred is particularly significant. Pondering the fascinating, alluring face of this mystery—nature, let us say—Otto emphasizes that the sacred conveys an intensely felt "energy," "a force . . . which is urgent, active, compelling, and alive" (p. 24). Here the holy fills us with a sense of wonder, grace, beauty, blessedness, gratitude, peace, and love. Turning to its other face, Otto shows that the holy can come across as immensely overpowering and terrifying. "This forms the numinous raw material for the feeling of religious humility" (Otto, p. 20). The natural world is among the most evident expressions of this awe-evoking mystery. Continuing, Otto speaks of the mystical "annihilation of self, and then, as its complement, of the transcendent as the sole and entire reality" (p. 21). As we have seen, this annihilating—surrendering, releasing, transcending—of self is not nihilistic but profoundly life affirming. Yet the life we usually try to affirm is not the one great life, but that of our supposedly self-sufficient ego. As Snyder (1990) remarked, "*Sacred* refers to that which helps take us . . . out of our little [egoic] selves" (p. 94). *But the ego usually recoils in the face of life's sacred depths.* What if we resist when the holy interrupts our egoic momentum and begins drawing us out of our habitually contracted self? What if we insist on clinging to this separate self in the face of the infinite depth and overwhelming power of the holy? What if we try to reinforce this small self and its wishes? *What if we try to say "No!" to nature's wild and sacred call, and "Yes" only to our own self, species, and agenda?* Well, we need only look around today. We generate a climate emergency and mass extinction. We taunt rattlesnakes with a stick. And we are haunted by a sense of confusion, lack, anxiety, insecurity, and craving.

These comments point to a crucial fact about the sacred's two-sided nature. When we lead with a self-centered agenda, nature's tremendous depth and power appears not as an awesome presence before which we are humbled and to which we respond with care, but as a threatening insult to our ego. Reacting to this—in a defensive turned offensive way—we often try to enforce our preestablished projects. Recall that the *wil-* in wilderness is associated with the word "will." This rightly suggests that nature has a kind of will and mind of its own, springing forth with a wild, multifarious force that vastly transcends our wishes. *The natural world expresses a noncentralized, alter-agency that functions outside my willful expectations, preferences, and power.* But when living via an egoic stance, I cannot tolerate this. The isolated insecure self, needing control and self-assurance, works to enforce its own will and (presumed) superiority. However, *nature rarely bends to my will.* (Think not only of the willfulness of an individual's ego but that of a corporation or a government.) Reacting with narcissistic rage to the inevitable frustration of my craving, I tend to reinstitute an excessive striving for mastery, safety, certainty, and acquisition, trying to reinforce my shaky identity and impose its wishes. A vicious circle of fear and defense is thereby perpetuated.

*Really being alive is far from safe.* When a particular other appears before me in all their holy depth and power, it is natural that I might feel afraid. Yet fear is not the actual problem, but what I do with it. No doubt, I am vulnerable to being hurt when I let myself be present with a radically open heart, when I sacrifice my merely individual self-interest and surrender my defenses. I can never know ahead of time how my relational partner will respond. It is risky to avail myself for such intimate contact. And yet, truly, this is "a fine risk to be run" (Levinas, 1981, p. 120). Being open to another is dangerous. Yet here is the decisive (turning) point: the far more common danger is remaining self-absorbed or closed off, thus deadening myself and letting my partner down. In the face of the wholly and holy other, life keeps giving us opportunities to take that fine risk. *Let us dare to be scared but not scared away.*

## Nature as Our Mentor:
## Lessons from Zen Master Dōgen

Zen teachers celebrate the life-giving value of embracing this risk. The way of intimate attunement and responsiveness is a real alternative to our ego-centered ways. A key passage from Zen master Dōgen's great "Genjōkōan" can help us appreciate this more fully. As a prelude, note that Dōgen insists on the nonduality of contemplative practice and awakening. *He consistently dispels the common notion that we practice meditation (or any other spiritual activity) in a utilitarian manner, with the intention of eventually achieving or acquiring something we are currently lacking, especially some imagined "enlightened" state in the future.* Similarly, notions such as "awakening" or "enlightenment" seem to suggest dramatic breakthroughs that happen only to supposedly elite spiritual beings. Momentous events and non-ordinary states of consciousness do occur, but that is not the heart of the matter. The "buddha way" or "essential way" is simply the heart of the down-to-earth human way, and it is not about special experiences or people. Dōgen deemphasizes isolated "enlightenment" experiences in favor of "practice-enlightenment," that is, an appreciation of life's intrinsic wakefulness and an ongoing consecrated devotion to seeing clearly and living wakefully and compassionately with our companions. Such "continuous practice" is the essential matter (Dōgen, 1999, pp. 114–116).

Given this context, let us ponder a splendid insight from Dōgen: "Conveying oneself toward all things to carry out practice-enlightenment is delusion. All things coming and carrying out practice-enlightenment through the self is realization [awakening, enlightenment]" (Okumura, 2010, p. 1). Dōgen is issuing a serious warning. Leading with a willful, ego-centered approach is radically misdirected. Caught in the grave confusion—"delusion"—that we are merely a separate ego, and *motivated unilaterally from the fear-filled experience of this superficial self*, we feel driven to advance and enforce our self-serving agenda. The momentum of this defensive, grasping, self-aggrandizing mode can actually co-opt genuine aspirations, even the devotion to awakening. If the ego is powerful enough to distort our most loving and wise intentions—and it surely is—then think of its unconscious effects in our usual circumstances. All too often we strive to master the natural world, and ego stakes its security and happiness on this. But nature rarely responds in just the ways we want. Nature is infinitely deeper than that. (Our human companions are as well.) Nature's wild-free expressivity is ultimately uncontrollable, far beyond even our best wishes, much less our habitual, ego-centered ones. Nonetheless, when the natural world asks something of us, it is easy to subsume its appeal into our preestablished agenda. This perverts the opportunity for a real dialogue and turns the encounter into a self-enclosed monologue: a rattlesnake becomes a mere play toy; a forest becomes mere lumber.

But we can take a different path: "All things coming and carrying out practice-enlightenment through the self is realization" (Dōgen, in Okumura, 2010, p. 1). Like Levinas, Dōgen begins with others—"all things"—and not with the ego-self. When we openly welcome the other's arrival we can craft a more apt reply. Here the primary source of realization (and healing as well) is not our self-centered effort, but all things: the whole of life in all its mystery, appearing as it ever does in the overtures of our particular present relational partner. As we emphasized earlier, nature comes first, as a kind of mentor or therapist, and our responsible reply follows. Let's say a new person comes into my life and I would like to get to know them. But I am also anxious because they are unfamiliar to me. In such a circumstance, I don't barge ahead arrogantly and try to dominate or control the interaction. Nor do I shut down and walk away. Rather, I might simply say, "Tell me about yourself." I give them space to share whatever they wish as I listen closely and respond in kind. A similar attitude facilitates our relations with the natural world, letting go of our ego-centered mode and letting go into an eco-centered one. When I am out birding it never works to run toward the singing or fluttering in the trees. That is a sure way *not* to make contact with these wondrous beings. Instead, it is best to stay still, silent, and attentive. Even if my initial entrance into their territory scared them away, when I am patient the winged ones relax and begin showing themselves again.

Until recently, listening to the meaningful messages of nature was central to ordinary daily life. There are signs that we are recovering this crucial capacity. Consider the growing interest in "biomimicry" (Benyus, 1997). This innovative approach endeavors to address human challenges by embracing nature as a teacher, thereby mimicking intelligent solutions already present in the more-than-human natural world. Life emerged on earth about 4.28 billion years ago, and it has been solving (co)existential concerns ever since! Thus, it is eminently wise to turn to nature for guidance. Across history, geniuses such as Leonardo da Vinci have apprenticed themselves to the natural world and incorporated natural design patterns into their technological creations. Now the interdisciplinary biomimicry movement is cultivating this keen approach anew. For example, Japan needed to minimize the window-rattling sonic booms that occurred when super-high-speed trains passed through tunnels. The problem stemmed from the transition from thinner air outside the tunnel to denser air inside. An engineer who was an avid birder then thought of a kingfisher. This bird's long narrow beak enables it to dive from the (thinner) air into (thicker) water with scarcely a splash. Working with this natural interrelational pattern, they redesigned the train's nose to mimic that of a kingfisher. And voilà, no more booms!

Biomimicry tends to focus on technological/engineering solutions for human problems. Yet, even more importantly, the natural world can mentor us about the inter-responsive structure and functioning of consciousness, self, and society. We have already explored Indra's Net and nature's conversational consciousness. And in a moment I will share an illustrative case from Yellowstone National Park. From all these examples we glean a crucial realization: interdependent conversational participation is the primary natural characteristic that we humans really need to cherish and "mimic." For example, let us consider what occurred when wild wolves were extirpated from Yellowstone (according to human wishes) and then later reintroduced (according to the wishes of the larger eco-community). Indigenous in North America, the gray wolf once flourished across the continent. However, because people were understandably wary of wolves and because ranchers viewed these predators as pests, wolves were utterly eradicated from almost all states. What was apparently the last survivor in Yellowstone Park was killed in 1926.

After humans wiped out Yellowstone's wolves, massive changes rippled throughout the ecosystem. First, ecologists observed a colossal increase in the elk population and a drastic demise in willows, cottonwoods, aspen, and other native flora. Because the elk could feed free from predators and competition, they devoured so much of the plant life that grassy meadows became barren and rivers began meandering due to erosion along their banks. "Trophic cascade" is the ecological term for this dynamic, interrelational phenomenon.[4] An organism's trophic level refers to its position in the ecological food chain (or food web). Organisms at different levels eat each other and are in turn eaten by others. A trophic cascade transpires inter-responsively, much like in the interdependent Jewel Net of Indra. (Appreciating that nature really comes first, it is more precise to say that Indra's Net functions like an ecosystem.) When an apex predator is removed or added, significant changes radiate throughout the whole eco-community. With the wolves gone, Yellowstone became terribly impoverished. Over time things became so bad that people began listening not only to loud human voices but to the more subtle voices of the natural world. Letting themselves be mentored by wild animals, plants, and elemental presences, ecologists began thinking like a mountain-valley-river ecosystem. They first tried to reduce the elk population by relocating or killing them. But this did not help. Eventually, sensitive researchers realized that *the natural community was calling for the repair of a relational rupture*. Therefore, in 1995–1996, 31 Canadian wolves were relocated to Yellowstone.

This move initiated an astounding recovery in terms of the park's biodiversity and beauty. The wolves not only killed many of the elk, but they also pushed them into safer but smaller havens. In an interdependent response, a variety of plants and other animals began to flourish once again. Willow, cottonwood, and aspen trees grew to maturity. Understory vegetation came back as well. When such habitat and forage sources (like berries and other browse) became more abundant, bison, grizzly bears, black bears, and songbirds soon started to increase. The bears also benefited from carrion left by wolves, as did scavengers such as bald eagles, golden eagles, and ravens. More bears preyed on elk calves, amplifying the impact made by wolves. The cascading interactions continued in countless other ways. Trees matured on riverbanks, providing food and building materials for beaver, decreasing soil erosion, and actually changing the shape of the river. Beaver dams created life-sustaining niches for moose, mink, muskrats, otters, waterfowl, wading birds, amphibians, reptiles, and fish. Wolves ate or drove away many coyotes, thus fostering a resurgence of smaller mammals such as foxes, badgers, weasels, rabbits, and mice. These then became food for hawks, whose numbers naturally grew. This astonishing portrayal only hints at the complex, interdependent metamorphosis in the park's eco-community.

These benefits came from the willingness of individuals and organizations to transform their relational sensibility: to welcome nature as a conversational partner, thus shifting from monologue to dialogue, from domination to participation, from power over to power with, from anthropocentrism to ecocentrism, from insisting on business as usual to hearkening nature's intelligent appeals, from seeking to master the natural world to listening to it and letting it be as it wished to be. Thus, the repair of the relational rupture was twofold, first between humans and Yellowstone and then between wolves and that eco-community. Heeding the call of a glorious but wounded ecosphere, humans said to nature: "Please, you take the lead. I'll follow."

## The World of Nature Is "Wholly Other."
## But Other than What?

It is important to acknowledge a fierce reality: Wild wolves are really scary. They can kill us. Nature is a tremendously mysterious and powerful force, both dreadful and alluring. Here I am circling back to Otto to help move us ahead. Along with many religious scholars, Otto contends that we experience G-d and the sacred (or holy) as that which is "wholly other"—"beyond the sphere of the usual, the intelligible, and the familiar" (Otto, 1978, p. 26). Levinas (1985) says the same about each person who comes to call upon us: "the other is absolutely other" (p. 66). When we look from our depths and see deeply, every relational partner teaches us that they go infinitely, sacramentally deep. "The face signifies the *Infinite*. . . . It is the exigency of holiness" (Levinas, 1985, p. 105). And as Blake (1988) says, "Every Minute Particular is Holy" (p. 223). This is all to say: *every single other is wholly other.* Wild wolves; wild hurricanes; the creaking of an old house; the sun; the moon; the great sentient-sapient earth; a dandelion; a moment's refreshing breath, which you might relish right now: each one infinitely mysterious and sacred, each one with its own idiomatic voice and appeal, these truly are *wholly other.*

Yet this appreciation carries an implicit question: *Other than what?* We have already shown that every other is other than who I think they are. Even with the most attentive contact, they inevitably transcend my presumptions, personal wishes, and will. Drawing from transpersonal psychology and contemplative practice, we can go further: every single being and presence who comes into my life is *wholly other than my conventional ego, but not other than or separate from my deepest being,* not other than my true self or true nature. When I realize this, nature's awesome powers may still induce fear but they do not induce reactions of domination and exploitation. When I grasp tightly to a sense of dualistic separation, reducing myself to a small, contracted ego, then the dreadful quality of the natural world becomes supremely pressing and frightening. When I experience any other as really separate from me, I usually construe them as more threatening than they actually are. As a great Hindu text puts it, "Where there is other, there is fear." Likewise, "where there is duality [separation], there is fear."[5] And where there is excessive fear, then excessive avoidance or aggression usually follow.

As long as I take myself to be a separate sovereign self (or species), I will perceive the world in a paranoid and greedy manner. *And*

*I will presume everyone else is driven in the same self-interested way.* In a vicious circle, my paranoia escalates as does my defensive avoidance, clinging, or even violence. In contrast, when I muster the resources to suspend my habitual reactivity, holding on to a thin thread of engaged awareness, then life freely gives me a profound teaching: namely, that I am not an isolated self thrown into the alien world of nature. Quite the contrary. Life shows me that I am (an inseparable mode of) nature; that my distinctive self is a unique form that nature is taking; that I am what nature is doing right here and now. Such a transpersonal realization can never take away nature's power to hurt or even kill me. But it can dissolve the *surplus* dread, defensiveness, and avarice that haunt me as a presumably separate self. I thereby open to the graceful, awesome, gloriously wild face of the sacred.

## The Animate Earth Is Calling. Who Is Being Called?

The fact that life—just as it is, in all its wildness—is wholly other than our best conceptions (much less our self-centered ones); that life transcends and disrupts even our best intentions (much less our efforts at control and domination); that life brings us things other than we wish and choose, including things that "should not happen" if our preferences could hold sway; that life challenges us with questions, claims, and pleas that are unbidden, unforeseeable, and uncontrollable; that life insists we face these and respond as best we can: well, this is what life does, unrelentingly so. But through and beyond its disruptive impact, these conditions can inspire awe, gratitude, and devotion. After all, our very existence—nature's, yours, mine—depends upon the overtures of others, the generosity of their gifts and the urgency of their needs.

The animate earth, in all its beauty, wisdom, love, and suffering, is ever addressing us. We are the ones summoned. This fervent assertion may seem quite clear at this stage in the present book. But there is more to it than first meets the eye. *You and I are being called upon, yes indeed. But which you? Which I?* Who is the self that is summoned? These questions may seem strange, but they are crucial. Even when I sense the natural world soliciting my reply, if I hear the appeal only through my contracted ego, then (by definition) my reply will be driven by confusion, fear, and greed. Alternately, what if I listened to the appeal from my deeper self, my transpersonal self? When nature sends forth its wild and sacred call, that call is coming from the very depths of life. To do justice to nature's appeal, I am asked to tap into my own depths. "Deep calls to deep in the voice of your waterfalls" (Psalm 47:7).

In the best of our day-to-day lives, we are already familiar with this kind of inter-responsiveness. In conversation with another person—if both of us are fortunate, attentive, courageous, and patient—a deeper way of listening and speaking with each other can emerge. In an uncanny process contingent mostly on mystery, but partly on our willingness to be open, vulnerable, and fallible, we may discover that we are involved in a true "heart to heart talk." Similarly, a song or a babbling brook can really speak to us and we "take it to heart." These common phrases celebrate the experience of fully meeting and being met by another. We each have these capacities. We each are given these responsibilities. But none of us are required to know precisely how to respond, much less to do so perfectly. That is not what life asks, nor anyone who comes to call upon us. In fact, Levinas points out that our best first reply may be a simple, humble avowal: "Here I am!," or "It's me here!" (*hineni*, in Hebrew). Invoking the prophet Isaiah (6:8), Levinas says that "'Here I am!' means 'send me'" (Levinas, 1981, p. 199). That is, I hear you calling me. I'm ready. I'm here for you. How may I lend a hand?

Even before our intentional freedom and consent, isn't it true that our tender bodies are touched by and drawn toward the bodies of others, toward (say) their suffering or beauty? Isn't this intimation the inception of bodying-forth a truly ethical, compassionate, loving, and just response? Doesn't this demonstrate that we are never really dissociated from others and the rest of nature, but intimately involved from the beginning (and even before every beginning)? Isn't it clear that our instantaneous bodily responsivity subverts (at least for a moment) all Cartesian dualism/separatism, radical individualism, and self-centeredness, revealing that we're always in this shared existence together? And doesn't it point to the fact—the urgent opportunity and responsibility—that we are in it not only *with* each other but *for* each other? Regardless of our preferences, everyday life keeps asking us to sustain an open, resilient receptivity in encounters that come from outside our self-centered wishes or expectations. This allows our response to be guided by the other's distinctive solicitation, let us say, by their holy or sacred summons. Such an alternative way may seem impossible. But surely we know, yes, that if we turn away from this radical opportunity and turn back to our usual reactions, if we perceive and act only according to our contracted, fear-filled stance, we will afflict others and continue to be afflicted ourselves.

The trapped rabbit, my beloved wife or children, a stranger in a store, or the rainforest being assaulted: one such as this comes to me, arriving with a plea that disrupts the flow of my day, that breaks through my plans and projects and (at times) my most cherished identity. Yet, when "will and grace are joined" (Buber, 1970, p. 58), I somehow find the resources to respond. In a mysterious and momentous way of being that bridges my conscious agency and a pure gift from the depths, I consent to release the supposedly separate self that is bent on mastery and control, and confide myself into an intimate responsiveness oriented by the welfare of the other. Somehow, indeed, it does transpire that this particular relational partner's summons is openly borne in body and heart, thereby metamorphosing into my authentic desire and consonant gesture of care, a responsive offering of my very being, freely given for my companion here and now, together with all the other others who are justly implicated in every encounter.

Chapter Eleven

# Love Is Our Nature, Our Calling, Our Path, Our Fruition

## It All Comes Down to This

Life's most persistent and urgent question is, What are you doing for others?

—Martin Luther King Jr. (1996, p. 17)

My religion is kindness.

—Tenzin Gyatso, the Fourteenth Dalai Lama (Gee, 2001, p. 23)

The life so short, the craft so long to learn. . . . All this mean I by Love.

—Geoffrey Chaucer (2014, p. 581)

## Overture

Love is our nature, calling, path, and fruition. When we realize this deeply, our conventional dissociation from the natural world falls away, the pathological structure of separation-elevation-devaluation-domination collapses. By way of this transformation of consciousness, the well-being of humankind and the rest of nature co-arise in concert.

## A Question of the Way

One summer day, when walking with our puppy in a community park, my wife was drawn to the sweet, ripe fruit beckoning in the brambles: Wild black raspberries! As she was enjoying the luscious treat, another woman came over to see what she was doing. Intrigued, but obviously anxious, she asked, "You're eating those berries?" "Yes," my wife replied. "Really, right off that plant?!" "*Yes. They're delicious. Try some.*" It may seem like a small thing that raspberries can appear threatening. But this event carries intimations of a grave psychocultural pathology: people's now normal but dissociative lack of familiarity with the natural world. Far more severe ecological maladies are also making it clear that we have lost our way. Life is beseeching us to find our way anew, for the indivisible well-being of humankind and the rest of nature. But what is the way? Is the way lost, or merely forgotten or obscured? How does each person discover and create their distinctive way? What about human cultures and the whole human species? How do we live in consonance with, and in the service of, life's great way?

Once upon a time, a pilgrim monk made an appeal to the Zen teacher Hsüan-sha:

"Please show me where to enter the Way."

"Do you hear the sound of the valley stream?" asked Hsüan-sha.

"Yes," said the monk.

"Enter there!" (Foster & Shoemaker 1996, p. vi).

What if the way truly is right here, right now? What if the real way can never really be lost? What if the way includes our getting lost along the way? And includes ever returning to the way; repairing, restoring, renewing, recreating the way's local manifestation, time and time again? Contemplative masters across the ages and contemporary transpersonal psychology both attest: the essential "way"—life's way, nature's way, G-d's way, the buddha way, our shared way—is always already presencing, giving itself freely in and as every encounter, and ceaselessly calling us to respond. "The real way circulates everywhere. . . . The essential teaching is fully available" (Dōgen, 1999, p. 33). The same testimony comes via the stream sounding through the valley, the tasty raspberries, even the dis-ease one might feel upon encountering that wild fruit or psychocultural disease of global warming: the way is ever right here. *This is it.*

Still, in the spirit of that monk's earnest inquiry, we might wonder, "What is this way?" We would do well to keep this question alive, for us to work on and for it to work on us. No one can really give a precise answer because "the way" is an ancient name for the great, unsayable, the unnamable, ungraspable mystery. Another classic name is the Dao. This Chinese word literally means "way," and at times it means nature: that is, "the *way* of Great Nature" (Snyder, 1990, p. 10). Neither the Buddha nor Socrates nor Jesus left us any written work. But Dōgen and Eckhart did in abundance, saying the unsayable in ways that foster revelatory, transformative experiences. It would be strangely incongruent for nondual traditions to dualistically split off words and texts (or anything else for that matter). This is true even though Bodhidharma described Zen as "a special transmission outside the scriptures. / No dependence on words or letters. / Pointing directly to the heart. / Seeing into our essential nature and becoming Buddha" (see Dumoulin, 1988, p. 85; Suzuki, 1955, p. 61). Hearsay is not enough. Even the most illuminating concepts fall short. We must realize the way through our direct experience, verify and clarify it endlessly, and give it form day by day as our responsive life. It is wonderful that Bodhidharma's words live on to remind us to not settle for words. Still, I hope that the words of this book serve as gates that open into fresh experience and renewed relationships.

## Love Is Our Nature, Calling, Path, and Fruition

What does it mean to "see our essential nature and become Buddha"? The same question could be put like this: What does it mean to enter the way by hearing the sounds of the stream? By eating wild raspberries? By transforming our nature-alienated consciousness and culture? Zen is renowned for going directly to the heart of life, right from the very start and always. Drawing inspiration from this approach I would like to offer a proposal, presented in a series of questions. *What if love is the way? What if the way is love? What if love is our shared nature, our calling, our path, and our fruition?* That is, what if we embraced intimate, understanding, compassionate involvement as the very essence of who we are? Inseparably, what if we felt this to be our deepest life calling?

And what if we welcomed this as an endless path, an ongoing practice by which we answer life's call by bringing our loving nature to fruition in tangible acts of love?

I am speaking up for love because illusory dualistic divisions are at the root of today's eco(psycho)logical maladies. Indeed, the real heart of ecopsychology consists of dissolving our fiercely felt sense of separation from each other and the rest of nature, surpassing our fear and greed, and allowing care to flow forth freely in response. That is what love does. That is what love is. If love is my nature, an essence that comes to fruition in answering a companion's ethical call, then the impoverishment of my capacity for intimacy with others in the natural world is a truly grave malady. Then the loss of my nonhuman relational partners is a grievous trauma. Then the belief that I am a separate self is a dreadfully afflictive delusion. Yet when I realize—vividly, experientially—that my essential nature is love, I can no longer cling to the fantasy of being merely a small, independent, self-interested self. I release my tight grip on this normal but pathological and pathogenic notion. Conversely, its tight grip on me is subverted. The misguided hubris that we are an exceptional species elevated above all the rest also falls away.

Since authentic love takes us to the heart of the great matter of life and death, I will venture to honor love in our relations with nature. But I do so with wary concern. Superficial sentimentality often shows up in the name of "love." And people tend to hear or utter the word in banal ways, presuming to instantly know what it means. Perhaps, instead, I should say that our essence is intimate responsiveness and response-ability. These words carry an etymology that accords with love in our version of transpersonal ecopsychology. It turns out that "*-spond*" arrives to us from ancient Latin and Greek roots that mean to pledge and to offer, as in making a sacred offering in a religious ritual. In each encounter the world does present itself to us and request something of us, thereby *sponsoring* a reply; we *re-spond* to this appeal, offering our very being(-in-relation) back to the world, particularly to the unique other right here before us. We reply more or less consonantly, consciously, compassionately to the call, hoping to *sponsor* the relational conditions for the other to further convey their own distinctive being. In this way, the call-and-response conversation continues. Quite crucially, such inter-responsive love includes the courageous, resilient practice of recovering from inevitable relational ruptures. The words responsiveness and responsibility may work better in some contexts, like when the one summoning us is a rainforest being destroyed or unknown people starving on the other side of the world. Or when a strongly assertive reply is required to stop acts of violence. Yet, in my view, love still applies in all these circumstances, not just in name but in engaged action.

Cutting through the spell of mawkishness and superficiality, I insist on the truly radical nature of love. It is heartening to share common ground with bell hooks (2009) on this: "It is the most militant, most radical intervention anyone can make to not only speak of love but to engage in the practice of love. For love as the foundation of all social movements for self-determination is the only way we create a world that domination and dominator thinking cannot destroy. Any time we do the work of love, we are doing the work of ending domination" (p. 248).

## Nature-Calling-Path-Fruition: Preliminary Suggestions

*Love is our nature or essence.* "That's my nature." "That is the nature of things." The word nature in these common phrases means the inherent way things are, the deep way and coherent functioning of self, life, being, or reality. By proposing that love is our nature, I am pointing to several essential aspects of our (co)existence. To begin with, we humans are relational beings. From prenatal life to the moment of death we become who we are, we are who we are, in and through our involvement with others. Love, or its absence, is crucial throughout. Further, as we explored with Levinas and Dōgen in chapter 10, our most authentic self comes into being not when we actively impose our preestablished wishes, but when we find the loving resources to respond well to the other's appeal. And recall that the spiritual traditions often present love as a name for our essential nature, our true self, transpersonal self, the essential dynamic functioning of the one great mystery. The Christian formulation is explicit: "G-d is love" (1 John 4:8).

Christ once posed a koan-like question to his disciples: "Who do you say I am?" (Matthew 16:15). On various occasions he answered his own query. Christ's most famous response is this: "My Father [G-d] and I are one" (John 10:30). In his supreme identity or essential nature, he knows himself to be no other than G-d. And since "G-d is love," we could say that Christ realizes that love is his essence. Although these exact words are not in the recorded sayings of Christ, he could well have proclaimed: *I am love.* Even if he did not say it overtly, his life was an expression of this truth. Like the Buddha before him, Christ taught that this deep realization is available for each of us (whether we identify as spiritual or not). Clearly, Christ wanted each of us to realize that *in our essential nature, we too are love.* Perhaps surprisingly, Buddhism offers the same message. My Zen teacher once shared a beautiful question that his teacher had previously posed for him: "Can we say that love is another name for our true nature?" To which my teacher replied, "Yes!" Meeting him right there, his teacher said, "I agree."

Given today's postmodern sensibilities, I understand that some readers may be suspicious of any talk about our "essence" or "nature." Such language might suggest a positivist or "essentialist" ontology that posits some reified, self-existent reality: objective, substantial, self-sufficient, static, permanent, simply given, merely present. However, this is not at all what I am proposing. The following discussion will make it obvious that the essence or nature I am exploring is coming into being ever anew, ceaselessly created inter-responsively with all our relations. This nondual essence is never a fixed delimited thing, nor some ideal world away from or other than the everyday world. As Nāgārjuna (ca. 150–250 CE) challenges us to see: "Whatever is the essence of the Tathāgata, / That is the essence of the world [and of you and me]. / The Tathāgata has no essence. / The world is without essence" (Garfield, 1995, p. 62). Tathāgata—"the one thus coming forth"—is a Sanskrit title for the historical Buddha. But far more deeply, it is a name for the buddha-nature of this very life, this very encounter. It derives from *tathatā*: the sheer suchness or how-it-is-ness of this presencing moment and of our essential nature. "This, *thusness*, is the nature of the nature of nature" (Snyder, 1990, p. 103). And this—precisely this!—is never other than you and me, never other than whatever is currently transpiring. We smile at our neighbor, lower our carbon footprint, engage in a conscious act of civil disobedience, care for an unknown cat struck by a car. In this way, love is a nonessentialist essence—inherently open, free, dynamic, ungraspable, yet tangibly responsive.

Let me acknowledge a curious fantasy: I just had an urge to take back much of what I had written so far in this chapter. What have I gotten us into by speaking of our essence or nature? Anything I say regarding our nature is not our nature itself (except insofar as the very *saying* is one phenomenal manifestation of *it*). Along life's great way, our true nature can be disclosed in any moment. And there are practices that can help us directly realize our essential nature: meditation, open conversation, sauntering in the natural world, lovemaking, psychotherapy, art, poetry, music, playing with dogs or cats, research, reading, gardening, ecopsychology, and so on. But it is impossible to grasp or define our essential nature. We can only really know our true nature by being it consciously. Hoping to evoke fresh experiences that carry our conversational life further, I will keep writing in that spirit, trusting that (for now) the following is a felicitous way of saying the unsayable: *love is our nature; our nature is love.*

Love is our *"calling."* This refers to a lifetime's ongoing developmental aspiration, how I am called to be and become; and, most importantly, to an ever-presencing ethical appeal given in my sensitive contact with everyone I meet. Each encounter asks something particular of me, but regardless of the specifics I am ever called to be understanding, compassionate, and loving.

Love is our *"path."* This refers to the path of relationally engaged practice—the devoted endeavor of discovering, personalizing, cultivating, and actualizing our inter-responsive nature and calling. "The life so short, the craft so long to learn. . . . All this mean I by Love" (p. 581). These beautiful words from Chaucer (2014) take us to the heart of this sacred path. To reply fittingly to the solicitations of others is an endless and precarious craft. There is no preestablished path, but it comes down to responding as best we can for the well-being of all our relations. Thus we discover and create our inter-responsive way as we walk along the inter-responsive way. We learn to love by engaging in loving relationships. This includes countless times of realizing that we are gripped by self-centeredness, and then humbly returning with care. The sage Shantideva states it directly: "The source of all misery in the world / Lies in thinking of oneself; / The source of all happiness / Lies in thinking of others" (Dalai Lama, 2000, p. 214). And the Dalai Lama avows, "My religion is kindness" (Gee, 2001, p. 23). To orient ourselves we can always ask: *For the time being, what is the most loving thing I can do for everyone involved?*

Love is our *"fruition."* "For one human being to love another: that is perhaps the most difficult of all our tasks, the ultimate, the last test and proof, the work for which all other work is but preparation" (Rilke, 1954, pp. 53–54). Love as our fruition refers to the tangible, daily actualization of our loving, compassionate, understanding, and just way of being-with-others, as completely as possible under the present circumstances. We might hold love as real value. We might see clearly that love is our true nature. We might feel called to be loving. All of this is good. But it does not take us nearly far enough. Going further, as far as we possibly can go: When we are actually loving in a particular encounter, well, that is really it! That is the fruition of life (here and now). And what a delicious fruit it is!

## Nature's Love for Us: A Mystical View of Biophilia

In crafting this chapter's story of love, I looked for illustrative examples to ensure that my theoretical views stayed grounded in lived experience. My encounter with the little rabbit from the previous chapter was the first thing that came to mind. But what about other examples? Pondering what to share as evidence, I felt my heart beating and realized, "Ah, this too is what I mean." If you are willing, place your fingers on the left side of your neck, on your carotid artery. Feel the pulsing of your heart, and really relish the sensation. Now notice that our heart continues to beat without us needing to do anything. Pulse by pulse, something far beyond our conscious self is ever beating our heart, ever sustaining our being, ever (dare I say) loving us into existence. Of course, the deep source of my heartbeat is not really a thing. But what is it? Might I deem it my cardiovascular system, or my whole body? Yes, but my body cannot do it alone, independently. What is the essential source that sustains my body (and thus keeps beating my heart)? Might I say nature? The earth in its dynamic, participatory functioning? G-d? The whole cosmos? Life? The Dao? The great, all-embracing way? Love? My deepest heart? In truth and gratitude, I happily say yes to all of these. But what are these? Looking intimately into direct experience, I have to acknowledge that I cannot say what they are. Yet it is undeniably evident that some unfathomable mystery is beating my heart, is bringing me (loving me) into being. This freely given blessing is completely ordinary and thoroughly awesome.

Christian mystics would say that G-d is beating our heart. They would also say that G-d is our essential nature or supreme identity. They would also say that "G-d is love." Speaking from this transpersonal realization, we could say: love itself is loving us into being, moment by moment, intimate contact by intimate contact. This is the spirit of Blake's (1988) joyous proclamation: "Eternity is in love with the productions of time" (p. 36). Eternity and time, the transcendent and the immanent, heaven and earth, G-d and you and me, these are never really two. The "productions of time"—all this phenomenal world—are the forms that eternity's love is taking, right here and now. As Eckhart (2009) proclaims, "God is creating the world *now* . . . God creates the world and all things in one present Now" (p. 338). Pulse . . . pulse . . . pulse . . .

My research on the sacred in everyday life is directly relevant here. I am thinking especially of Sarah's experience of the sunset sky changing colors. No longer was she a separate self, over here on the land, observing the red-purple sky over there. Rather, she said, "I was becoming a part of everything else. . . . Like a slowing down to a point where you, you really feel your own heartbeat. . . . But it was a large heartbeat. It was everything. . . . If the universe had a heartbeat it was the universal heartbeat." The transpersonal heartbeat. Our own most intimate heartbeat. Liberated from illusions of self-sufficiency, I may realize: *my true heart is not only mine, my true self is not only mine*—not only something that I (as an isolated body-mind) possess. My physical heart, my essential heart, and the heart of the cosmos are not separate from nor other than one another. Most deeply, they are one heart. No wonder that Zen speaks of our essential nature as our heart, our heartmind, our true heart, our heart ground, our heart center.

This exploration of love as our true nature places the experience of biophilia in a new light. As noted in chapter 1, the psychologist Erich Fromm coined the word by integrating *bio-*, life, and *-phila*, love. E. O. Wilson's biological research later emphasized how humans have an innate affinity with all living things: "Innate means hereditary and hence part of ultimate human nature" (Wilson, 1984, p. 3). Part of our essence or true nature, to use terms from the present chapter. Now, perhaps more than ever, biophilia points to our core calling and path: *to love all that is alive*. (And mountains, rivers, air, and other natural presences are alive in their own special ways.) When this great summons is welcomed via contemplative awareness, a crucially important, complementary dimension of biophilia is revealed. That is, our love for the natural world emerges from the (scientific and psychospiritual) fact that something infinitely deeper than our individual self is bringing us into being moment by moment. Stated differently, our *philia* for the *bios* is dependent upon the *philia* of the *bios* for us. Our love of nature grows from nature's love of us. Without that, we could not love at all, could not even be at all. And since we *are* (an embodiment of) nature, when we offer our care for the natural world, this is nature loving and caring for itself. In our relationships with people, love has to do with carefully tending to our partner so that they may come fully into being and flourish in their own distinctive way. This is akin to what the natural world does for each of us. I am certainly not claiming that nature is like an individual agent or anthropomorphic God who intervenes in our particular lives or directs love to us personally. Instead, *the very fact that we are at all, and that our existence is ever being created and sustained by the whole inter-responsive earth community—via breath, food, shelter, beauty, relationship, culture, and so forth—means that life is loving us into being right here, moment by moment, encounter by encounter.* When we know this, we also know that our *everyday engagement is correspondingly bringing life into being,* for our beloved ones—human and otherwise—and for unknown ones around the world.

## The Way of the Bodhisattva

We have already pondered Christ's avowal that love is our true calling: "love G-d with all your heart . . . love your neighbor as yourself" (Mark 12:28–31). Let us consider a Buddhist version of the same imperative. With its emphasis on wisdom—seeing our essential nature—Zen may appear from the outside to be less heart-centered than Christianity. Favoring the word compassion, Zen teachers speak explicitly of love only on special occasions. Yet love is implicit throughout all of Buddhism. We can catch this in the Buddha's famous avowal, "I teach only suffering and the transformation of suffering" (Nhat Hanh, 1998, p. 3). Zen and Tibetan Buddhism have long celebrated the way of the bodhisattva. The word *bodhi*—like *buddha*—means "being awake." *Bodhi* also carries connotations of courage and the intention to serve others, just as every buddha does. *Sattva* often denotes *a* being. Yet, most importantly, it means a *way of being.* A bodhisattva is one whose way of being is that of wakefulness, understanding, compassion, and love. Realizing deeply that no one can awaken alone (because detachment from each other is illusory), the bodhisattva devotes their life to the well-being of others— assisting all others in realizing their true nature and being liberated from suffering. This loving call and path are affirmed in a sacred pledge, the renowned "bodhisattva vow":

Beings are numberless, I vow to assist them all.

Greed, hatred, and delusion arise endlessly, I vow to clarify and release them all.

Dharma gates are infinite, I vow to enter them all.

The buddha-way is unsurpassable, I vow to realize it and embody it fully.[1]

Please be aware that the final line is not invoking the Buddhist way, but the buddha-way—the all-embracing, all-permeating way not limited to any tradition (nor, in fact, limited at all). The second line is addressing what Buddhism calls the "three poisons," three interconnected forms of suffering that are inevitable when we identify exclusively as a separate self: confused (deluded) that the ego is merely who we are, we become excessively afraid and resort to defensive/offensive reactions of hatred and greed. We will explore the vow's wondrous third line in the coda that follows this chapter. But now to the crucial first line. Aware that others are never really divorced from me, this sacred promise emerges from our inherent, interrelational response-ability and returns us to that very responsibility. Vimalakīrti, a lay disciple of the Buddha and a great bodhisattva, puts it powerfully: "This illness of mine is born of ignorance and feelings of attachment. Because all living beings are sick, therefore I am sick. If all living beings are relieved of their sickness, then my sickness will be mended. Why? Because the bodhisattva for the sake of living beings enters the realm of birth and death" (Watson, 1997, p. 65). The "ignorance" Vimalakīrti refers to is the "delusion" invoked in the vow: the way we often ignore our true, interdependently co-arising nature while (mis)taking ourselves to be separate sovereign subjects. The "realm of birth and death" is this very life of joy, beauty, pain, and suffering (*dukkha*). This includes our relations with the natural world. When we are sick, the earth is sick. When the earth is sick, we are sick. Thankfully, the converse is true too: the earth's wellness and ours are convivial and reciprocally constituted.

What is this life? Who am I? Who is the other? What is our relationship? How shall I live? What am I here for? These are core questions for us to answer with our very living, each in our own unique way. Yet we can all heed the loving message in Vimalakīrti's final comment. *We are in this world for the sake of others' well-being. To love and serve others, this is what we came into the world to do, what we are continually reentering the world (of relational involvement) to do.* "That's our mission, to fall in love with our world. We are made for that, you see, because we are dependently co-arising" (Joanna Macy, in Kaza & Kraft, 2000, p. 159). William Blake (1988) concurs: "We are put on earth a little space, / That we may learn to bear the beams of love" (p. 9). And so does Martin Luther King Jr. (1996): "An individual has not started living until he can rise above the narrow confines of his individualistic concerns to the broader concerns of all humanity. . . . Every man must decide whether he will walk in the light of creative altruism or the darkness of destructive selfishness. . . . Life's most persistent and urgent question is, What are you doing for others?" (p. 17). Vimalakīrti is an ancient bodhisattva, Blake a more recent one, Dr. King an even more recent one, Joanna Macy a contemporary one. So when I claim that love is what we are here for, I am in good company. This is just another way of saying that love is our nature and calling. However, doesn't Buddhism claim that awakening is what we are here for? Yes, but this cannot be disconnected from compassion-love. The Māhāyana traditions celebrate the nondual and reciprocal nature of these two essential dimensions. It is clear that real love fosters wakeful, liberating understanding; and wakeful wisdom fosters deep compassion and love. The Dalai Lama (2000) puts it strongly: "The practice of compassion is at the heart of the entire path" (p. 229).

## Who Is the One Who Answers the Call to Love?

The bodhisattva vow may sound impossible, much like Christ's appeal to love our neighbors and even our enemies as our very self (Mark 12:28–31; Matthew 5:44). To "assist *all* beings," how can I come close to fulfilling this pledge? We can draw insight from Dōgen's warning in the previous chapter: "Conveying oneself toward all things to carry out practice-en-lightenment is delusion" (Dōgen, in Okumura, 2010, p. 1). Unilaterally striving to assist all beings by way of my individual autonomy, power, and mastery: this attitude is a part of the delusion Dōgen is addressing. Even with the best of intentions, when I take this approach I unwittingly turn the bodhisattva vow into an ego project. Here I am not referring to crude self-aggrandizement, as in: "Aren't I great because I'm helping all beings!" The ego works in much subtler ways. *The bodhisattva vow becomes an ego project when I imagine that I alone, as a sovereign autonomous self, possess the power to liberate others from suffering; and when I am attached to controlling the outcome of my efforts to assist.* Thankfully, there is an alternative way. Quite crucially, the self that makes the vow to assist all beings is not my conventional, mastery-seeking, supposedly separate self. Rather, it is my (our) true or essential self. Life is infinitely deeper and wilder than my most loving capacities for mastery (much less my self-centered ones), so an individualistic, domineering approach will surely bring grief. I cannot fulfill the bodhisattva vow on my own, by way of my personal will and agency. Nor can I control the fruits of my offerings (as much as I wish I could). And yet "we must nonetheless take responsibility for a world that exceeds our capacity for saving it," as Jason Wirth (2017) says so beautifully (p. 31). Make no mistake, when another calls upon me—say in the form of global warming, a corporation dumping chemical wastes in the river, a spotted fawn frozen on the road when I am rushing to make a meeting—I am the one being implored to respond. No one else can assume this responsibility for me. Fortunately, the limits of my egoic mastery do not bring the journey to a dead end. Realization—seeing clearly, awakening, love—does not consist of independent self-assertion and control. Rather, it involves welcoming the overtures of my fellow participants in this great earth sangha, *allowing others to contact me and actualize their unique way through my unique involvement with them.* Herein, self and others are realized together, liberated together. To cite an ordinary example, it is not simply me as a completely self-directing person who, on my own, goes outside to put seeds in the birdfeeder. Instead, in the seamlessly interrelational flow of living, birds around the near-empty feeder catch my eye. My agentic actions follow naturally from being beckoned by the hungry birds and depleted feeder. Life sends me a request and I reply. That one was clear and easy. Many others are not.

Likewise, Dōgen alludes to the fact that it is not me as an autonomous agent who "achieves" enlightenment. That would be impossible. First of all, because vivid unconditioned wakefulness is the intrinsic nature of all that is. Since it was never absent in the first place, I cannot "attain" it but only realize it. Also, awakening is not an individual achievement because it inherently involves all beings and presences practicing-awakening together. Commenting on Dōgen's teaching, Zen master Shohaku Okumura (2010) says: "The subject of practice is not the personal self but all beings. . . . In other words, it is not I who practice, but rather Buddha carries out Buddha's practice through me" (p. 54). And what is meant here by "Buddha"? The word is familiar but truly ineffable and inconceivable. However, in this case it refers not to a particular person who lived in ancient India. Instead, "Dōgen defined Buddha as . . . 'whole great earth.' This is an expression for the self that is together with all beings" (Okumura, p. 54). Joining with Levinas, I know that when nature summons me to love, I myself am irreplaceably responsible. Joining with Dōgen, I know that this "I" is not me as an isolated skin-bounded ego. *I myself means life itself*—the whole great awake alive earth (and beyond) actualizing "practice-enlightenment" by way of my unique incorporation of its gifts and calls, and at best by way of my loving responses (say, to a little rabbit, to global warming, to the fresh air after a storm).

## Life Is Always Complete and Always Beseeching Us

Zen teachers insist that seeing into our essential nature is our supreme calling. This naturally sends us on a path of awakening, compassion, love. Yet they also emphasize that *we always already are that which we seek*. Our fruition is no other than our essence—but realized clearly and enacted lovingly. "Before you take even one step you have already arrived" (Bruce Harris, personal communication). As Hakuin, an eighteenth-century Zen master, sings: "All beings by nature are Buddha [wakefulness itself], as ice by nature is water. . . . How sad that people ignore the near and search for truth afar, like someone in the midst of water crying out in thirst. . . . This very place is the Lotus Land [*nirvāna*, buddha-nature, our true nature], this very body the Buddha" (Aitken, 1993, pp. 179–180). Nāgārjuna provides one of the most renowned formulations of this realization: "There is no specifiable difference whatsoever between *nirvāna* and the everyday world [*samsāra*]; there is no specifiable difference whatever between the everyday world and *nirvāna*" (Loy, 2000, p. 92). *Samsāra* is no other than *nirvāna*; *nirvāna* is no other than *samsāra*.

However, if this very life is *nirvāna*, if buddha-nature is always already present without the slightest lack, if there is a deep-vital-sacred-essential world inside our conventional one, then what about all the suffering in the world? What about ecological desecration, racism, poverty, and war? What about our personal wounds, conflicts, and confusions? What about the urgent *call* we feel and the *path* we walk to address these? What about the actual psychospiritual *practice* of living a compassionately engaged existence? Commenting on Nāgārjuna's proclamation, Garfield (1995) remarks: "Nirvāna is simply samsāra seen without reification [into separate selves and objects], without attachment, without delusion" (p. 331). *Nirvāna* is not some special place other than or removed from daily life, but it is responsively actualizing this very life in a radically alternative way. *Nirvāna* is *samsāra* lived via wakeful, loving consciousness.

From the view of Christian mysticism, we could say the same thing about heaven. Lived contemplatively, heaven is not some otherworldly place we go after we die, but a mode of consciousness and way of being with others here and now: "The kingdom of the Father is spread out upon the earth, but people do not see it" (Gospel of Thomas 113, in Pagels, 2003, p. 241). I once heard the story of a woman who, upon meeting G-d in a dream, asked about heaven and hell. G-d had her look into a room that was filled with hungry people, all screaming and cursing and attacking one another. Sitting around a big pot of soup, they were fighting because their spoons were longer than their arms and they could not find a way to get the food to their mouths. "That is hell!" said G-d. Then they looked into another room. The woman recoiled upon first glance, as the scene initially seemed the same: people with long spoons sitting around a pot of soup. But she noticed everybody was happy—smiling, laughing, eating gratefully. This was due to the loving-kindness of their companions, with each one filling a spoon and turning to feed their neighbor. And she realized, "That is heaven!" Buddhist lore gives us a similar story. A samurai warrior once asked a Zen master to teach him about heaven and hell. The Zen master scoffed strategically, claiming that the samurai was so confused and violent that he did not deserve such a precious teaching. Enraged, the warrior raised his sword and was about to behead the teacher. In a gesture infinitely sharper than the samurai's sword, the Zen master shouted, "That's hell!" Feeling his heart breaking open, the warrior stopped on the spot. With tears streaming from his eyes and loving gratitude flowing forth, he bowed to the Zen master for risking his life on his behalf. Thus heaven was disclosed for him.

## Forget Your Perfect Offering

*To assist all beings*: This vow may seem impossible, *and it is impossible to fulfill by one's supposedly separate self.* But we can take heart in Nhat Hanh's (1988) encouraging words: "All of us are sometimes bodhisattvas, and sometimes not" (p. 7). As the bodhisattva vow acknowledges, and as we agonizingly know from our daily life: ego-centered confusion, fear, and greed arise endlessly. In real relationships we will hurt each other, usually unintentionally, sometimes intentionally. Such is the case with other people and so too with the natural world. As a radically nondual tradition, Zen affirms that the great way is boundless, seamless, and all-embracing.

Therefore, uncannily, practice-awakening must include our hurtful reactivity to and alienation from others, including those in the natural world. This may be surprising but it is crucially important. It helps us cut through any idealization of spiritual life, helps us accept our fallibility and limited capacity to control our life, and helps us recover when we get lost.

It is crucial to understand that the bodhisattva vow is not a promise about the results of our actions. Even when we muster our best in the moment, things may still go awry. One day I found a ruby-throated hummingbird dead on our sidewalk. I had set out nectar feeders because I love to be in the presence of these awesome beings, and they need all the assistance we can offer these days. But sadly, the tiny bird had been killed by our beloved family cat, Rumi. He was a natural hunter, and I am sure he felt he was bringing us a gift. Earlier that morning the little hummer was flying freely through his world. His was an existence marvelous beyond conceiving. Now he was dead and I was responsible, in a way. My heart broke open upon seeing his limp lifeless body, the ruby-red glow fading from his throat. Offering an apology and a pledge, I put the feeders up higher and decided my next cat would live indoors. *We are responsible for answering the calls that arrive in our contact with others. But we are not responsible for controlling the outcome of our reply.* We are summoned to offer understanding, compassion, and love in the moment. What happens next is beyond us. Sometimes even our kindest responses turn out badly, generating suffering completely counter to our intentions.

Spiritual practitioners are often advised to let go of their attachment to the fruits of their actions; and to let go of their conventional identification as the independent, sovereign, self-sufficient agent of their actions. Yet along with this comes a core imperative: to never let go of their consecrated devotion to serve others. Thankfully, the conversation—*the interrelational participation that is our very life*—is ongoing. This sensibility is conveyed in "Anthem," a magnificent song by Leonard Cohen (1992): "Ring the bells that still can ring / Forget your perfect offering / There is a crack, a crack in everything / That's how the light gets in." The last two lines have garnered the most acclaim over the years, and they are exquisite. But I have been deeply moved by the first two as well. Life is immensely challenging. We and the rest of nature have surely been wounded. At times we are tempted to lose heart. And yet even so, *still,* we can find bells to ring, loving gifts to share in support of one another. But we cannot expect our offerings or their fruits to be perfect. Birds are killed, sometimes due to well-intentioned hands that filled birdfeeders or designed windmills for clean renewable energy. Whatever the situation, we will be waiting forever if we hold back until we are certain that we have come up with the perfect reply. We will be depriving the world of our real gifts—cracked, yet still precious just as they are. But when we do dare to make an imperfect yet heartfelt offering, we can trust that our gift will be carried onward in unfathomable ways via an infinite network of relationships, one that starts precisely where we are and radiates boundlessly. Touched by an other's overture, we are called to let love flow through us, let it be inflected with our unique being, and let it come forth in the service of all our relations. Such love is endless—imperfect and just right at the very same time.

## Love as Our Fruition:
## The Self Emerges as a Caring Response

Levinas and Buddhism may seem like an odd pairing, but they complement each other well. "The way I appear is a summons" (p. 139), declares Levinas (1981). Yet what can this mean? As conventionally construed, subjectivity or selfhood consists of the (presumed) autonomy of a preestablished separate self: willful, masterful, sovereign, agentic, self-sufficient, and so forth. As an ideal in the modern Euro-American world, this is often what parents and culture tell us we are, or should be. According to the familiar story, the self comes first. I am supposed to look out for "number one." But Levinas shows that our true subjectivity is structured otherwise. "The more I return to myself, the more I divest myself . . . of my freedom as a . . . willful, imperialist subject, the more I discover myself to be responsible" (Levinas, p. 112). Most deeply, the self comes not before but after and through the other. In what Levinas calls "the self emptying itself of itself" (p. 111), *the self comes as response and responsibility.* Far from existing as a skin-bounded ego, Levinas points out that "subjectivity" is actually "made out of assignation" (p. 111). This assignment is conferred upon me by the epiphany of the other's presencing. *I actually come into being in and as my responsible response to appeals arriving from beyond my egoic self.* In Levinas' (1969) phenomenological analysis—and this rings deeply true for me—such "responsibility" is "the essential, primary and fundamental structure of subjectivity" (p. 95). (In terms of the present chapter, love is our nature or essence.) Who am I? What am I here *for*? "I am first a servant of a neighbor"

(Levinas, 1981, p. 87). "I am . . . a responsibility . . . supporting the world" (p. 128). My true self is "incarnated in order to offer itself, to suffer and to give" (Levinas, p. 105). Crucially, when I listen carefully to the other's call rather than subsume it into my own preferences, the real self who emerges in reply is not a preestablished ego but a freshly resonant self-in-relation, (re)created by way of the unique particularities of the current interchange. "I exist through the other and for the other" (Levinas, 1981, p. 114), not as a self-imposing sovereign agent but a humble, sensitively responsive one. When I try to defend or bolster my preestablished ego, then the self that I assert is a stale, superficial, and often insensitive one. But in surrendering my need to aggrandize myself, *I become a gesture of loving-kindness that harmonizes with the soliciting gesture of my relational partner.*

I actually come into being only through, as, and (quintessentially) *for* my responsiveness to others. This is *who I am* and *that for which I am*—in this encounter, in this whole life. Correspondingly, *my relational partner also emerges into being anew in the present encounter, whether nourished or hurt by my reply.* Such immense responsibility is my very life. The singular being right here before me and, inseparably, the shared earth community: *these infinitely precious ones turn on my reply.*

## "Here I Am! Send Me!"

As in the bodhisattva vow, Levinas (1981) insists that "the word *I* means *here I am*, answering for everything and for everyone" (p. 114). And "'Here I am!' means 'send me'" (p. 199). (Notice that our being and loving are interwoven: "Here I am!" = being; "Send me!" = loving.) Replying to the beautiful, wounded earth, I avow: "Here I am! I'm with you. How may I be of service?" Moses uttered the same reverent response when G-d spoke to him from the burning bush (Exodus 3:4). When G-d called, Moses answered with the Hebrew word *hineni*. "Here I am!" Or, "It's me here." The urgent responsibility to embrace an other's plea is not reserved just for prophets. Every person is "a chosen one, called to leave . . . the concept of the ego . . . to respond with responsibility: me, that is, here I am for the others" (Levinas, 1981, p. 185). Let us appreciate that when we are chosen in an encounter, the deepest dimension of existence is making a claim upon us. "The dimension of the divine opens forth from the human face. . . . It is here that the Transcendent, infinitely other, solicits us and appeals to us" (Levinas, 1969, p. 78). And let us realize that our circle of love can expand such that the divine also opens forth from the face of our more-than-human fellows.

*Saying "here I am" is an acknowledgment that my relational partner's call has interrupted the momentum of my ego-centered ways, that the depths of life have touched my depths, and that I do not know quite what to offer in response, other than myself.* In actuality, *I myself am the offering.* Subverting the notion that there could be a separate self, Levinas (1981) remarks: " 'Here I am,' just that! . . . without having anything to identify myself with, but the sound of my voice or the figure of my gesture—the saying itself" (p. 149). A Zen teacher could easily have said the same thing. And the best of our everyday life actually functions just like this. Seeing my daughter burning with strep throat, or seeing the earth burning with human short-sightedness, I say, "Yes, I am here for you . . ." And love follows freely: giving her a cold washcloth for her forehead and antibiotics for that fierce bacteria, lowering my carbon footprint and practicing ecopsychology. In each of these instances it is not accurate to say that I, as an independent self, observed something apart from me out in the world and then acted to intervene. To posit such a reified entity is far removed from the actual unified interaction. Resonating with Levinas in the previous quote, with my daughter there is nothing that can really be identified as a preexisting "Dad" who is responding to her. My self actually *is* "the sound of my voice" and "the figure of my gesture." "Ah, my sweet full moon, you're on fire. Here's some water, and your medicine. And this cold washcloth might feel good on your forehead." For the time being, just that (!)—love—is what my self is. But even the last clause adds too much. The sheer reality is: Love. Fever. Pain. Water. Medicine. Cold cloth. Love. That's all! And that is everything.

## The Nonduality of Awakening and Love

In some versions of Buddhism it can appear that awakening—enlightenment, wisdom, deep understanding—comes first and then this gives rise to love and compassion. But love and awakening are two ways of describing the same unitive, conversational life. It is impossible to really say whether either one comes first. As individuals, don't we always begin (and begin again) in the middle, loving and awake to some extent and to some extent not? Still, in a chapter celebrating love as our essence and fruition, if I had to choose I would say that love and compassion are primary. Love comes at the beginning and at the end. And every ending initiates a new beginning. Dalai Lama (2000) says that "the aspiration to be of help to others has to be cultivated first" (p. 155). And Robert Aitken Rōshi (1991) remarks, "I must interact and through interaction find realization. . . . It is in engagement that we find our true nature—the true nature of the universe. This is the fact of mutual interdependence" (p. 30). Awakening "means . . . seeing into essential nature" (Aitken, 1991, p. 16). "This experience is called 'realization,' and it is also called 'intimacy'—the two words are synonyms in traditional Zen Buddhist literature" (Aitken, p. 14). "Dialogue is the Tao" (Aitken, 1984, p. 23). These contemporary affirmations join with the views of ancient masters. Jack Kornfield (1993) paraphrases Dōgen: "To be enlightened is to be intimate with all things" (p. 333). And Huineng, a great Chinese Zen ancestor, says: "Our true nature is open communication and fluidity" (translated by Bruce Harris, personal communication, May 2007). Or we could say: Our essential nature is love.

It is true that the more clearly we see, the more loving we are. Yet, equally, the more fully we love, the more clearly we see. For most of us, whether it be our own personal suffering or that of others, a heartfelt compassionate response to suffering is what initiates our psychospiritual quest. This is what happened for the young fellow who was to become the Buddha. Siddhartha Gautama had a privileged, sheltered life as a prince in a royal family. At age nine he attended a spring celebration for the year's initial plowing of the fields. In a long ceremony, people chanted scriptures, sang, and danced. Eventually the king, Siddhartha's father, ritually plowed the first row. Then the local farmers followed (Nhat Hanh, 1991, pp. 45–48). "As the plow turned the earth, Siddhartha noticed that the bodies of worms and other small creatures were being cut as well. As the worms writhed upon the ground, they were spotted by birds who flew down and grabbed them in their beaks. Then Siddhartha saw a large bird swoop down and grasp a small bird in its talons" (p. 47). Siddhartha was profoundly troubled, having never before witnessed such things. He walked over to the shade of a rose-apple tree to ponder what had just occurred. Sitting cross-legged with his eyes closed in the midst of the natural world, his reverie turned into a kind of spontaneous meditation. After being silent for a long time, he opened his eyes upon hearing his mother and some children from the village. " 'Mother,' he said, 'reciting the scriptures does nothing to help the worms and birds' "

(Nhat Hanh, 1991, p. 47). Soon Siddhartha noticed that the other children were quite poor, with tattered clothes and bodies thin from hunger. Going against the caste-oriented conventions of the culture, he invited them to come play with him at the royal picnic. Much later, when he was 29, Siddhartha underwent four encounters that inspired him to embark on a spiritual path. Venturing beyond the luxuries of the family palace, he saw an old man and was shaken by the pains that aging can bring. Later he met a sick man whom he wanted to help, but was unable to. Eventually, coming upon a dead man, he realized that suffering and death are inevitably part of everyone's life. Soon after he saw a wandering "holy man" whom, he learned, was devoting his life to the liberation from suffering. Moved by these events, and with compassion, grief, hope, and love rising in his heart, Siddhartha bid farewell to his family and left home on his transformative quest.

All these encounters took place before Siddhartha became the Buddha in an event of great enlightenment. Still, they are moments of real awakening and compassionate involvement. *Of all of life's circumstances, beauty, love, suffering, and death are the most likely to wake us up.* When we open to the depths of self and world, we see clearly that love and death are intertwined. Suffering is the first grace, so a classic mystical paradox claims. I am touched by pain—others', my own, these indivisibly—and this inspires love, practice, and realization. Our nature, calling, path, and fruition are all woven together. The Zen tradition has long used a series of contemplative "ox-herding pictures" to celebrate this sacred intertwining of awakening and love (Kapleau, 1980, pp. 313–325). Ten ink paintings, together with accompanying verses, depict a man's search for an ox that seems to be missing—with the ox representing our true self or essential nature. After he tracks, glimpses, tames, and eventually rides the ox with ongoing stability, and then sits serenely gazing at the sun setting over the mountains, the parable comes to an apparent conclusion in the eighth picture. Here we find a simple *enso*, a vast open circle. Complementing the image is a verse entitled "BOTH OX AND SELF FORGOTTEN" (p. 321). The picture and verse are meant to be a presentation of profound enlightenment. Earlier versions of the ox-herding pictures culminated with this one. However, in the nondual spirit of Zen, a twelfth-century Chinese master felt called to go deeper. So he added two more pictures. In the very last one we see the awakened man walking into the village. Smiling and thoroughly ordinary, he is looking for ways to provide loving assistance to the folks who live there.

The accompanying verse is called "ENTERING THE MARKETPLACE WITH HELPING HANDS" (p. 323). Truly, awakening/wisdom and love are different forms of one intimate way of being.

## Awakening in and with the Natural World

Our relationship with the natural world is one of the most auspicious sources of opening, realization, and transformation. Since nature has no ego to defend, aggrandize, or impose, it invites us to surrender our (fantasized) independent self and open into the interdependent play of life. Zen emphasizes that call-and-response contact is crucial for the transmission of the dharma, for realizing our essential nature. The "great way of Buddha ancestors is only giving and receiving face to face" (Dōgen, 1985, p. 180). Be assured, Dōgen is not only talking about a true meeting between two people, a Zen master and student. The giving he is referring to is the gift of each experience. The initiatory grace of the dharma is being offered all the time, even in challenging moments. Our everyday life is filled with (potential) moments of transmission. While the facilitating face we meet is often another person, it is significant that nonhuman presences were involved in the Buddha's awakening. So too for his first dharma heir, when the Buddha presented a flower and Mahākāśyapa smiled. In the Zen tradition, there are countless cases in which the source of realization was intimacy with the natural world: the *tock* of a pebble striking bamboo! a cricket *chirping!* the *kerplunking* (!) of a frog in an old pond.

Dōgen (1999) celebrated the poetic testimony of a lay practitioner whose enlightenment occurred upon *really hearing* a stream flowing through the valley: "Valley sounds are the long broad tongue [of Buddha]. / Mountain colors are no other than the unconditioned body [the buddha-body, our essential body] / Eighty-four thousand verses heard throughout the night [the natural presentation of the buddha-way]" (p. 60). Teachings like this can sound esoteric. But this is seriously misleading. In fact, the heart of Zen is available for all—mysterious yes, but never mystifying. D. T. Suzuki (1955, p. 251) tells the story of a scholar's query to a Zen master: "What is the ultimate secret of Zen?" The teacher replied: "You have a fine saying in your [Confucian] *Analects*: 'I have nothing to hide from you.' So Zen has nothing hidden from you." The scholar said that he did not understand. Later, when walking in the mountains with wild blossoms all around, the Zen master asked: "Do you smell the fragrance of the flowering tree?" Yes, replied the scholar. "Then," declared the master, "I have nothing to hide from you." Christ actually presents the very same teaching: "Recognize what is before your eyes, and the mysteries will be revealed to you. For there is nothing hidden that will not be revealed." (Gospel of Thomas 5, in Pagels, 2003, p. 227).

Since the "secret" is right there in the sweet fragrance (and everywhere else!), it is an ever open secret. Yet what this (non)secret *is* cannot be fully named, qualified, or defined. It is up to each of us to continually discover, create, and live it in our own singularly inter-responsive manner. *We come to know it by being it consciously.* Yet Dōgen (1985) provides pointers along the way: "Grass, trees, and lands . . . radiate a great light and expound the inconceivable, profound dharma" (p. 146). "Mountains and waters right now are the actualization of the ancient buddha way" (p. 97). The latter passage is from Dōgen's "Mountains and Waters Sūtra." *Sūtra* is a Sanskrit word referring to sacred Buddhist texts, primarily discourses of Shākyamuni Buddha but also other works held in high esteem. What is extraordinary about this particular text from Dōgen is that it is not a spiritual text *about* earth's mountains and waters. Instead, as Dōgen reverently discloses, *all particular mountains and rivers and other natural phenomena are themselves holy* sūtras. "The sūtras in question are the entire universe, mountains, rivers, and the great earth, plants and trees; they are the self and others, taking meals and wearing clothes, confusion and dignity" (Dōgen, in Kim, 2004, pp. 77–78). Similarly, the Christian mystical tradition has long honored two holy books, the Bible and "the book of nature." And in Shakespeare's eloquent words: "This our life. . . . Finds tongues in trees, books in the running brooks, Sermons in stones and good in everything" (Shakespeare, *As You Like It*, act 2, scene 1). Rejoining Dōgen, in the preceding passage he goes on to make a crucial claim: "Now we are born to meet these sūtras" (Kim, 2004, p. 78). Responding to the tutelage of mountains, rivers, trees, and stones, my vivid contact with nature's overtures reveal what this very life is, who I am, what I am here *for*. Wonder of wonders, life is ceaselessly giving itself to me as a *sūtra* or sermon, a holy teaching that is simultaneously a sacred appeal for loving-kindness. Simply and profoundly, I am being asked to listen and respond from my heart. *This is what I was born to do.*

In my view, *nature is actually more like a conversation than a text* (*sūtra*, holy scripture). My preferred metaphor is a call-and-response dialogue. Nonetheless, books can convey profound messages and sponsor fresh experiences. So what if we actually did meet the natural world as a holy *sūtra*? What if we allowed the nonhuman world to be a beloved, wise teacher, like the Buddha, Moses, Socrates, Christ, Muhammad, another revered mentor, our most trusted friend? This actually was John Muir's core attitude: "When I discovered a new plant, I sat down beside it for a minute or a day, to make its acquaintance and try to hear what it had to say" (Wolfe, 1938, p. 69). What am I being taught in each conversation with nature? What dharma is being transmitted by this particular relational partner? What reply is this event soliciting?

Our real answers must be discerned according to each unique encounter. How am I being claimed and how shall I respond to the wild orchid I discover on my walk; the corporation and township planning to build a factory that uses fracking gas to make plastic pellets? More generally, though, two inseparable messages are always being transmitted: (1) essential completeness; and (2) interdependent co-arising and responsibility. The teaching on essential completeness is expressed in various ways, such as Dōgen's declaration that "the sūtras are the whole body of the Tathāgata" (Kim, 2004, p. 78). In other words, the very body or reality of buddha, pure unconditioned presencing, wakefulness, aliveness, and love. As Dōgen pointed out, these *sūtras* are every person, other animal, plant, and elemental presence who touches me and carries out practice-enlightenment through me. To "meet the sūtras is to meet the Tathāgata" (Dōgen, in Kim 2004, p. 78). To really meet one of nature's sūtras is to be graced and mentored by buddha. "All-things-themselves-are-ultimate-reality here and now" (Dōgen, in Kim 2004, 78). Every encounter is holy and complete, just as it is. The essence, fulfillment, or fruition we yearn for—call it buddha-nature, G-d's presence, awakening, life, or love—is right here. It is no other than this very contact, ultimately and actually. "Our original Buddha-Nature is . . . omnipresent. . . . That which is before you is it, in all its fullness, utterly complete. There is naught beside" (Huang Po, in Blofeld, 1958, p. 35).

But how can we include the loss of even one glorious being in our essential nature, much less today's mass annihilation of species? Surely authentic Zen does not rest complacently in the face of suffering. No, Zen does not! Surely, in a chapter on love, I am not settling for this. No, I am not! Earlier I claimed that nature's *sūtras* appear in two indivisible ways. The previous paragraph addressed the essential way. The (inseparable) complementary way—let us call it the relative, inter-responsive, ethical way, the loving way of path and practice—is the palpable embodiment of the essential way. In fact, Zen discloses that the real way is nondual: absolute-as-relative and relative-as-absolute, transcendent-as-immanent, immanent-as-transcendent, indivisibly. This is to say: Yes, every encounter is inherently holy and complete—essence itself, fruition itself. And this also to say: Since essential completeness is never static or merely present, but impermanent and ceaselessly metamorphosing; since every explicit *presencing* gathers and carries forward implicit depths; then every encounter is summoning me into a wakeful-understanding-compassion-ate-just-loving response. *The other's beauty-filled or pain-filled call in one moment is precisely the way that essential reality is bearing fruit. And in the next fresh moment, my response is precisely the way essential, nondual reality is bearing fruit.*

The singular other before me, along with the complete undivided dynamic functioning reality itself, depend upon my reply. *This moment of contact, this intersection of time and eternity, is where my relative freedom and choice come into play. The whole of life is functioning through me, and I am irreplaceably responsible for the way it carries itself onward.* This is an awesome and crucial responsibility to bear. Thus, for the sake of the forsaken earth, I do all I can to subvert the anthropocentric and narcissistic forces generating global warming, mass extinction, and other eco(psycho)logical maladies. In the process, I am required to address my own woeful confusion, fear, and greed. "To be truly free one must take on the basic conditions as they are—painful, impermanent, open, imperfect—and then be grateful for impermanence and the freedom it grants us. With that freedom we improve the campsite, teach children, oust tyrants" (Snyder, 1990, p. 5). This too is an expression of the way.

Given the earth's severe wounds and our own wounds, it is intriguing that *sūtra* literally means thread. "Suture," in English, comes from this ancient Sanskrit word. Suture can be a noun, a thread or stitch, but for our present purposes let us hear it as a verb: *to suture*, as in rejoining or reuniting severed edges of a wound. Just as suturing helps an injury heal, stitching together flesh that has been torn asunder, the *sūtras* of nature's animate-intelligent expressions suture us: immediately closing the presumed gap between us and the natural world, healing our lived dissociation from earth's community, mending the apparent rupture in the nondual flesh of the world. I say "presumed" and "apparent" because *there can be no real rift in the flesh of being.* But in daily (co)existence, self/other, mind/body, human/nature ruptures are insidiously severe.

When we realize that love is our nature, calling, path, and fruition, all dualistic division falls away. In such intimacy, the natural world can never be construed merely as an objective commodity exploit or an impediment to our individual self-interests. Rather, we realize that nature is lovingly giving itself to us in and as this infinitely open life. We know our self and all others to be unique manifestations and co-creative participants in this all-embracing way. What "mysterious affinity," as Aitken Rōshi (2003, p. 219) sings. What mysterious love!

> All beings are made up by affinity. The whole universe . . .
> forms a vast net of affinity that is all of a piece. . . . With any
> movement within the web, everything moves. Each gesture,
> each blink brings a new kind of equilibrium and new kinds of
> interplay throughout the net. . . . Touches that bring joy and
> harmony bring new interplay and new equilibrium. Touches
> that cause suffering and death bring new interplay and new
> equilibrium as well. (Aitken, 2003, p. 220)

We are always being called upon. And we cannot not respond. *How* we respond really does make a difference. Again and again, each in our own absolutely irreplaceable way: may we keep awakening to *this* (*!*), this loving mystery, this wild and sacred fellowship of being, just as it shows itself here and now. Awakening *to* this, *in* this, *through* this, *as* this, and—quintessentially, lovingly, for the well-being of all our relations—awakening *for* this splendid, shared earth community.

# Coda

## Deep Calls to Deep—Deep Listens from Its Depths— Deep Serves Deep

Between every two pine trees there is a door leading to a new way of life.

—John Muir (Muir, n.d.)

I am the River, the River is me.

—Whanganui Māori proverb

The earth is *the* nurse. . . . And yet . . . we need to be there collaborating . . .

—Nora, Christian contemplative and research participant

## Overture

Life is structured and functions in a nondual, conversational, call-and-response manner. Yet not just any listening nor any reply will do. Rather, we are summoned to appreciate that earth is ceaselessly sending us a deep, wild, and sacred call; and that we are responsible for carrying it onward by way of our deep, sacred response. This is life's great way and the down-to-earth-human way: deep calls to deep, deep listens from the depths, deep responds lovingly to deep.

## Hallowing Our Relations with the Rest of Nature

*To begin with*, let us step outdoors and saunter in the natural world. It's a mysterious thing, but it seems just right to open our final chapter by saying "to begin with." The beginning I am proposing takes us right to a key point—the fact that sauntering is a nearly lost art: walking leisurely in nature; wandering wherever we feel drawn; stopping to listen, look, feel, touch, and be touched by this being (an iridescent dragonfly, a shy fox, a maroon trillium) or that presence (the sun's warmth, water gurgling over rocks, the ever-generous support of earth underfoot). I never used the word "saunter" until John Muir put a name to a sensibility I have long cherished. As the story goes, he was on a Sierra Club outing when another participant mentioned that he had heard Muir disliked the word "hike." In those days it held connotations of rushing to cover as much distance as possible. Muir's reply was wonderful: "Away back in the Middle Ages people used to go on pilgrimages to the Holy Land, and when people in the villages through which they passed asked where they were going, they would reply, 'A la sainte terre,' 'To the Holy Land.' And so they became known as sainte-terre-ers or saunterers. Now these mountains are our Holy Land, and we ought to saunter through them reverently, not 'hike' through them" (Palmer, 1911, pp. 27–28). Muir probably learned this etymology from Thoreau's writings, and it turns out that the word's history is more obscure ("John Muir and 'Saunter,'" 2019). Yet its psychospiritual truth is profound in this era of ecocide, nature-deficit disorder, and other eco(psycho)logical ills. Our perspective changes radically when we really know we are in the presence of holy lands, be they magnificent mountains like Muir revered, our local greenspaces, downtown sidewalks, or truly wherever we might be.

What a joy it is to saunter along with a friend, finding ourselves in conversation with each other and with the marvelous beings and presences still gracing our world . . . *Wait, I don't recognize that bird's song. Wonder what it is? A cuckoo! Yellow-billed or black-billed? I don't know, let's look more closely. Where did it go? Oh, now I see it. Wow, that bill really does glow yellow when touched by the sunlight . . . Hey, let's stop again. This moss is amazing—so soft and cool and moist . . .* I have never liked going fast in nature because so many beings and presences are beckoning. But now I consciously saunter along in sacred territory. However, if we do not embrace this opportunity—and the responsibility that comes with it—the consequences are truly dire. Wendell Berry

(2012) thus gives us an invitation, a warning, and an ethical imperative: "There are no unsacred places; / there are only sacred places / and
desecrated places" (p. 354). The difference depends completely upon
the depth of our consciousness and (sub)culture. When we look merely
from a superficial mode of consciousness we see a superficial world, say,
the natural world, as only a resource to exploit. In tandem with Berry,
Buber (1948) encourages us to refine our awareness such that we see
the sacred depths of others shining forth: "There is no not-holy, there
is only that which has not yet been hallowed" (pp. 135–136). *Not yet.*
With the natural world being desecrated—and thus our children and
generations to come—the hallowing of our relations with nature is a
core ingredient in the psychological-cultural-spiritual therapy that we
and the earth so urgently need.


## This Is Holy Ground:
## Take Off Your Sandals and Love Once Again

Way back in the introduction we pondered the story of Moses with the
burning bush, including G-d's beautiful declaration: "The place on which
you are standing is holy ground" (Exodus 3:5). Right before pointing
out the holiness of an apparently barren place, G-d gave Moses a keen
injunction, one that helped him open to the real depth of the experience:
"Take off your sandals." Take off your sandals so you can really feel the
sacramental nature of this very ground, this very encounter. Caught in
the momentum of our egoic existence, it is rarely obvious that we are
standing on holy ground (even though we *always* are). By removing
our sandals—actually and metaphorically—we can feel earth's touch far
more vividly. Our bare feet sensuously welcome nature's overture, and we
are drawn out of our small, contracted self. We appreciate the holiness
of the present relationship. And loving responses flow forth naturally.
Such encounters can transpire whenever we let go of unneeded barriers
that come between us. And the foundational (but illusory) barrier is our
exclusive self-representation as a separate sovereign ego and all the ways
we strive to bolster, aggrandize, and impose this mistaken identity. Of
course, some situations do call for defensive self-protection. And over
time the ego can learn to function not as a sovereign master but as a
servant of the mysterious life that ever transcends it. Indeed, our skillful
ego strengths keep working even as we know we are infinitely more than

ego. Still, embracing the radical implications of the metaphor in every circumstance that allows, let us not only take off our sandals, let us dare strip off all our protective armor—defenses, detachment, presumed superiority, self-centeredness—and stand before our companions with an open and naked heart. Whether human or otherwise, our fellows yearn for us to meet them like this, to join with them in their depths, in understanding and love. But that can only happen if we let our partner reach our depths, if we listen from the most intimate and tender place in our heart, if we respond from those sacred depths.

When someone arrives to call upon us—a smiling or crying person, a smiling or crying mountain or river—we are being summoned by an utterly unique precious presence that goes infinitely deep. As long as we realize this, it does not matter whether our relational partners are Ms. Smith or Mr. Jones or Kayford Mountain or the Allegheny River; or, say, life itself, nature itself; or, if we use spiritual language, the great mystery, the Dao, the beloved, or G-d (as in our touchstone psalm). The depths of each are essentially the same. "Deep calls to deep in the voice of your waterfalls" (Psalm 42:7). Such is the very structure and functioning of our conversational coexistence. The wild and sacred depths of nature are ceaselessly appealing to our own depths. Herein, life keeps presenting us with a core ethical opportunity: for deep to listen to deep, for deep to serve deep. Our health and that of all our relations turns on our embrace, or evasion, of this urgent responsibility. It is one thing to hear the call. It is another to really welcome it and listen with our heart. And, quintessentially, it is yet another to bring forth a reply from our heart-center. But when we do, what a precious gift we are providing! This is our great work, great opportunity, great responsibility. Open, sensitive attention is the most basic form of love. When we go out and consciously allow ourselves to be touched—out of our houses and out beyond our ego-centered ways—then caring responses will spring forth spontaneously. This we can trust.

## Where Did This Book Come From?

The *process* of writing and reading this book bears directly on core *themes* of ecopsychology and ecospirituality. Where did this book come from and where is it going? I said that it grew in response to my urgent questions about our troubled relations with the rest of nature. This is true, yet the full story is much more subtle. As the book was taking form, I realized that it was not simply that I had questions. At least not "I" as a fully independent autonomous agent. Instead, crucial concerns regarding the nature-human relationship were stirring in the air. I sensed that *life was asking me questions* and summoning me to join a critical and therapeutic conversation. The queries were coming to me from who knows where— from the depths of my self, the depths of culture, the depths of nature, from life itself, from all of these inseparably and identically.

Life itself. Or nature itself. Or even love itself. I take the liberty of using such phrases—as if life or nature or love could be a self, our true self (as various contemplatives say)—because that is how it felt. To discern whether the source of these questions was "inside" or "outside" of me is not just impossible, but irrelevant and nonsensical. Still, I will try to put it in words. I felt that I was being called by something infinitely deeper than my individual self (but not other than my true self), something—clearly not a thing—that precedes, exceeds, and includes my singular body-mind. The summons, it seemed to me, was emanating from a mysterious, subtle, dynamic, non-locatable but thoroughly ordinary source: life! nature! It was not only reaching out and making contact with me but addressing me with a kind of quasi-agency, asking something of me and imploring me to respond. I felt this transpersonal source beckoning me in the voices of other people (familiar ones, strangers, cherished authors); and in the voices of the more-than-human natural world (glorious mountains, besieged mountains). Intuitively, I felt the dynamic source to be—simply, but inconceivably—the seamless, all-embracing, all-permeating conversational field of this one great life we all share, ever gathered whole and complete across time and space into each encounter and its unique ethical appeal.

Here I am reminded of a passage from Rilke's "Duino Elegies," the luminous ninth one in which he contemplates life and death, what it is to be human, what we exist in this very life *for*. We are here, Rilke says, not for profit, nor curiosity, nor even happiness: "But because *truly* being here is so much; because everything here / apparently needs us, this fleeting world, which in some strange way / keeps calling to us. . . . / Speak and bear witness. More than ever / the Things that we might experience are vanishing. . . . / Earth, isn't this what you want: to arise within us. . . . / Superabundant being / wells up in my heart" (Rilke, 1989, pp. 199–203). This is what writing this book has felt like for me. And what everyday life feels like: given life, given death, given suffering, given joy, given beauty, given time, and—through it all—given love (by human companions and the earth itself), I feel nature's ineffable presence arising in my heart, asking me to bear witness, to speak, to act.

A close-at-hand example may be helpful. Not only did the questions of this book emerge from an unfathomably deep and mysterious source but so did the writing. There is no way that I could write this book as a sovereign, self-sufficient ego. Of course, the book did come through me and my particular sensibilities, somewhat like pure colorless sunlight shines through and is colored by a stained-glass window. The writing took form by way of my unique inflection of a larger conversation, the most understanding and loving reply I could offer right now. But that great dynamic conversation—life, nature, Indra's Net—is the consummate and continuous source. "I am not the one who loves, it's love that seizes me," as Leonard Cohen sings (Cohen & Robinson, 2001). The same song was sung by Rumi 800 years earlier. (It is an archetypal one after all.) Feeling the spirit of the beloved moving through him, Rumi (1995) proclaims: "I become the reed flute for your breath" (p. 138). It is such good fortune that we can borrow wise words from these great poets. But in truth, *all our words are borrowed (even as we articulate them anew)*. There really is no such thing as a self that stands alone.

A similar insight arose in my phenomenological research on the sacred in everyday life (Adams, 1996). In consciously experiencing the sacred—in intimate contact with another person, say, or with a splendid sunset—we realize that life involves an interpermeating communion between our individual self and the rest of existence. *In each encounter the being of others ceaselessly becomes part of our very being; and our being becomes part of theirs.* On the most basic level, such mutual permeation occurs outside our awareness and without us intentionally doing anything. The breath of trees (oxygen) actually becomes our body, nourishing and vitalizing us. Our breath (carbon dioxide) becomes the body of trees, nourishing and vitalizing them. Such self-world interchanges are transpiring all the time. All being is interbeing, as Thich Nhat Hanh says. Life is structured and functions in this nondual, inter-responsive way. However, this usually transpires unconsciously. It makes all the difference when we become aware of it, say, in the spontaneous revelation of the sacred or in a consciously cultivated bodhisattva path. Then we make the unconscious conscious, allowing us to live and love more freely. I am not talking about the personal repressed unconscious that psychoanalysis rightly encourages us to discover and befriend. Instead, this is an ontological or existential unconscious, a basic given of life that operates prereflectively. But it can be experienced consciously such that it guides our life. We suffer when this unconscious is not uncovered, because a sense of estrangement haunts our (co)existence: self versus others, humans versus nature, any exclusionary us versus them.

As we have seen in various ways, identifying exclusively as a separate self generates a chronically paranoid and greedy (co)existence. But when this delusion is dissolved, a different self, world, and life are disclosed. As I was eating a salad one evening I realized that I was eating the very body of the earth: the lettuce plant had drawn the soil's nutrients into its roots, thereby transforming the flesh of the earth into the very leaves I was enjoying. And I was eating the sun: the leaves had absorbed and incarnated the energy of the sun. And I was eating rain, rivers, lakes, oceans, clouds: the plant had taken in, transformed, and embodied the waters of the earth and sky. And I was eating the care and knowledge of the farmer who tended the lettuce; the labor of those who harvested it, took it to the market, and sold it to me; and the loving-kindness of my wife who prepared my meal. Further, through eating and metabolizing an ordinary lettuce leaf, *the body of the earth was becoming me (!)*—my *body, mind, heart, self.* The sun, rivers, labor, and loving-kindness were all becoming me. How astonishing! And completely commonplace.

When I was grieving the deaths of my beloved parents within six months of each other, a dear friend sent me a heartening card that addressed this core dynamic communion. Here is what she wrote: "May all the wisdom and love your parents shared live on in your heart and spring forth freshly your daily relationships" (Barbara Weaner, personal communication, July 2007). To be honest, I cannot recall precisely what she said long ago. But my rendering of her wise, loving response demon- strates the very point she was making, and one of the key points of this whole book. All our words, all our responses, indeed our very self and life—these are not ours alone but emerge from gifts others have already bestowed upon us. We recraft these gifts in our own idiomatic way and pass them onward. *Life truly is a grand giveaway.* Always wanting to be guided by an appreciation that nature comes first, let me affirm: *nature is the ultimate gift giver.* Some may say G-d or the Dao (or another version of the great mystery) is the ultimate benefactor, and I easily share this sensibility. But for now, I will say nature.

The key challenge is to live in a way that honors this great transper- sonal reality, instead of honoring, defending, and imposing our supposed

336 | A Wild and Sacred Call

great and self-sufficient ego. Strangely, even when we lead with our ego
it is still not us alone. (The ego is simply one expression of nature's great
way.) However, when we forget that our true self goes infinitely deeper,
our reactions tend to be tainted by excessive fear and greed. Therefore,
they are likely to be out of accord with the call life is sending us. We
would do well to help the ego step down from its self-presumed pinnacle,
thereby allowing the depths of life to work through us.

I have offered my best written response to today's eco(psycho)logical
peril, endeavoring to do justice to my human and more-than-human allies
and to the deep transpersonal source from which the book emerged. If
I have misrepresented any author, tradition, being, or presence, I want
to apologize. In any case, I hope my interpretations will help carry the
healing conversation further. But recall Nora's humble avowal: *Earth is
the real nurse.* In the same spirit, *earth is the real author.* In some mysterious way, everything I do or say or write is brought into being by the
whole wild and sacred earth. I appreciate that my words are far more
than "mine." Nature is ever imbuing my writing, and I have done what
I can to let this happen consciously. Relatedly, as a scholar I am happy
to use formal quotes and citations, presenting insightful testimony from
folks I respect and acknowledging my influences as best I can. But I often
cannot name what is theirs and what is "mine," because I and others
are not separate. In so many ways, these allies have inspired me deeply.
I have breathed in their words for decades, so much so that their gifts
are now part of who I am and how I live. Truth be told, for much of
this book it is impossible to say what has come from the Buddha, Christ,
Dōgen, Eckhart, Buber, Merleau-Ponty, Levinas, Goodall, Loy, Abram;
Bashō, Blake, Oliver, Snyder; my wife, daughter, son; friends, students,
patients, Zen teacher; trees, deer, birds, air, sun, mountains, rivers, the
great wide earth. I once heard someone say that the hands of G-d can
be found at the end of our arms. I am grateful that the world of nature
and all my scholarly and personal allies are coming through these typing
fingers. What a wonderful conversational mystery, *this life*! So, please,
never let yourself be burdened by the belief that you have to carry out
the great work on your own. You are indeed responsible, irreplaceably
so. But support from kindred allies in the human and more-than-human
communities is always available. When lost or despairing, find a comrade.

One day my wife, kids, and I were gazing into the treetops on a
hill high above the Allegheny River, just a few miles from our home.
We were marveling at a pair of bald eagles vying with two red-tailed

hawks to inhabit a big nest the hawks had already built for themselves. It was an astonishing contest to witness, with the eagles being three times larger but the hawks being far more agile in the air: screeching, soaring, swooping up and down, twisting, turning, locking talons, falling freely and then releasing just in time—and then doing it all again and again. With this fierce interplay the birds were carrying on a sacred compact initiated by their ancestors millions (!) of years ago, but one that has been severely disrupted by human lifestyles. The bald eagles were among three couples nesting around Pittsburgh after being missing for 150 years. Their absence was due to the unintended but still ruinous consequences of economic expansionism, industrial production, and associated pollution. In response to some wise social-political-ecological choices, the city's three rivers are again coming alive with fish, their predators such as eagles and osprey, and other wildlife. And this brings my family alive as well, since the rivers are part of our very being. We love seeing the exquisite birds; kayaking beside downtown skyscrapers; and biking, swimming, and fishing along a tributary of the Allegheny.

Just to let you know, the bald eagles took over the nest that year. Then the very next spring the red-tails won it back. And so the great way of nature flows on. However, there is a shadow side of this event. While being enchanted by the spectacular clash of raptors, we looked upstream and were assaulted by plumes of gray smoke rising above the land, a poisonous mix of ash and chemical compounds emitted (legally, for now) by a coal-fired power plant. Pittsburgh is no longer the "smoky city" dominated by steel mills, but its air remains some of the most polluted in all the country. At that moment the power plant was spewing toxins into vulnerable bodies, those of children and elderly folks, for sure; but also eagles, foxes, salamanders, beehives, creeks and rivers, wildflower fields, and other precious ones. As in this encounter, the wild and sacred earth keeps calling us—both with its wonders *and* its desecration.

Cherishing its beauty and wisdom, grieving its defilement, hearkening its appeal, I appreciate that nature crafted this book through me. This is a version of the fruitful circle we explored earlier: nature-healing-us-healing-nature-healing-us . . . Yet even this sounds too dualistic, because it is never nature over there, healing us over here, who then serve nature over there. *We are nature.* Transpersonal realizations such as this are a crucial aspect of the great turning of consciousness and culture currently underway. To say "we are nature" sounds odd to conventional ears, but it has long been completely obvious to indigenous peoples around the earth. "I am the River and the River is me," as the Whanganui Māori attest. Such nondual, transpersonal identification matters so much because ethical devotion follows. Thus the Māori affirm their "inalienable connection with, and responsibility to, Te Awa Tupua and its health and well-being" (Te Awa Tupua, 2017, p. 15). Recall that Te Awa Tupua is the whole integral river ecosystem—animate, aware, wise, loving—in all its physical and spiritual elements.

## Where Is This Book Going? Where Will You Take It?

The question "Where did this book come from?" implies a complementary one: "Where is this book going?" This really means, "What will readers do with what the book has offered?" My sincere hope is that it has touched you and that you will transmute what I have shared in your unique way, thereby allowing it to flow onward to touch others who will touch others, on and on. You do not have to do this on your own, since there is really no way to be totally on your own. (When a bodhisattva vows to assist all beings, the one making that holy pledge is never the supposedly separate self.) Nonetheless, you are the only one who can answer the particular appeals nature sends your particular way. After all, you are an utterly unique, utterly irreplaceable jewel in Indra's infinite net. No one else has the distinctive gifts that you can bring to the great work of our era. In this spirit, Dostoyevsky once articulated an ethos akin to that of a bodhisattva. "We are all responsible for everyone else—but I am more responsible than all the others" (from *The Brothers Karamazov*, in Cohen, 1986, p. 31). Each of us must hear the earth's wild and sacred call, allow its depths touch our depths, and thereby let nature work its magic through us. Simultaneously, each of us has a sacred duty to pass it on from our depths in accordance with our unique capacities. We could call this the great way of life, or the bodhisattva way, and it is. But I would say it is the heart of our down-to-earth human way.

Global warming. A snowflake on my tongue. Mass extinction of species. Purple coneflower blooming. Systemic racism and racist violence. My children's delight or distress, and privilege of being their dad in both instances. A patient's suicidal despair. Our puppy's gleeful greeting. Nature-deficit disorder. The vivid silence of meditation. Yet another email to answer. My wife's radiant heart. All these entreaties keep coming my way. In really being devoted to assisting all beings, which one do I answer? Clock time is limited. My heart aches in not being able to address each appeal right away, or to devote the time that would do justice to every single one. As a continuous practice, I keep returning to the touchstones that have guided us in this book. (1) I remember Dōgen's awesome insight about time. Deep time is not a quantity of hours that I have (or that have me when I am too stressed). *My time is who I am. My time is my very being, my very life.* That helps, because it reconnects me with life as it is transpiring right here and now. Thus I find a way of living time that is other than clock time. *Given the present circumstances, in the time being, what is the most loving offering I can make?* (2) What Dr. King (1986) called the "the interrelated structure of all reality" (p. 254), what Buddhism calls the interdependent co-arising of all phenomena, what ecologists call ecosystems: all these naturally come into play in this great venture. When I offer any gesture of understanding and care, it does not stop there. In answering another's call, my response lives on in my companion. They will carry it with them in some mysterious way, and it will serve as an incalculable influence—hopefully for good—when they go on to respond to the calls of others. The inextricable reality of our nondual, inter-responsive life carries crucial ethical implications. *The life of others turns on my response, as mine has turned on theirs and so will turn again.* "I make life what it is; life makes me what I am" (Dōgen, in Kim, 2004, p. 172). A wonderful artistic presentation of this is M. C. Escher's *Drawing Hands* (2016). Two hands—like self and others, self and nature—simultaneously drawing each other into being, into nondual co-creative coexistence. This is the way our life naturally functions. If people would really let this co-creative reality and responsibility sink in, I trust that they would tremble in awe and relate more sensitively from that moment on. (3) I keep remembering that it is not me alone who is responsible. ("Me alone" is never really who I am.) I do not have to be tyrannized by the idea that I am the sole agent of my offering. I am asked to show up for my partner. Yet, simultaneously and identically, nature is always working through me. "Such is the I that is life, the life that is I" (Dōgen, in Kim, 2004, p. 172). (4) I also breathe more fully when I remember that while I am obligated to respond, I am not responsible for controlling the outcome. I can only offer the best I can for the time being. What happens next is beyond me. Sensing things unfold, I respond again and again.

To make peace with the last point is a fierce challenge. The natural world is in dire need of our assistance, and we send forth our heart and hands in tangible acts of support. But even with goodwill and adept actions, things often do not turn out like we wish. Another species is driven extinct. Another mountain annihilated for a little coal (and a lot of money for a privileged few). Kids have more contact with screens and less with nature. Clinging to business as usual, corporate and political policies continue to amplify global warming. These terrible and often death-dealing things keep happening, even when we respond skillfully. That makes it all the more important to keep doing what we can for this glorious world. *Love is deeper than death.*

## Listening Deeply and Keeping the Conversation Going

Let us surrender the fantasy of a perfect offering and still give what we can, because it does make a difference. Bacon, Descartes, and company campaigned on the platform that we humans were entitled to be "masters and possessors of nature" (Descartes, 1998, p. 35). And they won (at least temporarily), capturing the minds and culture of Europe and North America for a very long time—400 years or so. But now things are turning. Increasingly we hear that humans must be better "stewards" of nature, and this indicates a significant transformation in our consciousness and culture. Yet stewardship still elevates humans to the position of managing the affairs of something that is truly unmanageable: wild nature. The metaphor I prefer is that of mutual conversation. Nature includes humankind yet goes infinitely deeper, so we are wise to let nature take the lead in the interchange. This is much like the relationship between a mentor and an apprentice. Even with all our great capacities, we are a young species with plenty to learn.

How we are treating the natural world is how we are treating the most beloved people in our lives, because these precious ones are always connected with nature and its well-being (or lack thereof). What we have learned about genuine human conversation can serve as a guide in these traumatic times. In an authentic heart-to-heart dialogue, people draw upon contemplative and phenomenological sensibilities without naming them as such. We open ourselves to our partner, really listening to their pain and cherishing their intelligence and beauty (especially the kind that goes way deeper than their skin); we notice our presumptions and reactivity regarding their words and actions; we handle these with critical reflexivity instead of enacting them blindly; we hospitably hold our companion's views in our heart-mind; we encourage our partner to come forth freshly and fully; we respond as best we can with loving care and understanding (the latter held tentatively, fallibly, and ever ready to be revised, the former unwavering regardless of how the conversation unfolds); we lose these response-abilities under stress, fear, self-absorption; we hurt others with these lapses and thereby rupture relationships; and still, devotedly, we return to open responsive contact time after time. Such a contemplative dialogical practice can be applied to our contacts with our nonhuman neighbors. All too commonly, though, rather than letting go into shared conversation we often become stuck in a tightly held, self-contained monologue. We strive for mastery and control, but the natural world rarely responds in the manner we prefer. Sometimes even our kindest actions go awry. But isn't this also true in relation with our human fellows? We cannot control life's wildness, but we can work and play and love skillfully with it. We cannot control the results of our caring actions, but we sure need to keep venturing them.

One spring a friend offered a big load of composted manure for our vegetable garden. We gratefully accepted, and soon the garden was filled with sprouts. Oddly, though, they did not look like the veggies we had planted. Nor did they look like weeds. It did not take long for us to realize that the cows had eaten lots of sunflower seeds. Now we had a garden totally comprised of sunflowers! It was definitely not what we had planned, but it was spectacular: giant yellow flowers glowing for all to see, making seeds for all to eat. My wife and I laughed when our neighbors told us how much they loved our garden—our neighbor next door and friend down the street, but also plenty of winged neighbors such as goldfinches and cardinals. It reminded us of the wise advice another friend had given us when we were about to depart for Europe. He remarked that things would certainly go awry occasionally as we navigated other cultures, with frustrating mishaps like missed trains and miscommunications being inevitable. So he said, "Whatever happens, see if you can make it either fun or funny!" (Peter Okun, personal communication, 2001). Turns out that the sunflower garden was both! Much of life is comprised of such unbidden, unforeseeable, uncontrollable twists and turns—and our response to these. In the film *Oh Brother, Where Art Thou?*, based loosely on Homer's *Odyssey*, three escaped convicts are scheming to get rich. They encounter a wise, elderly, blind Black man. As a kind of oracle, he declares: "You seek a great fortune, you three who are now in chains . . . And you will find a fortune—though it will not be the fortune you seek" (Coen & Coen, 2000). I hear this as a great truth. In a different year and a different garden, the plants are not growing well under our big black walnut tree. We eventually discover that these trees emit a substance called juglone that is toxic to some plants. So we choose to grow squash and foxglove instead of tomatoes and columbine. Likewise, thanks to the bodhisattva Rachel Carson, our society realizes that spring is becoming dreadfully silent. So we choose to ban pesticides such as DDT. Bald eagles, peregrine falcons, and others begin to recover. Some say that it is acceptable to spew millions of tons of carbon dioxide into the atmosphere every day, and earth becomes dangerously overheated. So we choose to . . . Well, this crucial choice is now hanging in the balance!

The world's eco(psycho)logical maladies are far more grave than the ones we faced in our garden. But their interrelational source and resolution are similar. Ecopsychology insists that we are inherently involved in a real relationship with the rest of nature, and that this relationship has been grievously ruptured. *Yet all close relationships will include painful rifts; and such ruptures can be healed.* This is true in relationships with other people and with the rest of nature. The key is for us to allow the rupture to turn into a message, a *sūtra*/suture let us say, one that reveals our nondual intimacy; reminds us that we are never actually cut off from each other; and teaches us how to (re)turn freshly, openly, vulnerably, compassionately to the conversation. In this spirit, when meeting with people for couples psychotherapy, I appeal to their depths in the very first session and recurrently throughout: As best you can day by day and, most crucially, moment by moment in tense exchanges with your partner (inside sessions and out), please listen from the deepest, most loving place in your heart. And trust that your partner is doing their best to speak from this deep place as well. Conversely, free yourself to be open and vulnerable, to speak from the deepest place in yourself—including giving voice to your hope and dread, anger and despair, pain and yearning, and most importantly your love—knowing that your equally vulnerable partner is listening with an open heart. Understand that your partner is fallible. And so are you. Know that you and they will slip into defensive attack or withdrawal at times. That comes with the territory of intimate relationship. Please commit to catching yourself when you lapse, acknowledge it to yourself and to your partner, apologize, listen again from your depths, and thereby find ways to repair the rupture. I also share a wonderful pointer with the couple, one I learned from

Gadamer's hermeneutic phenomenology. In dialogue with another, it is immensely helpful to "try to understand how what he is saying could be right" (Gadamer, 2011, p. 292). Please stretch yourself to appreciate where your partner is coming from. Look for the wisdom in what they are saying. Begin with that, before countering with your own views. This is not a directive to give up your sense of things, but to let real listening provide a bigger context.

Here is another way of saying all this: *please do not let your two egos ruin the deeper connection that you share, a connection that you can nurture and cultivate even further.* Tennessee Williams makes a brilliant observation regarding such matters. He is speaking about his famous play *A Streetcar Named Desire*, yet really about all close relationships:

> There are no "good" or "bad" people. Some are a little better or a little worse but all are activated more by misunderstanding than malice. A blindness to what is going on in each other's hearts. . . . Nobody sees anybody truly, but all through the flaws of their own ego. . . . Vanity, fear, desire, competi-tion—all such distortions within our own egos—condition our vision of those in relation to us. Add to those distortions in our own egos, the corresponding distortions in the egos of the others—and you see how cloudy the glass must become through which we look at each other. That's how it is in all living relationships except when there is that rare case of two people who love intensely enough to burn through all those layers of opacity and see each others naked hearts. (Devlin & Tischler, 2004, pp. 95–96)[1]

Placing all this in the context of ecopsychology, a basic (co)existential condition comes to our aid: *nature has no ego to impose or defend.* None-theless, a single ego is plenty enough to wreak havoc! Obviously, the egoism is ours—that of individuals, to be sure, but especially that of anthropocentric, capitalist, consumerist culture.

Often our best response to nature's wild and sacred call is not focused directly on the natural world but on ourselves, other people, and human institutions. Understanding global warming as a fever-filled plea from the animate earth, we learn how to reduce our personal and collective carbon footprint; joining with our neighbors, we speak up at the town council meeting in opposition to a fracking company's application to build wells near schools and neighborhoods; we *fight against* racist violence and oppression and *fight for* racial justice; we vote for ecologically committed candidates and lobby local, state, and national officials to enact legislation for sustainability; we support local organic farmers. In other situations, upon hearing the back-and-forth howling of a wolf pack, or a community of trees crashing down in a shortsighted clear-cut, the other who is calling upon us is a nonhuman participant in the shared earth fellowship. Many times we are summoned by humans and the rest of nature together, as in the coronavirus pandemic and the even more deadly pandemic of global warming.

## The Path Disappears and We Still Keep Going

I have suggested that love is the fruition of existence as well as the practical path to that fruition. I want to acknowledge that the path is often not very clear. The disaster is not looming. We are already in the midst of it. In these hard times, faced with profoundly hard things, we often do not know quite what to do. At one meditation retreat I attended there was an orientation meeting at the beginning. Someone asked the organizer for directions to a nearby waterfall they had heard about, and he replied: "There is a beautiful waterfall. It's not easy to find, and it's a difficult trek. But you can do it." Then he pointed over to the edge of the woods. "That opening is the beginning of a path. It winds down to a creek and you'll need to find a way to cross. Then follow the trail as it switches back and forth up a tall hill. It keeps getting narrower as it goes up. After climbing for quite a while you'll come to a dense thicket of rhododendrons. You're fairly close there. *But at that point the path disappears. And then you just keep going.*" A couple of us chuckled at this last remark. I'm pretty sure it was not consciously intended to be a Zen teaching, but I took it as one. My feeling was, well, that's how much of life is. In crucial moments the path disappears, and we must still dare to venture on. Søren Kierkegaard (1996), a great student of these existential turning points, put it this way: "Life must be understood backwards. But . . . it must be lived forwards" (p. 16). When we don't know precisely what to do to help make things better in our troubled relations with the natural world; when what we have already done appears to have had little effect; when mastery, certainty, and guaranteed results are impossible; when bouts of confusion, rage, or despair threaten to overwhelm us, we are still responsible for making a leap and carrying on. "Prayer and love are really learned in the hour when prayer becomes impossible and your heart turns to stone" (Merton, 1961, p. 221).

Life—be it in the form of a human or nonhuman neighbor—is ceaselessly beseeching our loving care. Although the path is often unclear out there in the distance and in the future, there is always a path right under our feet; or, more precisely, right in our embodied relational experience. *Really, the most crucial path is not one that takes us from here to somewhere else, but from being here superficially to being here more fully.* If love is the path, we do not have to go anywhere else to be loving, anywhere other than the present encounter. Indeed, direct awareness in the present moment is the best guide for responding well—awareness that is bolstered along the way by interpersonal allies and sociocultural and spiritual supports. This does not mean simply acting on any whim but intentionally being aware of our felt-and-thought sense of whatever life is sending our way. Such a sensitively attuned way of being involves "a perpetual uncalculated life in the present, and the maintenance, not of deliberate control, but of unsought, unshaken serenity in moments of greatest intimacy" (Coomaraswamy, 1985, p. 111). Consciously "perpetual" is perhaps too much to expect. We are fallible and will lose our way at times. However—with experiential practice across our life span, and instantaneously right now—we can attend openly and respond fittingly to the unbidden overtures of life.

To demystify this great imperative, and to counter any notion that my celebration of the bodhisattva way is somehow esoteric, consider this brief exchange between my wife and me. Anyone who knows Holly can attest that she is a true saint or bodhisattva (although she would humbly disavow any such depiction). During a thunderstorm one afternoon, I said to her: "Sweetheart, you came in from the garden just in time, right before that big downpour." She smiled and replied matter-of-factly: "I was listening to the birds. As long as they kept singing, I kept working. When they stopped, I stopped." We have been alienated from the rest of nature far too long. Therefore, throughout this book I have advocated for a radical transformation of our consciousness. My "Holly Lama's" response is exactly what I am talking about. Sociocultural transformation, urgently needed today, can only follow from such sensitive, grounded, inter-responsive awareness.

"*Beings are numberless, I vow to assist them all.*" Such is the heart of the bodhisattva vow. This core responsibility can feel overwhelming.

Fortunately, a key insight is embedded in a line from the vow that we did not address in the previous chapter: *"Dharma gates are infinite, I vow to enter them all."* Gates to the dharma, to the deep way, to our essential nature: these gates are infinite, so they must be opening everywhere and everywhen, always and in all ways in our daily relations. The "gate of heaven is everywhere," avows Merton (1968a, p. 158). And the Zen tradition has long pointed out that gates to the dharma are in fact "gateless gates" (Yamada, 2004), that all apparent barriers are "gateless barriers" (Aitken, 1991). Intense challenges included, the gates to real life are always wide open. Although he describes it differently, John Muir was aware that the gates of heaven—dharma gates—are in fact infinite and ever present, with nature continually offering auspicious opportunities for us to walk right in: "Between every two pine trees there is a door leading to a new way of life" (Muir, n.d.).[2]

There truly is another, deeper, life-enhancing world. And it is inside the one right here, right now—because, really, there is only one world. To see this deeper world we must access a deeper, seamlessly unified, relationally attuned consciousness. *The gateless gates to life's depths are always open. Yet let us beware: they always appear closed when our heart is closed.* When we release our contracted ego and self-preoccupied ways, we can saunter through pines, or walk out our front door, or settle into the presencing of this very encounter, and the sacred depths of this world will touch us. It is no accident that dharma also means "thing" or "phenomenon." Nothing is excluded from being a dharma gate: fresh white snow on a frozen pond, fish swimming slowly underneath, kids skating on top, fracking chemicals contaminating the pond and nearby wells. When welcomed intimately, every interchange—call it a dharma gate, heaven's gate, or this unique relational partner—teaches us how to respond (for the time being). Such responsibility is the heart of being human. *It is truly what we are in this life for.*

The world's beauty, wisdom, love, and suffering are ever calling us. In all these cases, our natural reply is compassion and loving-kindness. When you see your friend's kind face, you are spontaneously drawn to them in tender care. Later, when they become afflicted with COVID or cancer, your heart goes out to them. Deep care is the natural response once again. Likewise, imagine walking along a mountain ridge accompanied by a child with whom you are very close. Pausing for a moment, both of you are moved by the beauty of the place: spruce trees, ferns, wild blueberries; deer, woodpeckers, and trout; brooks, boulders, and fresh air. Rounding a bend you stop for a particularly lovely view of another mountain across the valley. Joy naturally arises as does real care—care for that holy ground, care for it to be preserved for your dear young companion and for generations to come. The child exclaims, "Let's come back soon!" And you heartily agree. A half year later you fulfill your promise and return to that mountain trail. The two of you are happily strolling along when you come around that same bend but are aghast to see the other mountain in rubble, demolished by mountain range annihilation mining. Through your breaking (open) heart, your compassion spontaneously flows forth. With grief, with anger, with dedication—all different forms of love—you say to your young partner, "Let's do what we can to stop this madness!" Heartbreak can induce our deeper heart to open. Ecological breakdown can induce real ecopsychological breakthroughs.

Across various circumstances, nature's wisdom, love, and beauty ask to be savored, celebrated, nurtured. Its suffering asks to be understood, healed, liberated. In both cases we can sense our love rising up. We feel this even if we turn away. Our act of avoidance shows that we were first connected with the one who called us, that we were in fact moved by their ethical appeal (but then abdicated it). However, we can always recover and turn again toward the other, turn to listen and turn to serve. Herein lies our awesome responsibility. Not only are we being called by the natural world, but called *upon. The call is incomplete without the response.*

## Nothing Can Get in the Way of the Way

In a wounded world that goes on to wound us, it is crucial that we stay grounded and resilient. Earlier in this coda I offered four touchstones that help me along the way, and that may serve you as well: deep time, which is our deep being; the way our responses ripple out as in Indra's Net; the truth that nature or life itself is the transpersonal source of our understanding and love; and the (co)existential fact that we must act but cannot control the fruits of our actions. The "koan" I'm about to articulate may serve as a fifth touchstone. Classic Zen koans are truly revelatory teaching stories. *Yet the real koan is the koan of our everyday life.* Day by day life addresses us from the depths and urges us to listen and respond accordingly. Over the last decade, I have consistently felt life sending me a particularly momentous koan. It is one that seems especially significant in this ecocidal era, when our care for the natural world (including humankind) is often met with yet another rise in global temperature or another species being extinguished. As best as I can convey it, this is what I hear life itself saying to me: *This shared world is inherently holy and complete just as is, for the time being. Now go work with all your heart to transform the world. You are inherently holy and complete just as you are, for the time being. Now go work with all your heart to transform your self, your consciousness, and your way of being with others.*

This sensibility came to me largely through my Zen practice, but an analogous perspective imbues the work of psychotherapy. Good therapists know that patients' symptoms are symbols—symbols of their suffering and their (current) best efforts to handle their suffering. Likewise, so-called defenses and resistances are the patient trying to manage their fear and pain as best they can (for now). It is never the case that we simply need to get rid of defenses so that the real therapy work can begin. Rather, working with defenses *is* the real work, for as long as the patient feels they are necessary. In the process we explore the wisdom of defenses, how they arose creatively and adaptively; how they initially saved the patient's life; how they may still serve the patient well in some circumstances; yet how, and in what circumstances, they not do not serve them well; how, in fact, patients may be depriving themselves by way of unconscious, reactive reliance on defensive patterns; and how they can experientially test whether or not they need to cling to these defenses. All the while we honor the patient's intelligence, resilience, and beauty as it shines through their symptoms, defenses, and resistances. Stated differently, we join with the patient exactly as they are, for the time being. All of this applies in the case of our defensive (mis)identification with our ego and also to humankind's defensive (turned offensive) stance of superiority over the rest of the natural world. In this spirit, in the midst of a terribly trying time in my life, the following realization came to me as I was wandering in the woods during a Zen *sesshin* (retreat).

> Nothing can get in the way of the way.
> Anything that appears to get in the way of the way,
> is itself the way.

Ultimately, yet practically as well, not a single thing can possibly get in the way of the great way (the Dao, G-d, life, nature, as you prefer): not global warming; not species extinction; not nature-deficit disorder; not people in power who—captivated by the poisons of separatist confusion, fear, and greed—want to build walls and fuel divisions; not our own confusion, fear, and greed. In some unfathomable manner, the great way includes today's catastrophic eco(psycho)logical afflictions. At the very same time, with unnecessary death and destruction all around us, we consecrate ourselves wholeheartedly to fostering a healthy, harmonious, peaceful, and just life. Imagine a world where people live in conscious caring appreciation of their inherent communion with each other and with the rest of nature. Imagine a world where biodiverse mountain communities are thriving instead of being annihilated, a world where coral reefs are teeming with vital color rather than being bleached white and lifeless by global warming. Imagine a world where sustainable economic systems—modeled on how ecosystems work for the well-being of all—center on the flourishing of the whole earth rather than centering on a contrived market and the wealth of a privileged few. Imagine a world where children feel a real affinity with the robins and maple trees around their home. To actualize these possibilities requires that we bring our distinctive gifts to a collaborative psycho-cultural-spiritual therapy, while remembering that nature itself is the real therapist. I believe our current eco(psycho)logical situation is the gravest existential crisis ever to confront humankind. Choices we make over the next decade or so will affect life on this planet for thousands of years.

This great endeavor can be intensely daunting. With nature being assaulted from the depths of oceans to the upper atmosphere; with sociocultural, economic, and political systems of oppression being so entrenched; with such pernicious forces often thwarting even our best efforts, we may wonder if our actions really matter. Despair and frustration definitely come with the territory of ecopsychology. It is crucial that we take these as a sign of our real care, and find ways to carry on in any case. The following story can lend us some energy, reminding us that every gesture matters. Walking along the beach on a hot summer day, a man noticed someone in the distance. Moving closer, he realized it was a young girl. She was gathering starfish who had been stranded when the tide went out and gently placing them back into the ocean. As if he knew better, the man scoffed and said, "There are thousands of those all up and down the beach. You can't make any difference by saving a few." Shaking her head in dismay, the girl lifted up another starfish and returned it to the water. Smiling, she looked directly into the man's eyes and replied: "I made a difference for that one."[3] And when we make a difference for one, we make a difference for innumerable others—because the first one is never isolated from all the rest.

## New Eco(psycho)logical Vows:
## Let's Do This Hard Thing, Together

So beautiful, so painful: such are the basic existential conditions of this one dear life we share. *This world is holy and complete! Let's go transform the world!* Changing the world, changing culture, changing our consciousness: These are immense ventures. A great turning surely requires great work—personally, interpersonally, and socioculturally. Once a schoolteacher was patiently helping a young student who was in tears over not understanding a math problem. Meeting the student right where they were, the teacher said: "This *is* a really hard thing. And you can do this hard thing."[4] Nature-deficit disorder; climate emergency; mass extinction; habitat destruction; toxic environments; water shortages; idolatry of capitalist expansion; entrancement by consumerism; sadness, grief, fear, and anger. These are tremendously hard challenges. *And we can handle these hard things, with each other and for each other.*

You, engaged reader, have accompanied me on a psychospiritual exploration of our relations with the rest of nature. In these traumatic times, it is a great privilege to join with unknown co-conspirators like you—countless allies breathing and thinking and acting together for the good of all. I have just a few more things to say, but I want to initiate a process of bidding you adieu. So I draw upon a marvelous word of both departure and greeting, one that comes to us from ancient Hinduism: *namaste*. I also draw upon its complementary gesture: bringing my two palms together at my heart center and bowing to you. These integrated expressions offer a chance to move toward saying farewell, while rephrasing the central points of transpersonal ecopsychology. Joining our hands in this way is called the *añjali mudra* in the Indian yogic traditions. But this familiar embodiment of communion and love is embraced across various spiritual traditions. Indeed, these "prayer hands" are a tangible enactment of Christ's nondual teaching: "When you make the two into one . . . then you will enter [the kingdom of heaven]" (Gospel of Thomas 22, in Pagels, 2003, p. 231). Self and nature, self and others: it is not even that these two need to be *made* into one, because they are never really divorced in the first place. And what of the bowing that comes with these united hands? The bow incarnates the ethical sensibility of the bodhisattva vow. And so too from Levinas (1969): "the Other is placed higher than me" (p. 291). And Saint Paul: "in humility, value others above yourself" (Philippians 2:3).

The Sanskrit *namaste* originated in India and has now become popular worldwide, largely by way of yoga classes. While often uttered rather superficially, its core psychospiritual meaning is identical to the ethos at the heart of transpersonal ecopsychology. That is, in really bowing to another, the bow comes not from my conventional ego. Nor is it offered to your ego. Rather, it emerges from my true self and is offered to yours. Thus *namaste* celebrates a sacred compact, conveying what cannot be said fully yet still must be said and enacted over and over: "From my divine depths I see, honor, and responsively serve your divine depths." This returns us to the heart of our shared life, to love as our nature-calling-path-fruition. Beyond being a formal gesture of greeting or parting, the spirit of *namaste* can imbue all our relationships: deep calls—deep hearkens—deep responds. We vividly feel the wild and sacred earth shining for us, speaking to us, flirting with us, serenading us, crying to us, appealing to us. Life gives us so much to grieve, so much to cherish and celebrate. There is wisdom in our heartbreak, wisdom in our joy. Staying faithful to both of these core experiences serves us and our companions well. In the voice of another person, in the voice of a waterfall or spring peepers or a desecrated forest: deep ever calls to us. But most crucial is our follow through: deep—each of us in our depths—listens to the call; not just listens, but responds; not just responds (since avoidance and violence are responses too) but responds with awareness, love, compassion, understanding, and justice. This is our essence and our calling, inherently so. We have the choice to consecrate it consciously as our everyday interrelational practice. In so doing, mutually beneficial fruits will follow (even though they grow far beyond our prediction or control).

Throughout this book my intention has been to plant seeds. In our relations with other people and with the rest of nature, a crucial seed-idea is that love can be lived as our shared nature-calling-path-fruition. In everyday encounters, what if this were completely obvious? What if we felt life's essential (ontological/ethical) structure and functioning to be ceaseless call-and-reply-responsibility? What if we embodied this as our deepest summons and aspiration? And what if we discovered that intimate responsiveness is the supreme path for actually nurturing into fruition this great holy yearning and appeal? What if we knew all this in our very marrow, as deep as deep can go, and put it into practice in our daily relationships? Whether such seeds are embraced in these terms or otherwise, life does ask us to undertake such a venture in our own distinctive way. Yet even when love comes to fruition—when we are enamored by an ordinary sparrow, or work to clean up our local river— our engaged practice circulates endlessly. *Fruit is seed-bearing, after all. That means it is both a culmination and a fresh origin, just like love!* Seeds sponsor new life to come into being, after having been dispersed by way of an interrelational process: by falling from a tree and being drawn into the earth, by a rabbit eating berries and leaving fertile pellets behind, by compassionate action for our local bioregion, by a reader taking up a single sentence and thereby living a little (or a lot) differently. In this way, nature's inter-responsive circle continues on and on. Love's inter-responsive circle continues on and on. Ultimately, these are two ways of describing the same sacred circle.

*To begin with:* let us place ourselves in a position to be touched by the nonhuman natural world. *Intimate aware contact* with nature, with other people, with our own self—this is the very first ecopsychological step. Beginning again and again is really what matters. "When you find your place where you are, practice occurs, actualizing the fundamental point. When you find your way at this moment, practice occurs, actualizing the fundamental point" (Dōgen, 1985, p. 72). Dōgen means the fundamental point of life, the fundamental point of our true, essential, inter-responsive and inter-responsible nature. This takes us directly to the great matter of life and death and love—here, now, always. Therefore, I propose that we venture a promise to all the beings and presences of this one precious earth; a pledge to everyone who is imploring us to listen deeply and respond from our depths; an affirmation of loving service for our two-legged, four-legged, winged, and finned companions, our rooted, rocky, watery, airy, and fiery fellows:

> Our place is here.
> Our time is now.
> May our hearts break . . . open . . . for each other . . .

This book is about to end, but the conversation will continue one way or another. Thus, eco-sisters and brothers, with palm to palm and with a bow and a smile, I say *namaste*. I have imagined you as a sympathetic eco-accomplice. I trust you will carry on in your own irreplaceable way. Perhaps, in moments, a heart-to-heart connection transpired via these pages. I have often hoped that my words would *speak to you*. (Even better, I would enjoy *speaking with you* in person. How sweet if it comes to pass that we are granted that opportunity!) I have insisted throughout that we are all summoned to the great work of caring for the mutual well-being of other people and the rest of nature; and that *everything turns on our response*. But even in invoking the inclusive "we," I would never presume to *speak in your place*. When it comes down to it, I dare speak only in my own name. That is especially true when making an intimate vow—as follows—that emerges from this book's inquiry.

Touched by nature's wild and sacred call; in gratitude, grief, anger, hope, and endless devotion; without quite knowing what to do and ever again after my efforts go awry; with tender, vulnerable body trembling and tears welling up; yet graced along the way by the wise and beautiful earth and by dear human allies; I offer my heart and hands in loving response, encounter by encounter by encounter.

*Yes!*

*Here I am!*

*What can I do for you?*

# Acknowledgments

I am happy to offer a great heartfelt thank you to my treasured allies. Without their generous, wise, loving gifts, the book you are holding in your hand could never have come into being. Somewhere along the way Meister Eckhart avowed that if saying "thank you" is the only contemplative practice we ever do, then that is plenty. For the time being, the following words of appreciation will have to be plenty. Yet, far more deeply than I can convey here, I sincerely hope that my dear allies know the immense gratitude I feel for their blessed presence in this book and in my larger life. It pains me that important people will inevitably be left out when I express thanks to particular ones. With apologies, I will venture ahead. At the outset, I want to thank you and every other reader of this book, for without your engaged involvement there would be no point in writing. May what I share touch you in some way and ripple outward in your world, with you touching others who touch others, endlessly so.

Holly, my beloved wife, has patiently encouraged me every step of the way, across years and years of writing, through innumerable delights and struggles. I hope this book does justice to her awesome love, love that graces and truly transforms my life every single day. Lily Claire and Eli, cherished daughter and son, have cheered me onward while also offering lots of well-deserved teasing in hopes that I would finally complete this long-unfolding labor of love. Sharing a life with these three glorious souls is the great joy of my existence. Lela and Bodhi, two sweet, furry four-legged members of our family pack, also deserve a warm nod, as they have mentored me in nature's ways and brought forth many a smile. The Ivory-billed Woodpecker and the Appalachian mountains, together with all the marvelous beings and presences of the shared earth community, must be included in this intimate group of companions. My life has been infinitely blessed by their wild and sacred presence. And this book is one form of my life.

The clear, luminous loving vision of my dear Zen teacher Bruce Sōun Harris Rōshi touches my heart with each encounter and imbues my life day by day. I hope the present work truly honors his profound and precious teaching. David Loy has clarified this ever mysterious life for me through deep-seeing, compassion-filled books and warm-hearted conversations. His impassioned foreword is a great gift. Like a brother to me, fellow ecopsychologist Jeff Beyer has shared his great earthy wisdom in countless birding adventures and talks over coffee. He also makes me laugh a lot! David Abram's kindness and generosity move me deeply, and his revelatory eloquence is a tremendous inspiration. I have embraced many different authors as dialogue partners in the explorations that follow. I'm grateful for the life-changing mentorship their writings have provided over the years.

My beloved mom and dad, Ann and Earl Adams, departed this world too soon, way before this book could come to fruition. Yet their love lives on in the words I've shared. My dear brother Mark Adams knows what I mean, and his camaraderie lives on in me as well. My parents-in-law, Jan and Jerry Smith, have generously offered steadfast support. I've been blessed by shining dharma friends in our Zen sangha, based at Saranam Retreat Center in West Virginia. Among so many dear ones, let me simply offer a deep bow to those I've been practicing with since our very beginning in Elkins way back in 1997: John Gallagher, Ruth Blackwell Rogers, Hugh Rogers, Susan Rosenblum, and Barbara Weaner. I was moved by the research participants whose wise testimony appears in the text: Joan, Nora, and Sarah. It's been a great privilege to participate in the Duquesne University Psychology community, with its distinctive human science, philosophical orientation. The wisdom and kindness of my colleagues has touched me profoundly. And I have learned so much from our gifted doctoral and undergraduate students, far too many to name. Countless ideas in this book were refined through conversations in and out of class. There are not many psych departments where I could teach ecopsychology, phenomenology, Buddhist psychology, Christian mysticism, and transpersonal psychology. Similarly, our Duquesne meditation group inspires me year after year. Duquesne University has generously supported my research by way of a Presidential Scholarship Award and a Paluse Faculty Research Grant.

James Peltz, associate director and editor-in-chief at SUNY Press, has stayed with me through the long and challenging phases of this project. That is to my great good fortune. Warm assistance from Alicia Brady, Aimee Harrison, and Eileen Nizer has been most welcome. Jonathan Rowe's sensitive copyediting made a real difference. My thinking and writing benefited immensely from the wisdom of generous readers: David Bajada, Jeff Beyer, Elizabeth Fein, Ruben Habito Rōshi, Roger Owens, Scott Staples, Silvia Tibaduiza, and Jason Wirth. This book is blessed by endorsements from authors whose writings have been profoundly transformative for me: David Abram, James Finley, Ruben Habito, Donna Orange, and Jason Wirth.

To all these precious allies and endless others, I am so grateful that we are co-conspirators in the truly great work of this era: cultivating a shared life that nourishes us and all our relations together, both human and otherwise.

*A Wild and Sacred Call* is a thoroughly new work of scholarship. Still, earlier versions of some sections of the book have appeared in the following journals: *British Gestalt Journal, Existential Analysis, The Humanistic Psychologist, Journal of Humanistic Psychology, Journal of Phenomenological Psychology, Journal of Transpersonal Psychology,* and *ReVision.* And in these anthologies: *Ecopsychology, Phenomenology, and the Environment,* edited by Douglas Vakoch and Fernando Castrillón; *Embodied Relational Gestalt,* edited by Michael C. Clemmens; *Integral Ecology,* edited by Gerard Magill and Jordan Potter; and *The Qualitative Vision for Psychology: An Invitation to a Human Science Approach,* edited by Constance Fischer, Leswin Laubscher, and Roger Brooke.

# Notes

## Preface

1. Unless indicated otherwise, all brackets within quotes are my gloss on the passage.

2. When I came upon this revealing proclamation it was attributed to the French surrealist poet Paul Éluard (Tarrant, 1998, p. 4, without the italics I added). Later I found the same attribution in other books, but a source was never cited. It turns out that Éluard did not use those exact words, but something much like them (Llewelyn, 2009, p. 452). And he was paraphrasing someone else who had made a similar remark.

3. For convenience, I will speak of "the mystics." While there are significant differences across practitioners and traditions, a comparative discussion is beyond the scope of this book. Still, I am wary of totalizing claims. So when I invoke "mystics" or "contemplatives," I mean the spiritual teachers and sensibilities explored in this book.

4. Scholars have not been able to determine whether Bashō actually wrote this, or if it was an oral teaching from him that was passed on by students.

5. This study was previously unpublished. "Nora," a self-chosen pseudonym, was (at the time of our interview) a 62-year-old, White, Christian contemplative who worked as an educator.

## Introduction

1. The etymologies in the present book have been drawn from *The Compact Oxford English Dictionary* (1971) and the multisource *Online Etymology Dictionary* (2021).

2. At this first mention of John Muir, let me strongly condemn the racist views he held toward Indigenous American and Black people, especially when he was young. In contrast, regarding nature, I find his views to be beautiful and revelatory, indeed deeply resonant (ironically) with sensibilities of first peoples.

In today's cultural context I imagine Muir would readily open his heart to all. But who knows, that may be wishful thinking.

3. I do my best to surpass language that perpetuates gender bias. Unfortunately, many authors were not aware of this important issue when they were writing. I critically inserted *sic* here, but for ease of reading I will not include this notation every time.

4. Heidegger does not figure prominently in the present text, but I cannot cite his work without condemning his terrible complicity with the Nazi regime. In fact, there are indications that fascist views infected his philosophy. As I see it, two gaps in his work are consistent with an authoritarian stance: the absence of a philosophy of relationship with a unique singular other, and the lack of a philosophy of the body. I work with the best of his insights while critiquing his egregious conduct and views.

5. Wade-Giles and pinyin are the most common systems for transliterating Chinese into the Latin alphabet. With thanks to Jason Wirth, I use pinyin because it is the most widely accepted. Thus, Laozi instead of Lao Tzu. However, if authors I cite use Wade-Giles, I retain that form of romanization so as to quote them verbatim. Thus, Tao instead of Dao.

6. Zen is the Japanese translation of the Chinese word Chán, which itself is a translation of the Sanskrit word *dhyāna*, which basically means meditation. Zen/Chán refers to a school of Māhāyana Buddhism that emerged in sixth-century China. Integrating Buddhism and Daoism, this tradition focuses on meditative, experiential realization of our nondual "true nature." Like most authors, I use "Zen" even when referring to a Chinese Chán teacher, as in Zen master Linji.

7. In this era of mass extinction and other death-wielding catastrophes, *choosing life* seems a good way to carry on together! After years of bringing "life" to mind (and heart) when I heard the word G-d, I was pleased to discover many esteemed precedents. Speaking from his supreme identity as G-d, Christ said: "I am . . . the life" (John 14:6). Meister Eckhart remarks, "God's isness is my life" (1980, p. 90). Regarding G-d, the sixteenth-century saint Teresa of Ávila (2003) sings, "Oh life of my life!" (p. 271). I am tempted to use italics or capitals to honor the depth dimension of that which I am invoking, as in *life* or Life. But I want to make it clear that I am referring to our shared daily life. This ordinary life goes infinitely deep. Likewise, I am inclined to capitalize nature, buddha-nature, love, being, mystery, and so forth. But this would mislead us into thinking that the unnamable mystery is separate from or other than our everyday coexistence. G-d and Dao are almost always capitalized in English, so I will follow that tradition.

## Chapter 1. Seeing Those Peach Blossoms Changed My Life

1. I have taken the liberty of combining different translations from several sources. See, for instance, Dōgen, 2012, p. 88; Miura & Sasaki, 1966, p. 292.

2. Tales of this event originated in the Zen tradition. Scholars believe that the story is probably apocryphal. While it may not be historically accurate, it is true psychospiritually.

3. The Zen school in which Harris Rōshi and I practice is called Sanbō Zen, formerly Sanbō Kyōdan. A tradition for lay practitioners that integrates Soto and Rinzai Zen, its recent lineage includes the following rōshi (esteemed teachers): Harada Daiun Sogaku, Yasutani Haku'un, Yamada Kōun, Kubota Juin, and Yamada Ryōun. American Zen teachers Robert Aitken, Philip Kapleau, and David Loy trained in this school.

4. Merton died in a suspicious but apparent accident when he was only 53, during a pilgrimage in Asia largely devoted to encounters with Buddhist teachers and sacred sites.

## Chapter 3. All Real Living Is Meeting

1. Of course, we don't have to wait until we are on our deathbed. Long before asking "Did I love well?" at the very end, we can ask, "Am I loving well right now?"

2. I include these overlapping schools: object relations, interpersonal psychoanalysis, attachment theory, self psychology, intersubjective and phenomenological psychoanalysis, and relational-cultural theory.

3. Traditional attachment theory addresses only our involvement with other humans. As the present book emphasizes, our attachment to the larger natural world is also crucial.

4. "Interior" and "exterior" are conventional terms that I use provisionally. Close attention shows that any presumed separation of these dimensions is a misleading abstraction from the actual nondual arising of living experience.

5. To be edible, milkweed buds have to be boiled three times because they harbor a natural toxin. Interestingly, when monarch caterpillars feed on milkweed they incorporate this poison but are immune to its effects. Because of the toxin, birds have learned to avoid eating them.

## Chapter 4. The Dissociative Madness of Modernity's Shadow

1. "APA" refers to the American Psychological Association, the world's most influential psychological organization.

2. This phrase was coined by sociologists Peter Berger and Thomas Luckman (1966).

3. Castaneda's early books were based upon extensive anthropological fieldwork in Mexico, including a participatory apprenticeship with an indigenous

shaman. It appears that his later texts were largely fictionalized elaborations derived from his actual experiences.

4. The following survey draws appreciatively from the work of scholars such as Martin Heidegger (1977b), Carolyn Merchant (1980, 1995), Morris Berman (1981), Fritjof Capra (1983), and David Loy (2002, 2010).

## Chapter 5. The Supposedly Separate Ego

1. The following discussion is my integration of transpersonal developmental theory. See Wilber, 1977, 1980, 2000b; Washburn, 1995; Ferrer, 2002; Engler, 2003; and Loy, 2018b.

2. This quote comes from notes I took while watching a talk by Thomas Berry on YouTube. I cannot locate the video in which he shared this beautiful view.

3. The stage names and characterizations (What's good for all of us?, etc.) come from Wilber (2000a). The comments in parentheses are my adaptation and elaboration.

4. I encourage you to view one of the many YouTube videos that show Harlow interacting with monkeys in his lab. But a warning is in order: these videos are tremendously disturbing.

## Chapter 6. No Longer I

1. I speak of "the" Christian mystical tradition" only as an orienting generalization. There are certainly differences across various mystics and various branches of the larger tradition.

2. The physicist Brian Swimme was a collaborator with Thomas Berry.

3. This is a translation from Augustine's *Tractates on the Gospel of John*, 38.10.

4. We could equally say that the whole world is the *love, awareness, spirit*, or *being* of G-d. But here we will stay with a fleshy, earthy metaphor and intuit G-d embodied.

5. Muhammad's often-cited teaching comes from the Sufi oral tradition, not the Koran.

6. See also John Welwood's (2000) important work on "spiritual bypassing."

7. The Heraclitus quote is from Fragment B45. The text I presented is an integration of various English translations.

8. Conversely, immature, prerational, prepersonal experiences are sometimes overly elevated and construed to be mature, transpersonal realizations.

9. Recent reports have indicated that Mother Teresa's mission was tainted by her conflicts regarding classic concerns such as sensual pleasure, pain, money, and power. I do not know the inside story, but I can welcome wise teachings without necessarily embracing the teacher.

10. This is the same passage, in two translations.

11. After working with this realization for several years I found something quite similar in a book by Elaine MacInnes (2007, p. 27), a Catholic nun and Zen teacher.

12. This translation is an often-seen free rendering of Augustine's (1997) words in the *Confessions* (book 3, section 6.11): "You [G-d] are more intimately present to me than my innermost being" (*interior intimo meo et superior summo meo*).

## Chapter 7. Nature's Conversational Consciousness

1. With the ascendance of mechanical metaphors in the modern era, G-d was no longer felt to be immanent in nature. Instead, placed far away in an imagined heavenly realm, an exclusively transcendent, otherworldly G-d was imagined to be the creator and operator of the great universal machine. In this major psychocultural change, people's sense of the holy, intelligent, harmonious functioning of the natural world was lost.

2. An odd example for an ecopsych book, granted. So let's imagine a dead tree about to fall on your house!

3. I encourage you to listen to loons singing at the wonderful website of the Cornell Lab of Ornithology: www.allaboutbirds.org/guide/Common_Loon/sounds. Better yet, find a real loon at your first opportunity!

4. When Bateson was writing the situation was so bad that the lake and its tributaries had caught fire (!) at least 13 times. Following the notorious 1969 Cuyahoga River fire, Congress established the Environmental Protection Agency (1970) and the Clean Water Act (1972).

5. My appreciative understanding of the Whanganui Māori sensibility comes from reading about their culture. If I have misrepresented their views in any way, I offer my sincere apologies.

## Chapter 8. Bashō's Contemplative Therapy for Narcissus

1. The poet Allen Ginsberg gives us the onomatopoeic "kerplunk!"

2. This translation comes from Bruce Sōun Harris Rōshi. See also Aitken, 1991, p. 12.

## Chapter 9. Nature-Healing-Body-Healing-Nature-Healing Body

1. I first heard this poem long ago. I have searched to no avail for its textual source.

2. Intriguingly, "interbeing" is a key notion for the Zen teacher Thich Nhat Hanh.

3. For a powerful sense of the ongoing calamity, please see the documentary film *The Last Mountain* (Haney, 2011); or even better, visit an active mine site in Appalachia.

4. Larry's comments brought tears to my eyes. When my wife saw this video she teared up as well, sighed deeply, and said, "I'm so glad we got to meet that man." So, so grateful indeed.

5. Instead of invoking the transpersonal "life" that we are, I could say transpersonal being, energy, spirit, awareness, or love—with all of these appearing as your body and mine and that of an oak tree and in fact the whole wide earth. I often opt for "life" because I find this word more experientially accessible.

6. If you feel any aversion to dogs, please substitute another animal for whom you feel warm affection.

## Chapter 10. Living Means Being Addressed

1. The same day I wrote this passage my wife brought home a note from one of her first grade students: "Ms. Adams, you are a great teacher because you let us be ourselves. ♥" Not just a random coincidence it seemed, but a meaningful one—real synchronicity, as Jung would say.

2. At some point even a stance of meditative witnessing needs to be spontaneously surrendered, thereby allowing the contemplative practitioner to open into (and as) the seamless nondual flow of experience. Otherwise a subtle dualistic separation is maintained, reinforcing our fundamental affliction: namely, the *apparent* gap between a supposedly separate self observing a supposedly separate object. Still, the mature capacity to witness our experience in relative freedom from reactive aversion or attachment, is a skillful "dualism" indeed.

3. The bracketed additions are mine. Regarding the first, these were my wife's words when a multicolored painted bunting showed up serendipitously in Pittsburgh one winter! In the third, I hope you understand the context for my obscene allusion. But this is not an apology because my anger fits the circumstances. The real obscenity is nature's desecration.

4. The information about Yellowstone's trophic cascade was gathered from Ripple and Beschta, 2012, and an amazing YouTube video, "How Wolves Change Rivers" (2014).

5. *Brihadaranyaka Upanishad* 1.4.2. I have drawn from several different translations.

## Chapter 11. Love Is Our Nature, Our Calling, Our Path, Our Fruition

1. There are many versions of the bodhisattva vow. This one is adapted from my Zen training with Bruce Harris Rōshi.

## Coda

1. This is rendered verbatim from Devlin and Tischler's text. I presume they quoted Williams' original letter precisely. This includes misspelling "others"— instead of other's—in the final sentence. Because of the way it would *sound*, I could not bring myself to write "each others [sic] naked hearts." Far from being sick, opening our naked hearts for each other is the healthiest gesture of all, truly the essence-calling-path-fruition of being human!

2. This revelatory comment is one that Muir penned by hand on the back flyleaf of his personal copy of *The Prose Works of Ralph Waldo Emerson, Volume I.*

3. This is my adaptation of a story I first heard from David Loy. Over the years it has been presented in various versions that differ significantly (as mine also does) from the apparent original: "The Star Thrower," an essay by Loren Eiseley. In pondering the story, I learned that marine scientists are encouraging people to call these amazing animals "sea stars," because they are not actually fish. But that is not the most important thing I learned from the story!

4. The extraordinary singer-songwriter Carrie Newcomer spoke and sang about this encounter during a concert in Pittsburgh (ca. 2014).

# References

Abe, M. (1992). *A study of Dōgen*. State University of New York Press.

Abram, D. (1996). *The spell of the sensuous: Perception and language in a more-than-human world*. Random House.

Abram, D. (2010). *Becoming animal: An earthly cosmology*. Random House.

Abrams, G. (1987, May 27). Conversation with Joseph Campbell. Retrieved from the *Los Angeles Times* web page, https://www.latimes.com/archives/la-xpm-1987-05-27-vw-1659-story.html.

Adams, W. (1996). Discovering the sacred in everyday life: An empirical phenomenological study. *Humanistic Psychologist, 24*(3), 28–54.

Ainsworth, M. D. S., Blehar, M. C., Waters, E., & Wall, S. (1978). *Patterns of attachment*. Psychology Press.

Aitken, R. (1978). *A Zen wave: Basho's haiku and Zen*. Weatherhill.

Aitken, R. (1984). *The mind of clover*. North Point Press.

Aitken, R. (1991). *The gateless barrier*. North Point Press.

Aitken, R. (1993). *Encouraging words*. Pantheon.

Aitken, R. (1996). *Original dwelling place*. Counterpoint.

Aitken, R. (2003). *The morning star*. Shoemaker Hoard.

Albert, G. (2017). Tupua Te Kawa. Retrieved from the 23rd Annual River Symposium web page, http://riversymposium.com/wp-content/uploads/2017/09/Gerrard-Albert.pdf.

Armstrong, R. J., & Brady, I. C. (1982). *Francis and Clare*. Paulist Press.

Arvay, C. G. (2018). *The biophilia effect*. Sounds True.

Atlantic cod. (2014). Retrieved from the National Oceanic and Atmospheric Administration FishWatch website, http://www.fishwatch.gov/seafood_profiles/species/cod/species_pages/atlantic_cod.htm.

Augustine, Saint. (1997). *The confessions* (ca. 400) (M. Boulding, Trans.). Vintage.

Badè, W. F. (1924). *The life and letters of John Muir, vol. I*. Houghton Mifflin.

Bashō, M. (1966). *The narrow road to the deep north and other travel sketches* (N. Yuasa, Trans.). Penguin.

Bashō, M. (1998). *Narrow road to the interior* (S. Hamill, Trans.). Shambhala.

Bashō, M. (2004). *Bashō's haiku* (D. L. Barnhill, Trans.). State University of New York Press.

Bateson, G. (1972). *Steps to an ecology of mind.* Ballantine.

Baxter, D. E., & Pelletier, L. G. (2019). Is nature relatedness a basic human psychological need? *Canadian Psychology, 60*(1), 21–34.

Becker, E. (1973). *The denial of death.* Free Press.

Beckwith, R. T. (2017, September 27). President Trump won't say if he still thinks climate change is a hoax. Here's why. Retrieved from the *Time* website, https://time.com/4959233/donald-trump-climate-change-hoax-question/.

Behar, R. (1996). *The vulnerable observer.* Beacon.

Benyus, J. M. (1997). *Biomimicry.* Harper Perennial.

Berger, P. L., & Luckman, T. (1966). *The social construction of reality.* Anchor.

Berman, M. (1981). *The reenchantment of the world.* Cornell University Press.

Bernasconi, R., & Wood, D. (Eds.). (1988). *The provocation of Levinas.* Routledge.

Berry, T. (1988). *The dream of the earth.* Sierra Club.

Berry, T. (1999). *The great work.* Bell Tower.

Berry, W. (2012). *New collected poems.* Counterpoint.

Beyer, J. D. (1999). *Experiencing the self as being part of nature.* UMI.

Beyer, J. (2014). A phenomenology of intimate relating and identification with the whole (and the tale of the woefully misguided aspirations of the common land barnacle). In D. Vakoch & F. Castrillón (Eds.), *Ecopsychology, phenomenology, and the environment* (pp. 127–140). Springer.

Biomimicry Institute. (2020). https://biomimicry.org/.

Blake, W. (1946). From Crabb Robinson's reminiscences (1869). In A. Kazin (Ed.), *The portable Blake* (pp. 675–694). Viking.

Blake, W. (1988). *The complete poetry and prose of William Blake,* newly revised edition (D. V. Erdman, Ed.). Anchor Doubleday.

Blofeld, J. (1958). *The Zen teaching of Huang Po.* Grove Press.

Blum, D. (1994). *The monkey wars.* Oxford University Press.

Blum, D. (2002). *Love at Goon Park: Harry Harlow and the science of affection.* Basic Books.

Bly, R. (1980). *News of the universe.* Sierra Club Books.

Bodhi, B. (Ed.). (1995). *The middle length discourses of the Buddha.* Wisdom Publications.

Bowlby, J. (1969). *Attachment.* Basic Books.

Bowlby, J. (1979). *The making and breaking of affectional bonds.* Tavistock.

Brown, N. O. (1959). *Life against death.* Wesleyan University Press.

Brune, M. (2015). Oil drilling makes whales deaf. Mass email posted by the Sierra Club.

Buber, M. (1948). *Hasidism.* Philosophical Library.

Buber, M. (1952). *At the turning*. Farrar, Straus and Young.

Buber, M. (1958). *I and Thou* (1923) (R. G. Smith, Trans.). Charles Scribner's Sons.

Buber, M. (1965). *Between man and man*. Beacon Press.

Buber, M. (1970). *I and Thou* (1923) (W. Kaufmann, Trans.). Touchstone.

Campbell, J. (1988). *The power of myth*. Doubleday.

Capra, F. (1983). *The turning point*. Bantam.

Caputo, J. D. (1997). *The prayers and tears of Jacques Derrida*. Indiana University Press.

Cashore, D. (2019). *Listen for the desert: An ecopsychological autoethnography*. [Doctoral dissertation, Duquesne University, Pittsburgh, PA]. From https://dsc.duq.edu/etd/1801.

Castaneda, C. (1972). *Journey to Ixtlan*. Simon & Schuster.

Catherine of Genoa. (1989). *The spiritual doctrine of Saint Catherine of Genoa*. TAN Books.

Chaucer, G. (2014). *The Canterbury tales and other poems*. Lerner.

Christian, R. F. (Ed. & Trans.). (1978). *Tolstoy's letters, vol. I*. Charles Scribner's Sons.

Clayton, S., Manning, C. M., Krygsman, K., & Speiser, M. (2017). *Mental health and our changing climate*. American Psychological Association.

Cleary, T., & Cleary, J. C. (2005). *The blue cliff record*. Shambhala.

Coen, E., & Coen, J. (2000). *Oh Brother, Where Art Thou?* Touchstone Pictures and Universal Pictures. Screenplay retrieved from the Internet Movie Script Database, http://nldslab.soe.ucsc.edu/charactercreator/film_corpus/film_2010 0519/all_imsdb_05_19_10/O-Brother-Where-Art-Thou%253f.html.

Cohen, L. (1992). Anthem. In L. Cohen, *The future*. Sony Music.

Cohen, L., & Robinson, S. (2001). You have loved enough. In L. Cohen, *Ten New Songs*. Sony Music.

Cohen, R. (Ed). (1986). *Face to face with Levinas*. State University of New York Press.

*Compact edition of the Oxford English dictionary* (OED). (1971). Oxford University Press.

Cook, F. H. (1977). *Hua-yen Buddhism: The jewel net of Indra*. Penn State University Press.

Coomaraswamy, A. (1985). *The dance of Śiva*. Dover.

Dalai Lama. (2000). *The Dalai Lama's little book of wisdom*. Hampton Roads.

Day, D. (1948). *On pilgrimage*. Catholic Worker Books.

Davis, J. H. (2018). Trump calls some unauthorized immigrants "animals" in rant. Retrieved May 16, 2018, from the *New York Times* web page, https://www.nytimes.com/2018/05/16/us/politics/trump-undocumented-immigrants-animals.html.

Dellinger, D. (2011). Hieroglyphic stairway. In *Love letter to the Milky Way*. White Cloud Press.

Descartes, R. (1984). *The philosophical writings of Descartes, volume II* (1641). Cambridge University Press.

Descartes, R. (1998). *Discourse on method and meditations on first philosophy* (1637). (D. A. Cress, Trans.). Hackett.

Devlin, A. J., & Tischler, N. M. (Eds.). (2004). *The selected letters of Tennessee Williams, vol. II, 1945–1957*. New Directions.

De Vos, J. M., Joppa, L. N., Gittleman, J. L., Stephens, P. R., & Pimm, S. L. (2015). Estimating the normal background rate of extinction. *Conservation Biology, 29*(2), 452–462.

Deignan, K. (Ed.). (2003). *When the trees say nothing*. Sorin Books.

Dillard, A. (1974). *Pilgrim at Tinker Creek*. Harper Perennial.

Dōgen, E. (1985). *Moon in a dewdrop* (K. Tanahashi, Trans.). North Point Press.

Dōgen, E. (1999). *Enlightenment unfolds* (K. Tanahashi, Ed.). Shambhala.

Dōgen, E. (2012). *Treasury of the true dharma-eye: Zen master Dōgen's Shobo Genzo* (K. Tanahashi, Ed.). Shambhala.

Donne, J. (1999). *Devotions upon emergent occasions* and *Death's dual* (1624). Vintage Books.

Doré, F., & Prévost, M.-L. (Eds.). (1990). *Selected letters of Romain Rolland*. Oxford University Press.

Dumoulin, H. (1988). *Zen Buddhism*. Macmillan.

Duncan, D. (2009). *The national parks: America's best idea*. Knopf.

Dwyer, C. (2018, July 31). After calf's death, orca mother carries it for days in "tragic tour of grief." Retrieved from the National Public Radio website, https://www.npr.org/2018/07/31/634314741/after-calfs-death-orca-mother-carries-it-for-days-in-tragic-tour-of-grief.

Dylan, B. (1965). Subterranean homesick blues. In B. Dylan, *Bringing it all back home* [Audio compact disc]. Columbia Records.

Easwaran, E. (1987). *The Upanishads*. Nilgiri Press.

Eckhart, M. (1980). *Breakthrough: Meister Eckhart's creation spirituality in new translation* (M. Fox, Ed.). Image Books.

Eckhart, M. (2007). *Meister Eckhart's sermons*. Cosimo Classics.

Eckhart, M. (2009). *The complete mystical works of Meister Eckhart* (M. O'C. Walshe, Trans. & Ed.). Crossroad.

Einstein, A. (1950). Letter to Norman Salit, March 4, 1950. Reprinted in the *New York Times*, March 29,1972, https://www.nytimes.com/1972/03/29/archives/the-einstein-papers-a-man-of-many-parts-the-einstein-papers-man-of.html; archived in the Einstein Archives Online, http://alberteinstein.info/vufind1/Record/EAR000025410.

Eliot, T. S. (1962). *The complete poems and plays*. Harcourt, Brace & World.

Engler, J. (2003). Being somebody and being nobody. In J. Safran (Ed.), *Psychoanalysis and Buddhism* (pp. 35–79). Wisdom Publications.

Erikson, E. (1980). *Identity and the life cycle.* Norton.

Erlich, P. R., Dobkin, D. S., & Wheye, D. (1988). *The birder's handbook.* Simon & Schuster.

Escher, M. C. (2016). *Drawing Hands.* Retrieved from http://www.mcescher.com/gallery/back-in-holland/drawing-hands/.

Ferrer, J. N. (2002). *Revisioning transpersonal theory.* State University of New York Press.

Ferrer, J. N. (2008). Spiritual knowing as participatory enaction: An answer to the question of religious pluralism. In J. N. Ferrer & J. H. Sherman (Eds.), *The participatory turn* (pp. 135–169). State University of New York Press.

Fimrite, P. (2009, August 9). Park ranger asks: Where are the black visitors? Sunday Profile: Shelton Johnson. Retrieved from the SF Gate website of the *San Francisco Chronicle,* June 24, 2019, https://www.sfgate.com/outdoors/article/Park-ranger-asks-Where-are-the-black-visitors-3222468.php.

Finley, James. (2004). *Christian meditation.* Harper.

Firmage, G. J. (Ed.). (1994). *E. E. Cummings: Complete poems.* Liveright.

Fischer, C. T., Laubscher, L., & R. Brooke (Eds.). (2016). *The qualitative vision for psychology: Invitation to a human science approach.* Duquesne University Press.

Fisher, A. (2013). *Radical Ecopsychology,* 2nd ed. State University of New York Press.

Fitzpatrick, J. W., Lammertink, M., Luneau, D., Gallagher, T., Harrison, B., & Sparling, G. (2005, April 28). Ivory-billed Woodpecker (*Campephilus principalis*) persists in continental North America. Retrieved April 28, 2005, from the *Science Magazine* website, http://www.sciencemag.org/cgi/content/abstract/1114103.

Fleischman, L., & Franklin, M. (2017). Fumes across the fence-line: The health impacts from oil and gas facilities on African American communities. Retrieved from the NAACP website, https://www.naacp.org/wpcontent/uploads/2017/11/Fumes-Across-the-Fence-Line_NAACP-and-CATF-Study.pdf.

Foster, N., & Shoemaker, J. (Eds). (1996). *The roaring stream.* Ecco Press.

Fox, W. (1990). *Toward a transpersonal ecology.* Shambhala.

Freud. S. (1955). A difficulty in the path of psycho-analysis (1917). In J. Strachey (Ed. & Trans.), *The standard edition of the complete psychological works of Sigmund Freud, volume XVII* (pp. 137–144). Hogarth Press.

Freud. S. (1957). Repression (1915). In J. Strachey (Ed. & Trans.), *The standard edition of the complete psychological works of Sigmund Freud, volume XIV* (pp. 141–158). Hogarth Press.

Freud, S. (1964). On narcissism (1914). In J. Strachey (Ed.), *The standard edition of the complete psychological works of Sigmund Freud, volume XIV (1914–1916)* (pp. 67–102). Hogarth Press.

Freud, S. (1966). *Introductory lectures on psychoanalysis* (1917) (J. Strachey, Trans. & Ed.). Norton.

Freud, S. (2010). *Civilization and its discontents* (1930) (J. Strachey, Trans.). Norton.

Freud, Sigmund. (2012). *The future of an illusion* (1927) (G. C. Richter, Trans.). Broadview.

Friedman, H. L., & Hartelius, G. (Eds.). (2013). *The Wiley Blackwell handbook of transpersonal psychology.* Wiley Blackwell.

From billions to none: The passenger pigeon's flight to extinction. (2015). Retrieved from http://www.billionstonone.com/index.html.

Fromm, E. (1955). *The sane society.* Henry Holt.

Fromm, E. (1964). *The heart of man.* Harper & Row.

Gach, G. (1998). *What book!? Buddha poems from beat to hiphop.* Parallax Press.

Gadamer, H.-G. (2011). *Truth and method,* second revised ed. (1960) (J. Wiensheimer & D. G. Marshall, Trans.). Continuum.

Gallagher, T. (2005). *The grail bird.* Houghton Mifflin.

Gallup, G. G. (1970). Chimpanzees: Self-recognition. *Science, 167*(3914), 86–87.

Garfield, Jay L. (1995). *The fundamental wisdom of the Middle Way: Nāgārjuna's Mūlamadhyamakakārikā.* Oxford University Press.

Gee, M. (Ed.). (2001). *Words of wisdom.* Andrews McMeel.

Geertz, C. (1983). *Local knowledge.* Basic Books.

Gibson, L. (2019). Retrieved from the Earthjustice website, https://earthjustice.org/mountain-heroes/larry-gibson.

Gilchrist, A. (1969). *Life of William Blake, vol. I.* Phaeton Press.

Gonnerman, M. (2015). *A sense of the whole.* Counterpoint.

Goodall, J. (1990). *Through a window.* Houghton Mifflin.

Goodall, J. (1999). *Reason for hope: A spiritual journey.* Warner Books.

Goodall, J. (2001). *The chimpanzees I love.* Scholastic Press.

Goodall, J., & Beckoff, M. (2002). *The ten trusts.* Harper.

Goodall, J. (2016). #JaneGoodall#WednesdayWisdom. "If we kill off the wild, then we are killing a part of our souls." Retrieved from JaneGoodallInstitute@JaneGoodallInst.

Goleman, D. (2006). *Social intelligence.* Bantam.

Greenberg, J. (2014). *A feathered river across the sky.* Bloomsbury.

Hamilton, E., & Cairns, H. (Eds.). (1973). *The collected dialogues of Plato.* Princeton University Press.

Haney, B. (Director). (2011). *The last mountain.* [Motion picture]. Solid Ground Films.

Hardy, T. (2001). *Thomas Hardy: The complete poems* (J. Gibson, Ed.). Palgrave.

Harlow, H. F. (1986). The nature of love. In C. M. Mears (Ed.), *From learning to love: The selected papers of H. F. Harlow* (pp. 101–120). Praeger.

Harlow, H. F., Gluck, J. P., & Suomi, S. J. (1986). Generalization of behavioral data between nonhuman and human animals. In C. M. Mears (Ed.), *From learning to love: The selected papers of H. F. Harlow* (pp. 61–74). Praeger.

Harlow, H. F., Harlow, M. K., & Suomi, S. J. (1971). From thought to therapy: Lessons from a primate laboratory. *American Scientist 59,* 538–549.

Harlow, H. F., & Mears, C. (1979). *The human model*. V. H. Winston & Sons.

Harlow, H. F., & Suomi, S. J. (1970). Induced psychopathology in monkeys. *Engineering Science, 33*, 8–14.

Harlow, H. F., & Suomi, S. J. (1986). Nature of love—simplified. In C. M. Mears (Ed.), *From learning to love: The selected papers of H. F. Harlow* (pp. 121–134). Praeger.

Harlow's studies on dependency in monkeys. (2010, Dec. 16). Retrieved from YouTube, https://www.youtube.com/watch?v=OrNBEhzjg8I.

Hass, R. (Ed.). (1994). *The essential haiku*. Ecco Press.

Haxton, B. (2001). *Fragments: The collected wisdom of Heraclitus*. Viking.

Heidegger, M. (1966). *Discourse on thinking* (1959) (J. Anderson & H. Freund, Trans.). Harper & Row.

Heidegger, M. (1977a). On the essence of truth (J. Sallis, Trans.). In D. F. Krell (Ed.), *Martin Heidegger: Basic writings* (pp. 117–141). Harper & Row.

Heidegger, M. (1977b). *The question concerning technology and other essays* (1954) (W. Lovitt, Trans.). Harper & Row.

Heidegger, M. (1996). *Being and time* (1927) (J. Stambaugh, Trans.). State University of New York Press.

Henderson, H. G. (1958). *An introduction to haiku*. Doubleday Anchor.

A hero doesn't get used to this. (2012, August 3). Retrieved from YouTube, https://www.youtube.com/watch?v=0V3ajs7Boi4.

Hertsgaard, M. (2019, January 28). The climate kids are coming. Retrieved from the *Nation* website, https://www.thenation.com/article/archive/greta-thunberg-climate-change-davos/.

Hirshfield, J. (2015). *Ten windows*. Knopf.

hooks, b. (2009). Lorde: The imagination of justice. In R. P. Byrd, J. B. Cole, & B. Guy-Sheftall (Eds.), *I am your sister* (pp. 242–248). Oxford University Press.

How Dr. Jane Goodall used the lessons she learned from chimps to raise her own children. (October 20, 2017). Retrieved from the *Today* website, https://www.youtube.com/watch?v=QYFj2feOjLA.

How wolves change rivers. (2014, Feb. 14). Sustainable Human. Retrieved from YouTube, https://www.youtube.com/watch?v=ysa5OBhXz-Q.

Hughes, T. (1997). *Tales from Ovid*. Farrar, Straus and Giroux.

Hunter, R., & Garcia, J. (1970). Ripple. In The Grateful Dead, *American Beauty*. [Audio compact disc]. Warner Bros.

Husserl, E. (1970). *Logical investigations, vol. I* (1900) (J. N. Findley, Trans.). Humanities Press.

IPCC. (2018a). *Global warming of 1.5°C: An IPCC special report on the impacts of global warming*.

IPCC. (2018b). Summary for policymakers of IPCC special report on global warming of 1.5°C approved by governments. Retrieved October 20, 2018, from the United Nations Intergovernmental Panel on Climate Change (IPCC) website, https://www.ipcc.ch/2018/10/08/summary-for-policymakers-of-ipcc-special-report-on-global-warming-of-1-5c-approved-by-governments/.

Ivory-billed Woodpecker. (2005). Retrieved July 15, 2005, from the Nature Conservancy website, http://nature.org/ivorybill/.

IUCN Red List of Threatened Species. (2020). Retrieved from IUCN website, https://www.iucnredlist.org.

Jackson, J. (2006). Ivory-billed Woodpecker (*Campephilus principalis*). *The Auk, 123*(1), 1–15.

Jamail, D. (2020, May 21). Grieving my way into loving the planet. Retrieved from the *Yes!* website, https://www.yesmagazine.org/health-happiness/2020/05/21/grief-climate-change/?utm_medium=email&utm_campaign=YTW_20200522&utm_content=YTW_20200522+CID_6952aa3207789a573c5e92a67a090420&utm_source=CM.

John Muir and "Saunter." (2019, October 26). Retrieved from *Online etymology dictionary*, https://www.etymonline.com/columns/post/john-muir-and-'saunter.'

John of the Cross. (1991). *The collected works of Saint John of the Cross* (K. Kavanaugh & O. Rodriguez, Trans.). ICS.

John of the Cross. (2007). *A spiritual canticle of the soul and The bridegroom of Christ* (D. Lewis, Trans.). Cosimo Classics.

Jones, D. N. (February 26, 2006). Almost level, West Virginia. *Pittsburgh Post-Gazette.*

Jordan, J. V. (2010). *Relational-cultural therapy.* American Psychological Association.

Jung, C. G. (1959). *Aion.* Princeton University Press.

Kalin, N. H. (2015, December 22). Effects of early experience on the development of anxiety and its neural substrate. University of Wisconsin-Madison Animal Care and Use Protocol Review Form (pp. 1–27). Retrieved from https://animalresearch.wisc.edu/content/uploads/2016/02/protocol_2016.pdf.

Kaplan, R. (1993). The role of nature in the context of the workplace. *Landscape and Urban Planning, 26,* 193–210.

Kaplan, R., & Kaplan, S. (1989). *The experience of nature.* Cambridge University Press.

Kaplan, R., Kaplan, S., & Ryan, R. L. (1998). *With people in mind.* Island Press.

Kapleau, P. (1980). *The three pillars of Zen.* Anchor Books.

Kaza, S., & Kraft, K. (Eds.). (2000). *Dharma rain.* Shambhala.

Keating, T. (1986). *Open mind, open heart.* Amity House.

Keats, J. (1959). *John Keats: Selected poems and letters.* Houghton Mifflin.

Kellert, S. R., & Wilson, E. O. (Eds.). (1993). *The biophilia hypothesis.* Island Press.

Kelly-Gagni, C. (2006). *Mother Teresa.* Barnes & Noble.

Kepner, J. (1987). *Body process.* Gestalt Press.

Kierkegaard, S. (1996). *Søren Kierkegaard: Papers and journals.* Penguin.

Kim, Hee-Jin. (2004). *Eihei Dōgen: Mystical realist*. Wisdom Publications.

King, C. S. (Ed.). (1996). *The words of Martin Luther King, Jr*. New Market.

King, M. L. (1968). Remaining awake through a great revolution. National Cathedral, March 31, 1968. Retrieved from YouTube/African American History, https://www.youtube.com/watch?v=SLsXZXJAURk.

King, M. L. (1986). A Christmas sermon on peace (1967). In J. M. Washington (Ed.), *A testament of hope* (pp. 253–258). Harper Collins.

Kohut, H. (1984). *How does analysis cure?* University of Chicago Press.

Kohlberg, L. (1981). *The philosophy of moral development, vol. I*. Harper & Row.

Kolbert, E. (2014). The sixth extinction: An unnatural history. Henry Holt.

Kornfield, J. (1993). *A path with heart*. Bantam.

Korten, D. (2006). *The great turning*. Berrett-Koehler.

Lacan, J. (1977). The mirror stage as formative of the function of the I. In A. Sheridan (Trans.), *Écrits* (pp. 1–7). W. W. Norton.

Ladinsky, D. (2002). *Love poems from God*. Penguin Compass.

Laing, R. D. (1967). *The politics of experience*. Pantheon.

Lame Deer, J. F., & Erdoes, R. (1972). *Lame Deer*. Pocket Books.

Latta, S. C., Michaels, M. A., Scheifler, D., Michot, T. C., Shrum, P. L., Johnson, P., Tischendorf, J., Weeks, M., Trochet, J., & Ford, B. (2022, April 8). Multiple lines of evidence indicate survival of the Ivory-billed Woodpecker in Louisiana. bioRxiv preprint, 1–38. doi: https://doi.org/10.1101/2022.04.06.487399.

Leiss, W. (1972). *The domination of nature*. Beacon Press.

Leopold, A. (1949). *A Sand County almanac*. Oxford.

Leopold, A. (1993). *Round river*. Oxford University Press.

Levinas, E. (1969). *Totality and infinity* (1961) (A. Lingis, Trans.). Duquesne University Press.

Levinas, E. (1981). *Otherwise than being, or beyond essence* (1974) (A. Lingis, Trans.). Duquesne University Press.

Levinas, E. (1984). Ethics as first philosophy (S. Hand & M. Temple, Trans.). In S. Hand (Ed.), *The Levinas reader* (pp. 75–87). Blackwell.

Levinas, E. (1985). *Ethics and infinity* (R. A. Cohen, Trans.). Duquesne University Press.

Lilla Watson: "Let us work together." (n.d.). Retrieved from Uniting Church in Australia Assembly web page, https://uniting.church/lilla-watson-let-us-work-together/.

Llewlyn, J. (2009). *Margins of religion*. Indiana University Press.

Lopez, B. (1978). *Of wolves and men*. Simon & Schuster.

Louv, R. (2008). *Last child in the woods*. Algonquin Books.

Loy, D. R. (2002). *A Buddhist history of the west*. State University of New York Press.

Loy, D. R. (2008). *Money sex war karma*. Wisdom Publications.

Loy, D. R. (2010). *The world is made of stories*. Wisdom Publications.

Loy, D. R. (2015). *A new Buddhist path*. Wisdom Publications.

Loy, D. R. (2018a). *Ecodharma*. Wisdom Publications.

Loy, D. R. (2018b). *Lack and transcendence* (1996). Wisdom Publications.

MacInnes, E. (2007). *The flowing bridge*. Wisdom Publications.

Macfarlane, R. (2016, August 7). The secrets of the wood wide web. Retrieved from the *New Yorker* website, https://www.newyorker.com/tech/annals-of-technology/the-secrets-of-the-wood-wide-web.

Macy, J. (1991). *World as lover, world as self*. Parallax Press.

Macy, J., & Brown, M. Y. (2014). *Coming back to life*. New Society.

Macy, J., & Johnstone, C. (2012). *Active hope*. New World Library.

Mahler, M., Pine, F., & Bergman, A. (1975). *The psychological birth of the human infant*. Basic Books.

Mascaró, J. (Ed.). (1965). *The Upanishads*. Penguin.

Maslow, A. (1968). *Toward a psychology of being*, 2nd ed. Van Nostrand Reinhold.

Maslow, A. (1971). *The farther reaches of human nature*. Viking.

Mbiti, J. S. (1969). *African religions and philosophies*. Heinemann.

McFague, S. (1993). *The body of God: An ecological theology*. Fortress Press.

McWilliams, N. (1994). *Psychoanalytic diagnosis*. Guilford Press.

Mears, C. M. (Ed.). (1986). *From learning to love: The selected papers of H. F. Harlow*. Praeger.

Meng, H., & Freud, E. L. (1963). *Psychoanalysis and faith*. Basic Books.

Mental health by the numbers. (2019). Retrieved from the National Alliance on Mental Illness website, https://www.nami.org/learn-more/mental-health-by-the-numbers.

Merchant, C. (1980). *The death of nature*. Harper Collins.

Merchant, C. (1995). *Earthcare: Women and the environment*. Routledge.

Merchant, N. (2018). Immigrant kids seen held in fenced cages at border facility. Retrieved June 18, 2018, from the Associated Press website, https://apnews.com/6e04c6ee01dd46669eddba9d3333f6d5.

Merleau-Ponty, M. (1962). *Phenomenology of perception* (1945) (C. Smith, Trans.). Routledge & Kegan Paul.

Merleau-Ponty, M. (1968). *The visible and the invisible* (1964) (A. Lingis, Trans.). Northwestern University Press.

Merleau-Ponty, M. (2003). *Nature: Course notes from the College de France* (R. Vallier, Trans.). Northwestern University Press.

Merton, T. (1953). *The sign of Jonas*. Harvest.

Merton, T. (1961). *New seeds of contemplation*. New Directions.

Merton, T. (1967). *Mystics and Zen masters*. Farrar, Straus and Giroux.

Merton, T. (1968a). *Conjectures of a guilty bystander*. Image Books.

Merton, T. (1968b). *Zen and the birds of appetite*. New Directions.

Merton, T. (1995). *Passion for peace*. Crossroad.

Merton, T. (1996). *A search for solitude.* Harper.

Mitchell, S. (1988). *Tao Te Ching.* Harper & Row.

Mitchell, S. (Ed.). (1989). *The enlightened heart.* Harper Perennial.

Mitchell, S. (Ed. & Trans). (1995). *Ahead of all parting.* Modern Library.

Mitchell, S. A. (1988). *Relational concepts in psychoanalysis.* Harvard University Press.

Mitchell, S. (1993). *Hope and dread in psychoanalysis.* Basic Books.

Mitchell, S. A., & Aron, L. (Eds.). (1999). *Relational psychoanalysis.* Analytic Press.

Miura, I., & Fuller Sasaki, R. (1966). *Zen dust.* Harcourt, Brace & World University Press.

Monkey to the rescue. (2014, December 21). Retrieved from the *New York Times* website, https://www.nytimes.com/video/multimedia/100000003386019/monkey-to-the-rescue.html.

Mother Teresa. (1999). *In the heart of the world.* New World Library.

Mountaintop removal 101. (July 18, 2019). Retrieved from Appalachian Voices website, http://appvoices.org/end-mountaintop-removal/mtr101/.

Moyers, B. (2009, May 15). *Bill Moyers Journal.* Retrieved from the Public Broadcasting System website, http://www.pbs.org/moyers/journal/05152009/transcript2.html.

Muir, J. (n.d.). John Muir's handwritten note on the back flyleaf of his personal copy of *The prose works of Ralph Waldo Emerson, volume I*, in the Beinecke Rare Book and Manuscript Library of Yale University, Catalog Number Za Em34 C869 1 Copy 3.

Muir, J. (1988). *My first summer in the Sierra.* Sierra Club Books.

Muir, J. (2013). *John Muir: Spiritual writings.* Orbis Books.

Mullany, G. (2017, January 17). World's 8 richest have as much wealth as bottom half, Oxfam says. Retrieved from *New York Times* website, https://www.nytimes.com/2017/01/16/world/eight-richest-wealth-oxfam.html?_r=0.

Nelson, R. K. (1983). *Make prayers to the raven.* University of Chicago Press.

Nhat Hanh, T. (1988). *The heart of understanding.* Parallax Press.

Nhat Hanh, T. (1991). *Old path white clouds.* Parallax Press.

Nhat Hanh, T. (1998). *The heart of the Buddha's teaching.* Broadway Books.

Nhat Hanh, T. (2008). *The world we have.* Parallax Press.

Nietzsche, F. (1974). *The gay science* (W. Kaufmann, Trans.). Vintage.

O'Keeffe, G. (1939). Georgia O'Keeffe: Exhibition of oils and pastels, January 22–March 17, 1939; An American Place [art gallery], New York City. [Commentary by O'Keeffe in the catalogue for this art show]. Retrieved from https://brbl-dl.library.yale.edu/vufind/Record/4212776 (Yale University Library).

Okumura, S. (2010). *Realizing Genjōkōan.* Wisdom Publications.

*Online etymology dictionary.* (2021). http://www.etymonline.com/.

Oliver, M. (1992). *New and selected poems.* Beacon Press.

Oliver, M. (2004). *Long life: Essays and other writings*. Da Capo Press.

Oliver, M. (2005). *New and selected poems, volume two*. Beacon Press.

Oliver, M. (2016). *Felicity*. Penguin Press.

Orange, D. (2011). *The suffering stranger*. Routledge.

Otto, R. (1978). *The idea of the holy* (1923) (J. W. Harvey, Trans.). Oxford University Press.

Ovid. (1986). *Metamorphoses* (A. D. Melville, Trans.). Oxford.

Ovid. (1994). *The metamorphoses of Ovid*. Johns Hopkins University Press.

Pachniewska, A. (2015). List of animals that have passed the mirror test. Retrieved on April 15, 2015, from the Animal Cognition website, http://www.animal cognition.org/2015/04/15/list-of-animals-that-have-passed-the-mirror-test/.

Pagels, E. (1998, April). The gospel of Thomas. Retrieved from the *Frontline* website, https://www.pbs.org/wgbh/pages/frontline/shows/religion/story/thomas.html.

Pagels, E. (2003). *Beyond belief*. Random House.

Palmer, A. W. (1911). *The mountain trail and its message*. Pilgrim Press.

Perls, F., Hefferline, R. F., & Goodman, P. (1951). *Gestalt therapy*. Dell.

Pope Francis. (2015). *Laudato Si': On Care for Our Common Home* [Encyclical].

Porete, M. (1993). *The mirror of simple souls*. (E. Babinsky, Trans.). Paulist Press.

Pyle, R. M. (1992). Intimate relations and the extinction of experience. *Left Bank* (2), 61–69.

Pyle, R. M. (2005). Cosmic convergence. *Orion, 24*(3), 68–69.

Rajala, A. Z., Reininger, K. R., Lancaster, K. M., & Populin, L. C. (2010). Rhesus monkeys (*Macaca mulatta*) do recognize themselves in the mirror: Implications for the evolution of self-recognition. *PLOS One* 5: e12865, doi:10.1371/journal.pone.0012865, PMC 2947497, PMID 20927365, https://www.ncbi.nlm.nih.gov/pmc/articles/PMC2947497/.

Reece, E. (2006). *Lost mountain*. Riverhead Books.

Rilke, R. M. (1954). *Letters to a young poet*, revised ed. W. W. Norton.

Rilke, R. M. (1989). *The selected poetry of Rainer Maria Rilke* (S. Mitchell, Ed. & Trans.) Vintage.

Ripple, W. J., & Beschta, R. L. (2012). Trophic cascades in Yellowstone: The first 15 years after wolf reintroduction. *Biological Conservation 145*, 205–213.

Robinson, J. M. (Ed.) (1977). *The Nag Hammadi Library*. Harper & Row.

Rodriguez, A. (2016). Marin man faces $25,000 fine for cutting down 100-year-old redwood tree. Retrieved November 7, 2016, from Mercury News website, *Marin Independent Journal*, https://www.mercurynews.com/2016/11/07/marin-man-faces-25000-fine-for-cutting-down-100-year-old-redwood-tree/.

Rolland, R. (1929). *The life of Ramakrishna*. Advaita Ashrama.

Roszak, T., Gomes, M. E., & Kanner, A. D. (Eds.). (1995). *Ecopsychology: Restoring the earth, healing the mind*. Sierra Club Books.

Rumi. (1992). *A garden beyond paradise: The mystical poetry of Rumi*. Bantam.

Rumi. (1995). *The essential Rumi* (C. Barks, Trans.). Harper Collins.

Safran, J. D. (Ed.) (2003). *Psychoanalysis and Buddhism*. Wisdom Publications.

Safran, J. D., & Muran, J. C. (2000). *Negotiating the therapeutic alliance*. Guilford Press.

Sale, K. (1990). *The conquest of paradise*. Alfred A. Knopf.

Search for the Ivory-billed Woodpecker. (2015). Retrieved from the Cornell Lab of Ornithology website, http://www.birds.cornell.edu/ivory/.

Seismic surveys. (2015). Retrieved June 29, 2015, from Beachapedia website, http://www.beachapedia.org/Seismic_Surveys.

Sells, M. (1994). *Mystical languages of unsaying*. University of Chicago Press.

Seng-ts'an. (2001). *Hsin-hsin ming* (ca. 600) (R. Clarke, Trans.). White Pine Press.

Seung, S. (2012). *Connectome*. Houghton Mifflin Harcourt.

Shannon, W. H., & Bochen, C. M. (Eds.). *Thomas Merton: A life in letters*. Ave Maria Press.

Shepard, P. (1973). *The tender carnivore and the sacred game*. Charles Scribner's Sons.

Simard, S. (2016, August 30). How trees talk to each other. Retrieved from the TED website, https://www.youtube.com/watch?v=Un2yBgIAxYs.

Simons, I. (2010). Does raping the earth make us crazy? Ecopsychology says that mental health depends on environmental health. Retrieved from *Psychology Today* website, https://www.psychologytoday.com/blog/the-literary-mind/201002/does-raping-the-earth-make-us-crazy.

Singer, P. (1990). *Animal liberation*. Avon Books.

Slater, L. (2004). *Opening Skinner's box*. Norton.

Slobodchikoff, C. (2012). *Chasing Doctor Doolittle*. St. Martin's Press.

Slobodchikoff, C. (2019). Con Slobodchikoff: Blending science with empathy for all living beings. Retrieved from Slobodchikoff's website, http://con-slobodchikoff.com/.

Small, R. (1983). Nietzsche and a Platonist tradition of the cosmos: Center everywhere and circumference nowhere. *Journal of the History of Ideas*, 44(1), 89–104.

Snell, M. (1997, November/December). The world of religion according to Huston Smith. *Mother Jones*, 40–43.

Snyder, G. (1980). *The real work*. New Directions.

Snyder, G. (1990). *The practice of the wild*. North Point Press.

Snyder, G. (1992). *No nature*. Pantheon.

Snyder, G. (2007). *Back on the fire*. Shoemaker & Hoard.

Snyder, G. (2008a). Gary Snyder on ecology and poetry—part 3. Retrieved November 4, 2008, from YouTube website, http://www.youtube.com/watch?v=jPaPYNsjmN4&feature=related.

Snyder, G. (2008b). Gary Snyder on ecology and poetry—part 4. Retrieved November 4, 2008, from YouTube website, http://www.youtube.com/watch?v=u6aK_FqYuaw&feature=related.

Star, J., & Shiva, S. (2005). *A garden beyond paradise: Love poems of Rumi*. Theone Press.

Suzuki, D. T. (1955). *Zen Buddhism*. Doubleday Anchor.

Suzuki, S. (1970). *Zen mind, beginner's mind*. Weatherhill.

Swimme, B. (1984). *The universe is a green dragon*. Bear & Company.

Swimme, B., & Berry, T. (1992). *The universe story*. Harper.

Tardiff, M. (Ed.). (1995). *At home in the world*. Orbis Books.

Tarrant, J. (1998). *The light inside the dark*. HarperCollins.

Te Awa Tupua (Whanganui River Claims Settlement) Act 2017. (2017, March 20). Retrieved from the New Zealand Parliamentary Counsel Office website, http://www.legislation.govt.nz/act/public/2017/0007/latest/whole.html.

Teresa of Ávila (2003). *The interior castle* (M. Starr, Trans.). Riverhead.

Teresa of Ávila (2007). *The book of my life* (M. Starr, Trans.). New Seeds.

Tremblay, B. (2002). *The search for the Ivory-billed Woodpecker*. Retrieved July 15, 2005, from Living on Earth website, http://www.loe.org/shows/shows.htm?programID=02-P13-00010#feature1.

Tuchman, B. W. (1978). *A distant mirror*. Ballantine.

Vakoch, D. A., & Castrillón, F. (Eds.). (2014). *Ecopsychology, phenomenology, and the environment: The experience of nature*. Springer.

VandenBos, G. R. (Ed.). (2007). *APA dictionary of psychology*. APA.

Van Houten, C. (2016). The first official climate refugees in the U.S. race against time. Retrieved May 25, 2016, from https://news.nationalgeographic.com/2016/05/160525-isle-de-jean-charles-louisiana-sinking-climate-change-refugees/.

Vogt, E. W. (Ed.). (1996). *The complete poetry of St. Teresa of Avila*. University of the South.

Wahlberg, D. (2015, March 13). Controversial UW-Madison monkey study won't remove newborns from mothers. Retrieved from Madison.com website, https://madison.com/news/local/education/university/controversial-uw-madison-monkey-study-wont-remove-newborns-from-mothers/article_e8a288f4-5d1a-5ab2-ab50-64b24920b2e3.html#.

Warne, K. (2019). A voice for nature. Retrieved from *National Geographic* website, https://www.nationalgeographic.com/culture/2019/04/maori-river-in-new-zealand-is-a-legal-person/.

A warning on climate and the risk of societal collapse. (2020, December 6). Retrieved from the *Guardian* website, https://www.theguardian.com/environment/2020/dec/06/a-warning-on-climate-and-the-risk-of-societal-collapse.

Warren, K. J. (1997). Taking empirical data seriously. In K. J. Warren, *Ecofeminism: Women, culture, nature* (pp. 3–20). Indiana University Press.

Washburn, M. (1995). *The ego and the dynamic ground*. State University of New York Press.

Watson, B. (1993). *The Zen teachings of Master Lin-Chi*. Shambhala.

Watson, B. (1997). *The Vimalakirti sutra*. Columbia University Press.

Watson, J. B. (1928). *Psychological care of the infant and child*. Norton.

Watts, A. W. (1957). *The way of Zen*. Vintage Books.

Weber, M. (2004). *The vocation lectures*. Hackett.

Welwood, J. (2000). *Toward a psychology of awakening*. Shambhala.

White, L. (1967). The historic roots of our ecologic crisis. *Science, 155*(3767), 1203–1207.

Wick, G. S. (2005). *The book of equanimity*. Wisdom Publications.

Wilber, K. (1977). *The spectrum of consciousness*. Quest Books.

Wilber, K. (1980). *The atman project*. Quest Books.

Wilber, K. (1983). *Eye to eye*. Anchor Books

Wilber, K. (1999). *One taste*. Shambhala.

Wilber, K. (2000a). *Integral psychology*. Shambhala.

Wilber, K. (2000b). *Sex, ecology, spirituality*, 2nd ed. Shambhala.

Williams, N. (1994). *Psychoanalytic diagnosis*. Guilford Press.

Williams, R. (2015). *Keywords*. Oxford University Press.

Wilson, E. O. (1984). *Biophilia*. Harvard University Press.

Wilson, E. O. (1992). *The diversity of life*. Norton.

Winnicott, D. W. (1965). *The maturational processes and the facilitating environment*. International Universities Press.

Winnicott, D. W. (1971). *Playing and reality*. Tavistock.

Winnicott, D. W. (1987). *The child, the family, and the outside world*. Perseus.

Wirth, J. M. (2017). *Mountains, rivers, and the great earth: Reading Gary Snyder and Dōgen in an age of ecological crisis*. State University of New York Press.

Wolfe, L. M. (Ed.). (1938). *John of the mountains*. University of Wisconsin Press.

Yamada, K. (2004). *The gateless gate*. Wisdom Publications.

# Index

Abram, David, xiii, xviii, xxii,
93–94, 96, 99, 111, 117, 212, 220,
222, 249, 257, 259, 269
Advaita Vedanta, 175, 271
Aitken, Robert, 237, 239–241, 322,
328, 361n3 (chap. 1), 363n2
(chap. 8)
animal experimentation, contemporary,
156–157; Harry Harlow's, 152–160
anthropocentrism, 64, 108, 150, 217,
297. *See also* human-centered
anthropomorphism, 63–64; and God,
29, 183, 312
aporia, 26. *See also* unnamable;
unsayable
appeal. *See* ethical/relational call
attachment theory, 88–91, 147,
152–153, 361n2 & n3 (chap. 3)
Augustine, Saint, 170, 174, 176, 203,
363n12 (chap. 6)
aversion. *See* avoidance; dissociation;
repression
avoidance, 2, 5, 57–58, 69, 76, 78,
125–128, 147, 161, 238, 256–257,
272, 287–288, 298–299. *See also*
repression; dissociation
awakening, xiii, xvi, 18, 22, 28,
34–35, 49–50, 71–72, 134,
167–172, 185–187, 206, 237–248,
294–295; as interdependent

co-arising, 86–87, 214–217, 223; as
loving service, 190–195, 312–328

Bacon, Francis, 103, 119, 125
Bashō, Matsuo, xix, 16, 86–87,
233–248, 359n4 (preface)
Bateson, Gregory, 122, 205, 206,
217–219, 225–226
beauty, xviii, xxi, xxiii, 33–54, 71,
204, 233, 271–272, 300, 323, 346,
350
Becker, Ernest, 146, 149, 257
Berry, Thomas, ix, xxi, xxvi, 68, 105,
128–129, 140
Berry, Wendell, 330–331
Beyer, Jeff, 20, 142–143, 201
biodiversity, ix, 42–43; and loss of
our relational partners, 55–73
biomimicry, 295–297
biophilia, 43–44; a mystical/
contemplative view of, 310–312
Blake, William, xv, 18, 110, 113,
115, 163, 167–168, 177, 195, 204,
298, 310, 313–314
Bodhidharma, 30, 305
bodhisattva, 312–321, 328, 345–346
body. *See* embodiment
Bowlby, John, 88–89, 152, 158
breakdown and breakthrough, x,
xxiii, 71, 100–101, 200, 204, 347

# About the Author

Will W. Adams serves as a psychology professor at Duquesne University in Pittsburgh, Pennsylvania, and as an ecopsychologist, psychotherapist, and meditation teacher. He completed a BS at the University of North Carolina–Chapel Hill, an MA in psychology at West Georgia College, a PhD in clinical psychology at Duquesne University, and a clinical fellowship in psychology at McLean Hospital/Harvard Medical School. Will's training includes 35 years of practice with esteemed meditation teachers, both Christian and Buddhist. For the last 23 years he has studied Zen with Bruce Harris Rōshi, who has heartily encouraged him to share his practice with others. This takes place by way of university teaching, meditation groups, and experiential workshops in the woods. His special interests include contemplative/meditative/mystical spirituality (especially Buddhism and Christian mysticism), ecopsychology/ecospirituality, and psychotherapy. His previous scholarly work has appeared in numerous academic journals and anthologies. Will is blessed with a saint, or a bodhisattva, for a wife—she really is both—and with two marvelous teenage children.

Printed in the USA
CPSIA information can be obtained
at www.ICGtesting.com
LVHW051225111123
763485LV00065B/2141

9 781438 492063